NATURE OF THE BEAST

By Adam Mansbach and Douglas Mcgowan

Art by Owen Brozman

Color by MATT ROTA
with Eric Collins & Stavros Pavlides

Soft Skull Press
an imprint of COUNTERPOINT

BERKELEY

Library of Congress Cataloging-in-Publication Data is available.

HC ISBN 978-1-59376-447-0
PB ISBN 978-1-59376-245-2

The creators wish to thank Johnny Dwyer and Langdon Foss.

Soft Skull Press
An imprint of COUNTERPOINT
1919 Fifth Street
Berkeley, CA 94710
www.softskull.com

Distributed by Publishers Group West
Printed in the United States of America

10 9 8 7 6 5 4 3 2 1

NATURE OF THE BEAST

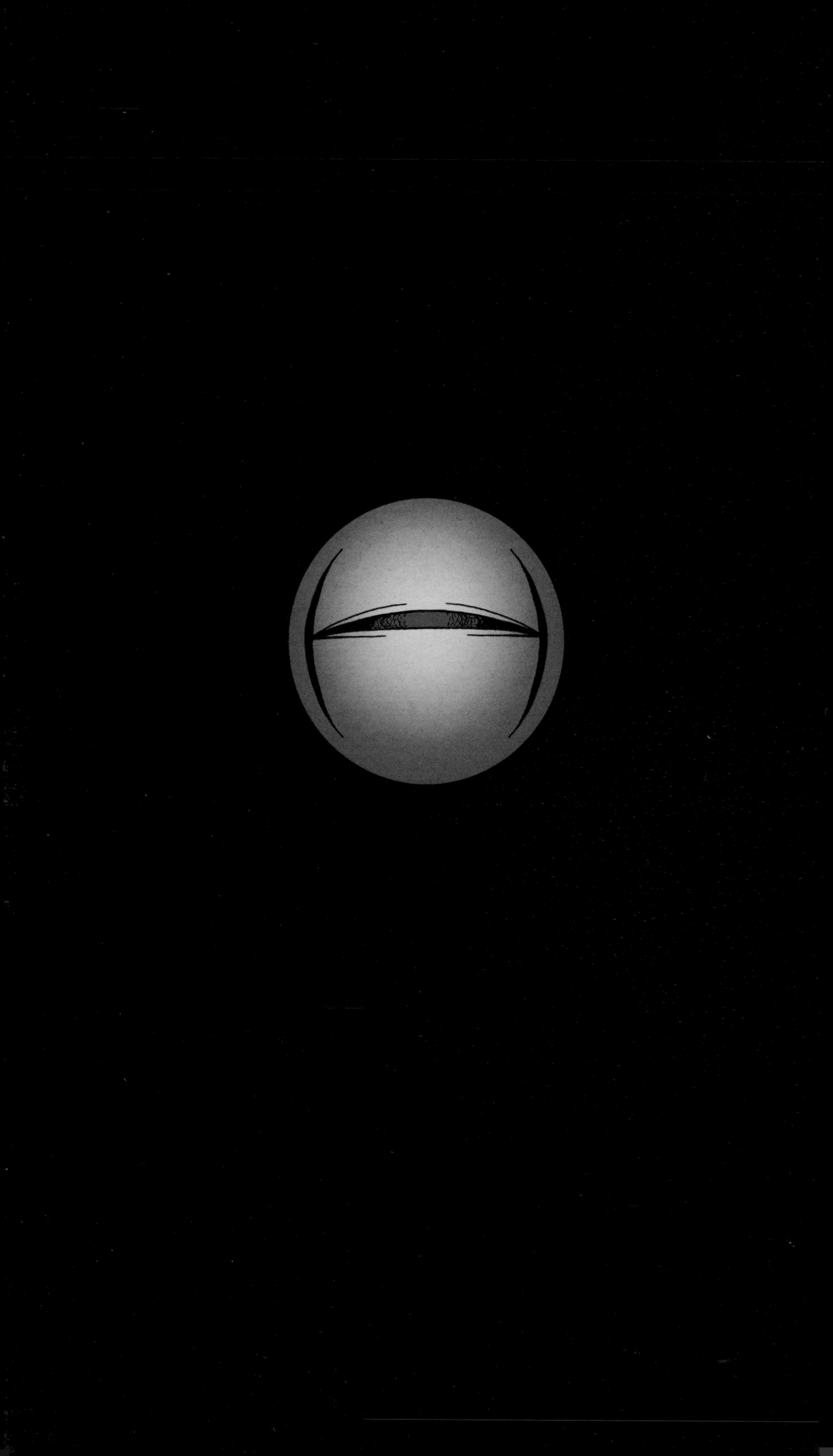

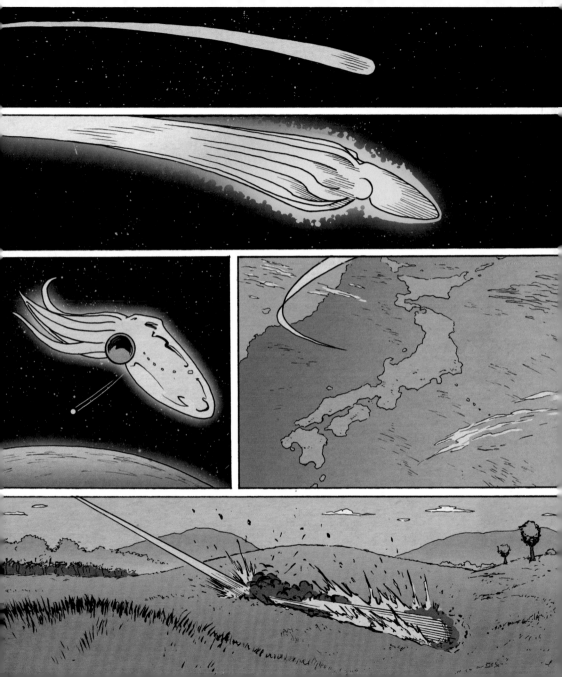

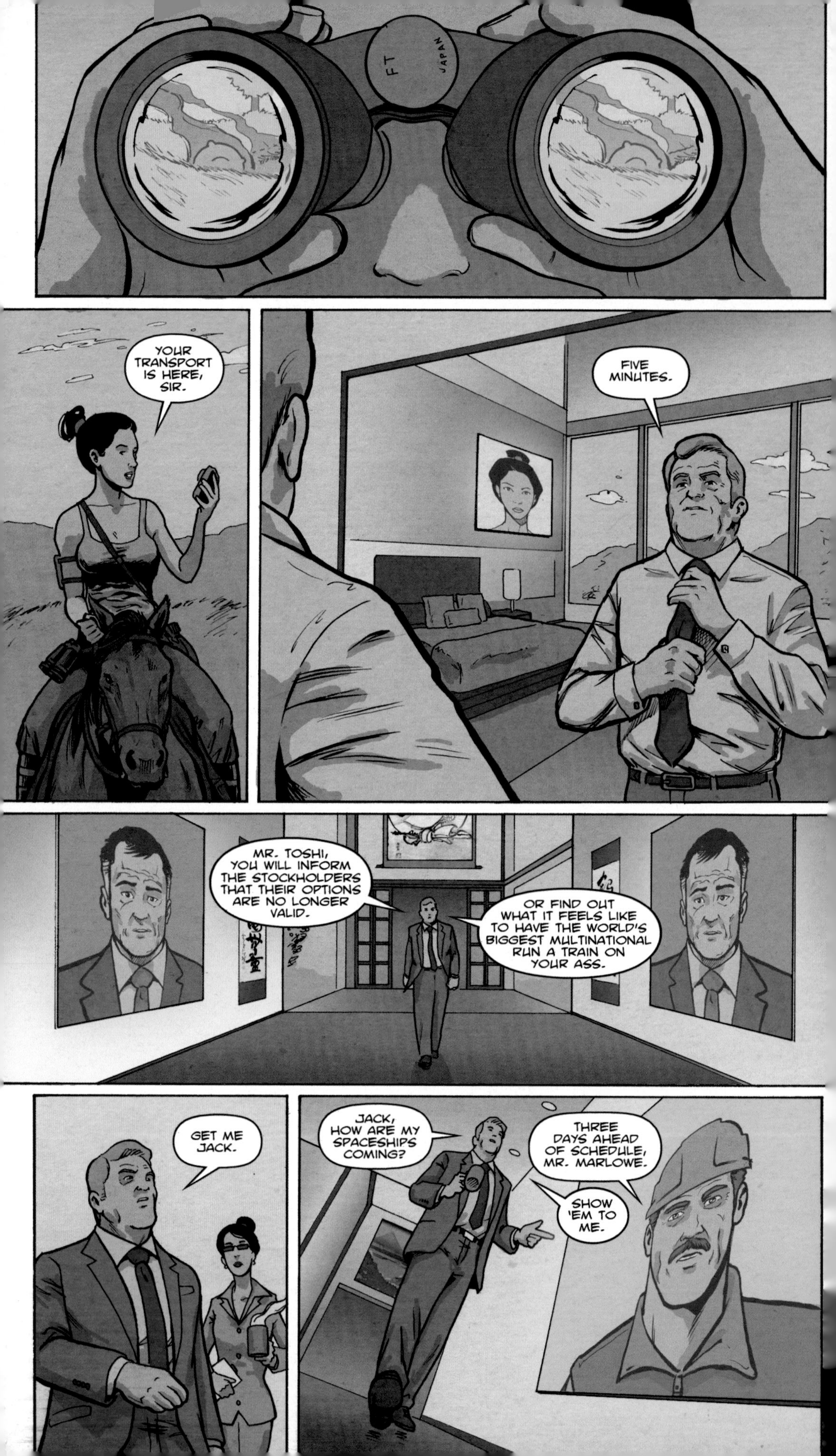
FT
JAPAN
YOUR TRANSPORT IS HERE, SIR.
FIVE MINUTES.
MR. TOSHI, YOU WILL INFORM THE STOCKHOLDERS THAT THEIR OPTIONS ARE NO LONGER VALID.
OR FIND OUT WHAT IT FEELS LIKE TO HAVE THE WORLD'S BIGGEST MULTINATIONAL RUN A TRAIN ON YOUR ASS.
GET ME JACK.
JACK, HOW ARE MY SPACESHIPS COMING?
THREE DAYS AHEAD OF SCHEDULE, MR. MARLOWE.
SHOW 'EM TO ME.

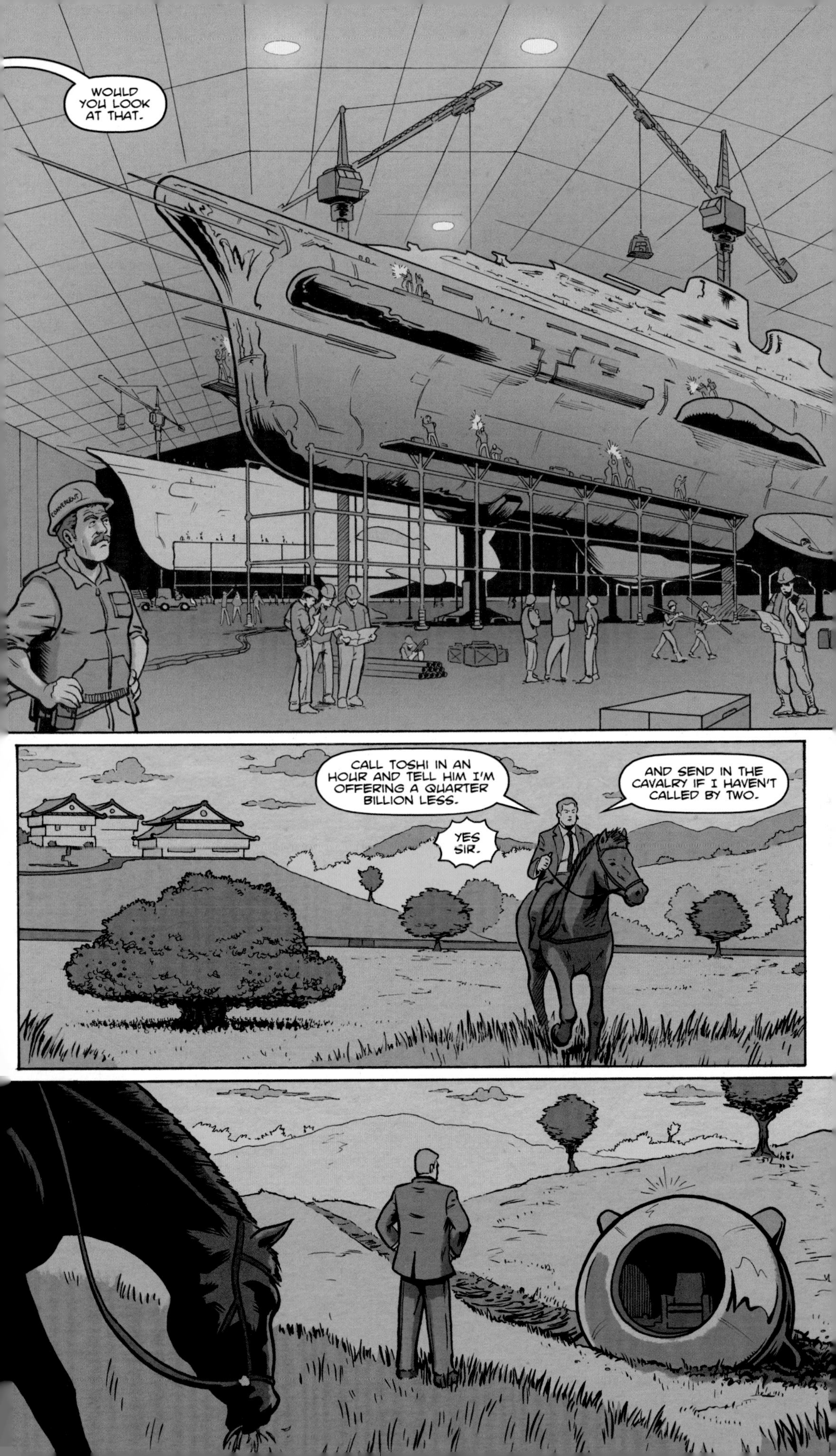
WOULD YOU LOOK AT THAT.
CALL TOSHI IN AN HOUR AND TELL HIM I'M OFFERING A QUARTER BILLION LESS.
YES SIR.
AND SEND IN THE CAVALRY IF I HAVEN'T CALLED BY TWO.

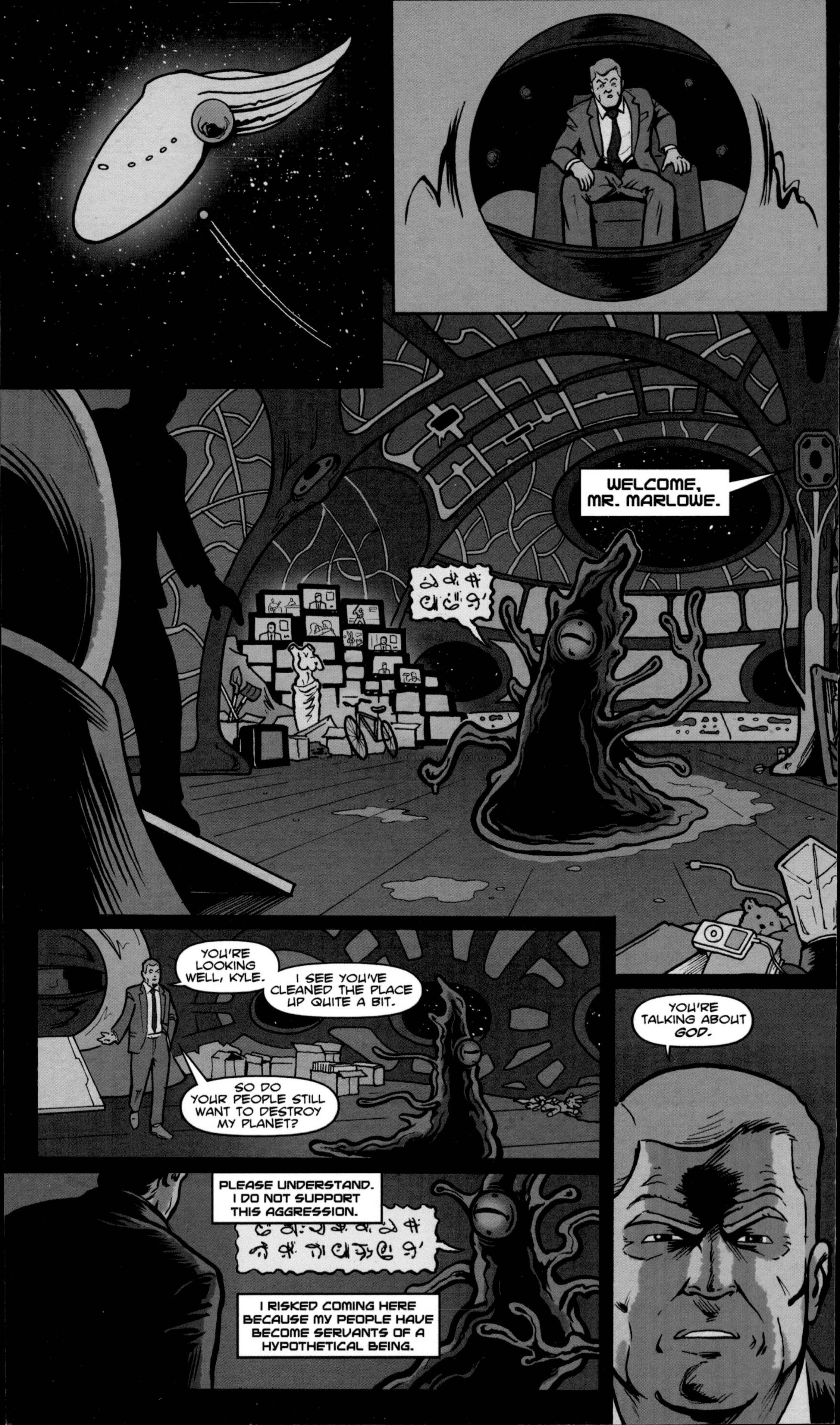
WELCOME, MR. MARLOWE.
YOU'RE LOOKING WELL, KYLE.
I SEE YOU'VE CLEANED THE PLACE UP QUITE A BIT.
SO DO YOUR PEOPLE STILL WANT TO DESTROY MY PLANET?
PLEASE UNDERSTAND. I DO NOT SUPPORT THIS AGGRESSION.
I RISKED COMING HERE BECAUSE MY PEOPLE HAVE BECOME SERVANTS OF A HYPOTHETICAL BEING.
YOU'RE TALKING ABOUT *GOD*.

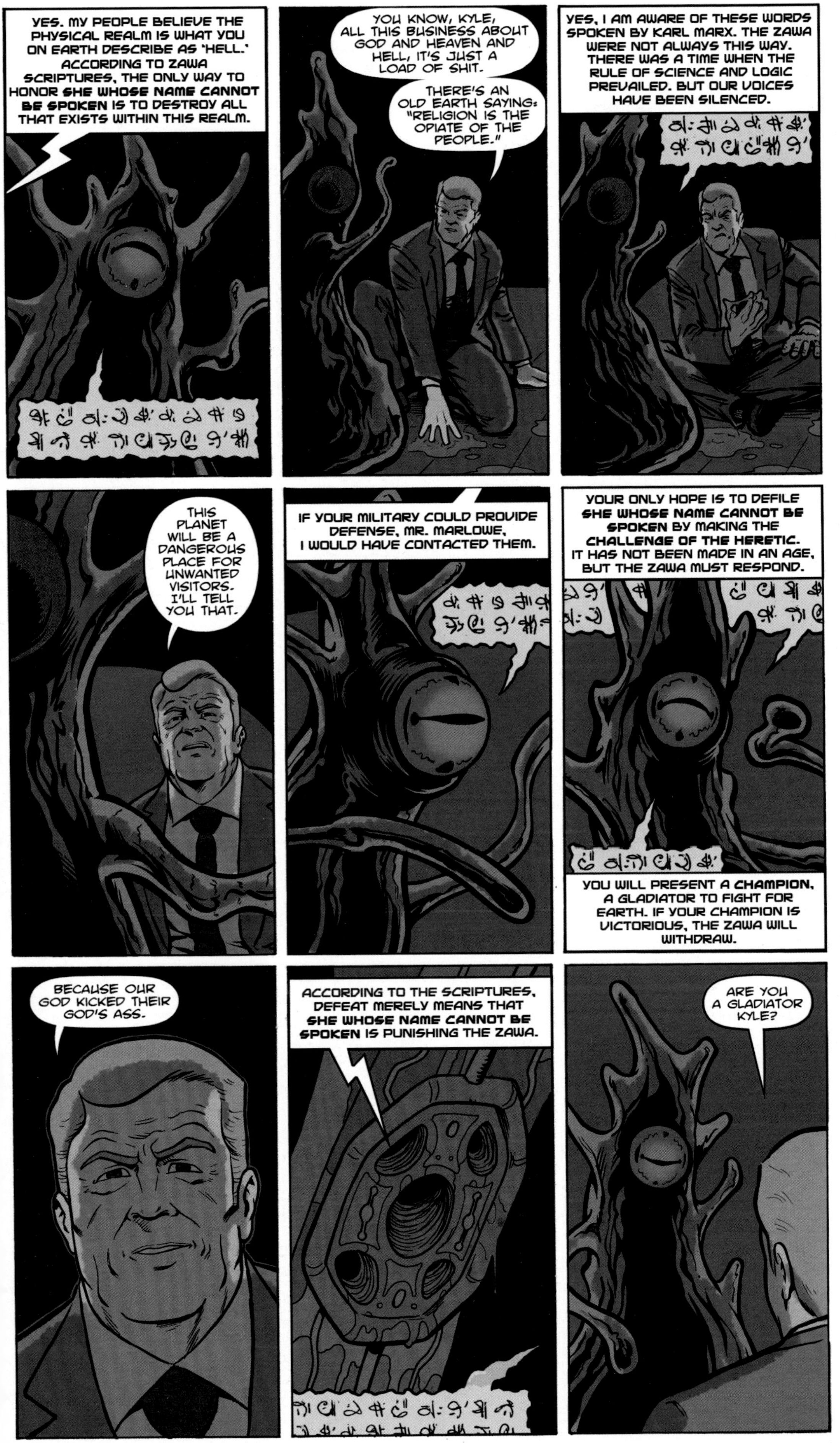
YES. MY PEOPLE BELIEVE THE PHYSICAL REALM IS WHAT YOU ON EARTH DESCRIBE AS 'HELL.' ACCORDING TO ZAWA SCRIPTURES, THE ONLY WAY TO HONOR SHE WHOSE NAME CANNOT BE SPOKEN IS TO DESTROY ALL THAT EXISTS WITHIN THIS REALM.
YOU KNOW, KYLE, ALL THIS BUSINESS ABOUT GOD AND HEAVEN AND HELL, IT'S JUST A LOAD OF SHIT.
THERE'S AN OLD EARTH SAYING: "RELIGION IS THE OPIATE OF THE PEOPLE."
YES, I AM AWARE OF THESE WORDS SPOKEN BY KARL MARX. THE ZAWA WERE NOT ALWAYS THIS WAY. THERE WAS A TIME WHEN THE RULE OF SCIENCE AND LOGIC PREVAILED. BUT OUR VOICES HAVE BEEN SILENCED.
THIS PLANET WILL BE A DANGEROUS PLACE FOR UNWANTED VISITORS. I'LL TELL YOU THAT.
IF YOUR MILITARY COULD PROVIDE DEFENSE, MR. MARLOWE, I WOULD HAVE CONTACTED THEM.
YOUR ONLY HOPE IS TO DEFILE SHE WHOSE NAME CANNOT BE SPOKEN BY MAKING THE CHALLENGE OF THE HERETIC. IT HAS NOT BEEN MADE IN AN AGE, BUT THE ZAWA MUST RESPOND.
YOU WILL PRESENT A CHAMPION, A GLADIATOR TO FIGHT FOR EARTH. IF YOUR CHAMPION IS VICTORIOUS, THE ZAWA WILL WITHDRAW.
BECAUSE OUR GOD KICKED THEIR GOD'S ASS.
ACCORDING TO THE SCRIPTURES, DEFEAT MERELY MEANS THAT SHE WHOSE NAME CANNOT BE SPOKEN IS PUNISHING THE ZAWA.
ARE YOU A GLADIATOR KYLE?

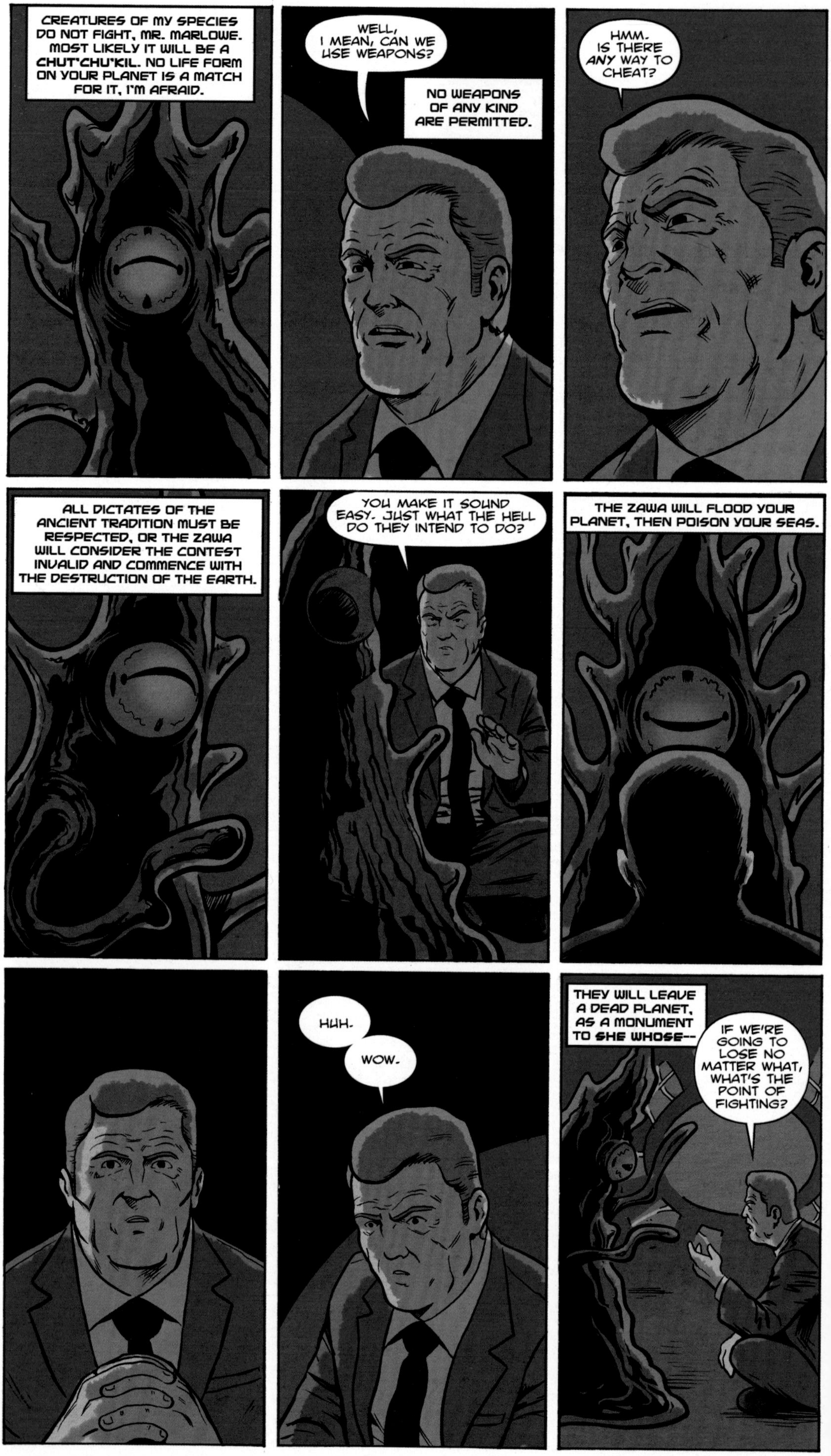
CREATURES OF MY SPECIES DO NOT FIGHT, MR. MARLOWE. MOST LIKELY IT WILL BE A CHUT'CHU'KIL. NO LIFE FORM ON YOUR PLANET IS A MATCH FOR IT, I'M AFRAID.
WELL, I MEAN, CAN WE USE WEAPONS?
NO WEAPONS OF ANY KIND ARE PERMITTED.
HMM. IS THERE *ANY* WAY TO CHEAT?
ALL DICTATES OF THE ANCIENT TRADITION MUST BE RESPECTED, OR THE ZAWA WILL CONSIDER THE CONTEST INVALID AND COMMENCE WITH THE DESTRUCTION OF THE EARTH.
YOU MAKE IT SOUND EASY. JUST WHAT THE HELL DO THEY INTEND TO DO?
THE ZAWA WILL FLOOD YOUR PLANET, THEN POISON YOUR SEAS.
HUH.
WOW.
THEY WILL LEAVE A DEAD PLANET, AS A MONUMENT TO **SHE WHOSE--**
IF WE'RE GOING TO LOSE NO MATTER WHAT, WHAT'S THE POINT OF FIGHTING?

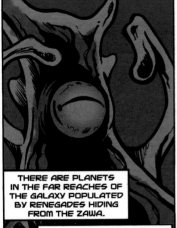

IN THE TIME THE ZAWA SPEND ON RITUAL PREPARATION, YOU CAN COLLECT YOUR CRUCIAL WORKS AND LIFE FORMS AND ESCAPE INTO SPACE.

THERE ARE PLANETS IN THE FAR REACHES OF THE GALAXY POPULATED BY RENEGADES HIDING FROM THE ZAWA.

A FEW SMALL SHIPS COULD ESCAPE AND JOIN THEM.

AND I'M STILL THE ONLY ONE WHO KNOWS ABOUT THIS?

YES. WE HAVE DETERMINED YOU TO BE EARTH'S MOST POWERFUL BEING.

WELL, MAYBE. BUT AS FAR AS DECLARING OUR GOD SUPERIOR...

HUMANS AREN'T UNITED IN ANY PARTICULAR BELIEF, KYLE. PEOPLE BELIEVE ALL KINDS OF THINGS.

CONSENSUS IS NOT NECESSARY. AS THE REPRESENTATIVE OF EARTH, YOU SHALL MAKE THE CHALLENGE OF THE HERETIC.

BUT KYLE, I DON'T BELIEVE IN ANYTHING.

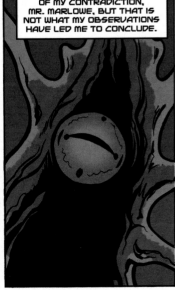

PLEASE FORGIVE THE INSULT OF MY CONTRADICTION, MR. MARLOWE, BUT THAT IS NOT WHAT MY OBSERVATIONS HAVE LED ME TO CONCLUDE.

OH YEAH?

YOU BELIEVE IN THE SURVIVAL OF THE FITTEST.

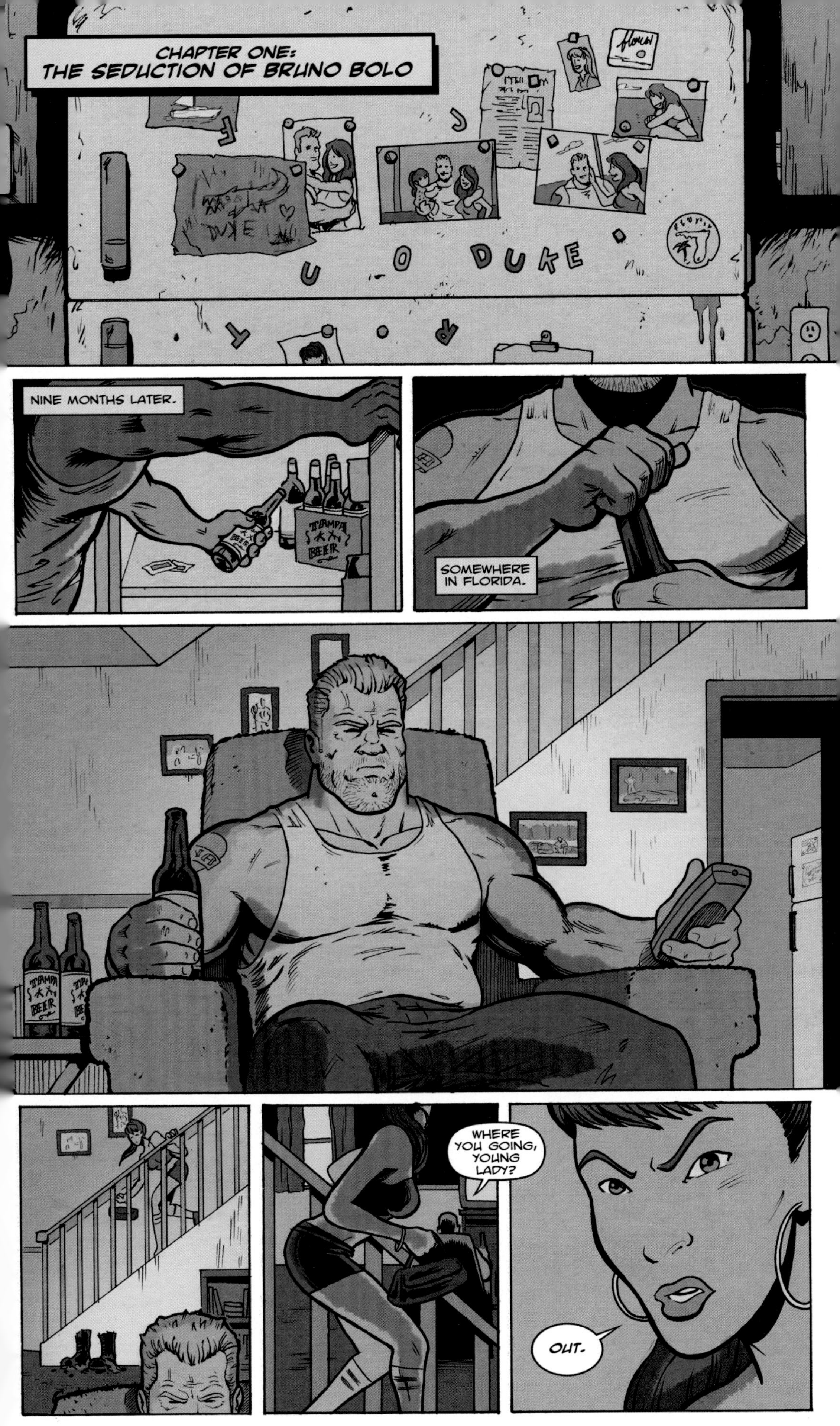
CHAPTER ONE:
THE SEDUCTION OF BRUNO BOLO
DUKE
NINE MONTHS LATER.
TAMPA BEER
SOMEWHERE IN FLORIDA.
WHERE YOU GOING, YOUNG LADY?
OUT.

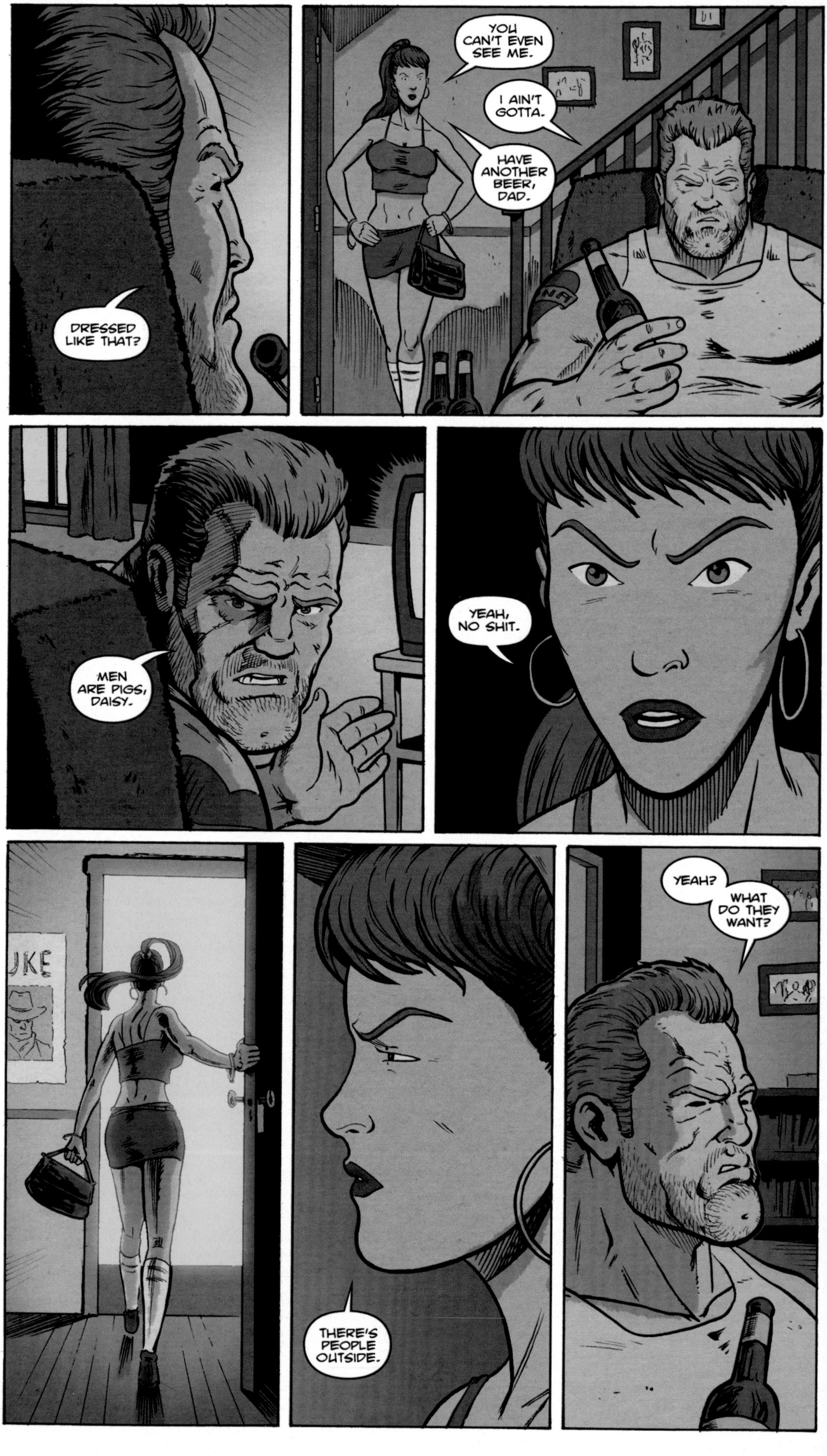
DRESSED LIKE THAT?
YOU CAN'T EVEN SEE ME.
I AIN'T GOTTA.
HAVE ANOTHER BEER, DAD.
MEN ARE PIGS, DAISY.
YEAH, NO SHIT.
UKE
THERE'S PEOPLE OUTSIDE.
YEAH?
WHAT DO THEY WANT?

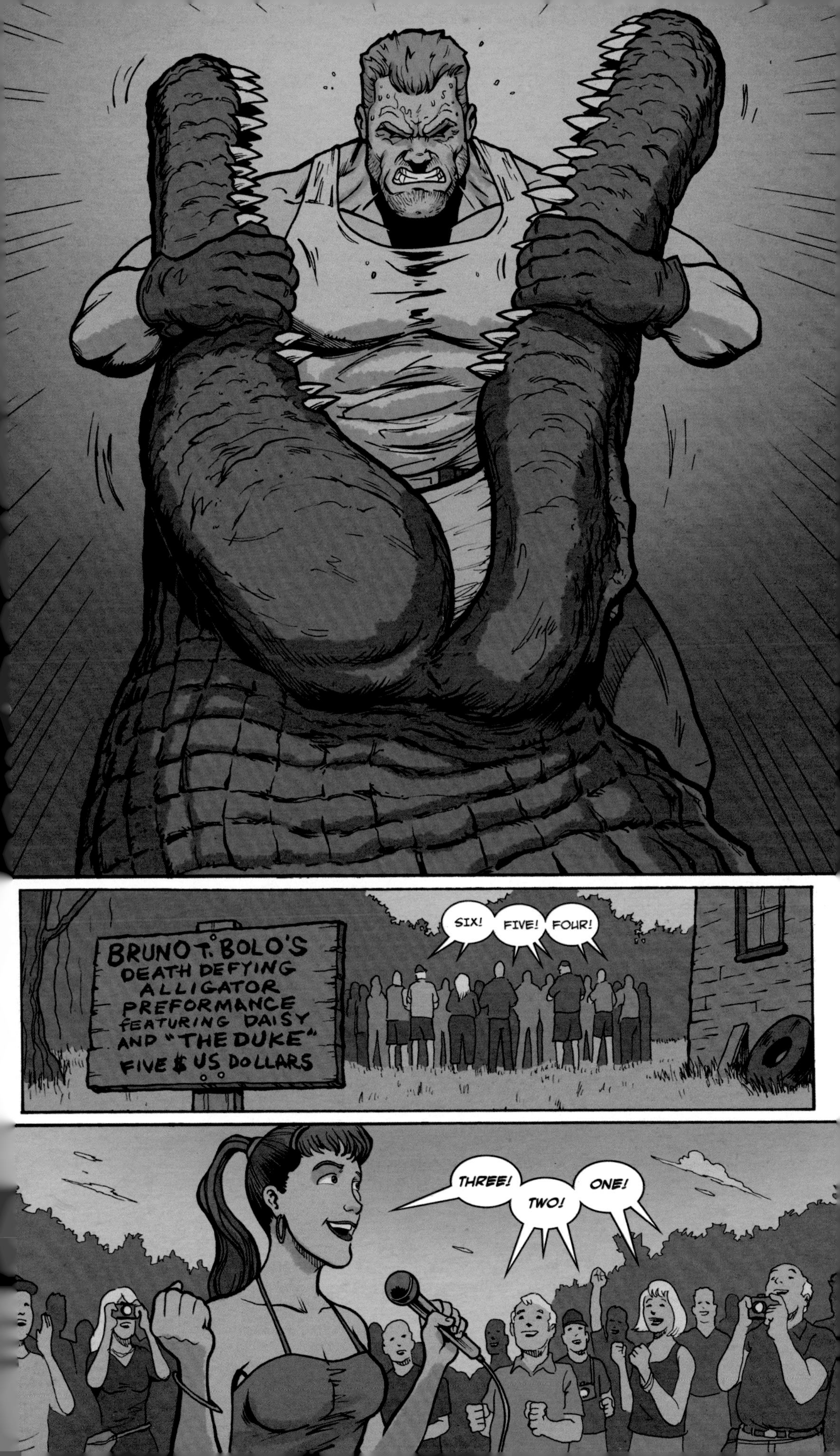
BRUNO T. BOLO'S DEATH DEFYING ALLIGATOR PREFORMANCE FEATURING DAISY AND "THE DUKE" FIVE $ U.S. DOLLARS
SIX!
FIVE!
FOUR!
THREE!
TWO!
ONE!

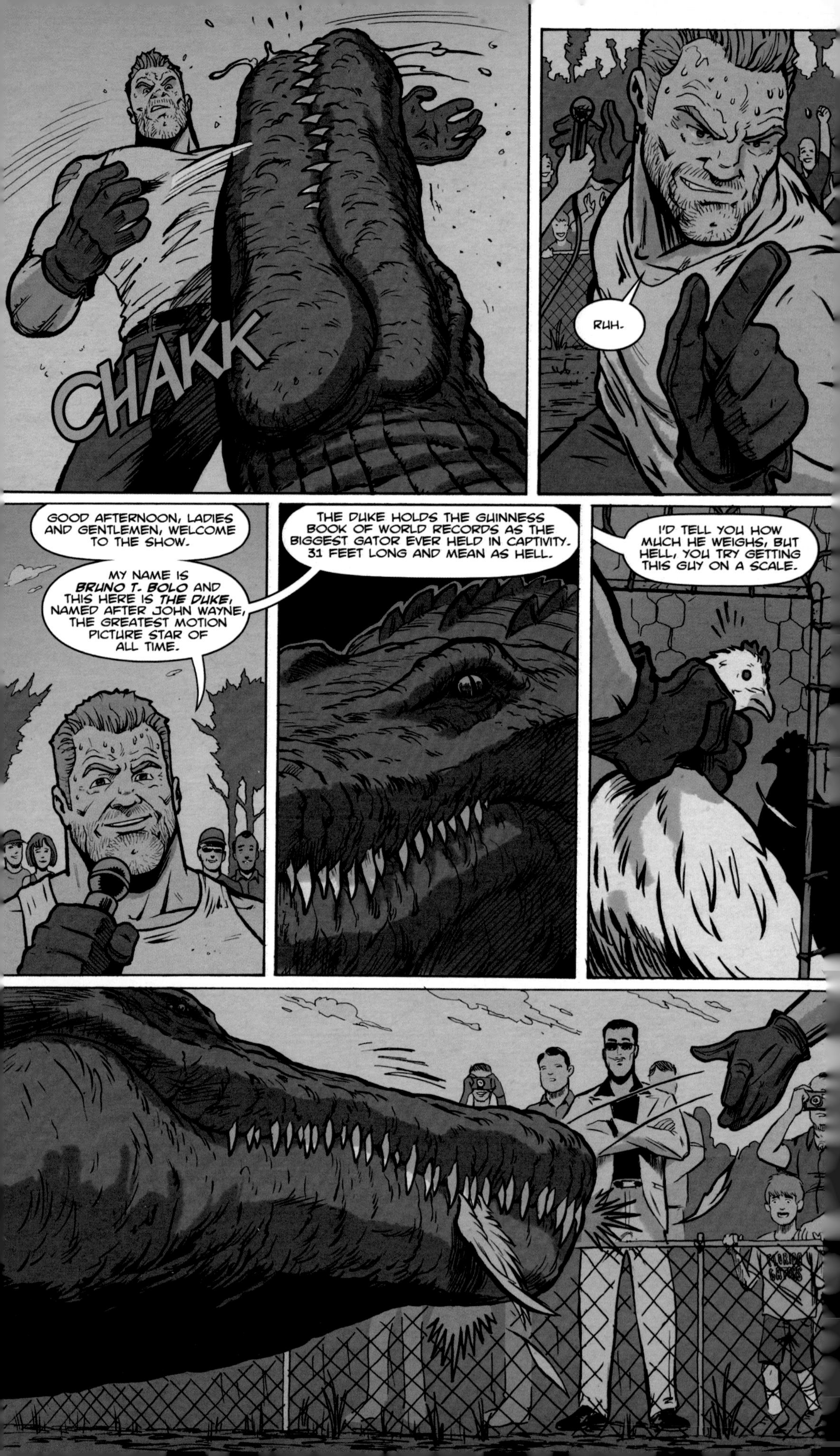
CHAKK
RUH.
GOOD AFTERNOON, LADIES AND GENTLEMEN, WELCOME TO THE SHOW.
MY NAME IS BRUNO T. BOLO AND THIS HERE IS THE DUKE, NAMED AFTER JOHN WAYNE, THE GREATEST MOTION PICTURE STAR OF ALL TIME.
THE DUKE HOLDS THE GUINNESS BOOK OF WORLD RECORDS AS THE BIGGEST GATOR EVER HELD IN CAPTIVITY. 31 FEET LONG AND MEAN AS HELL.
I'D TELL YOU HOW MUCH HE WEIGHS, BUT HELL, YOU TRY GETTING THIS GUY ON A SCALE.

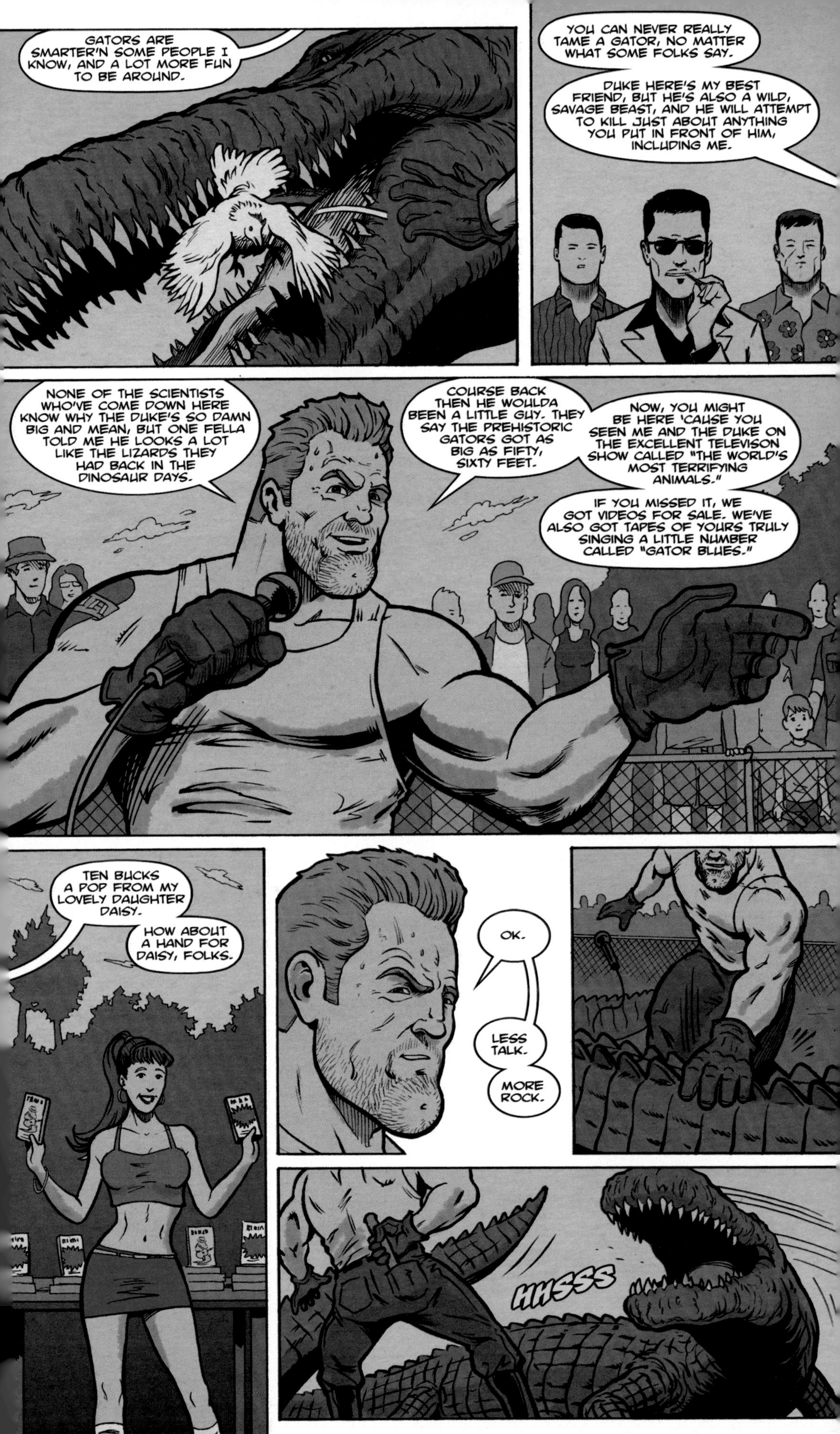
GATORS ARE SMARTER'N SOME PEOPLE I KNOW, AND A LOT MORE FUN TO BE AROUND.
YOU CAN NEVER REALLY TAME A GATOR, NO MATTER WHAT SOME FOLKS SAY.
DUKE HERE'S MY BEST FRIEND, BUT HE'S ALSO A WILD, SAVAGE BEAST, AND HE WILL ATTEMPT TO KILL JUST ABOUT ANYTHING YOU PUT IN FRONT OF HIM, INCLUDING ME.
NONE OF THE SCIENTISTS WHO'VE COME DOWN HERE KNOW WHY THE DUKE'S SO DAMN BIG AND MEAN, BUT ONE FELLA TOLD ME HE LOOKS A LOT LIKE THE LIZARDS THEY HAD BACK IN THE DINOSAUR DAYS.
COURSE BACK THEN HE WOULDA BEEN A LITTLE GUY. THEY SAY THE PREHISTORIC GATORS GOT AS BIG AS FIFTY, SIXTY FEET.
NOW, YOU MIGHT BE HERE 'CAUSE YOU SEEN ME AND THE DUKE ON THE EXCELLENT TELEVISON SHOW CALLED "THE WORLD'S MOST TERRIFYING ANIMALS."
IF YOU MISSED IT, WE GOT VIDEOS FOR SALE. WE'VE ALSO GOT TAPES OF YOURS TRULY SINGING A LITTLE NUMBER CALLED "GATOR BLUES."
TEN BUCKS A POP FROM MY LOVELY DAUGHTER DAISY.
HOW ABOUT A HAND FOR DAISY, FOLKS.
OK.
LESS TALK.
MORE ROCK.
HHSSS

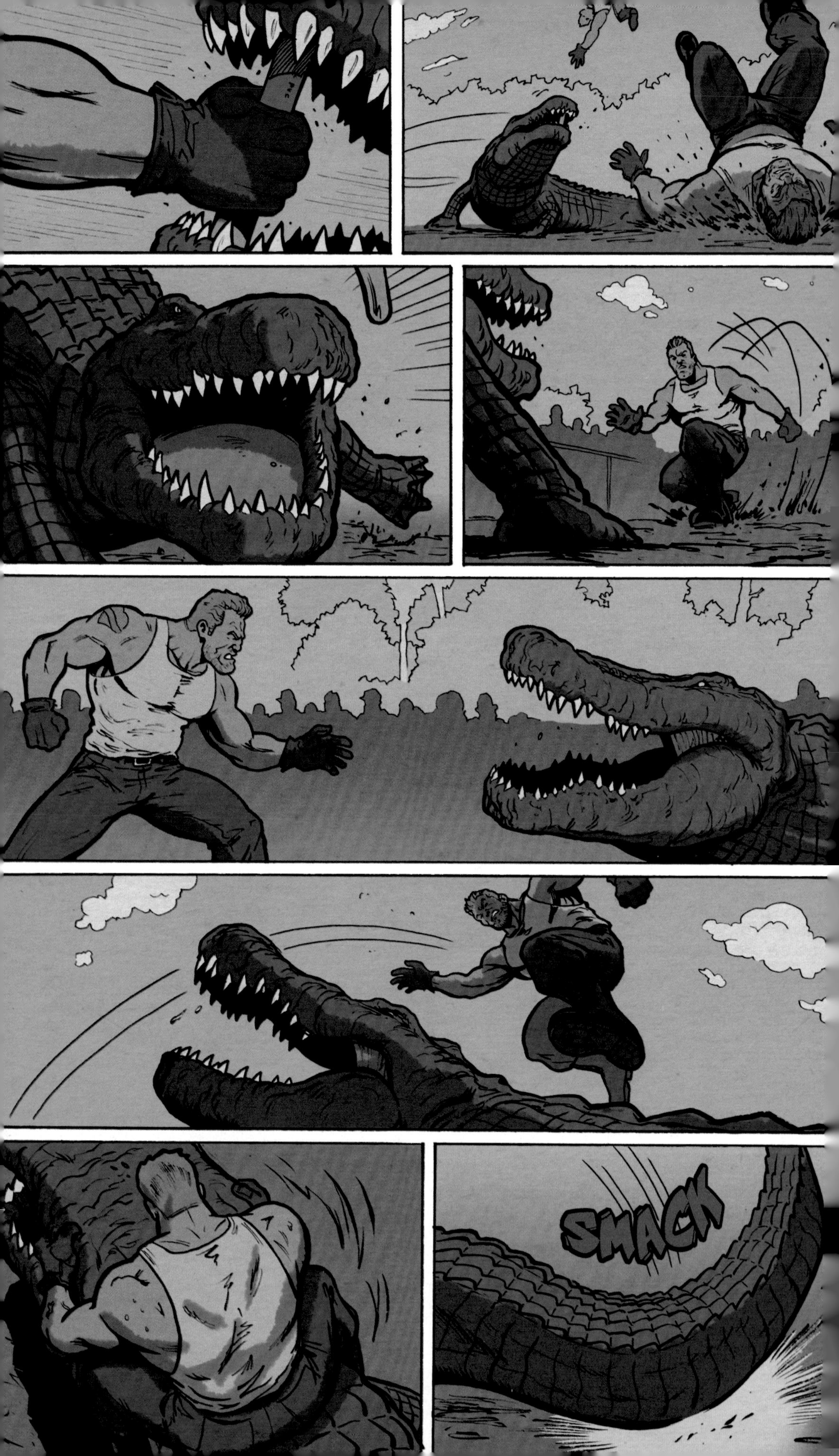
SMACK

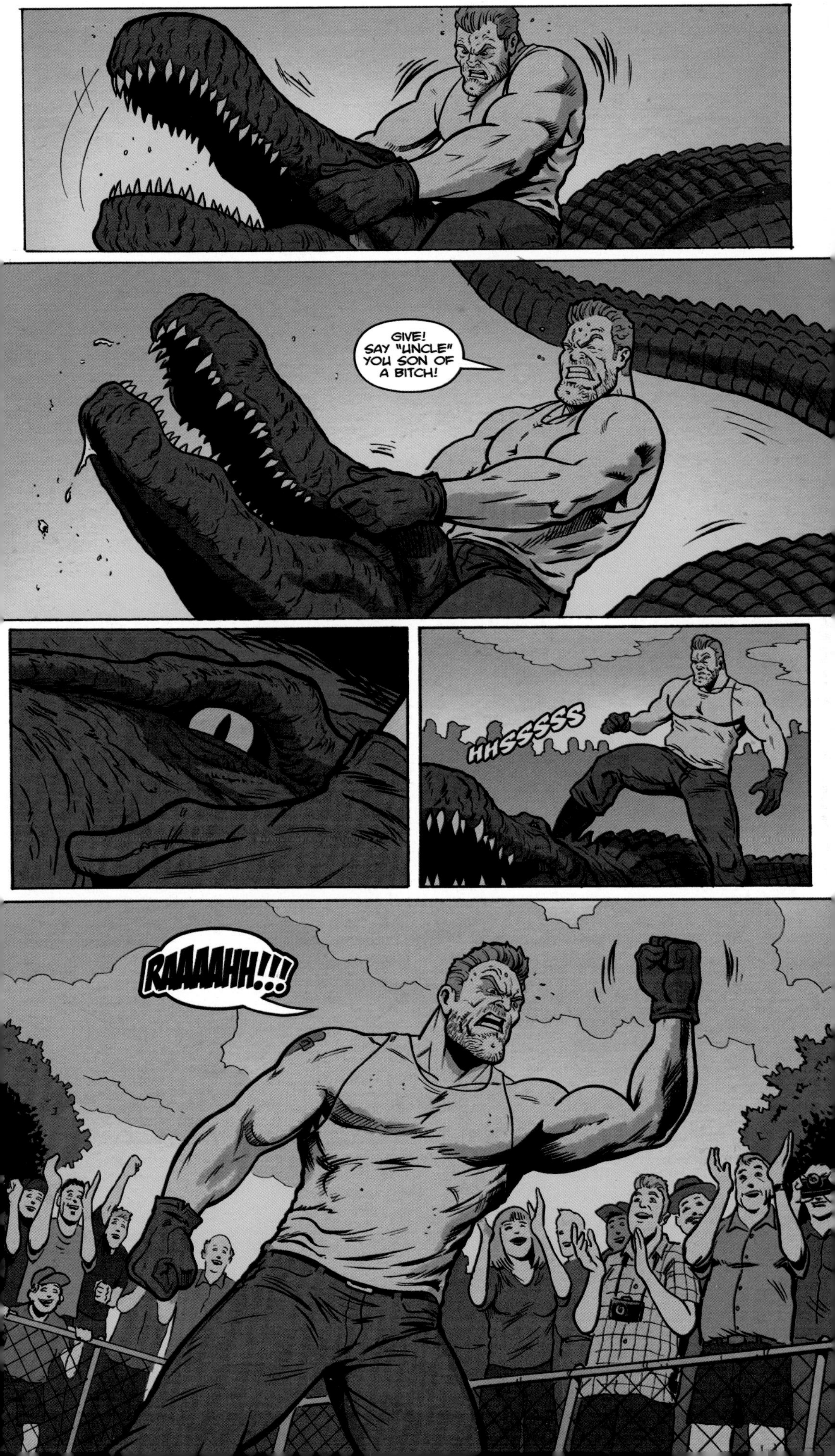
GIVE! SAY "UNCLE" YOU SON OF A BITCH!
HHSSSSS
RAAAAHH!!!

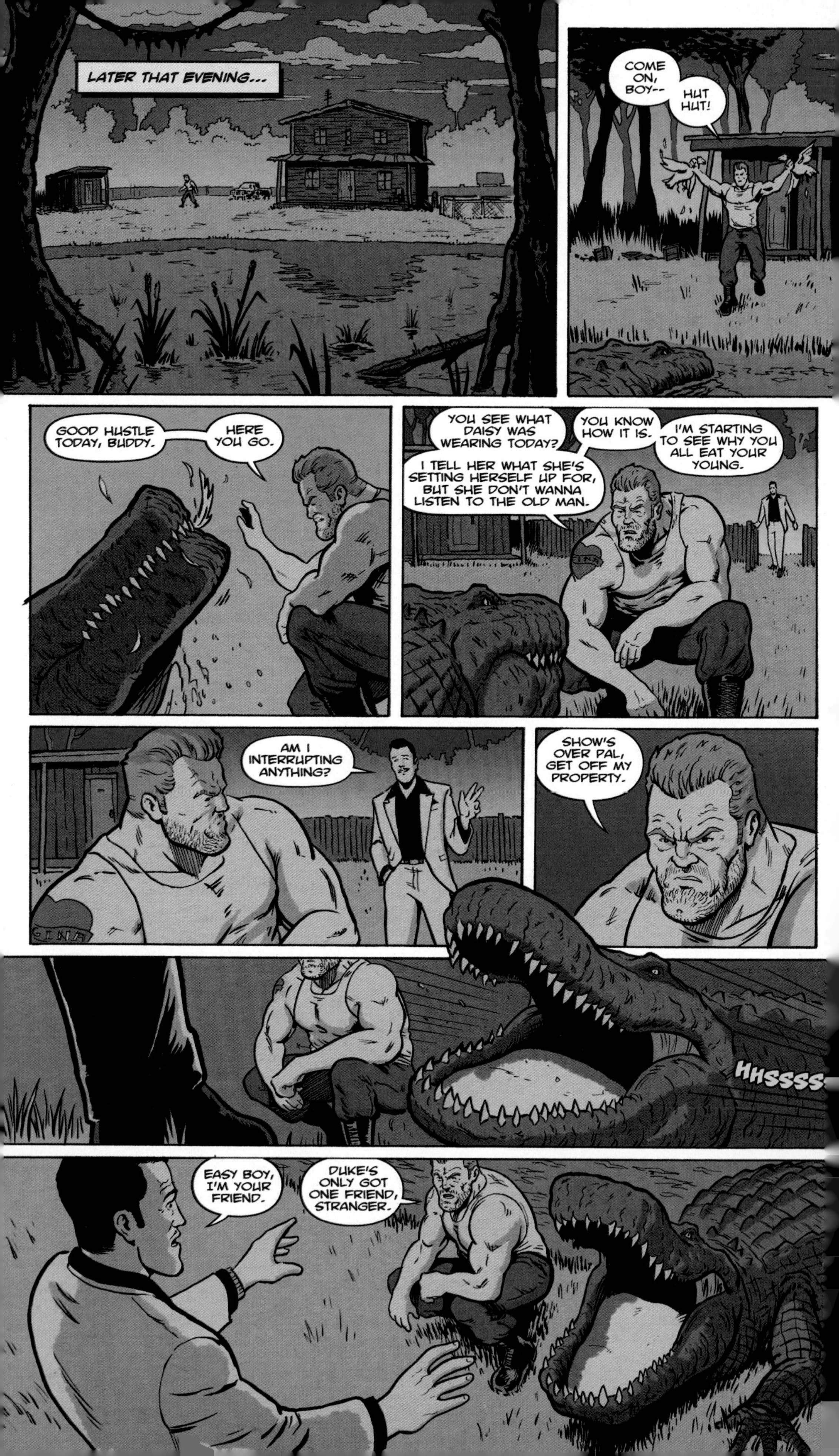
LATER THAT EVENING...
COME ON, BOY--
HUT HUT!
GOOD HUSTLE TODAY, BUDDY.
HERE YOU GO.
YOU SEE WHAT DAISY WAS WEARING TODAY?
I TELL HER WHAT SHE'S SETTING HERSELF UP FOR, BUT SHE DON'T WANNA LISTEN TO THE OLD MAN.
YOU KNOW HOW IT IS.
I'M STARTING TO SEE WHY YOU ALL EAT YOUR YOUNG.
AM I INTERRUPTING ANYTHING?
SHOW'S OVER PAL, GET OFF MY PROPERTY.
HHSSSS
EASY BOY, I'M YOUR FRIEND.
DUKE'S ONLY GOT ONE FRIEND, STRANGER.

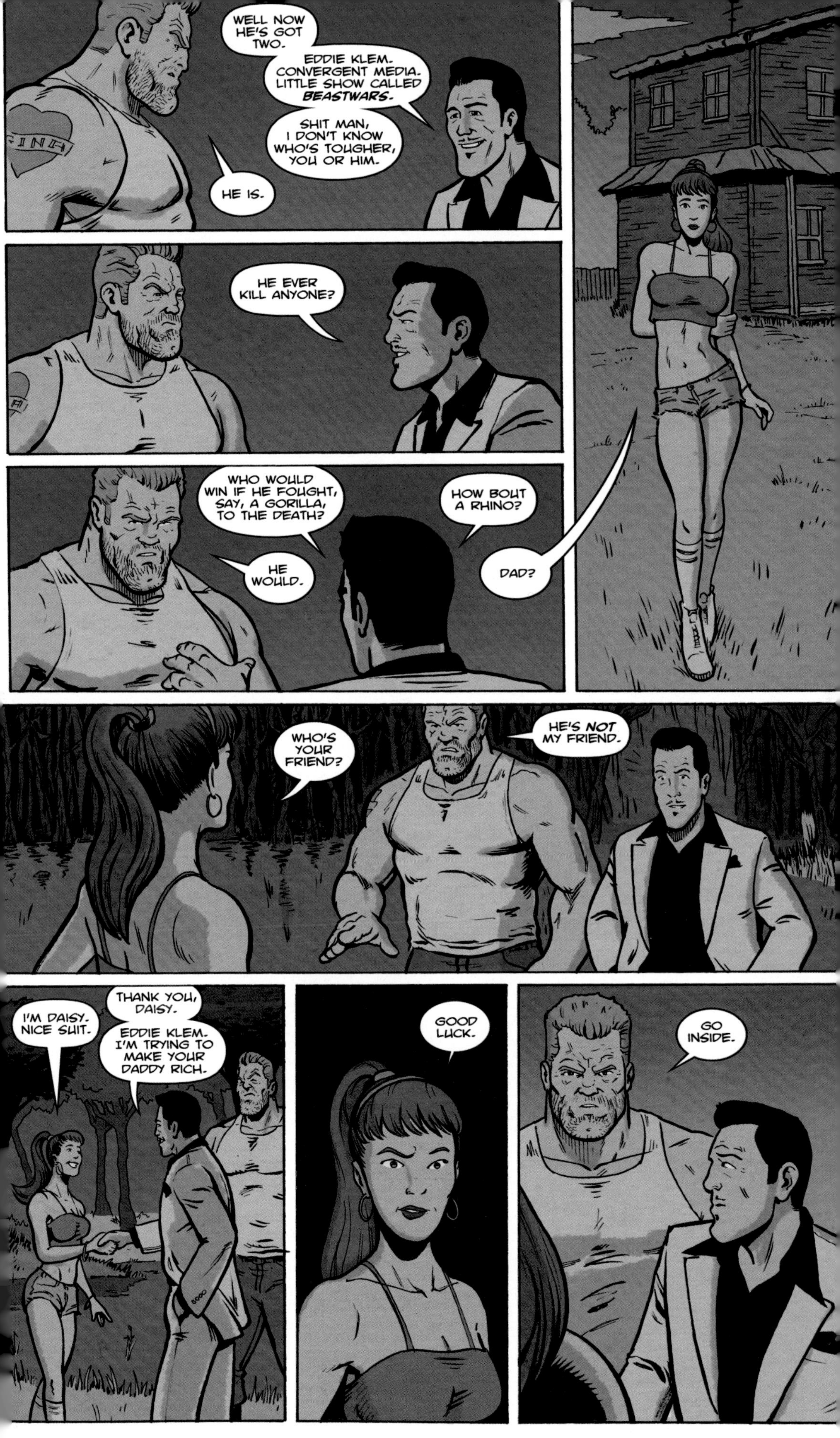
WELL NOW HE'S GOT TWO.
EDDIE KLEM. CONVERGENT MEDIA. LITTLE SHOW CALLED BEASTWARS.
SHIT MAN, I DON'T KNOW WHO'S TOUGHER, YOU OR HIM.
HE IS.
HE EVER KILL ANYONE?
WHO WOULD WIN IF HE FOUGHT, SAY, A GORILLA, TO THE DEATH?
HE WOULD.
HOW BOUT A RHINO?
DAD?
WHO'S YOUR FRIEND?
HE'S NOT MY FRIEND.
I'M DAISY. NICE SUIT.
THANK YOU, DAISY.
EDDIE KLEM. I'M TRYING TO MAKE YOUR DADDY RICH.
GOOD LUCK.
GO INSIDE.

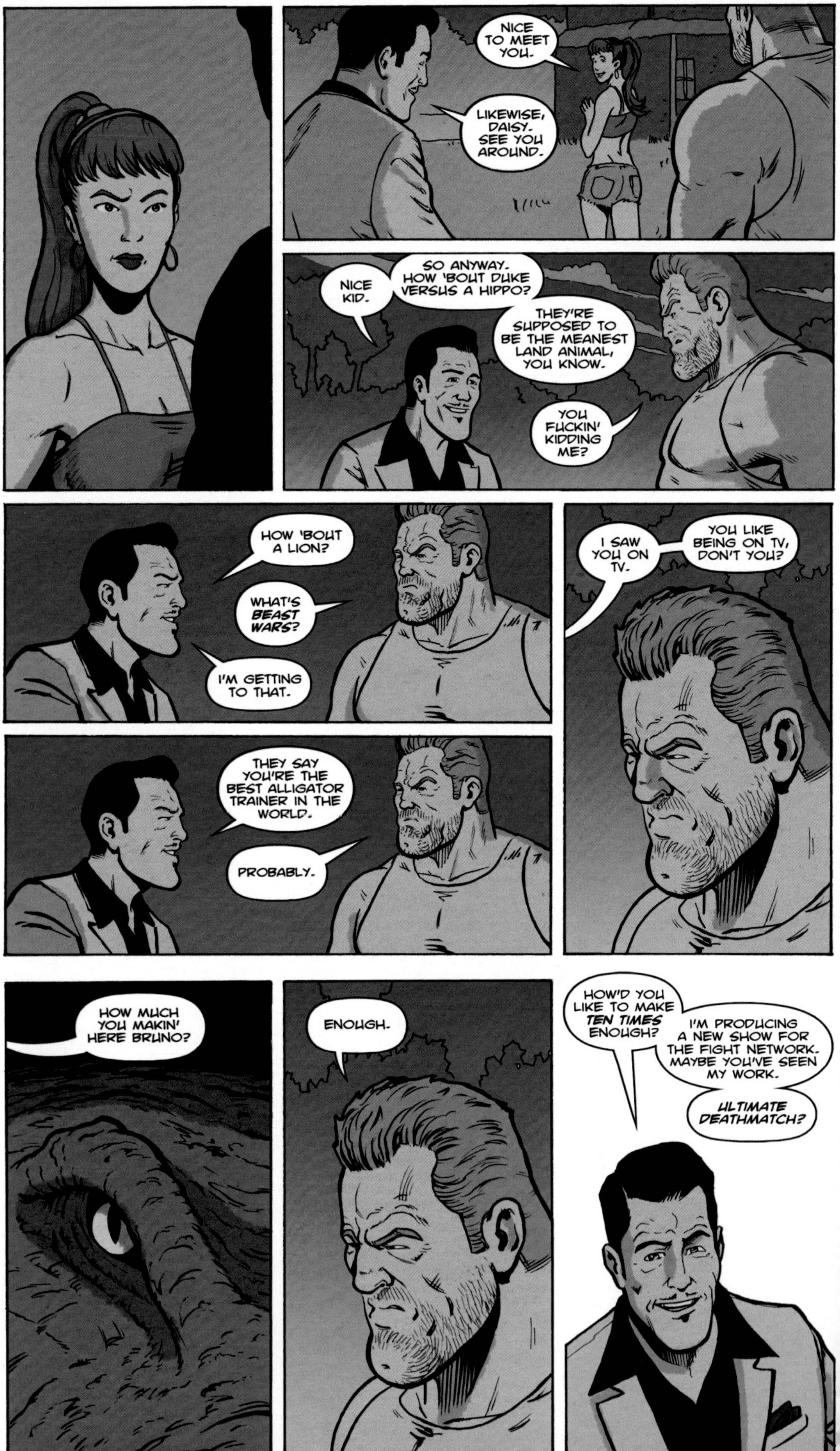
NICE TO MEET YOU.
LIKEWISE, DAISY. SEE YOU AROUND.
NICE KID.
SO ANYWAY. HOW 'BOUT DUKE VERSUS A HIPPO?
THEY'RE SUPPOSED TO BE THE MEANEST LAND ANIMAL, YOU KNOW.
YOU FUCKIN' KIDDING ME?
HOW 'BOUT A LION?
WHAT'S *BEAST WARS*?
I'M GETTING TO THAT.
THEY SAY YOU'RE THE BEST ALLIGATOR TRAINER IN THE WORLD.
PROBABLY.
I SAW YOU ON TV.
YOU LIKE BEING ON TV, DON'T YOU?
HOW MUCH YOU MAKIN' HERE BRUNO?
ENOUGH.
HOW'D YOU LIKE TO MAKE *TEN TIMES* ENOUGH?
I'M PRODUCING A NEW SHOW FOR THE FIGHT NETWORK. MAYBE YOU'VE SEEN MY WORK.
ULTIMATE DEATHMATCH?

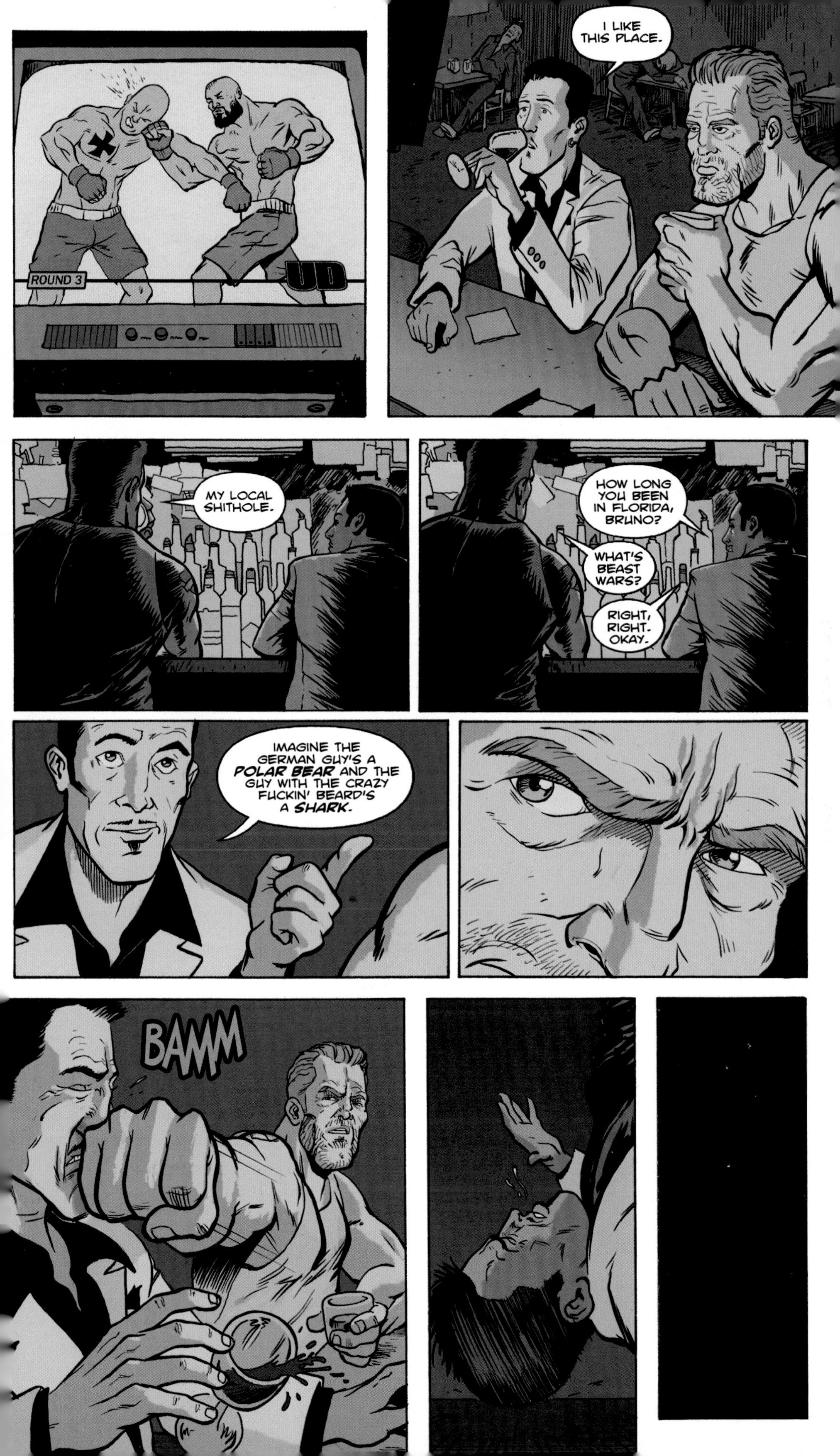
ROUND 3
UD
I LIKE THIS PLACE.
MY LOCAL SHITHOLE.
HOW LONG YOU BEEN IN FLORIDA, BRUNO?
WHAT'S BEAST WARS?
RIGHT, RIGHT. OKAY.
IMAGINE THE GERMAN GUY'S A POLAR BEAR AND THE GUY WITH THE CRAZY FUCKIN' BEARD'S A SHARK.
BAMM

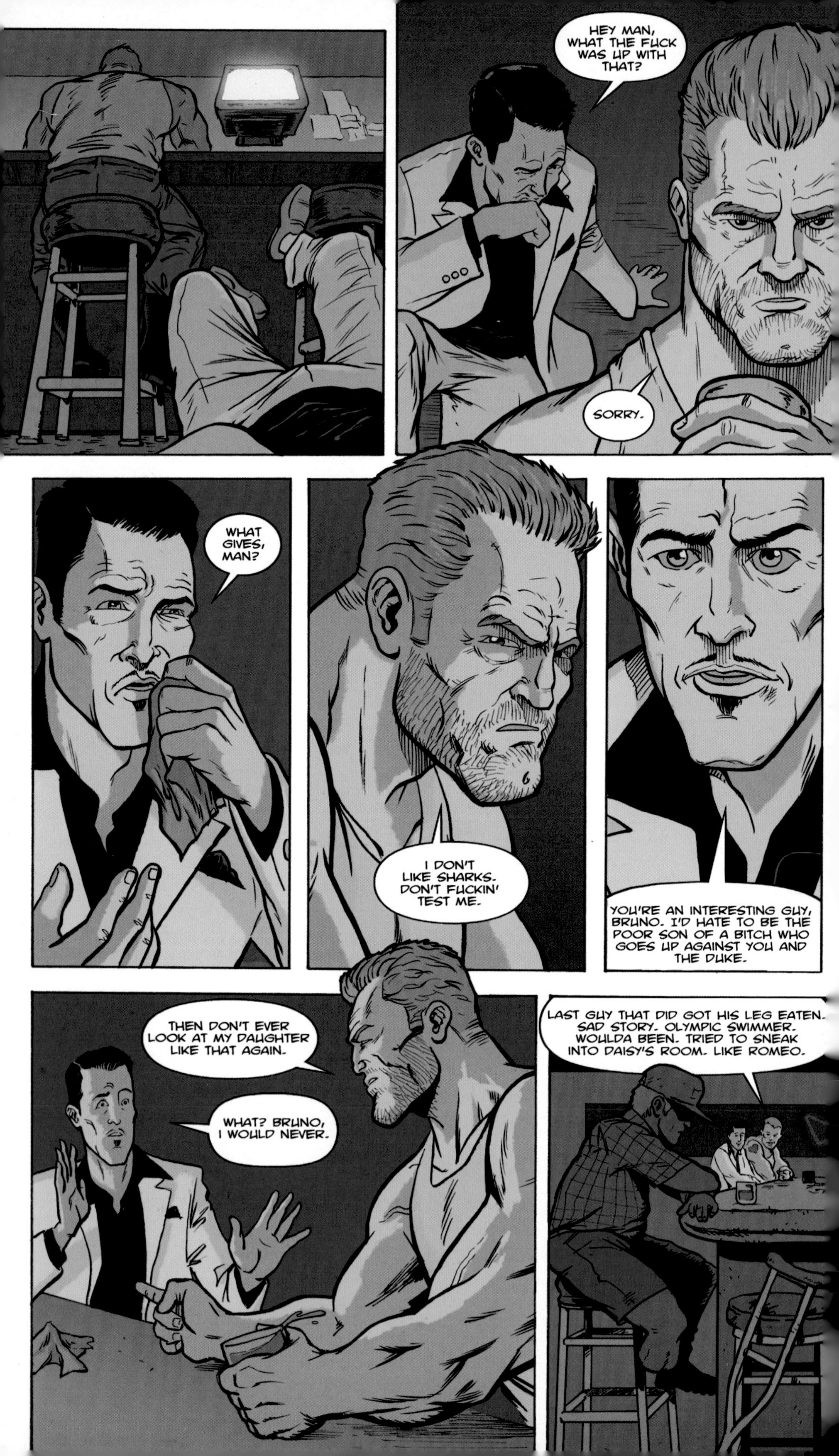
HEY MAN, WHAT THE FUCK WAS UP WITH THAT?
SORRY.
WHAT GIVES, MAN?
I DON'T LIKE SHARKS. DON'T FUCKIN' TEST ME.
YOU'RE AN INTERESTING GUY, BRUNO. I'D HATE TO BE THE POOR SON OF A BITCH WHO GOES UP AGAINST YOU AND THE DUKE.
THEN DON'T EVER LOOK AT MY DAUGHTER LIKE THAT AGAIN.
WHAT? BRUNO, I WOULD NEVER.
LAST GUY THAT DID GOT HIS LEG EATEN. SAD STORY. OLYMPIC SWIMMER. WOULDA BEEN. TRIED TO SNEAK INTO DAISY'S ROOM. LIKE ROMEO.

SEE THAT GUY BRUNO?

APOCALYPSE.

YEAH. APOCALYPSE. BEST IN THE BUSINESS. WE PAY HIM A HUNDRED GS A MATCH.

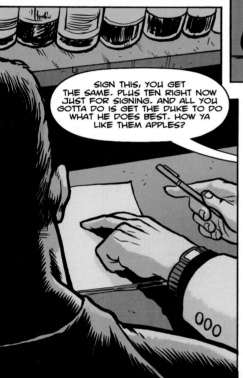

SIGN THIS, YOU GET THE SAME. PLUS TEN RIGHT NOW JUST FOR SIGNING. AND ALL YOU GOTTA DO IS GET THE DUKE TO DO WHAT HE DOES BEST. HOW YA LIKE THEM APPLES?

SOUNDS LIKE A SCAM.

WHAT HAVE YOU GOT WORTH SCAMMING, BRUNO?

NOTHING.

HOW SOON CAN YOU GET PACKED?

SLOW DOWN, PAL. DRINK.

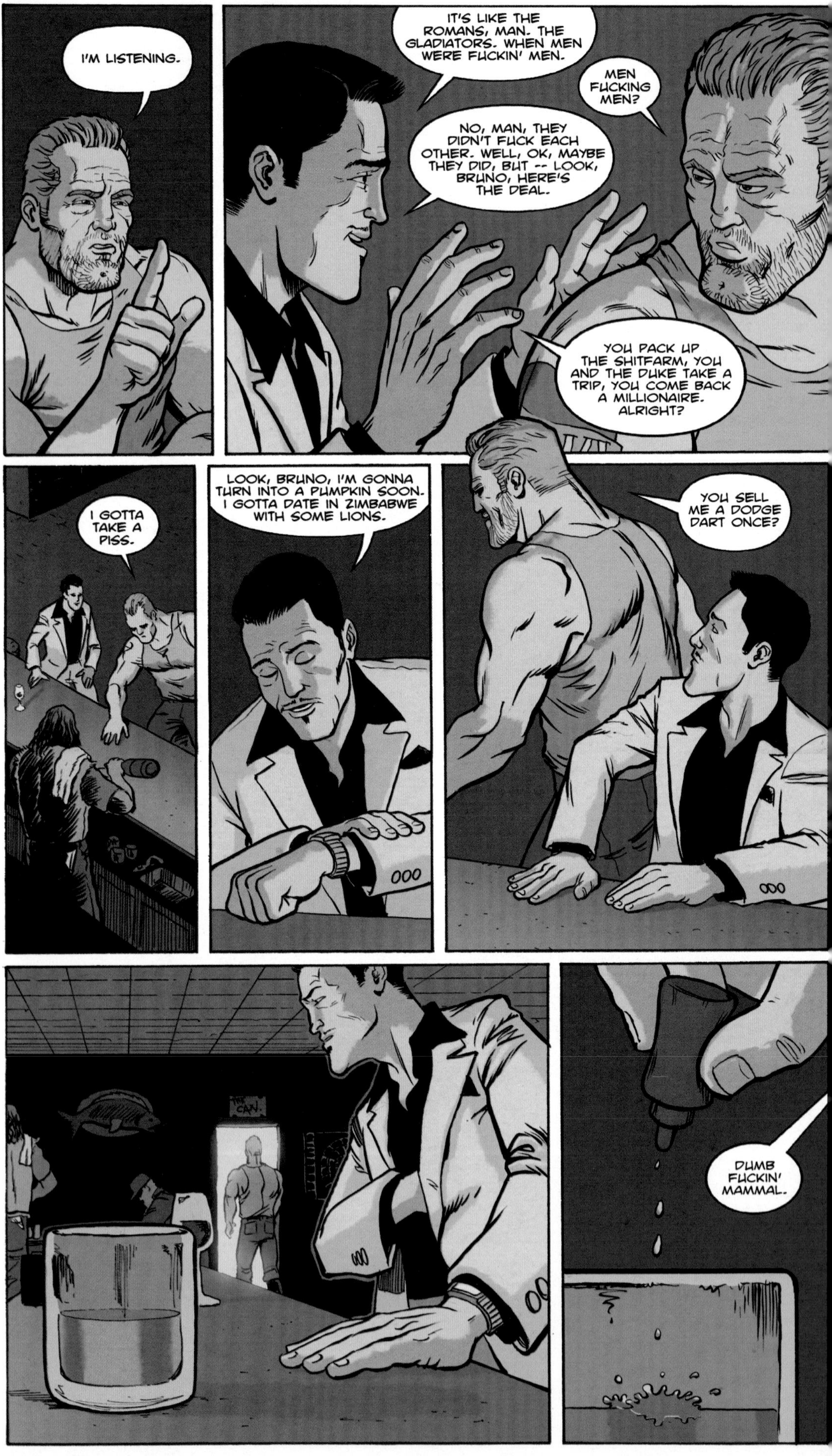
I'M LISTENING.
IT'S LIKE THE ROMANS, MAN. THE GLADIATORS. WHEN MEN WERE FUCKIN' MEN.
MEN FUCKING MEN?
NO, MAN, THEY DIDN'T FUCK EACH OTHER. WELL, OK, MAYBE THEY DID, BUT -- LOOK, BRUNO, HERE'S THE DEAL.
YOU PACK UP THE SHITFARM, YOU AND THE DUKE TAKE A TRIP, YOU COME BACK A MILLIONAIRE. ALRIGHT?
I GOTTA TAKE A PISS.
LOOK, BRUNO, I'M GONNA TURN INTO A PUMPKIN SOON. I GOTTA DATE IN ZIMBABWE WITH SOME LIONS.
YOU SELL ME A DODGE DART ONCE?
THE CAN
DUMB FUCKIN' MAMMAL.

I DO SOME OF MY BEST THINKING IN THE CAN.

LET'S KICK SOME ASS.

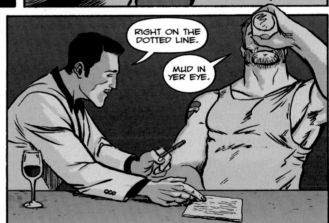

RIGHT ON THE DOTTED LINE.

MUD IN YER EYE.

GODDAMN. HOW MANY I HAD?

ENOUGH, BUDDY, ENOUGH.

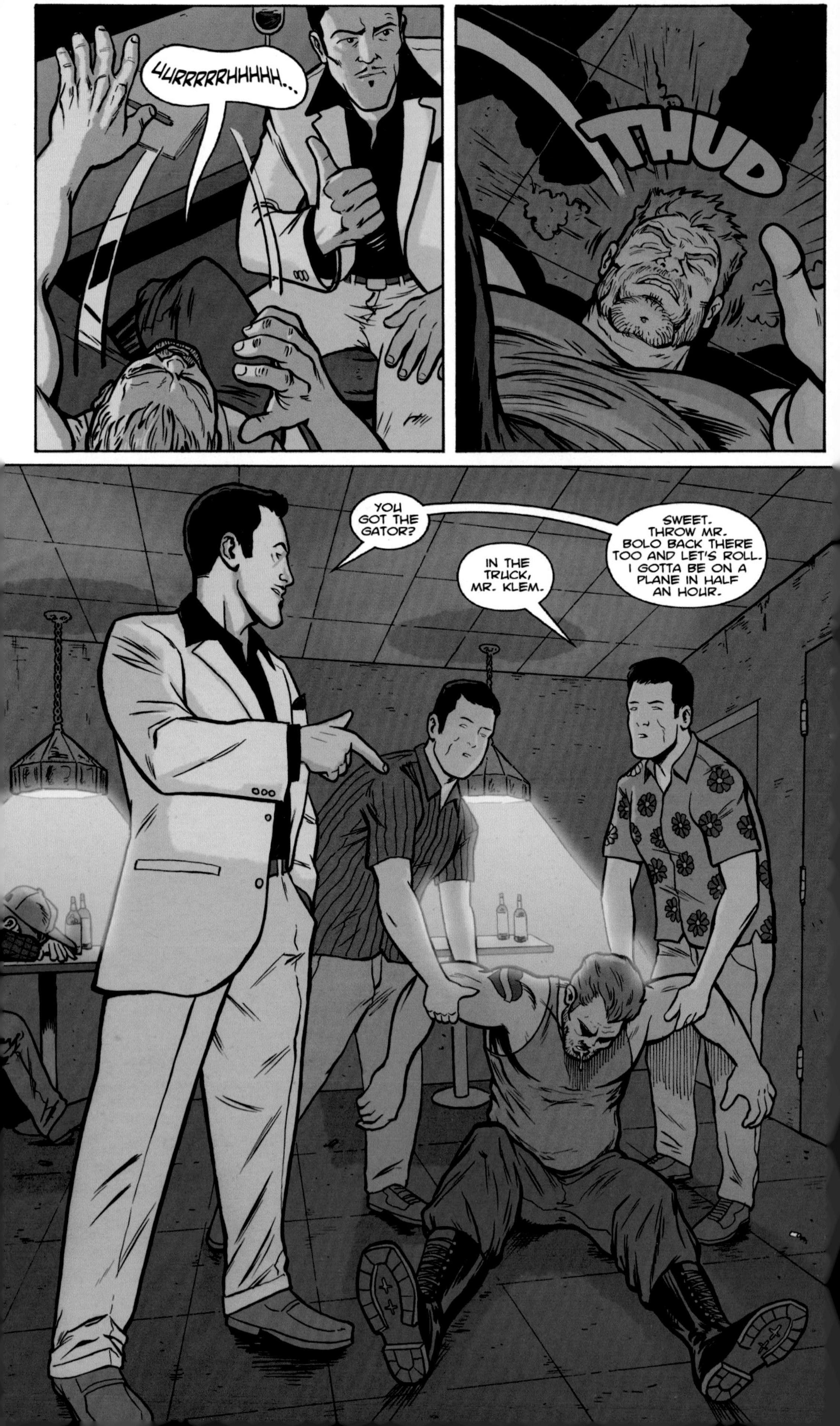
UURRRRRHHHHH...
THUD
YOU GOT THE GATOR?
IN THE TRUCK, MR. KLEM.
SWEET. THROW MR. BOLO BACK THERE TOO AND LET'S ROLL. I GOTTA BE ON A PLANE IN HALF AN HOUR.

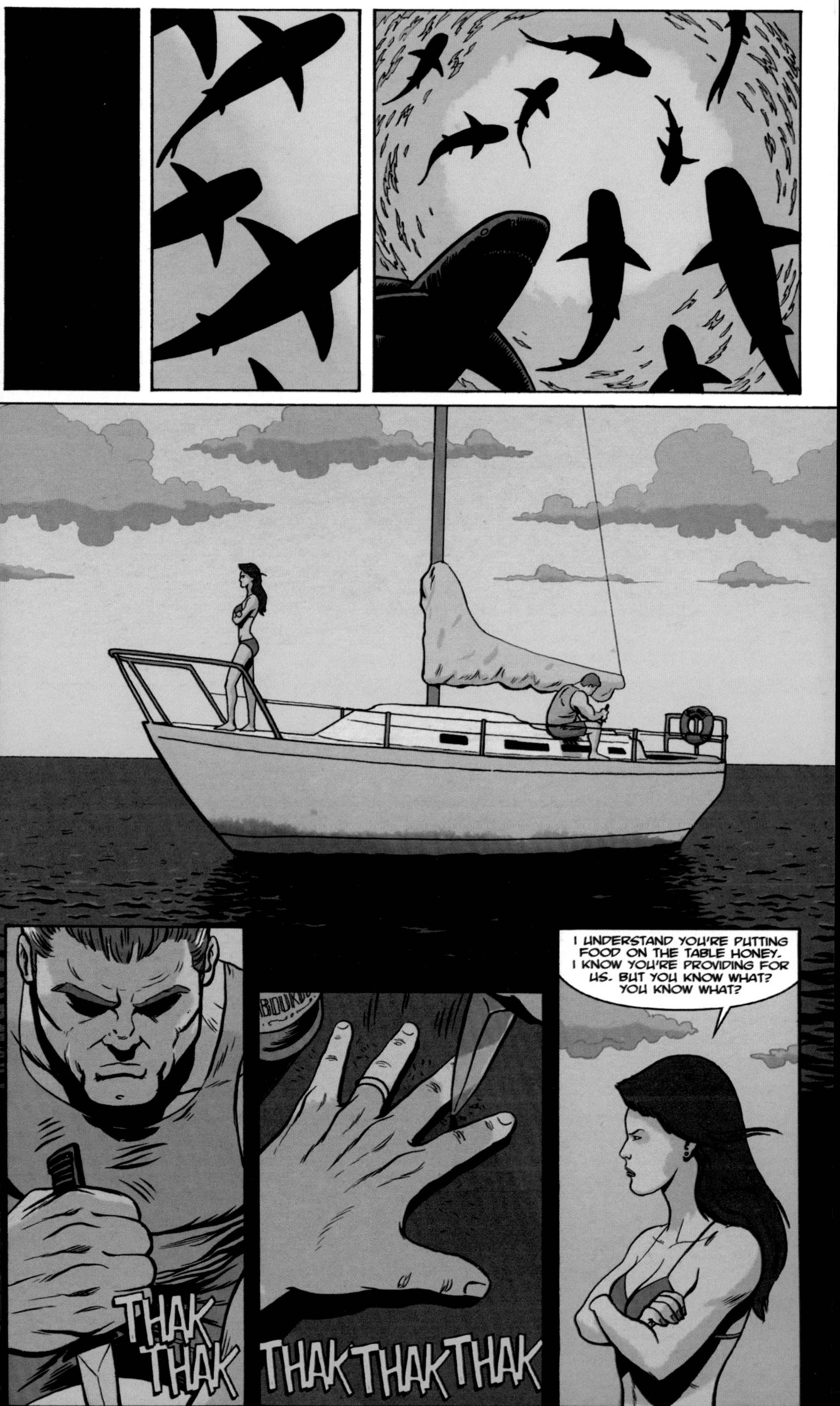

I UNDERSTAND YOU'RE PUTTING FOOD ON THE TABLE HONEY. I KNOW YOU'RE PROVIDING FOR US. BUT YOU KNOW WHAT? YOU KNOW WHAT?
THAK THAK
THAK THAK THAK

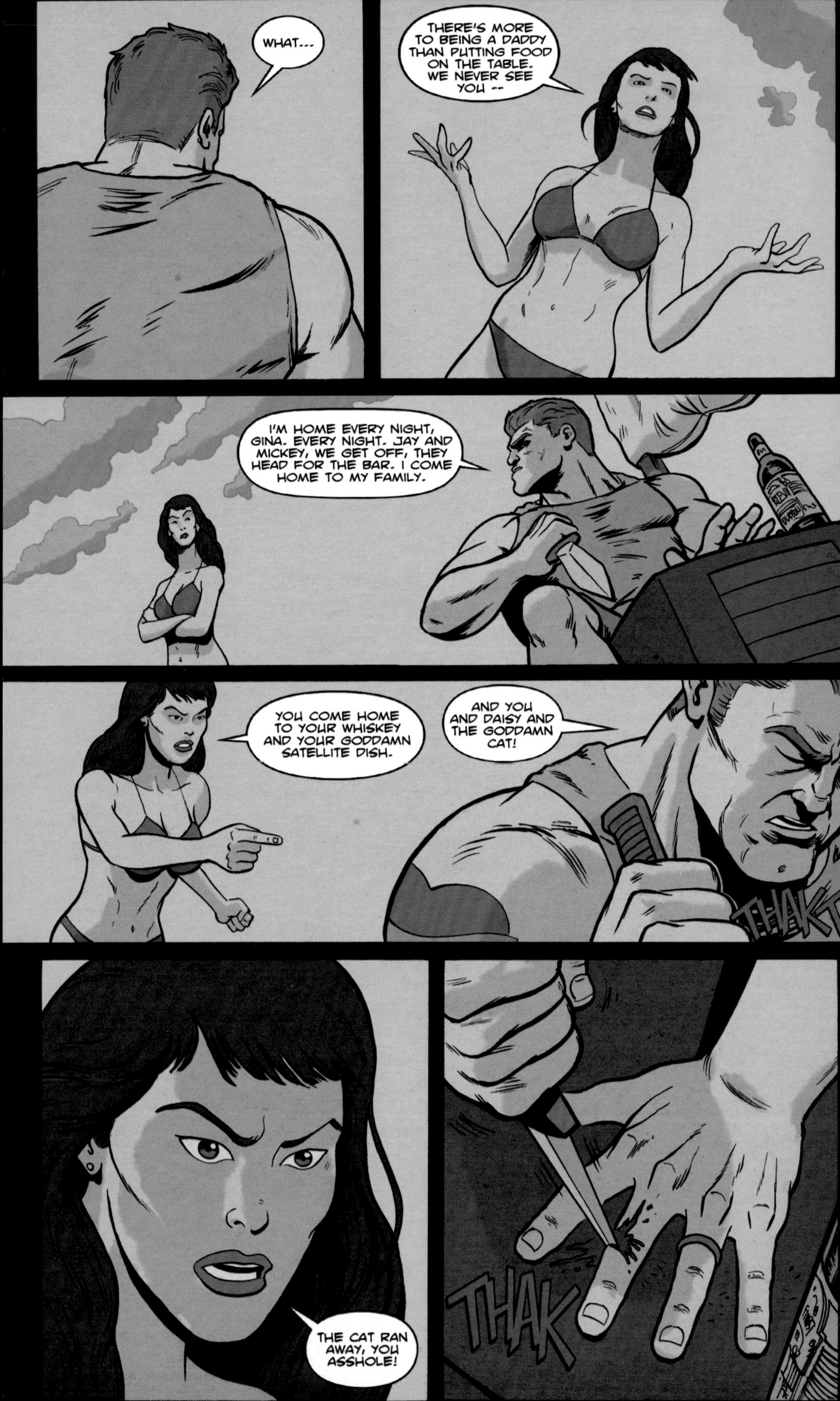

WHAT...
THERE'S MORE TO BEING A DADDY THAN PUTTING FOOD ON THE TABLE. WE NEVER SEE YOU --
I'M HOME EVERY NIGHT, GINA. EVERY NIGHT. JAY AND MICKEY, WE GET OFF, THEY HEAD FOR THE BAR. I COME HOME TO MY FAMILY.
YOU COME HOME TO YOUR WHISKEY AND YOUR GODDAMN SATELLITE DISH.
AND YOU AND DAISY AND THE GODDAMN CAT!
THAKT
THE CAT RAN AWAY, YOU ASSHOLE!
THAK

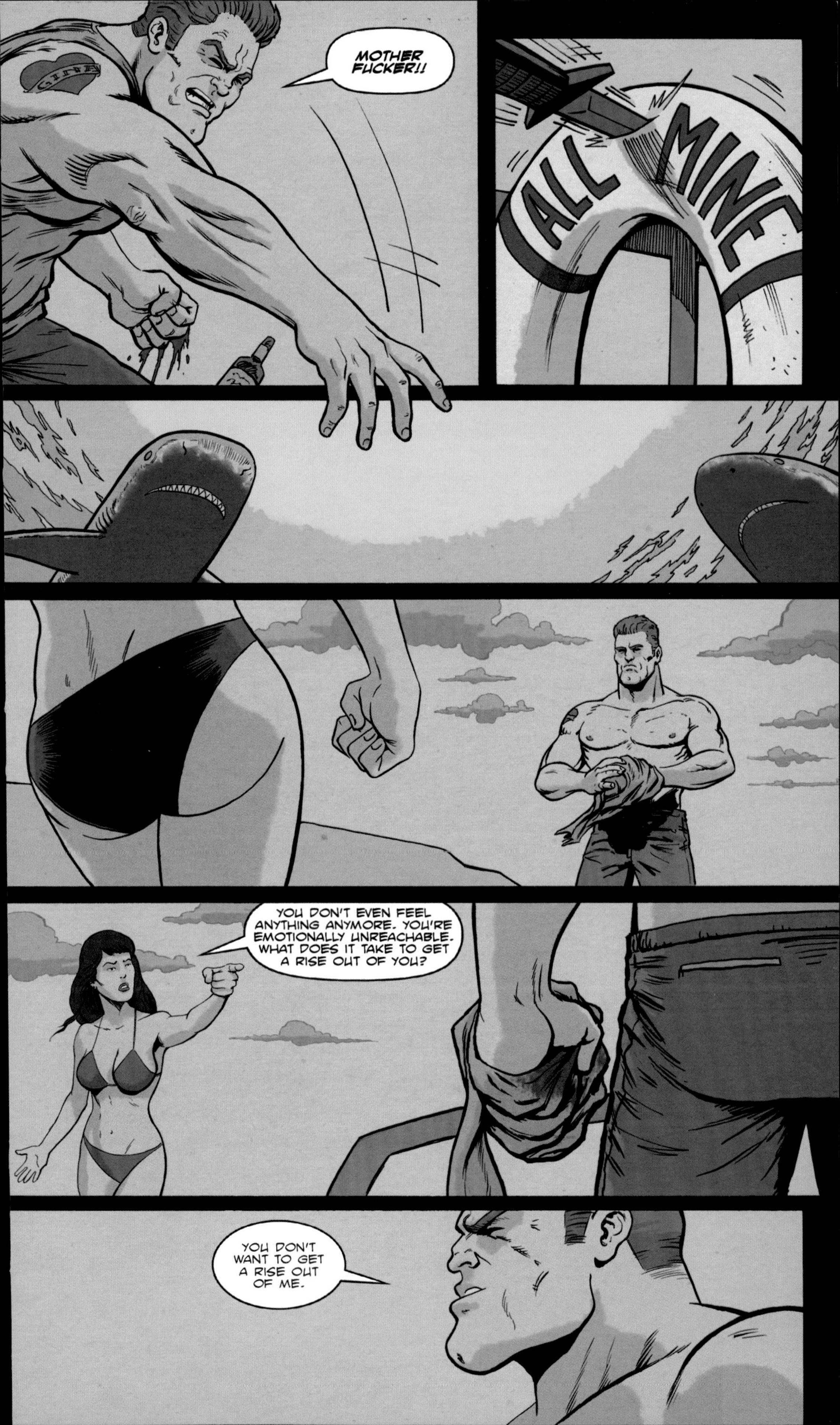
MOTHER FUCKER!!
ALL MINE
YOU DON'T EVEN FEEL ANYTHING ANYMORE. YOU'RE EMOTIONALLY UNREACHABLE. WHAT DOES IT TAKE TO GET A RISE OUT OF YOU?
YOU DON'T WANT TO GET A RISE OUT OF ME.

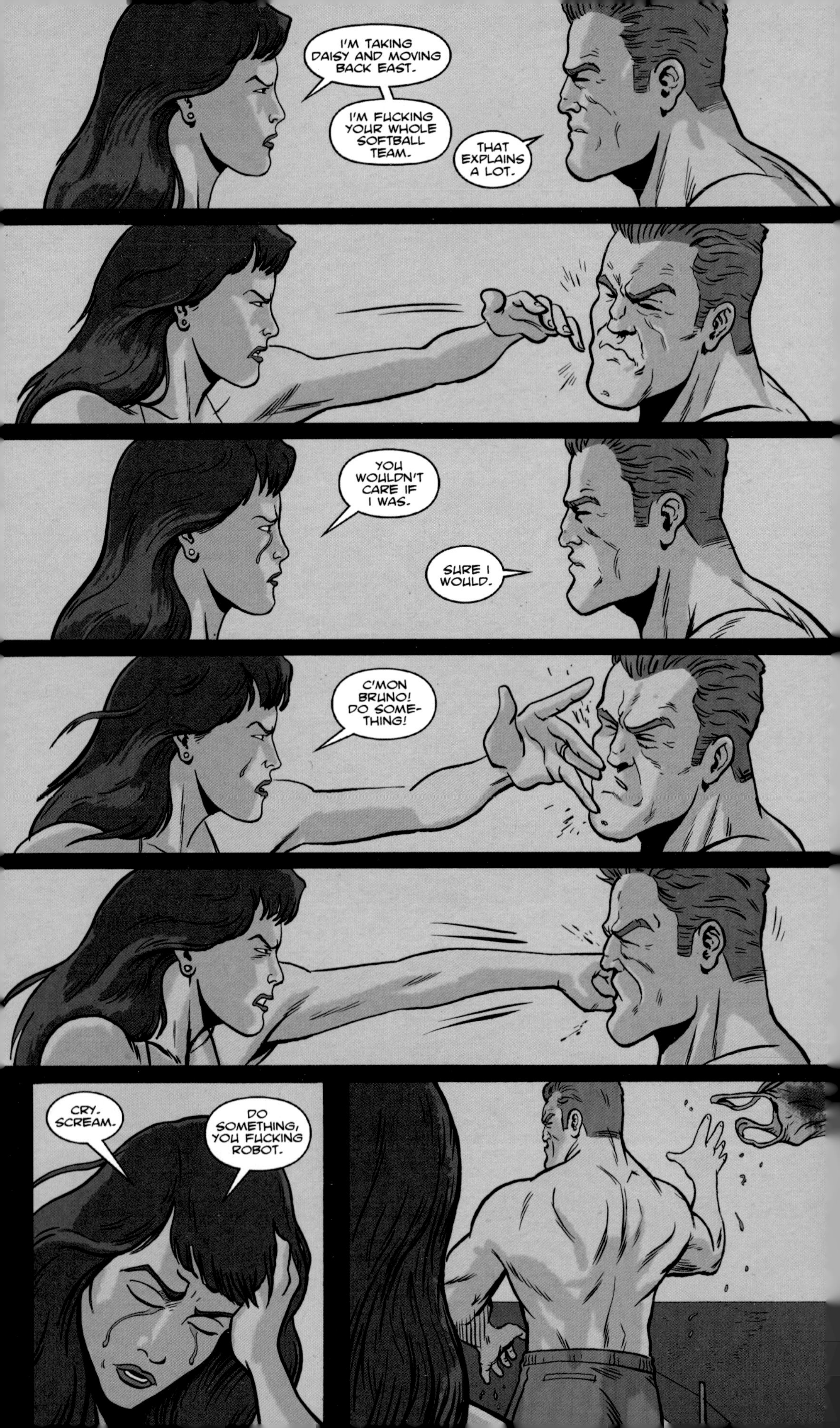
I'M TAKING DAISY AND MOVING BACK EAST.
I'M FUCKING YOUR WHOLE SOFTBALL TEAM.
THAT EXPLAINS A LOT.
YOU WOULDN'T CARE IF I WAS.
SURE I WOULD.
C'MON BRUNO! DO SOME-THING!
CRY. SCREAM.
DO SOMETHING, YOU FUCKING ROBOT.

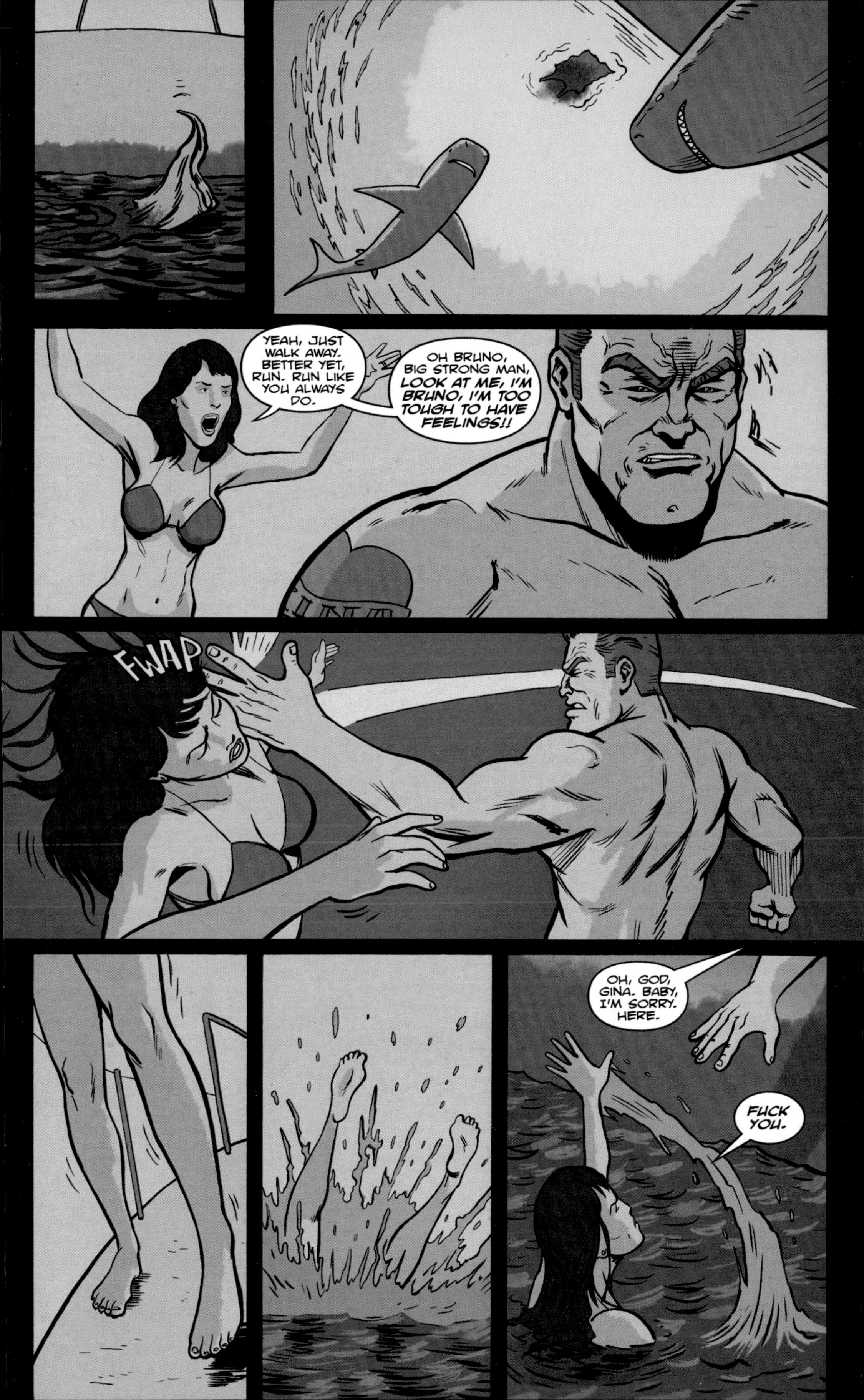
YEAH, JUST WALK AWAY. BETTER YET, RUN. RUN LIKE YOU ALWAYS DO.
OH BRUNO, BIG STRONG MAN, LOOK AT ME, I'M BRUNO, I'M TOO TOUGH TO HAVE FEELINGS!!
FWAP
OH, GOD, GINA. BABY, I'M SORRY. HERE.
FUCK YOU.

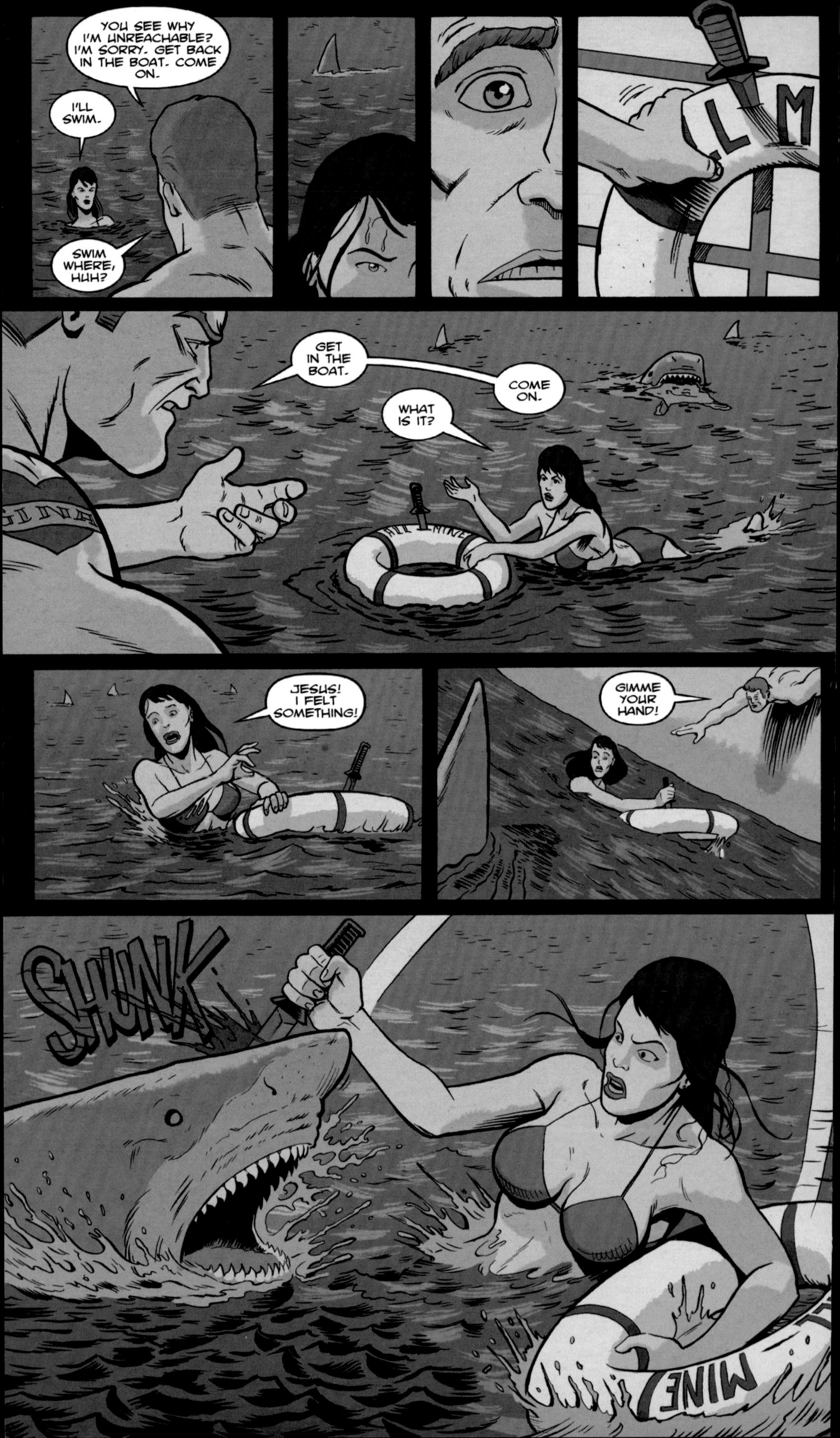
YOU SEE WHY I'M UNREACHABLE? I'M SORRY. GET BACK IN THE BOAT. COME ON.
I'LL SWIM.
SWIM WHERE, HUH?
GET IN THE BOAT.
COME ON.
WHAT IS IT?
JESUS! I FELT SOMETHING!
GIMME YOUR HAND!
SHUNK

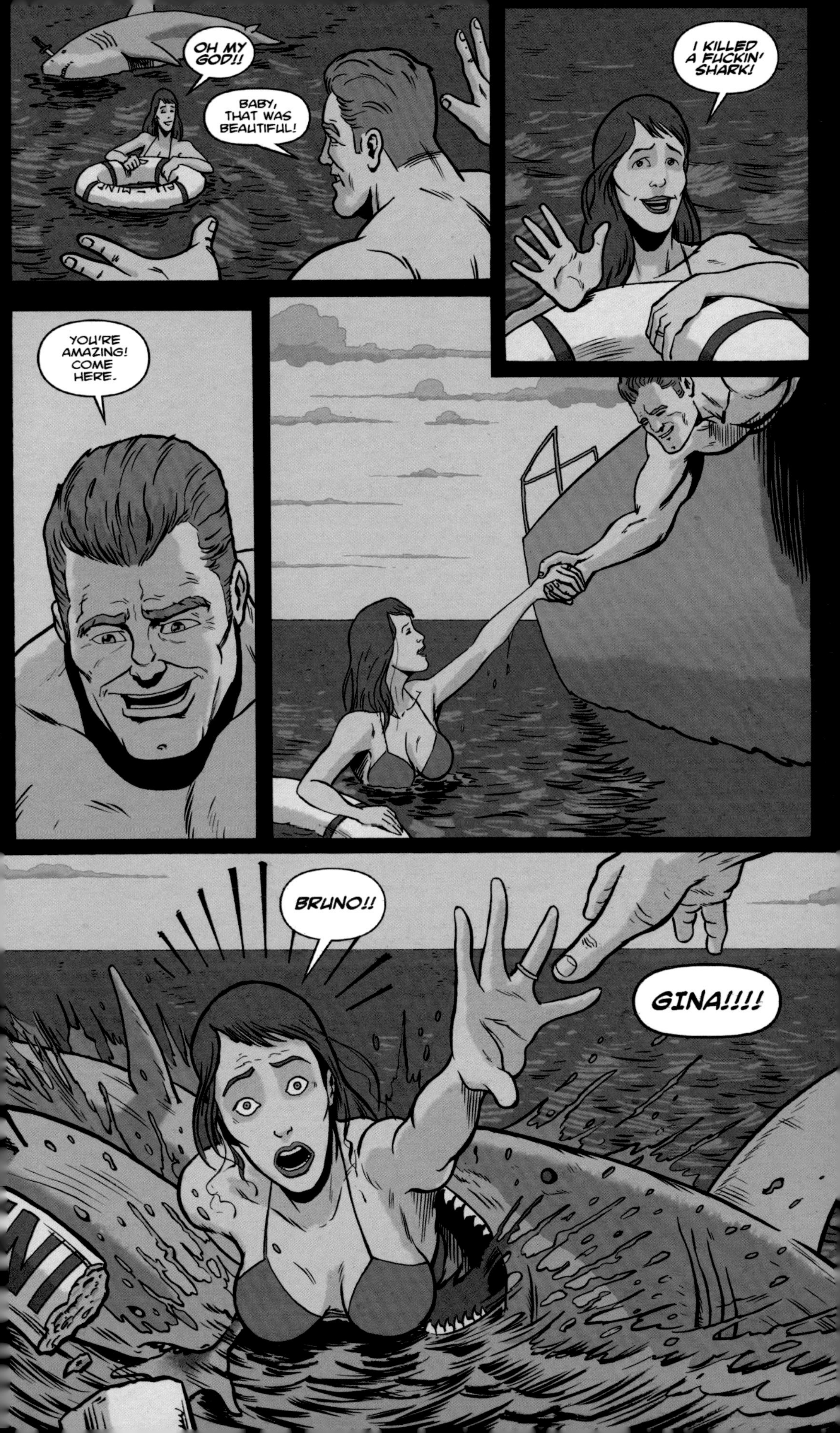
OH MY GOD!!
BABY, THAT WAS BEAUTIFUL!
I KILLED A FUCKIN' SHARK!
YOU'RE AMAZING! COME HERE.
BRUNO!!
GINA!!!!

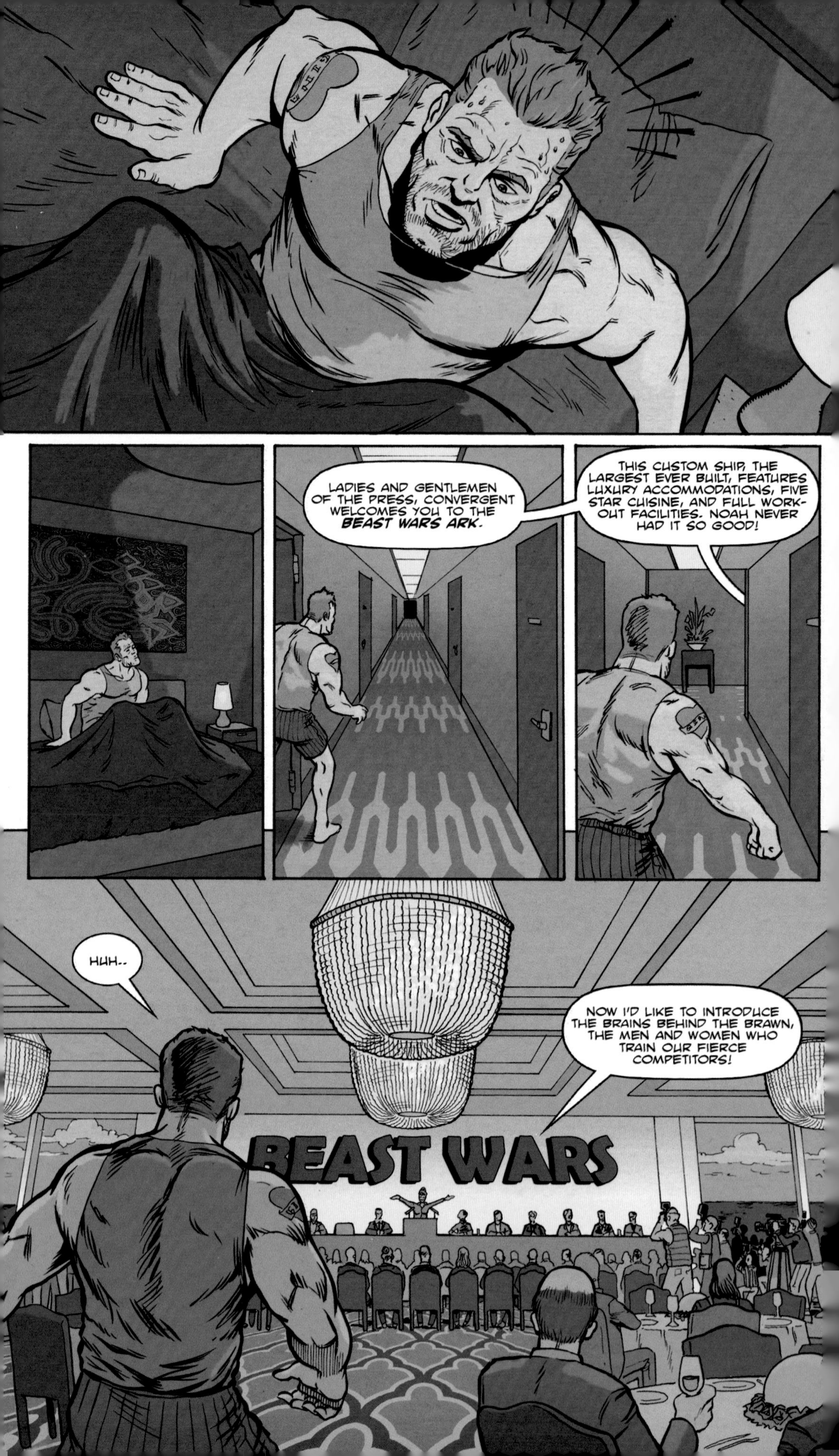
LADIES AND GENTLEMEN OF THE PRESS, CONVERGENT WELCOMES YOU TO THE *BEAST WARS ARK*.
THIS CUSTOM SHIP, THE LARGEST EVER BUILT, FEATURES LUXURY ACCOMMODATIONS, FIVE STAR CUISINE, AND FULL WORK-OUT FACILITIES. NOAH NEVER HAD IT SO GOOD!
HUH--
NOW I'D LIKE TO INTRODUCE THE BRAINS BEHIND THE BRAWN, THE MEN AND WOMEN WHO TRAIN OUR FIERCE COMPETITORS!
BEAST WARS

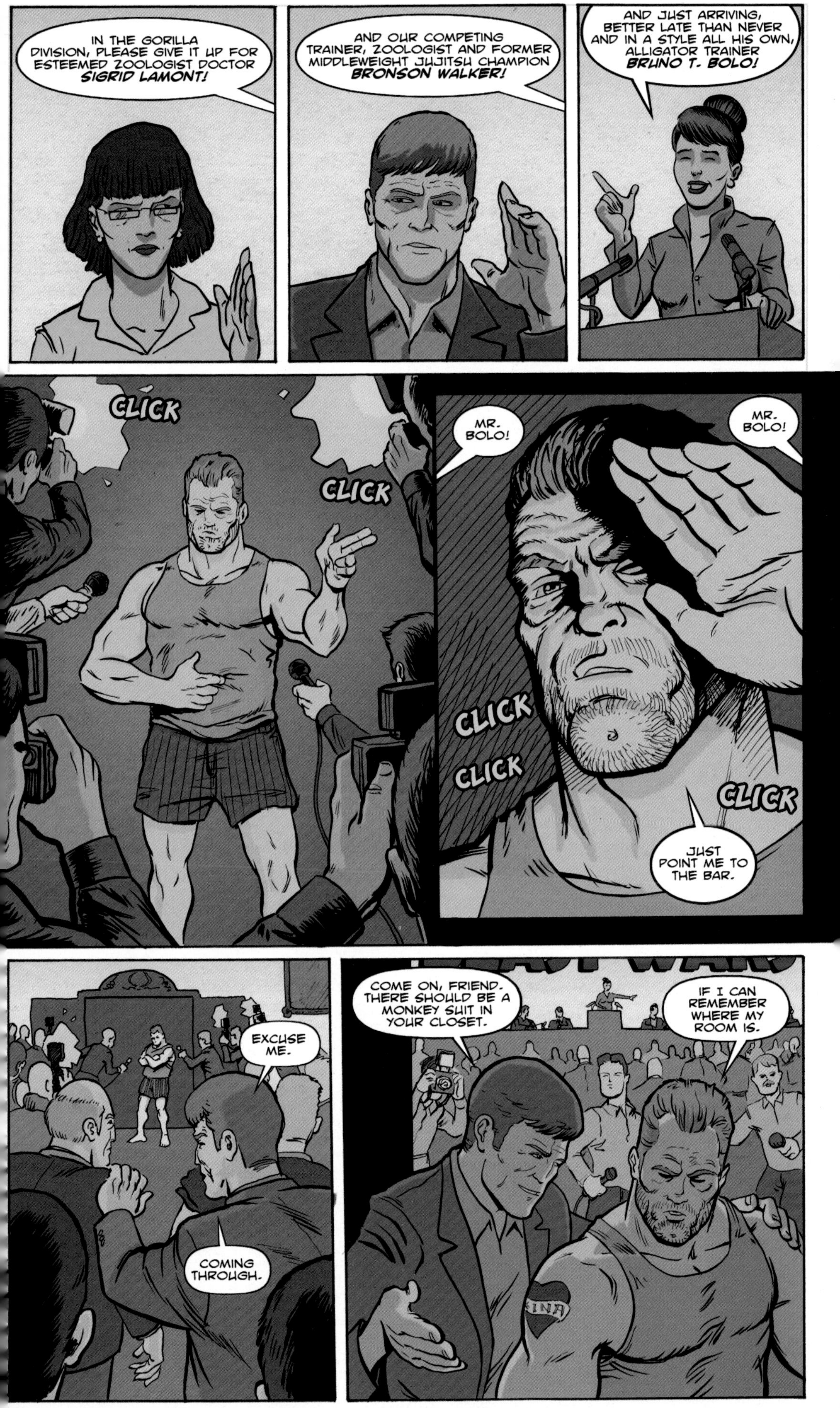
IN THE GORILLA DIVISION, PLEASE GIVE IT UP FOR ESTEEMED ZOOLOGIST DOCTOR SIGRID LAMONT!
AND OUR COMPETING TRAINER, ZOOLOGIST AND FORMER MIDDLEWEIGHT JUJITSU CHAMPION BRONSON WALKER!
AND JUST ARRIVING, BETTER LATE THAN NEVER AND IN A STYLE ALL HIS OWN, ALLIGATOR TRAINER BRUNO T. BOLO!
CLICK
CLICK
MR. BOLO!
MR. BOLO!
CLICK
CLICK
CLICK
JUST POINT ME TO THE BAR.
EXCUSE ME.
COMING THROUGH.
COME ON, FRIEND. THERE SHOULD BE A MONKEY SUIT IN YOUR CLOSET.
IF I CAN REMEMBER WHERE MY ROOM IS.

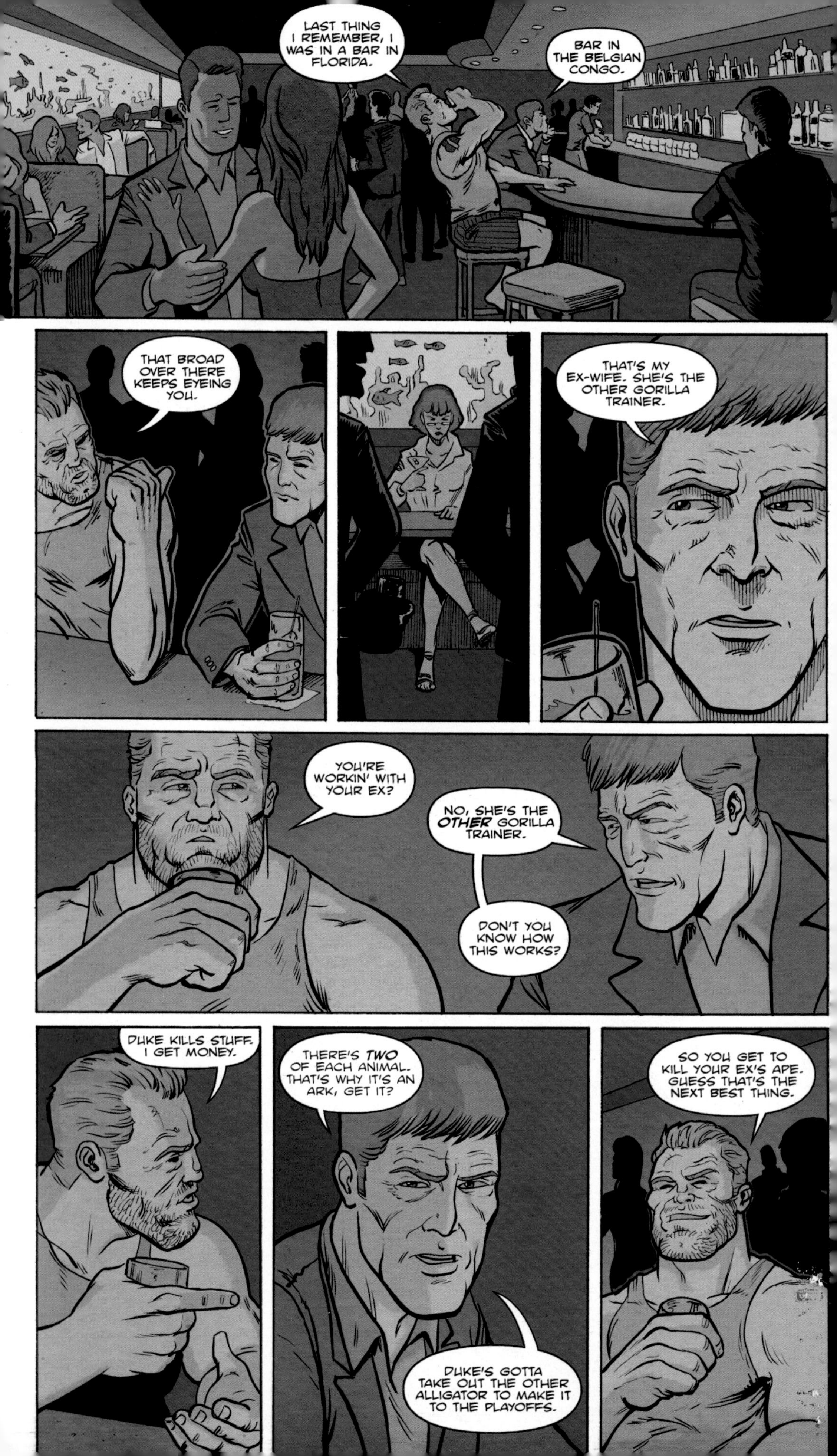

LAST THING I REMEMBER, I WAS IN A BAR IN FLORIDA.
BAR IN THE BELGIAN CONGO.
THAT BROAD OVER THERE KEEPS EYEING YOU.
THAT'S MY EX-WIFE. SHE'S THE OTHER GORILLA TRAINER.
YOU'RE WORKIN' WITH YOUR EX?
NO, SHE'S THE OTHER GORILLA TRAINER.
DON'T YOU KNOW HOW THIS WORKS?
DUKE KILLS STUFF. I GET MONEY.
THERE'S TWO OF EACH ANIMAL. THAT'S WHY IT'S AN ARK, GET IT?
DUKE'S GOTTA TAKE OUT THE OTHER ALLIGATOR TO MAKE IT TO THE PLAYOFFS.
SO YOU GET TO KILL YOUR EX'S APE. GUESS THAT'S THE NEXT BEST THING.

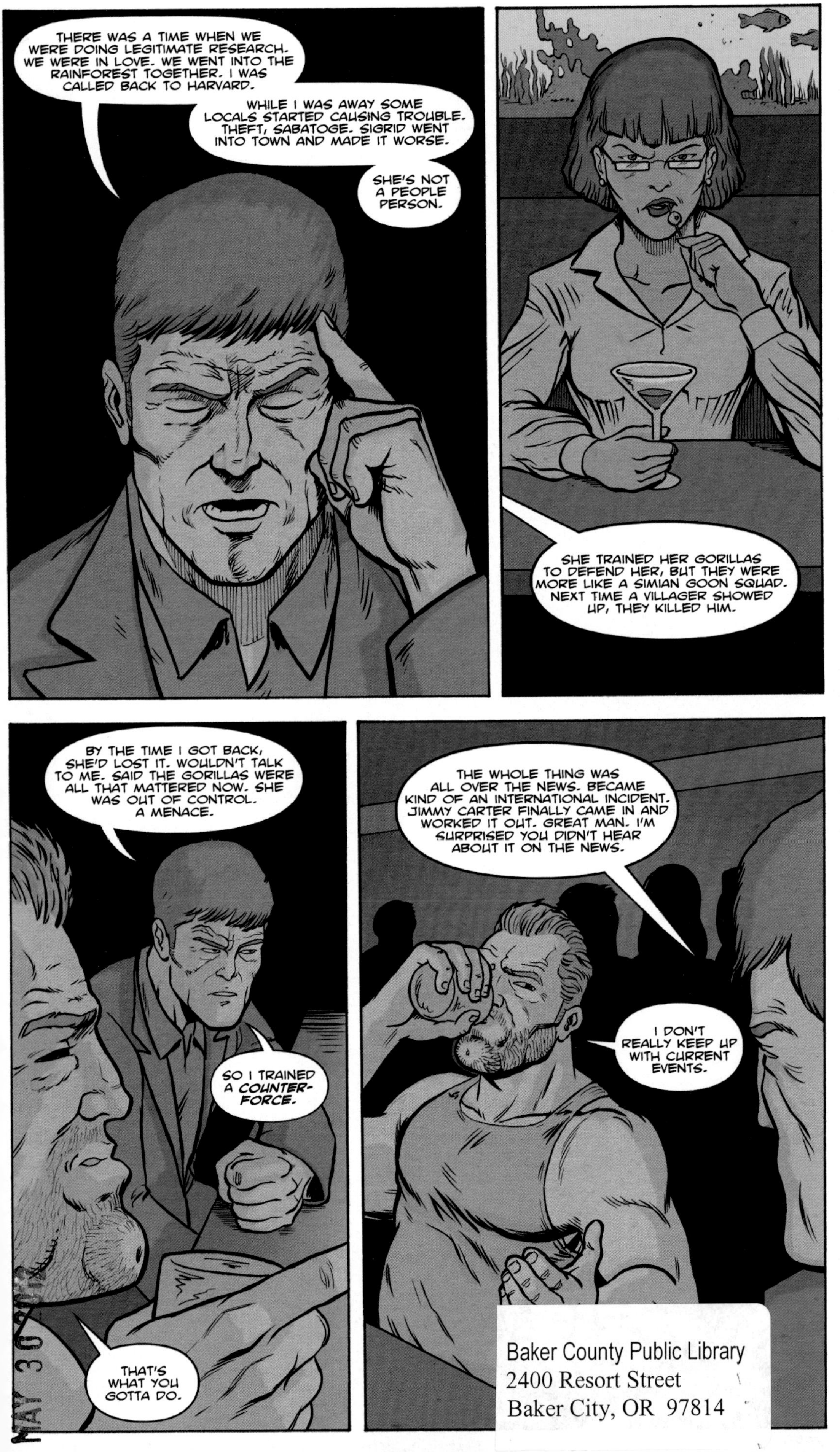
THERE WAS A TIME WHEN WE WERE DOING LEGITIMATE RESEARCH. WE WERE IN LOVE. WE WENT INTO THE RAINFOREST TOGETHER. I WAS CALLED BACK TO HARVARD.
WHILE I WAS AWAY SOME LOCALS STARTED CAUSING TROUBLE. THEFT, SABATOGE. SIGRID WENT INTO TOWN AND MADE IT WORSE.
SHE'S NOT A PEOPLE PERSON.
SHE TRAINED HER GORILLAS TO DEFEND HER, BUT THEY WERE MORE LIKE A SIMIAN GOON SQUAD. NEXT TIME A VILLAGER SHOWED UP, THEY KILLED HIM.
BY THE TIME I GOT BACK, SHE'D LOST IT. WOULDN'T TALK TO ME. SAID THE GORILLAS WERE ALL THAT MATTERED NOW. SHE WAS OUT OF CONTROL. A MENACE.
SO I TRAINED A *COUNTER-FORCE.*
THAT'S WHAT YOU GOTTA DO.
THE WHOLE THING WAS ALL OVER THE NEWS. BECAME KIND OF AN INTERNATIONAL INCIDENT. JIMMY CARTER FINALLY CAME IN AND WORKED IT OUT. GREAT MAN. I'M SURPRISED YOU DIDN'T HEAR ABOUT IT ON THE NEWS.
I DON'T REALLY KEEP UP WITH CURRENT EVENTS.

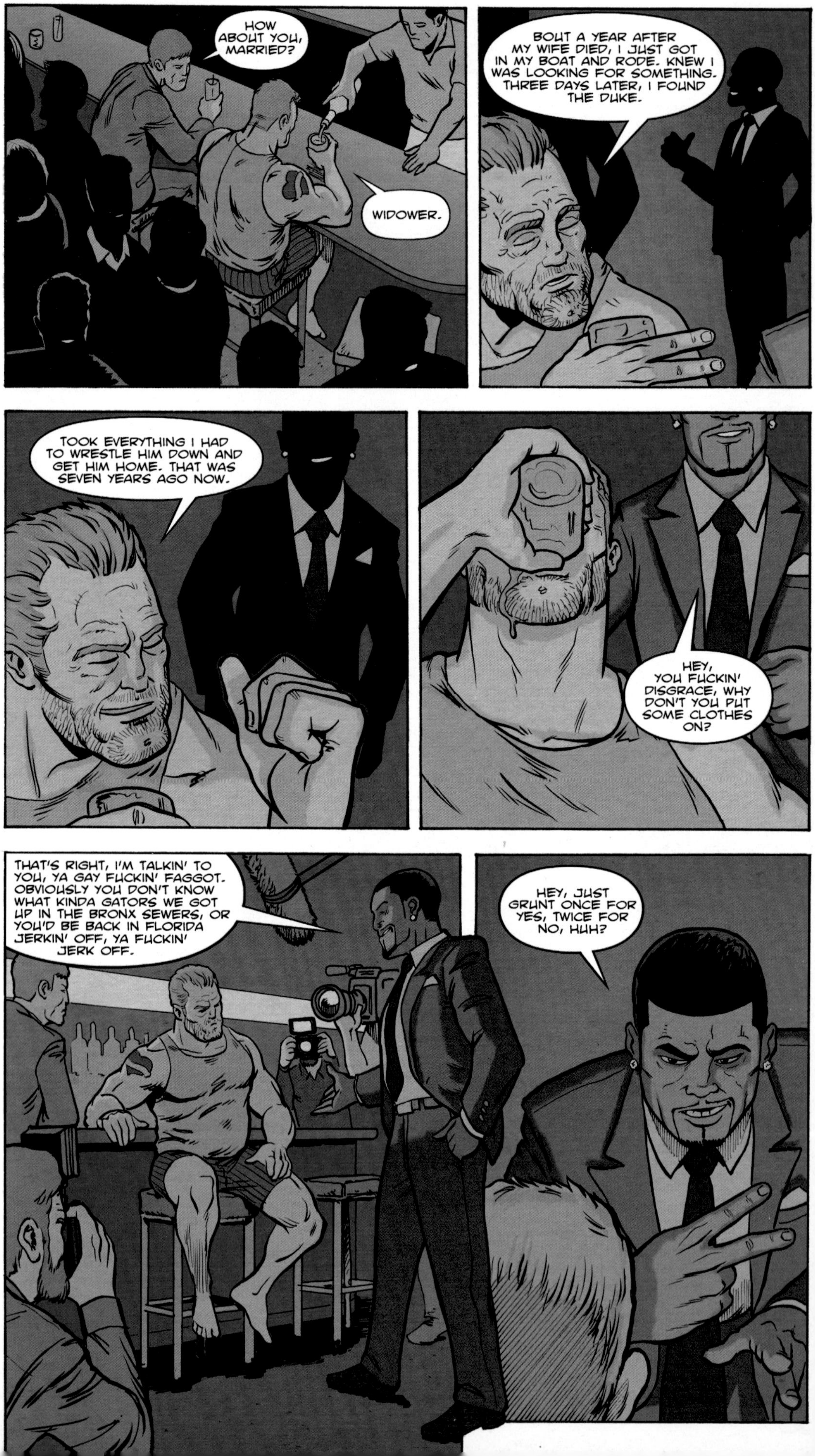
HOW ABOUT YOU, MARRIED?
WIDOWER.
BOUT A YEAR AFTER MY WIFE DIED, I JUST GOT IN MY BOAT AND RODE. KNEW I WAS LOOKING FOR SOMETHING. THREE DAYS LATER, I FOUND THE DUKE.
TOOK EVERYTHING I HAD TO WRESTLE HIM DOWN AND GET HIM HOME. THAT WAS SEVEN YEARS AGO NOW.
HEY, YOU FUCKIN' DISGRACE, WHY DON'T YOU PUT SOME CLOTHES ON?
THAT'S RIGHT, I'M TALKIN' TO YOU, YA GAY FUCKIN' FAGGOT. OBVIOUSLY YOU DON'T KNOW WHAT KINDA GATORS WE GOT UP IN THE BRONX SEWERS, OR YOU'D BE BACK IN FLORIDA JERKIN' OFF, YA FUCKIN' JERK OFF.
HEY, JUST GRUNT ONCE FOR YES, TWICE FOR NO, HUH?

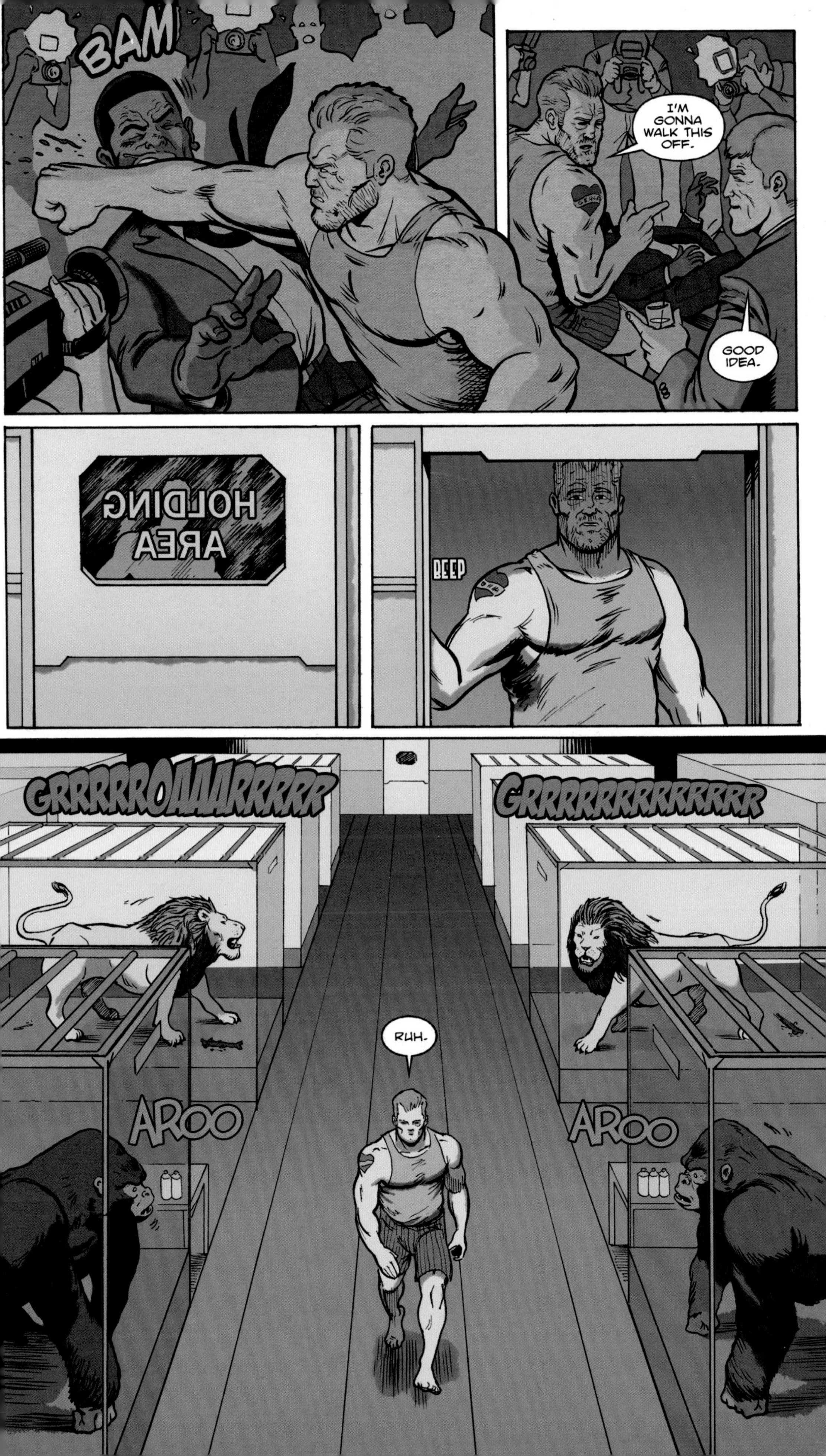
BAM
I'M GONNA WALK THIS OFF.
GOOD IDEA.
HOLDING AREA
BEEP
GRRRRROAAARRRRRR
GRRRRRRRRRRRRR
RUH.
AROO
AROO

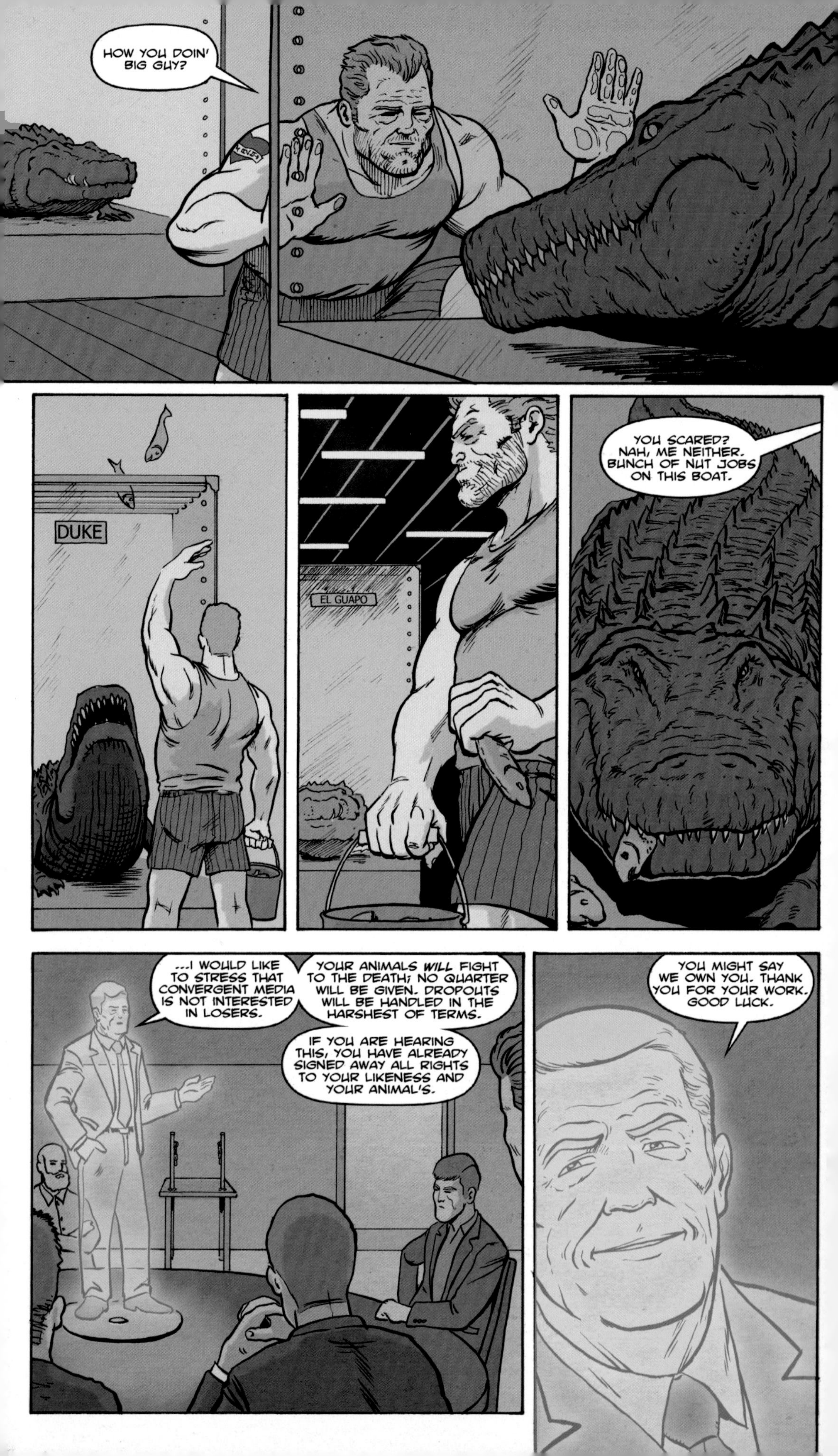
HOW YOU DOIN' BIG GUY?
DUKE
EL GUAPO
YOU SCARED? NAH, ME NEITHER. BUNCH OF NUT JOBS ON THIS BOAT.
...I WOULD LIKE TO STRESS THAT CONVERGENT MEDIA IS NOT INTERESTED IN LOSERS.
YOUR ANIMALS WILL FIGHT TO THE DEATH; NO QUARTER WILL BE GIVEN. DROPOUTS WILL BE HANDLED IN THE HARSHEST OF TERMS.
IF YOU ARE HEARING THIS, YOU HAVE ALREADY SIGNED AWAY ALL RIGHTS TO YOUR LIKENESS AND YOUR ANIMAL'S.
YOU MIGHT SAY WE OWN YOU. THANK YOU FOR YOUR WORK. GOOD LUCK.

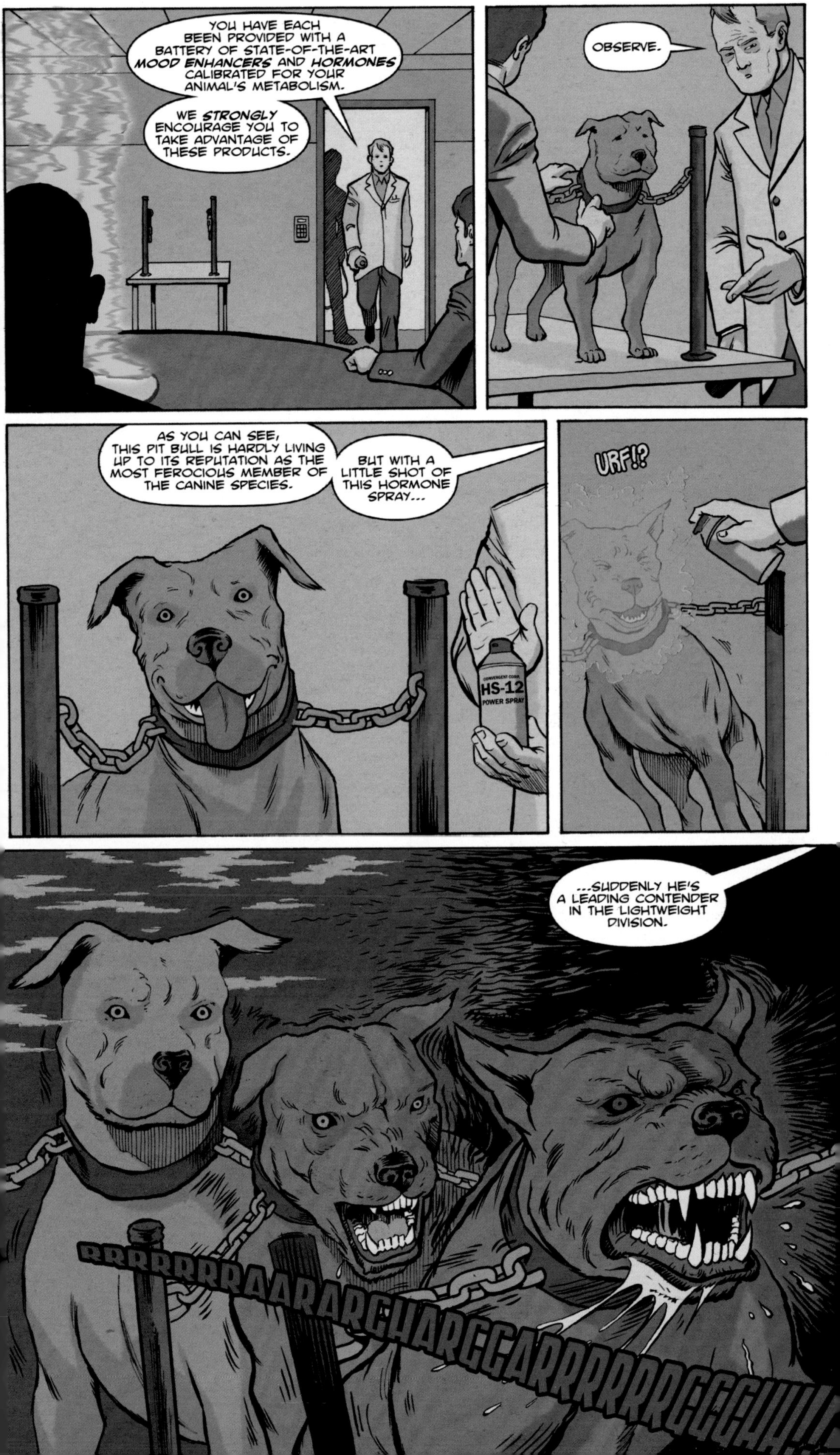
YOU HAVE EACH BEEN PROVIDED WITH A BATTERY OF STATE-OF-THE-ART MOOD ENHANCERS AND HORMONES CALIBRATED FOR YOUR ANIMAL'S METABOLISM.
WE STRONGLY ENCOURAGE YOU TO TAKE ADVANTAGE OF THESE PRODUCTS.
OBSERVE.
AS YOU CAN SEE, THIS PIT BULL IS HARDLY LIVING UP TO ITS REPUTATION AS THE MOST FEROCIOUS MEMBER OF THE CANINE SPECIES.
BUT WITH A LITTLE SHOT OF THIS HORMONE SPRAY...
CONVERGENT CORP.
HS-12
POWER SPRAY
URF!?
...SUDDENLY HE'S A LEADING CONTENDER IN THE LIGHTWEIGHT DIVISION.
RRRRRRRRAARARGHARGGARRRRRRRGGGHH!!

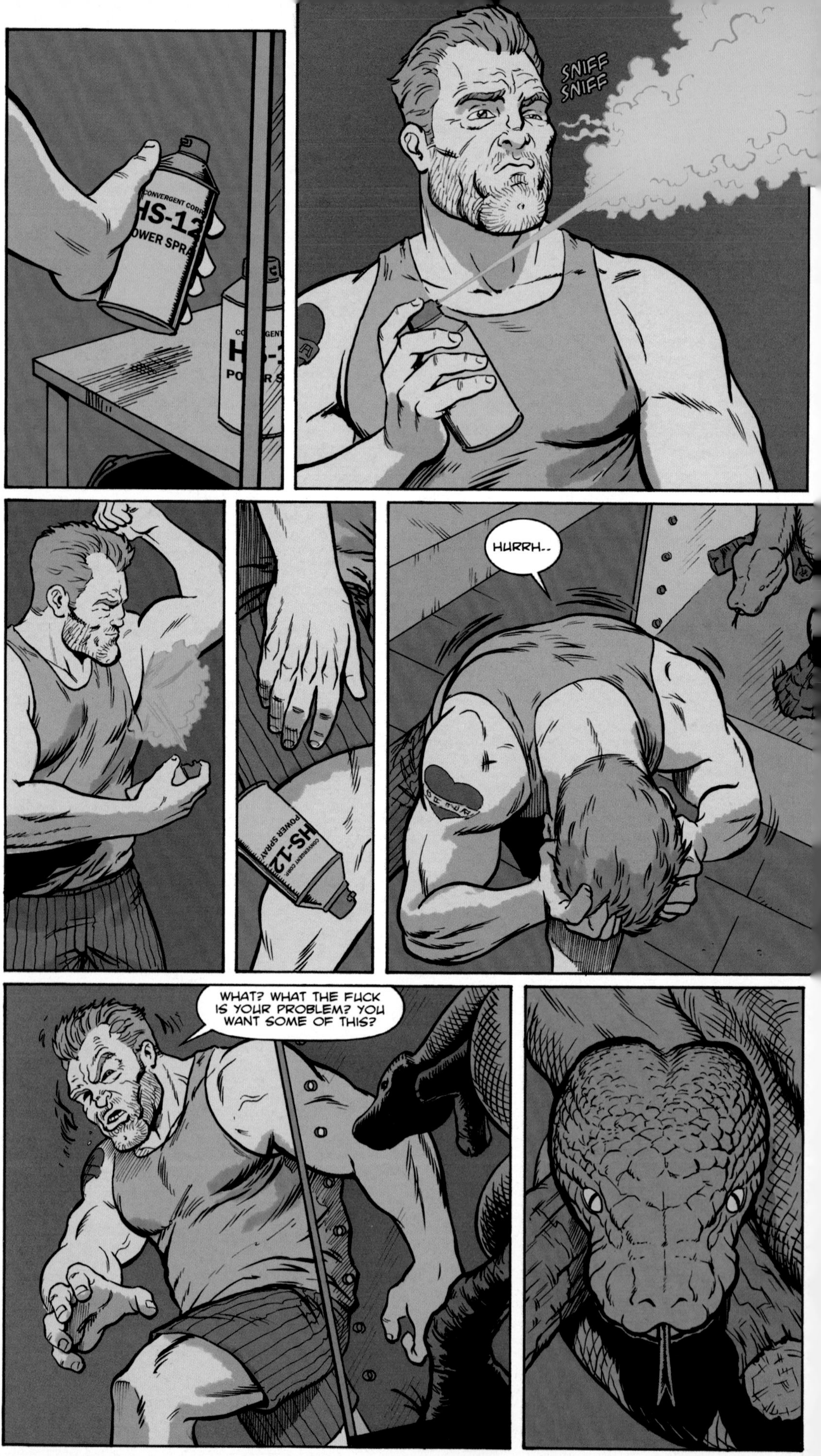
CONVERGENT CORP.
HS-12
POWER SPRAY
SNIFF
SNIFF
CONVERGENT CORP.
HS-12
POWER SPRAY
HURRH..
WHAT? WHAT THE FUCK IS YOUR PROBLEM? YOU WANT SOME OF THIS?

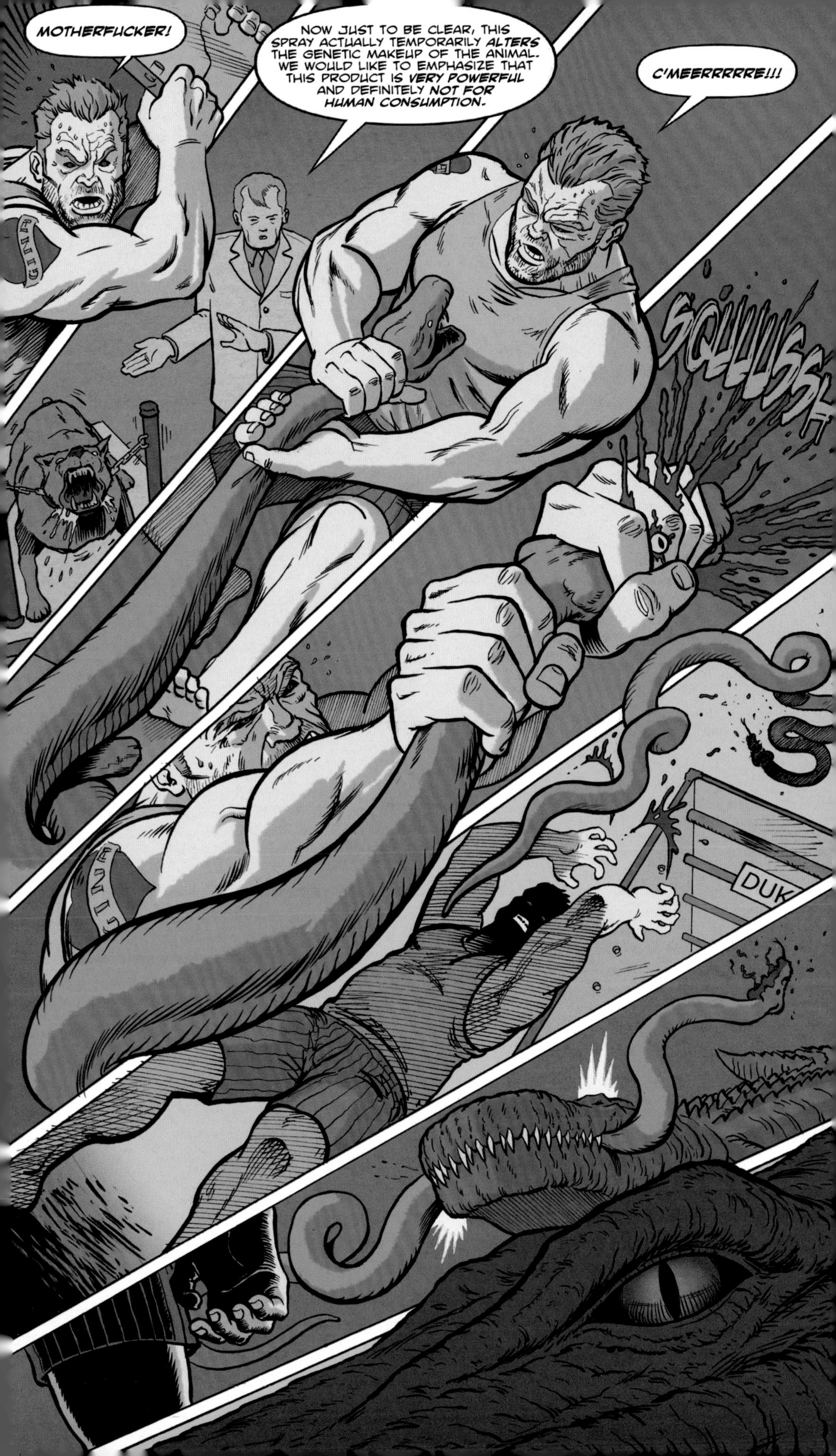
MOTHERFUCKER!
NOW JUST TO BE CLEAR, THIS SPRAY ACTUALLY TEMPORARILY ALTERS THE GENETIC MAKEUP OF THE ANIMAL. WE WOULD LIKE TO EMPHASIZE THAT THIS PRODUCT IS VERY POWERFUL AND DEFINITELY NOT FOR HUMAN CONSUMPTION.
C'MEERRRRRE!!!
SQUUSSH
DUK

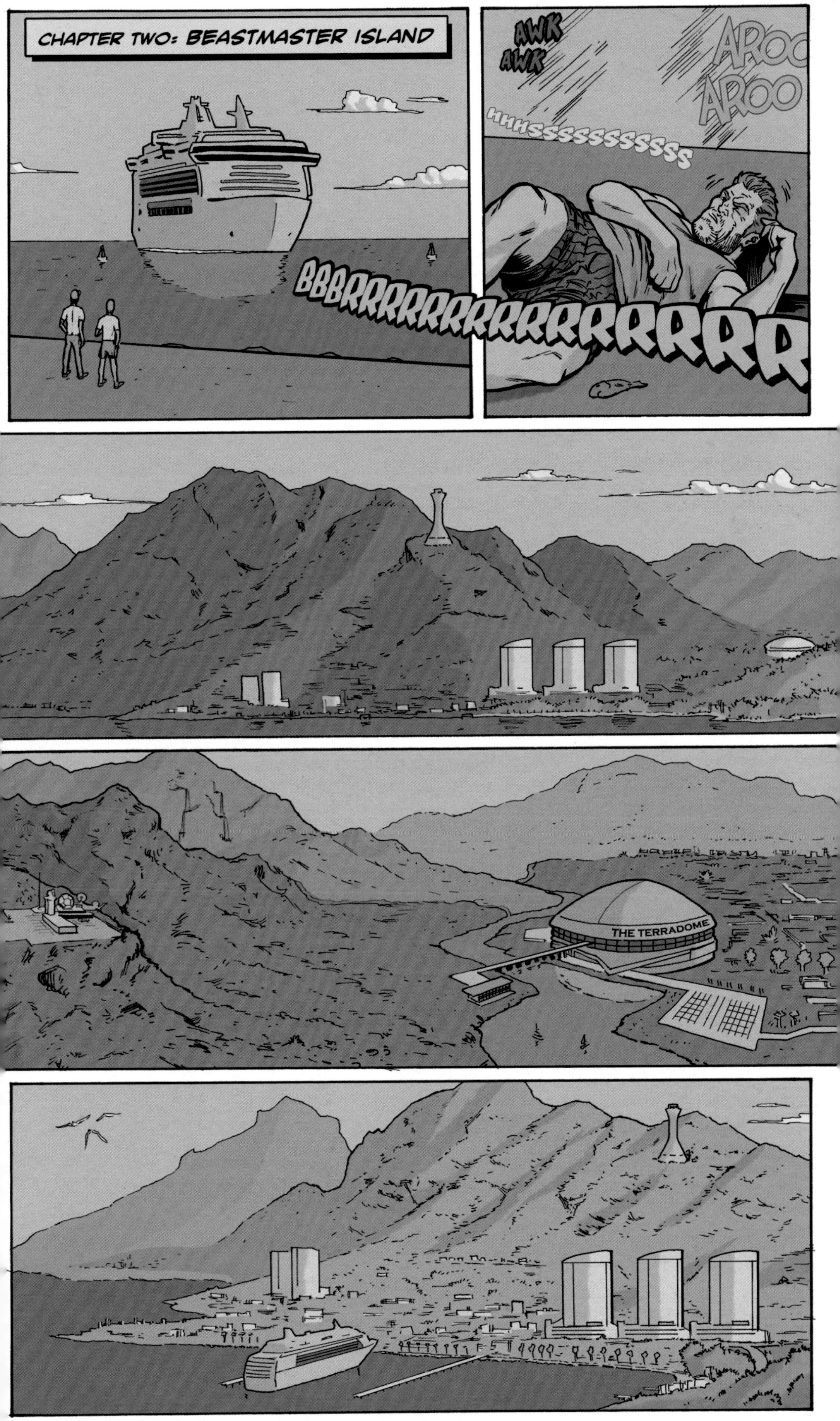
CHAPTER TWO: BEASTMASTER ISLAND
AWK
AWK
AROO
AROO
HHHSSSSSSSSSSSS
BBBRRRRRRRRRRRRRRRRR
THE TERRADOME

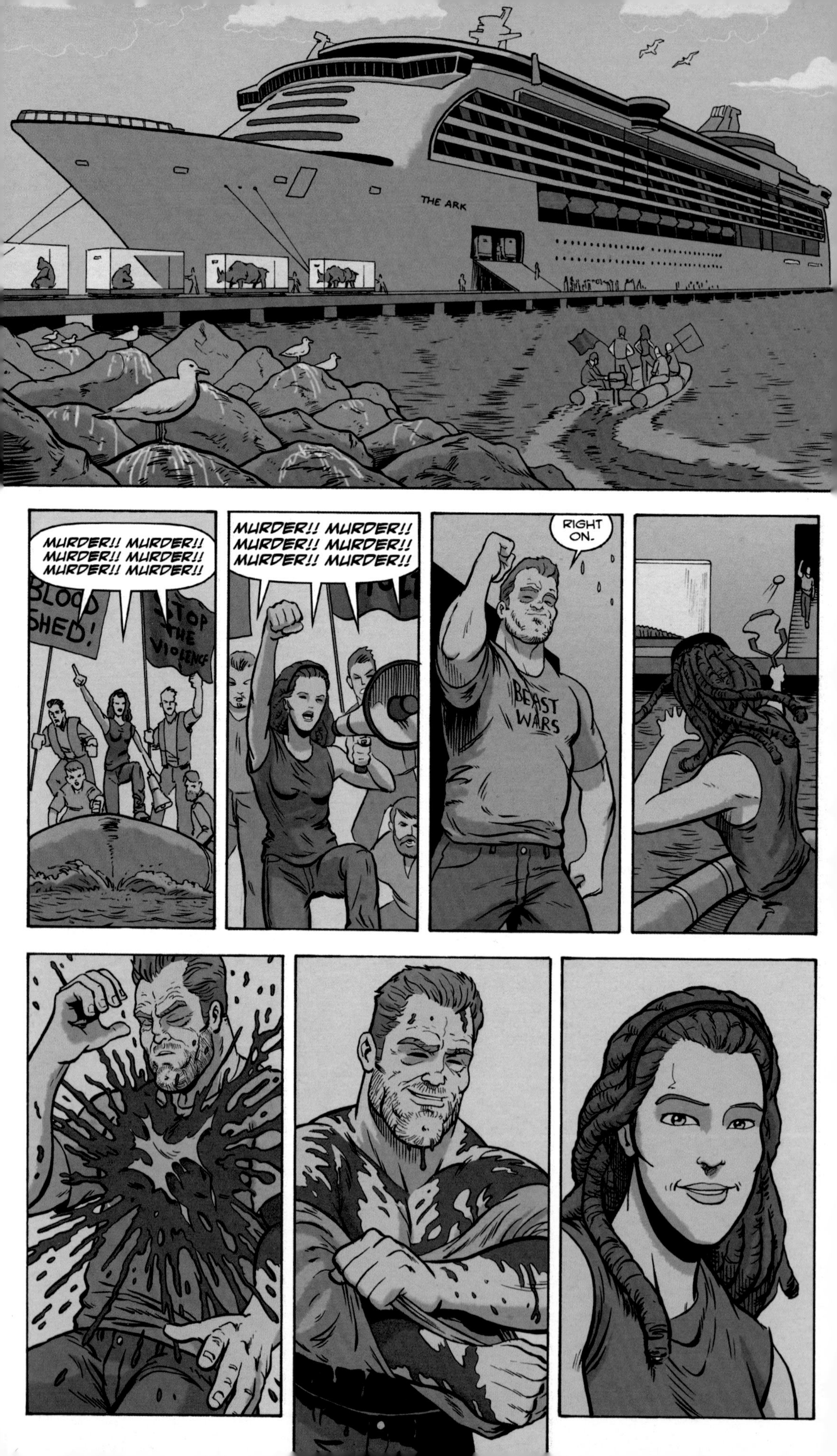
THE ARK
MURDER!! MURDER!! MURDER!! MURDER!! MURDER!! MURDER!!
BLOOD SHED!
STOP THE VIOLENCE
MURDER!! MURDER!! MURDER!! MURDER!! MURDER!! MURDER!!
RIGHT ON.
BEAST WARS

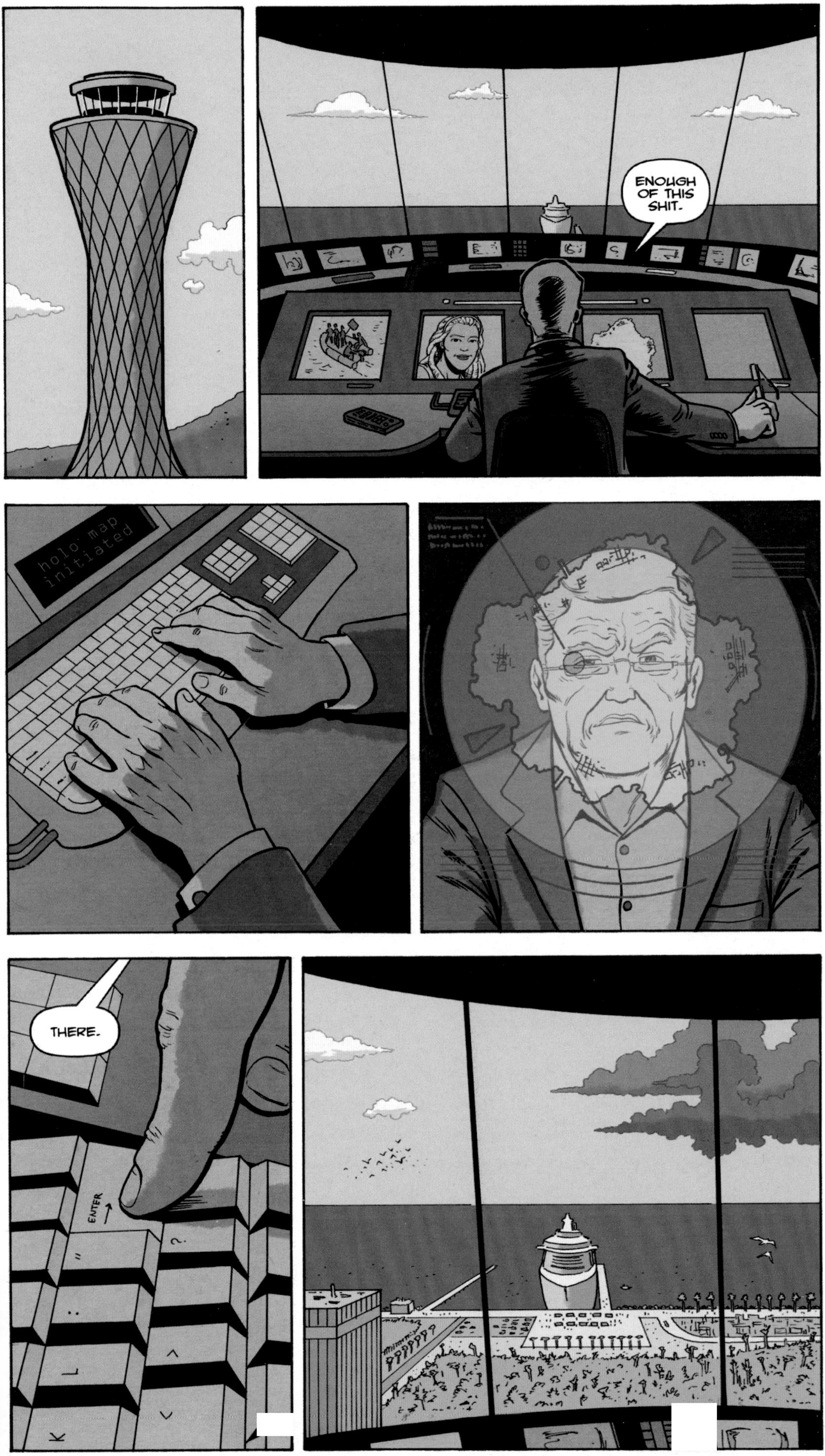
ENOUGH OF THIS SHIT.
holo map initiated
THERE.
ENTER

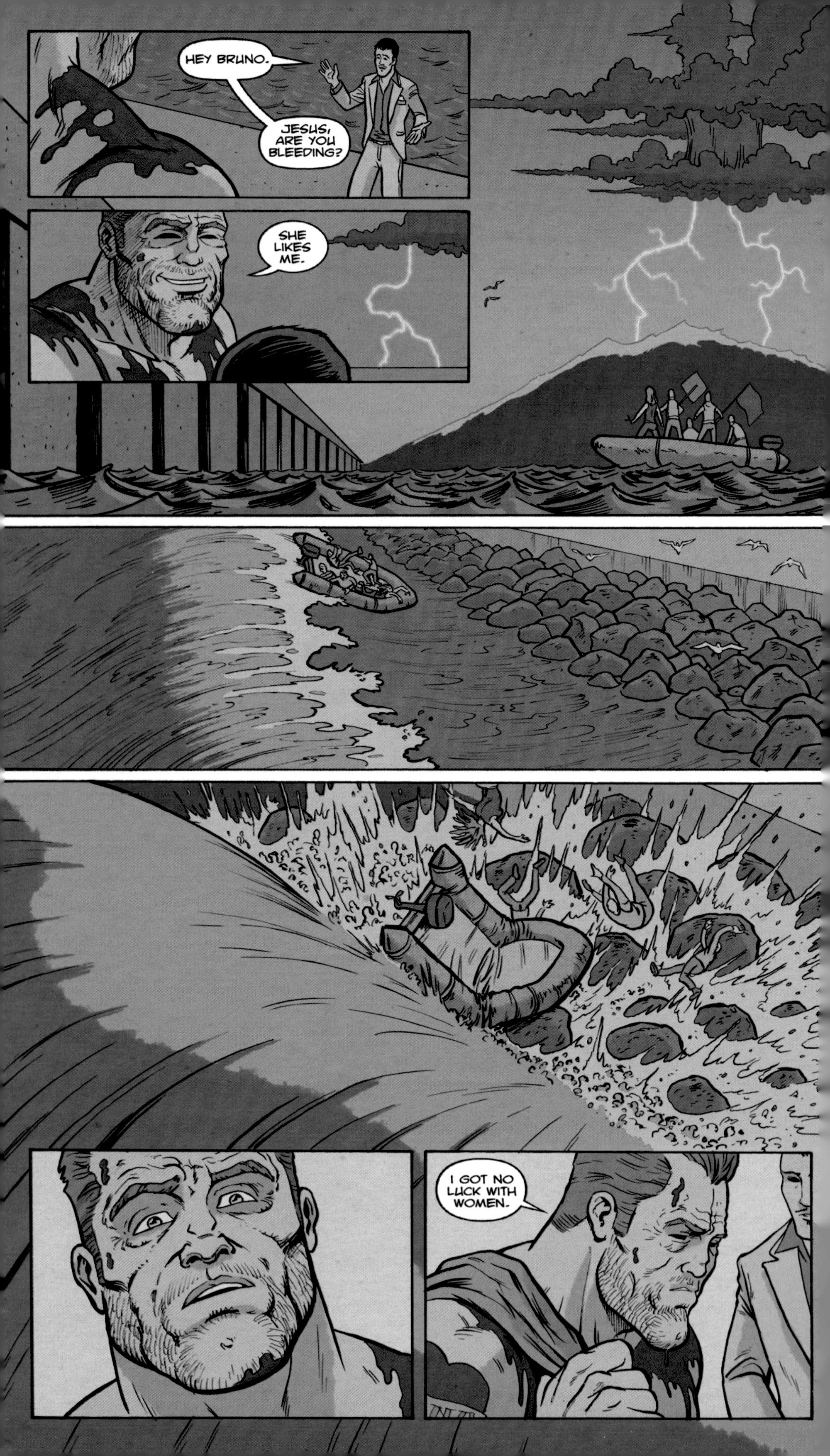
HEY BRUNO.
JESUS, ARE YOU BLEEDING?
SHE LIKES ME.
I GOT NO LUCK WITH WOMEN.

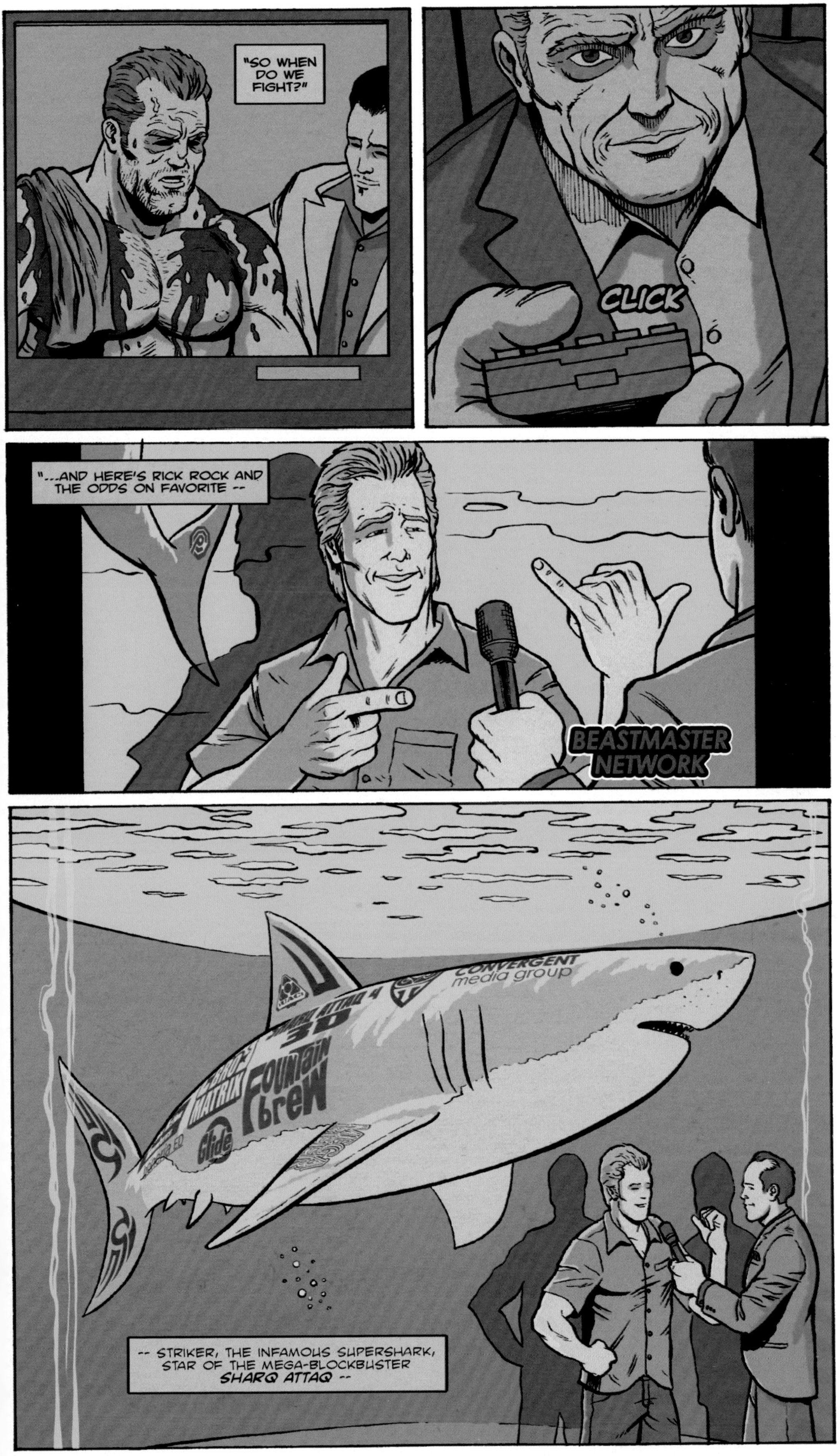
"SO WHEN DO WE FIGHT?"
CLICK
"...AND HERE'S RICK ROCK AND THE ODDS ON FAVORITE --
BEASTMASTER NETWORK
CONVERGENT media group
SHARQ ATTAQ 4 3D
Fountain brew
MATRIX
Glide
-- STRIKER, THE INFAMOUS SUPERSHARK, STAR OF THE MEGA-BLOCKBUSTER *SHARQ ATTAQ* --

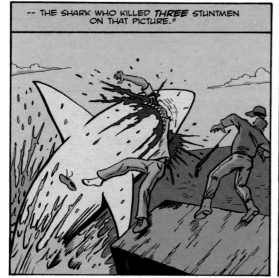

-- THE SHARK WHO KILLED THREE STUNTMEN ON THAT PICTURE."
"THAT'S RIGHT, BOB, HE'S ONE MOVIE STAR WHO ACTUALLY DOES HIS OWN STUNTS, AND THERE ARE SOME PEOPLE WHO DON'T THINK STRIKER SHOULD EVEN BE ALLOWED TO COMPETE HERE TODAY."
TWORK BEASTMASTER NETWORK BE
"OF COURSE I REGRET THE LOSS OF HUMAN LIFE, BUT I THINK PEOPLE HAVE TO UNDERSTAND THAT, YOU KNOW, THAT'S THE NATURE OF THE BEAST. STRIKER'S A SHARK. AND THAT'S NOT A CRIME."
"THE FANS ARE JUST RIPPED ABOUT THIS ONE, BOB. IMAGINE, IN JUST A FEW SHORT DAYS WE'RE GOING TO SEE IF STRIKER CAN HANDLE A MEMBER OF HIS OWN SPECIES LIKE HE DID THOSE STUNTMEN, AND THEN, WHO KNOWS? WE MIGHT SEE STRIKER TAKE ON ONE OF THE GORILLAS, OR A POLAR BEAR. ANYTHING CAN HAPPEN."
ASTER NETWORK BEASTMASTER NETW
WORK BEASTMASTER NETWORK
THIS IS SOME -- FUCKED UP SHIT.

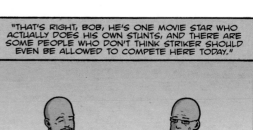

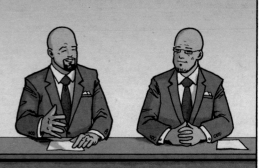

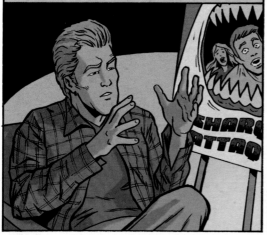

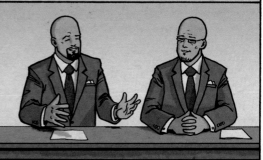

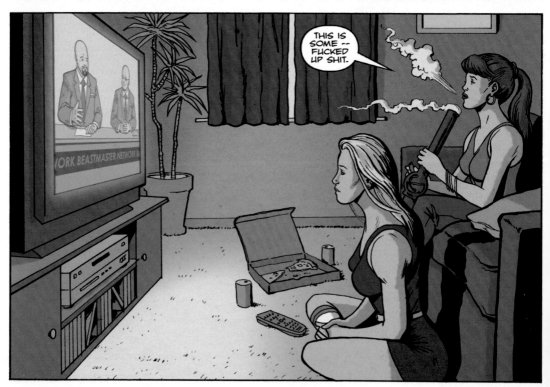

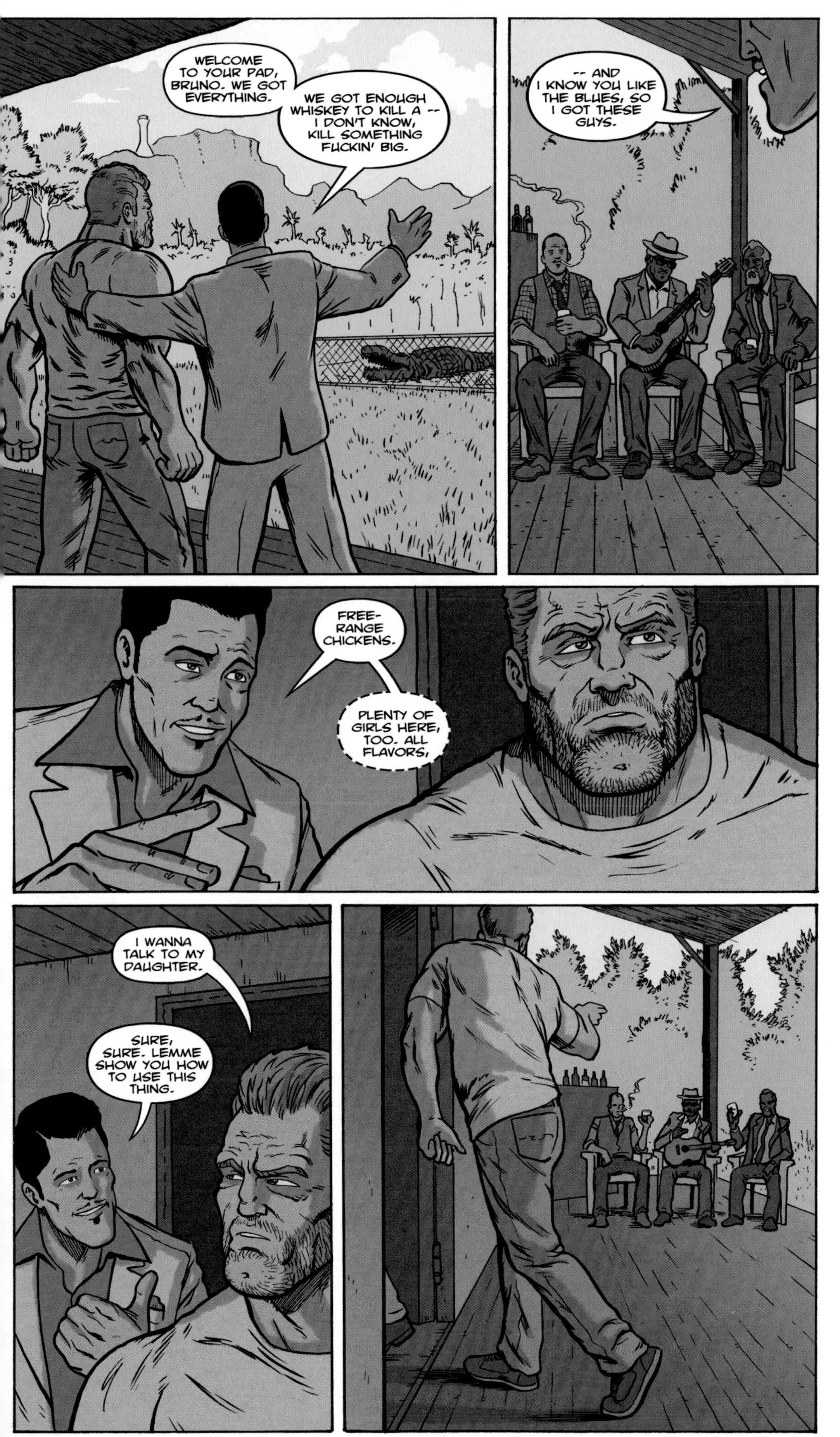
WELCOME TO YOUR PAD, BRUNO. WE GOT EVERYTHING.
WE GOT ENOUGH WHISKEY TO KILL A -- I DON'T KNOW, KILL SOMETHING FUCKIN' BIG.
-- AND I KNOW YOU LIKE THE BLUES, SO I GOT THESE GUYS.
FREE-RANGE CHICKENS.
PLENTY OF GIRLS HERE, TOO. ALL FLAVORS,
I WANNA TALK TO MY DAUGHTER.
SURE, SURE. LEMME SHOW YOU HOW TO USE THIS THING.

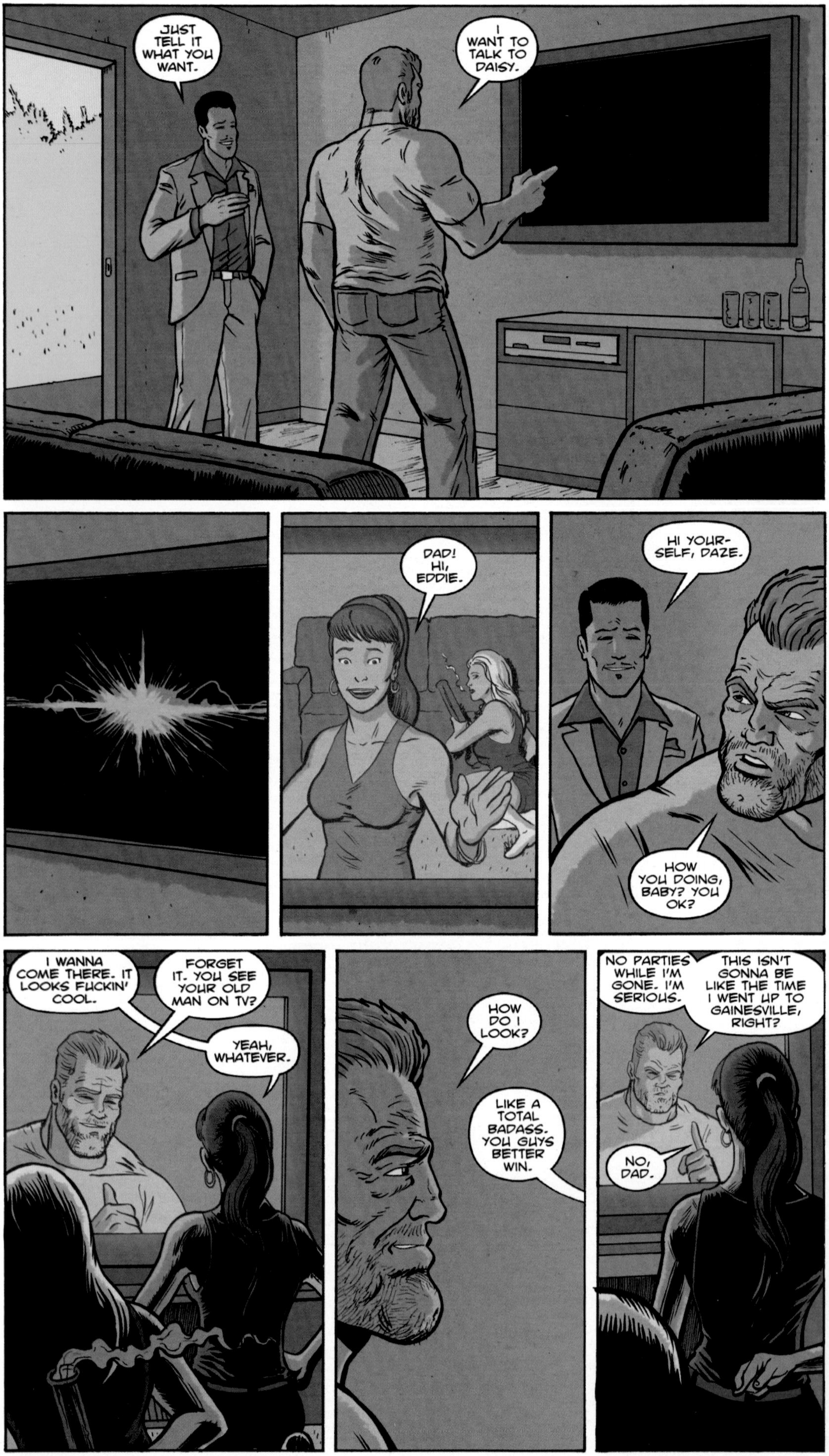
JUST TELL IT WHAT YOU WANT.
I WANT TO TALK TO DAISY.
DAD! HI, EDDIE.
HI YOURSELF, DAZE.
HOW YOU DOING, BABY? YOU OK?
I WANNA COME THERE. IT LOOKS FUCKIN' COOL.
FORGET IT. YOU SEE YOUR OLD MAN ON TV?
YEAH, WHATEVER.
HOW DO I LOOK?
LIKE A TOTAL BADASS. YOU GUYS BETTER WIN.
NO PARTIES WHILE I'M GONE. I'M SERIOUS.
THIS ISN'T GONNA BE LIKE THE TIME I WENT UP TO GAINESVILLE, RIGHT?
NO, DAD.

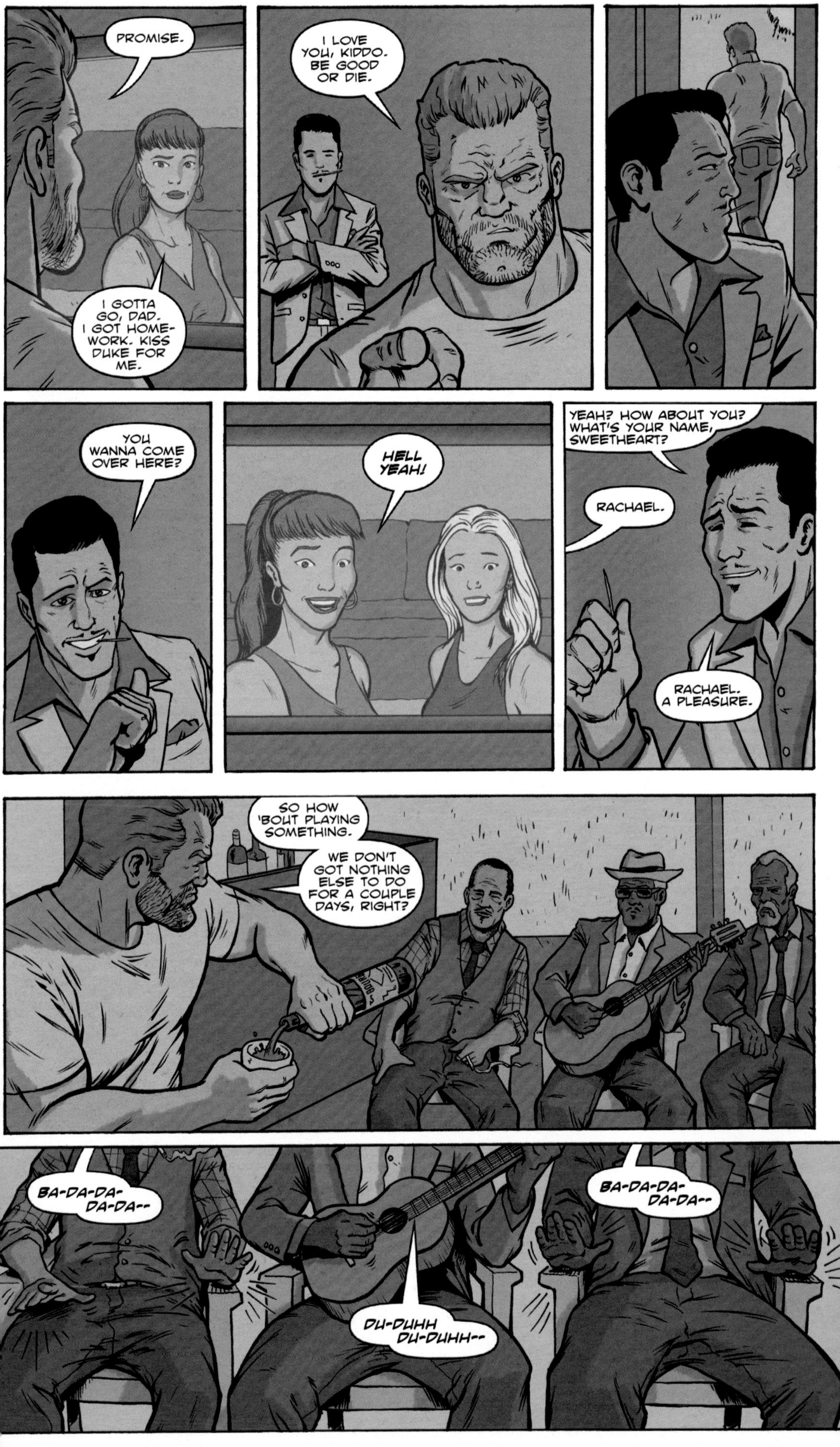
PROMISE.
I GOTTA GO, DAD. I GOT HOME-WORK. KISS DUKE FOR ME.
I LOVE YOU, KIDDO. BE GOOD OR DIE.
YOU WANNA COME OVER HERE?
HELL YEAH!
YEAH? HOW ABOUT YOU? WHAT'S YOUR NAME, SWEETHEART?
RACHAEL.
RACHAEL. A PLEASURE.
SO HOW 'BOUT PLAYING SOMETHING.
WE DON'T GOT NOTHING ELSE TO DO FOR A COUPLE DAYS, RIGHT?
BA-DA-DA-DA-DA--
BA-DA-DA-DA-DA--
DU-DUHH DU-DUHH--

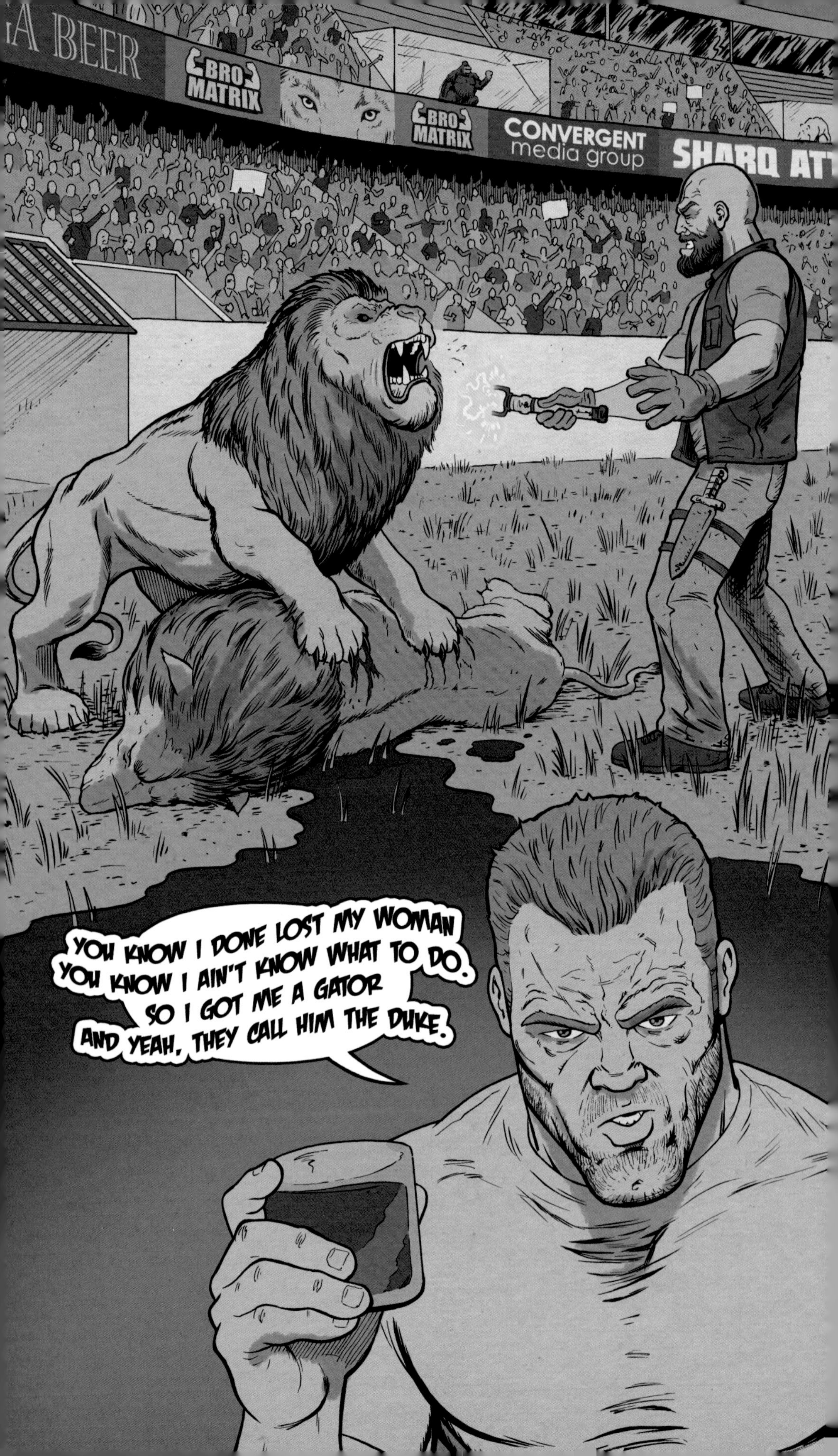
BEER
BRO MATRIX
BRO MATRIX
CONVERGENT media group
YOU KNOW I DONE LOST MY WOMAN
YOU KNOW I AIN'T KNOW WHAT TO DO.
SO I GOT ME A GATOR
AND YEAH, THEY CALL HIM THE DUKE.

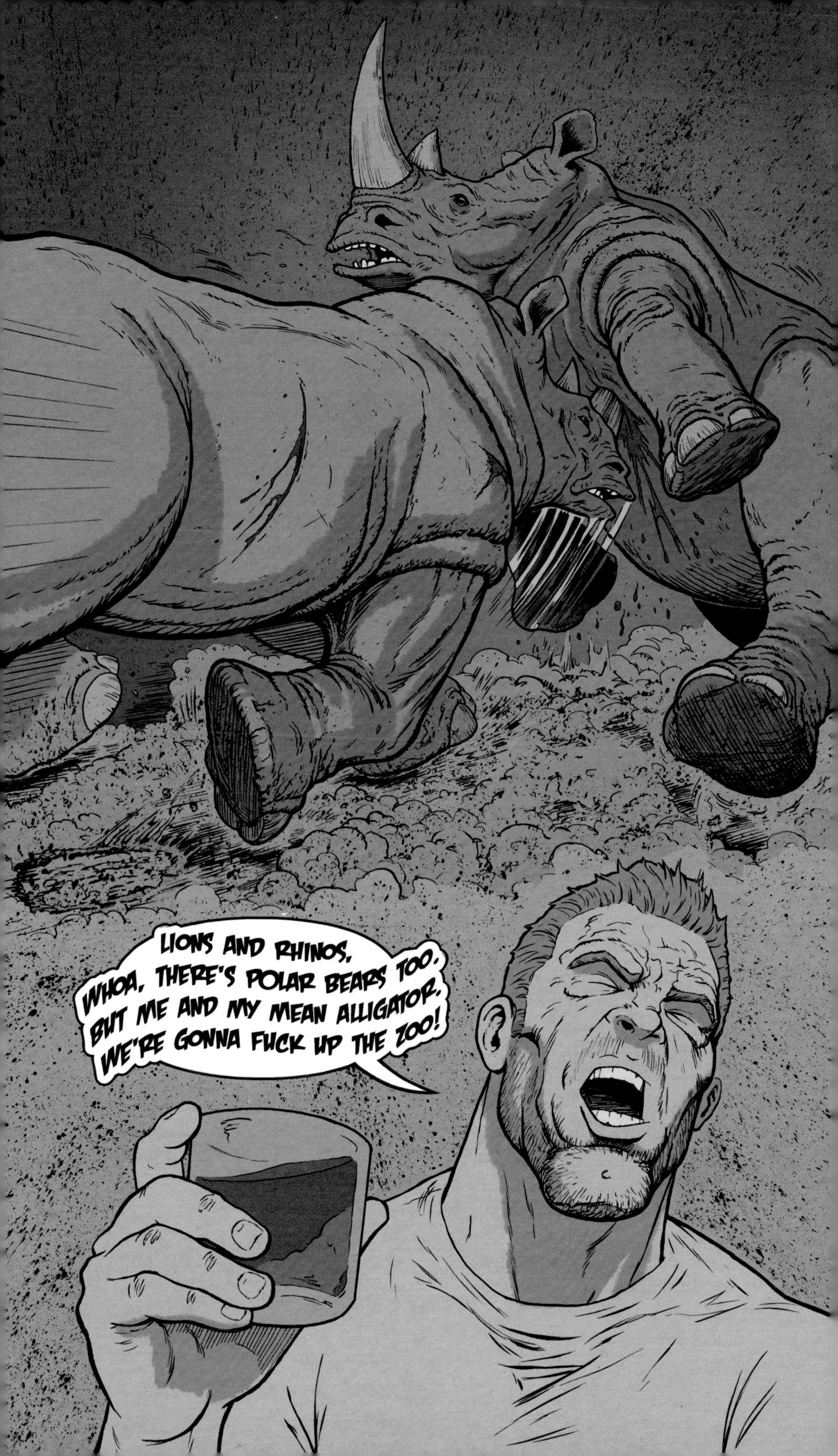
LIONS AND RHINOS, WHOA, THERE'S POLAR BEARS TOO, BUT ME AND MY MEAN ALLIGATOR, WE'RE GONNA FUCK UP THE ZOO!

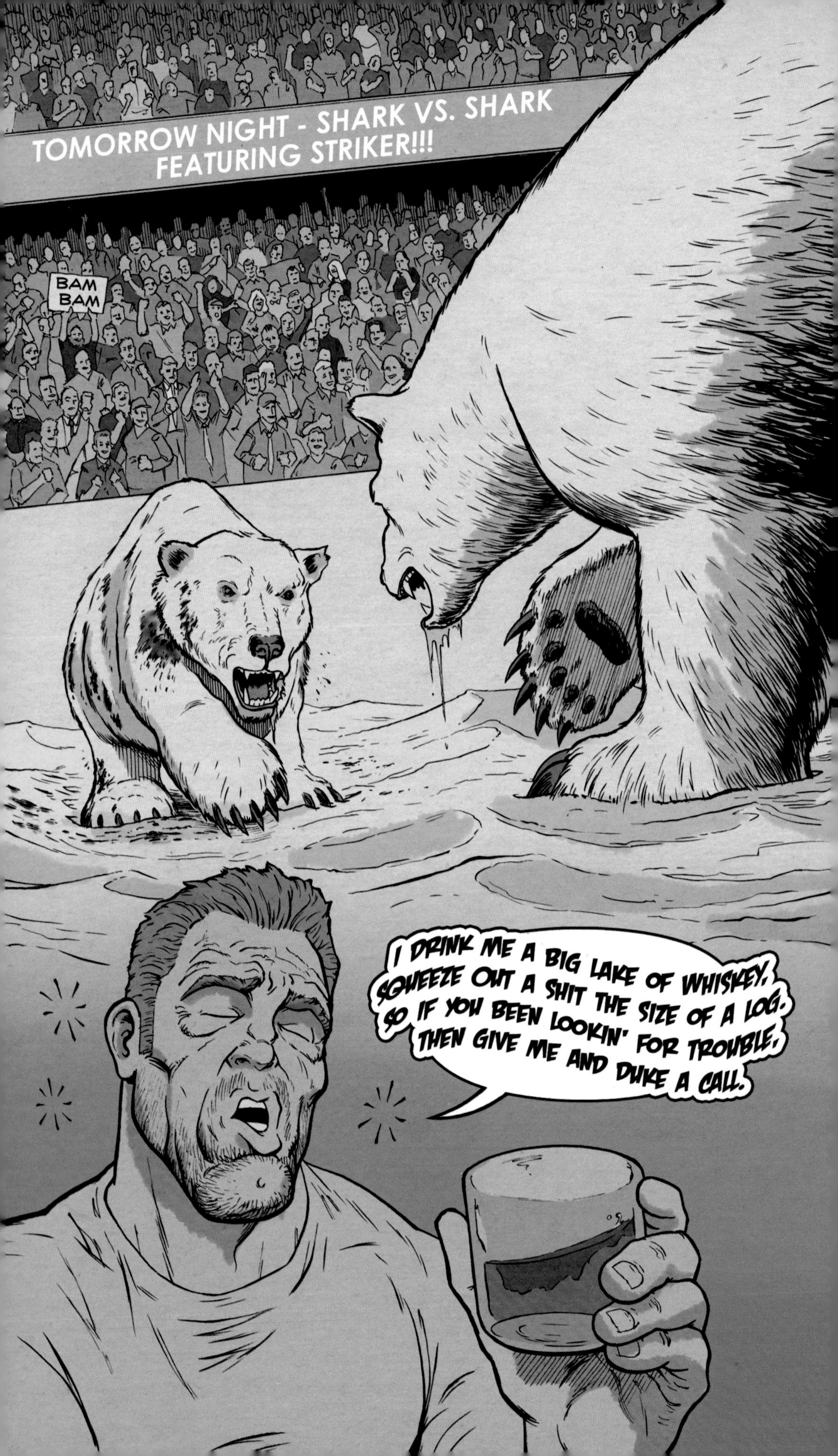
TOMORROW NIGHT - SHARK VS. SHARK FEATURING STRIKER!!!
BAM BAM
I DRINK ME A BIG LAKE OF WHISKEY, SQUEEZE OUT A SHIT THE SIZE OF A LOG. SO IF YOU BEEN LOOKIN' FOR TROUBLE, THEN GIVE ME AND DUKE A CALL.

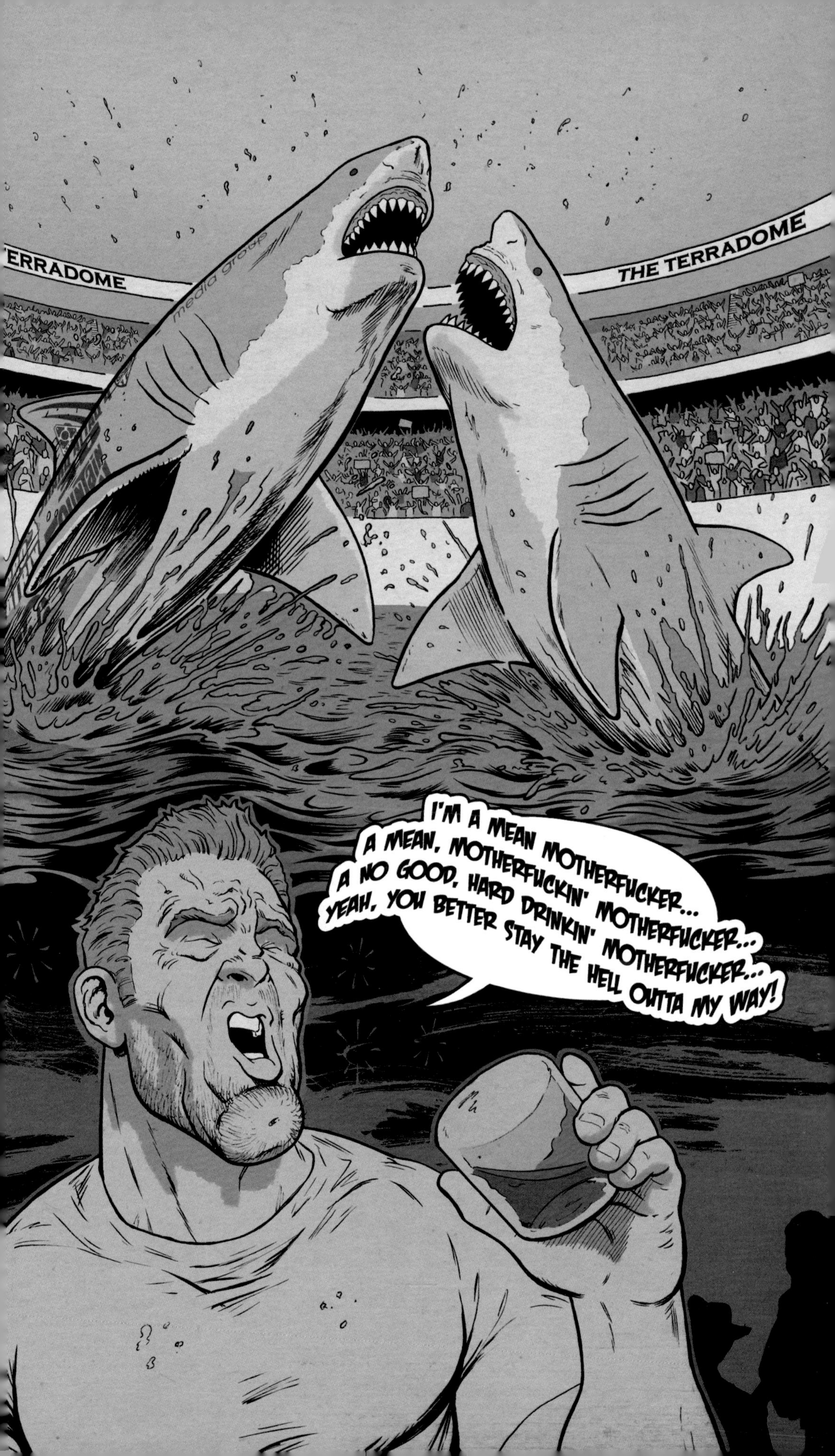

THE TERRADOME
ERRADOME
media group
I'M A MEAN MOTHERFUCKER...
A MEAN, MOTHERFUCKIN' MOTHERFUCKER...
A NO GOOD, HARD DRINKIN' MOTHERFUCKER...
YEAH, YOU BETTER STAY THE HELL OUTTA MY WAY!

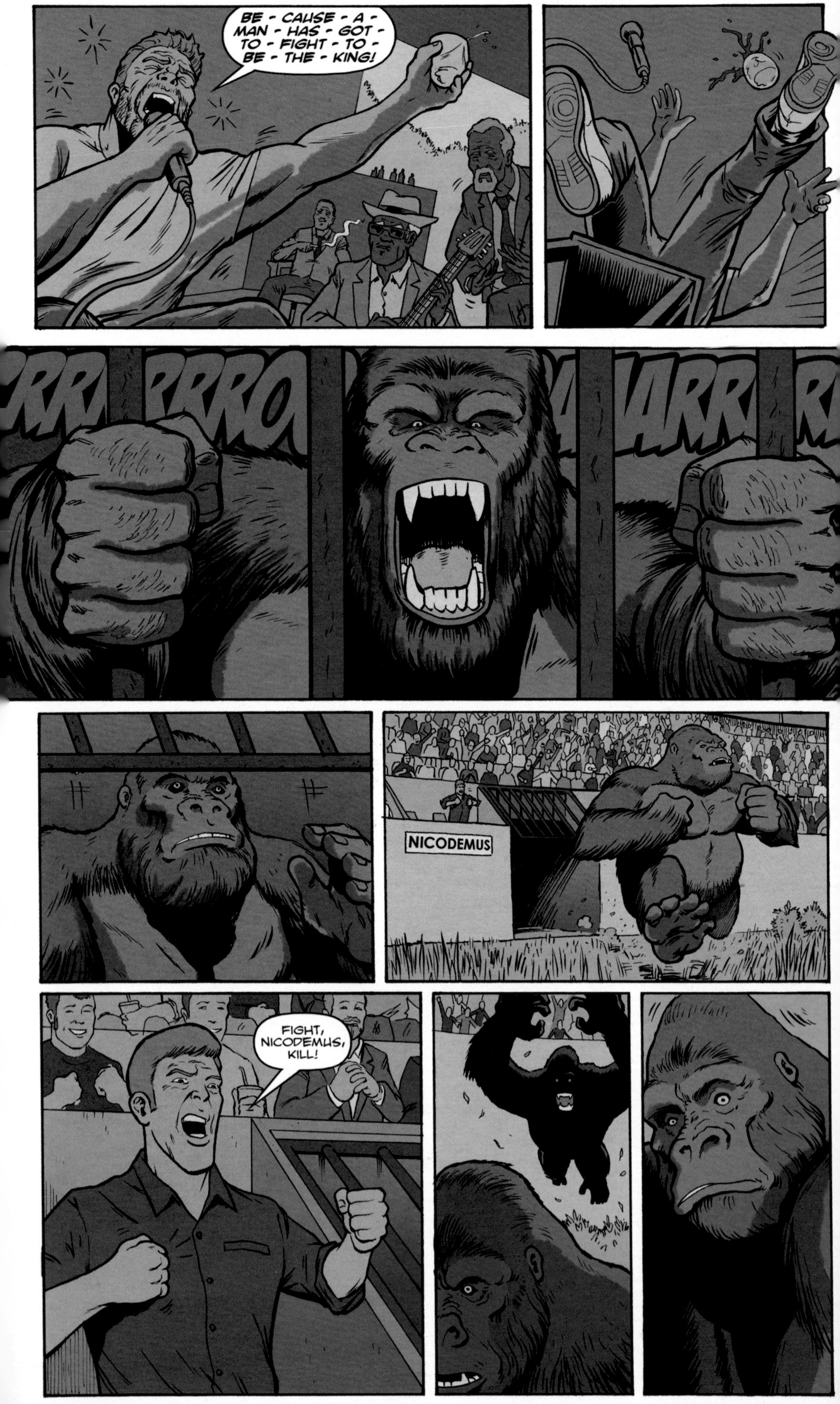
BE - CAUSE - A - MAN - HAS - GOT - TO - FIGHT - TO - BE - THE - KING!
NICODEMUS
FIGHT, NICODEMUS, KILL!

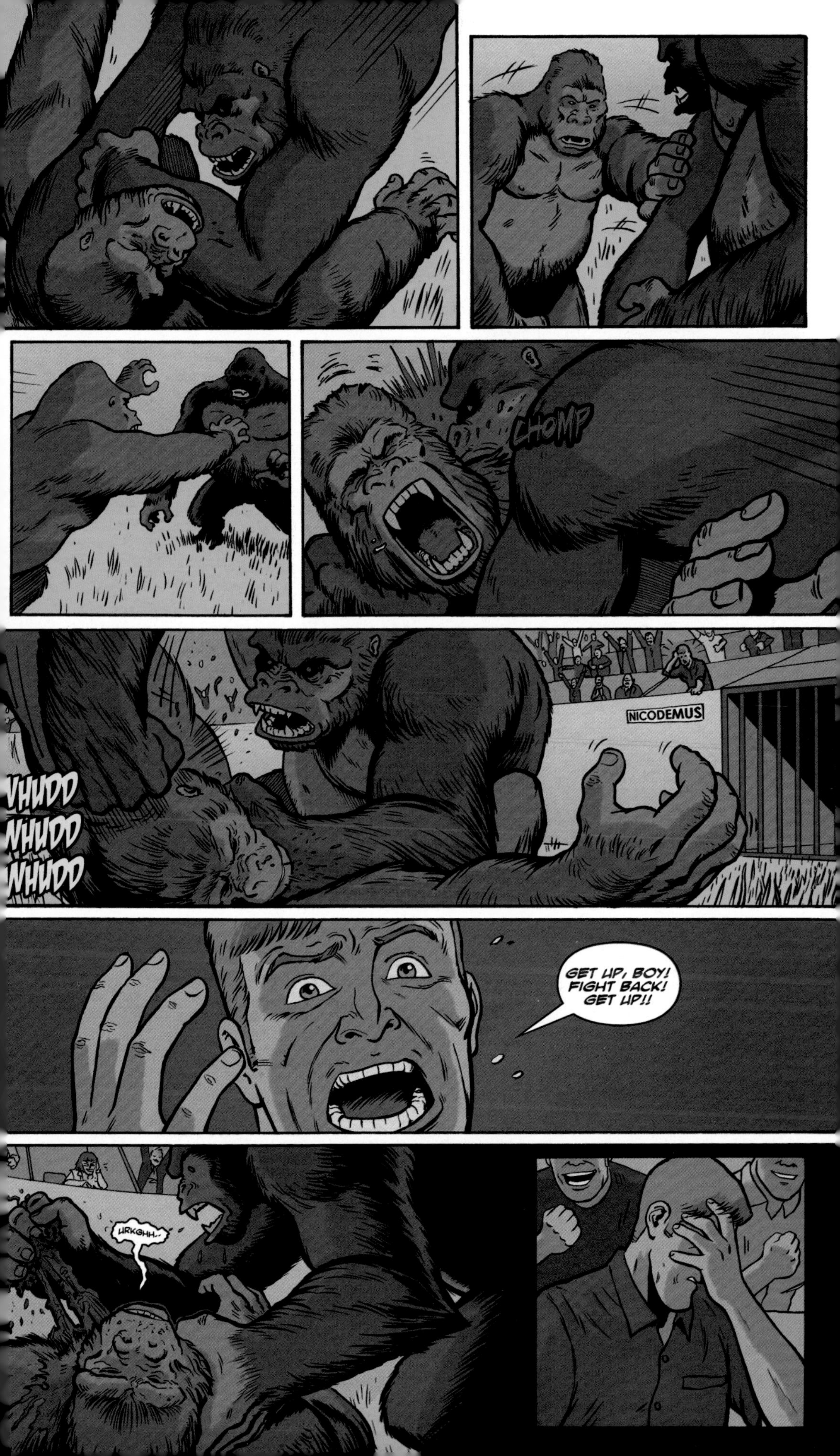
CHOMP
NICODEMUS
WHUDD
WHUDD
WHUDD
GET UP, BOY! FIGHT BACK! GET UP!!
URKGHH..

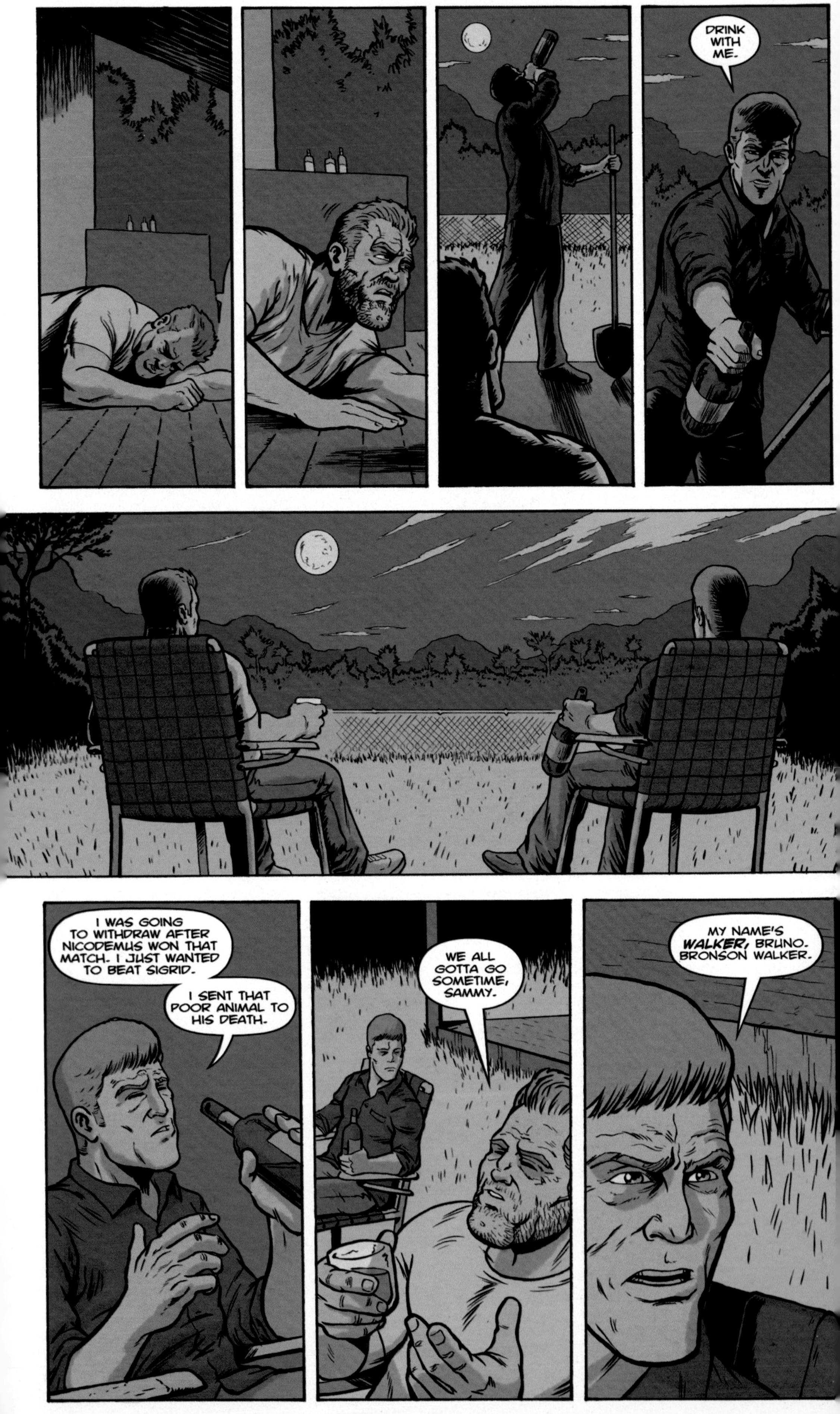
DRINK WITH ME.
I WAS GOING TO WITHDRAW AFTER NICODEMUS WON THAT MATCH. I JUST WANTED TO BEAT SIGRID.
I SENT THAT POOR ANIMAL TO HIS DEATH.
WE ALL GOTTA GO SOMETIME, SAMMY.
MY NAME'S WALKER, BRUNO. BRONSON WALKER.

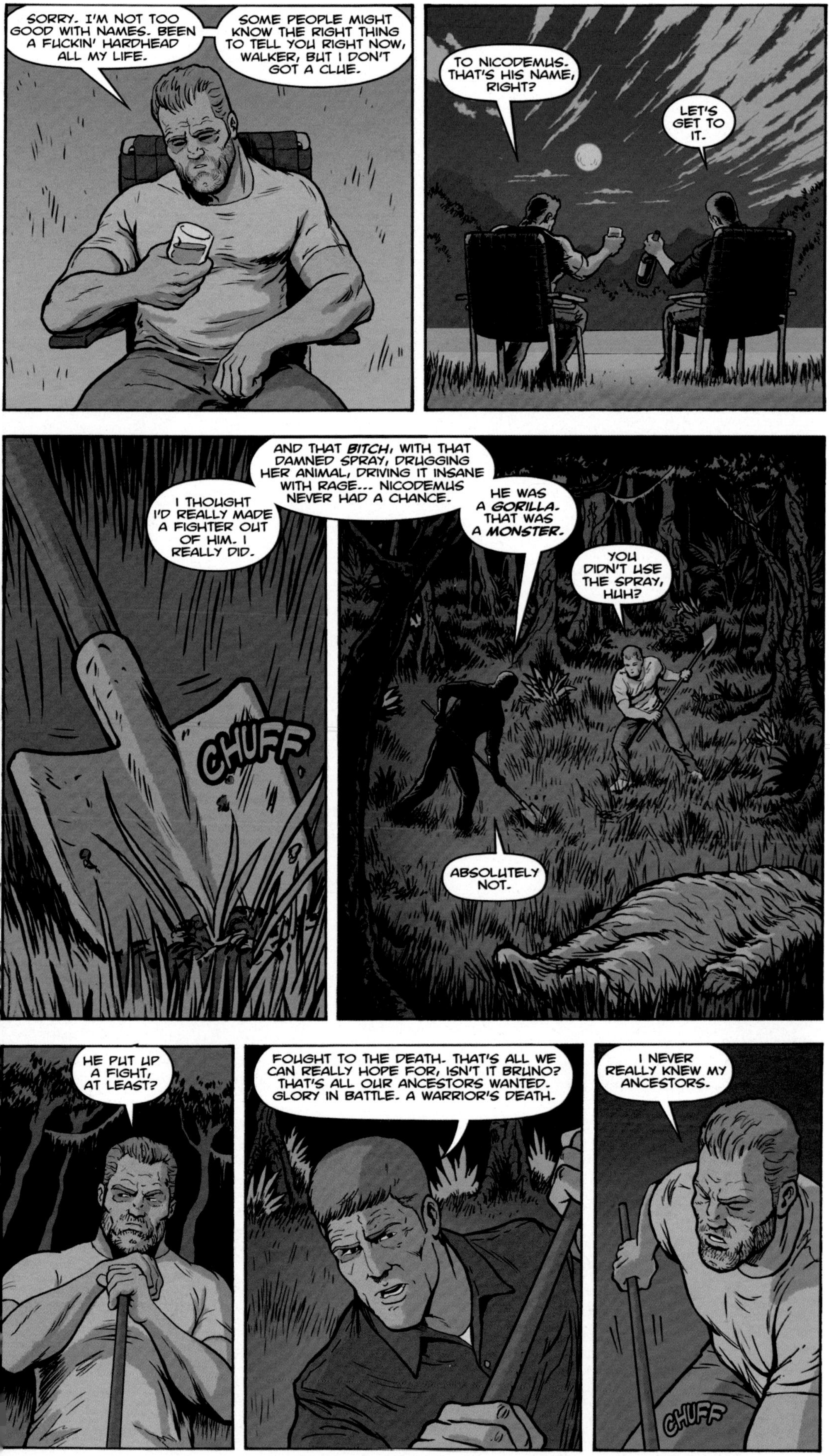
SORRY. I'M NOT TOO GOOD WITH NAMES. BEEN A FUCKIN' HARDHEAD ALL MY LIFE.
SOME PEOPLE MIGHT KNOW THE RIGHT THING TO TELL YOU RIGHT NOW, WALKER, BUT I DON'T GOT A CLUE.
TO NICODEMUS. THAT'S HIS NAME, RIGHT?
LET'S GET TO IT.
I THOUGHT I'D REALLY MADE A FIGHTER OUT OF HIM. I REALLY DID.
AND THAT BITCH, WITH THAT DAMNED SPRAY, DRUGGING HER ANIMAL, DRIVING IT INSANE WITH RAGE... NICODEMUS NEVER HAD A CHANCE.
CHUFF
HE WAS A GORILLA. THAT WAS A MONSTER.
YOU DIDN'T USE THE SPRAY, HUH?
ABSOLUTELY NOT.
HE PUT UP A FIGHT, AT LEAST?
FOUGHT TO THE DEATH. THAT'S ALL WE CAN REALLY HOPE FOR, ISN'T IT BRUNO? THAT'S ALL OUR ANCESTORS WANTED. GLORY IN BATTLE. A WARRIOR'S DEATH.
I NEVER REALLY KNEW MY ANCESTORS.
CHUFF

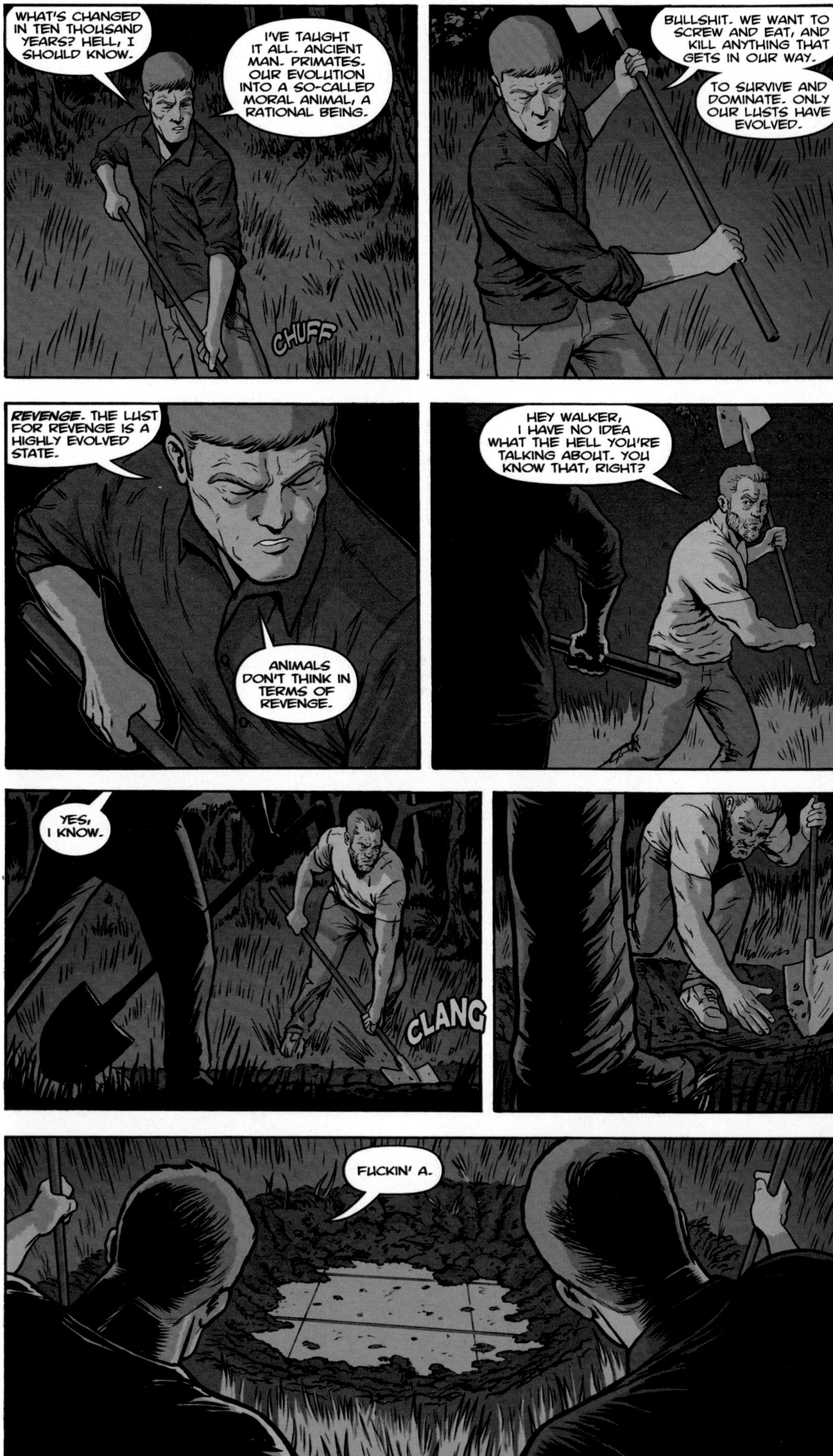
WHAT'S CHANGED IN TEN THOUSAND YEARS? HELL, I SHOULD KNOW.
I'VE TAUGHT IT ALL. ANCIENT MAN. PRIMATES. OUR EVOLUTION INTO A SO-CALLED MORAL ANIMAL, A RATIONAL BEING.
CHUFF
BULLSHIT. WE WANT TO SCREW AND EAT, AND KILL ANYTHING THAT GETS IN OUR WAY.
TO SURVIVE AND DOMINATE. ONLY OUR LUSTS HAVE EVOLVED.
REVENGE. THE LUST FOR REVENGE IS A HIGHLY EVOLVED STATE.
ANIMALS DON'T THINK IN TERMS OF REVENGE.
HEY WALKER, I HAVE NO IDEA WHAT THE HELL YOU'RE TALKING ABOUT. YOU KNOW THAT, RIGHT?
YES, I KNOW.
CLANG
FUCKIN' A.

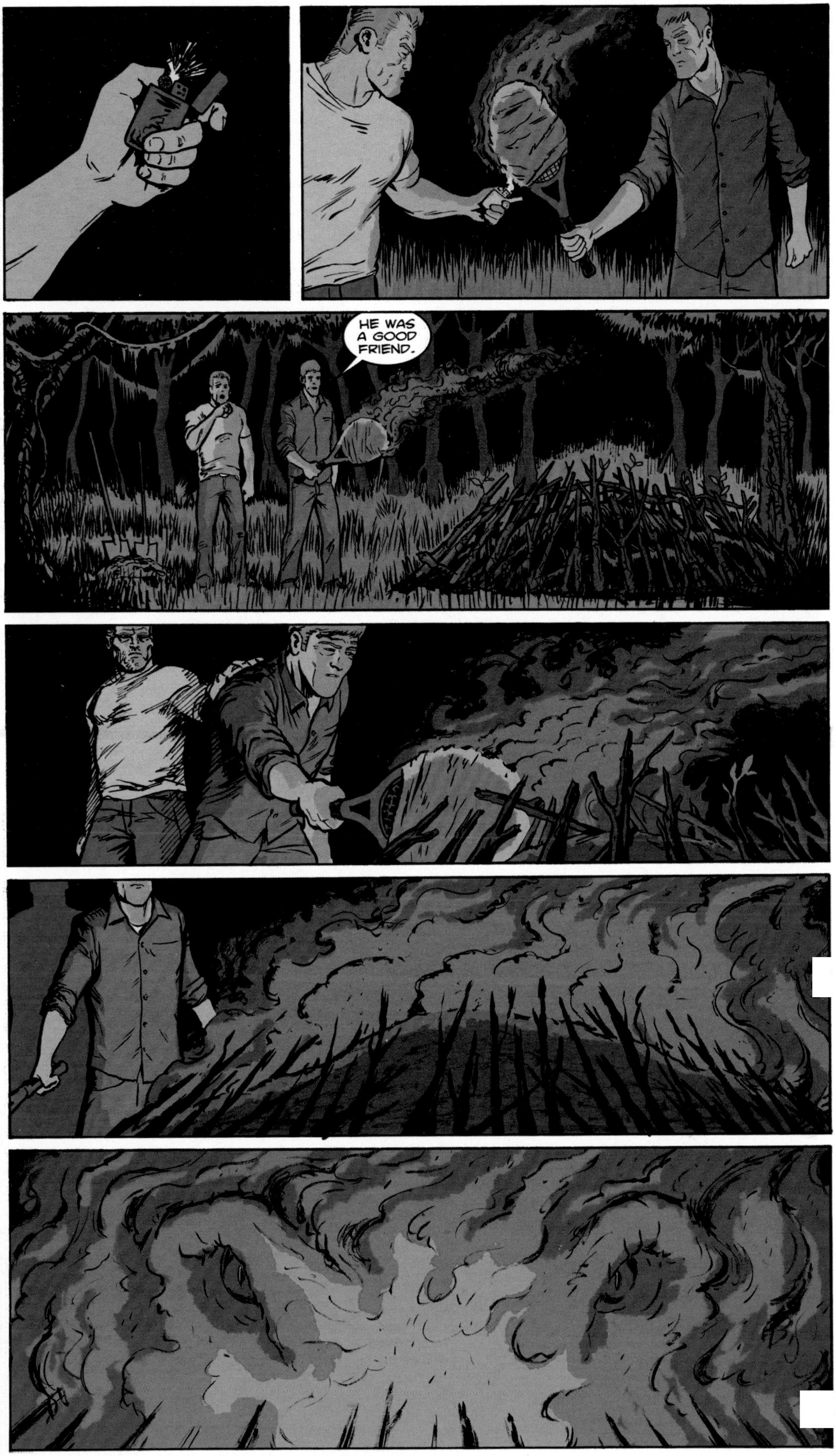
HE WAS A GOOD FRIEND.

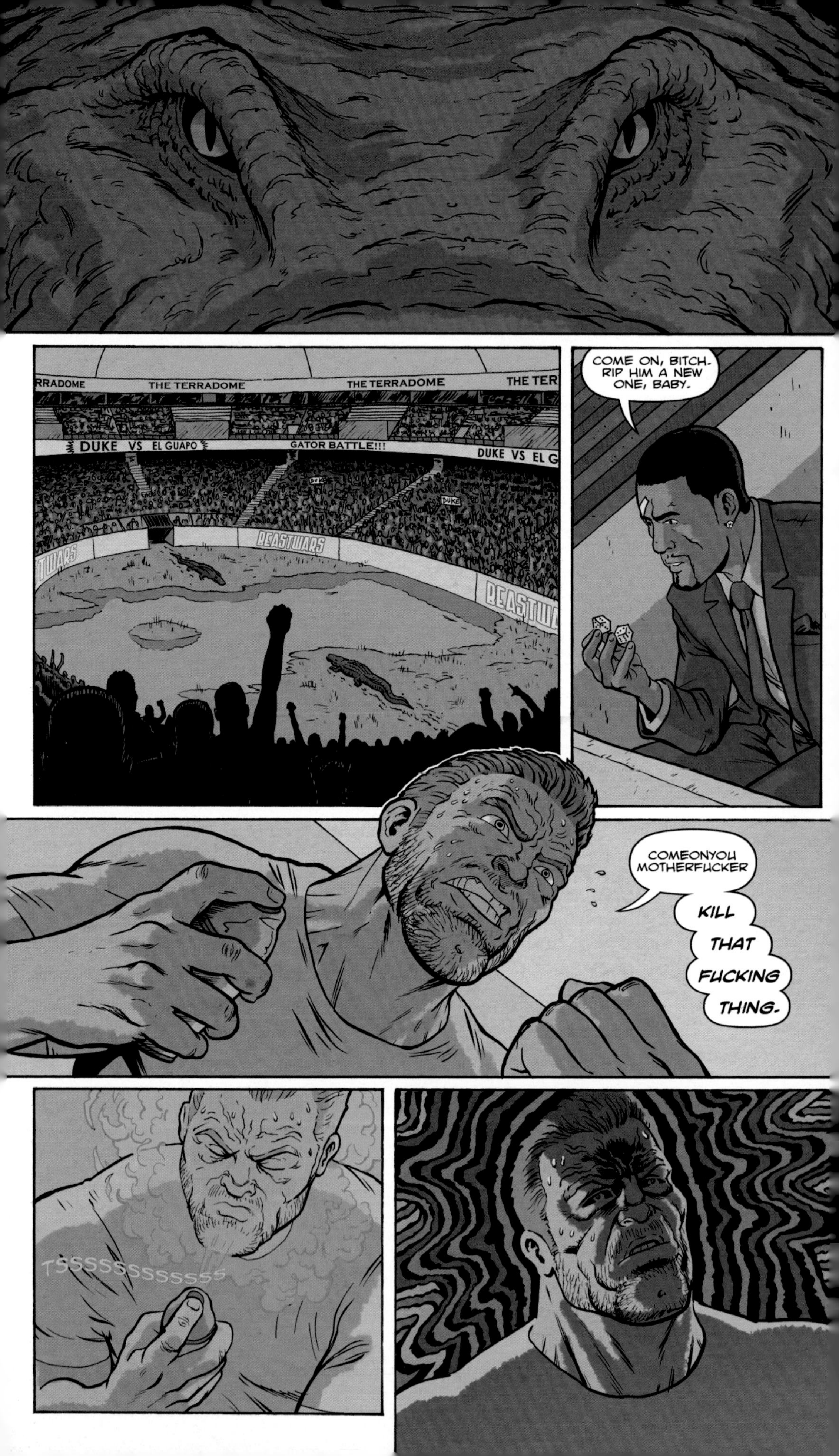

THE TERRADOME
DUKE VS EL GUAPO GATOR BATTLE!!!
BEASTWARS
COME ON, BITCH. RIP HIM A NEW ONE, BABY.
COMEONYOU MOTHERFUCKER
KILL THAT FUCKING THING.
TSSSSSSSSSSSS

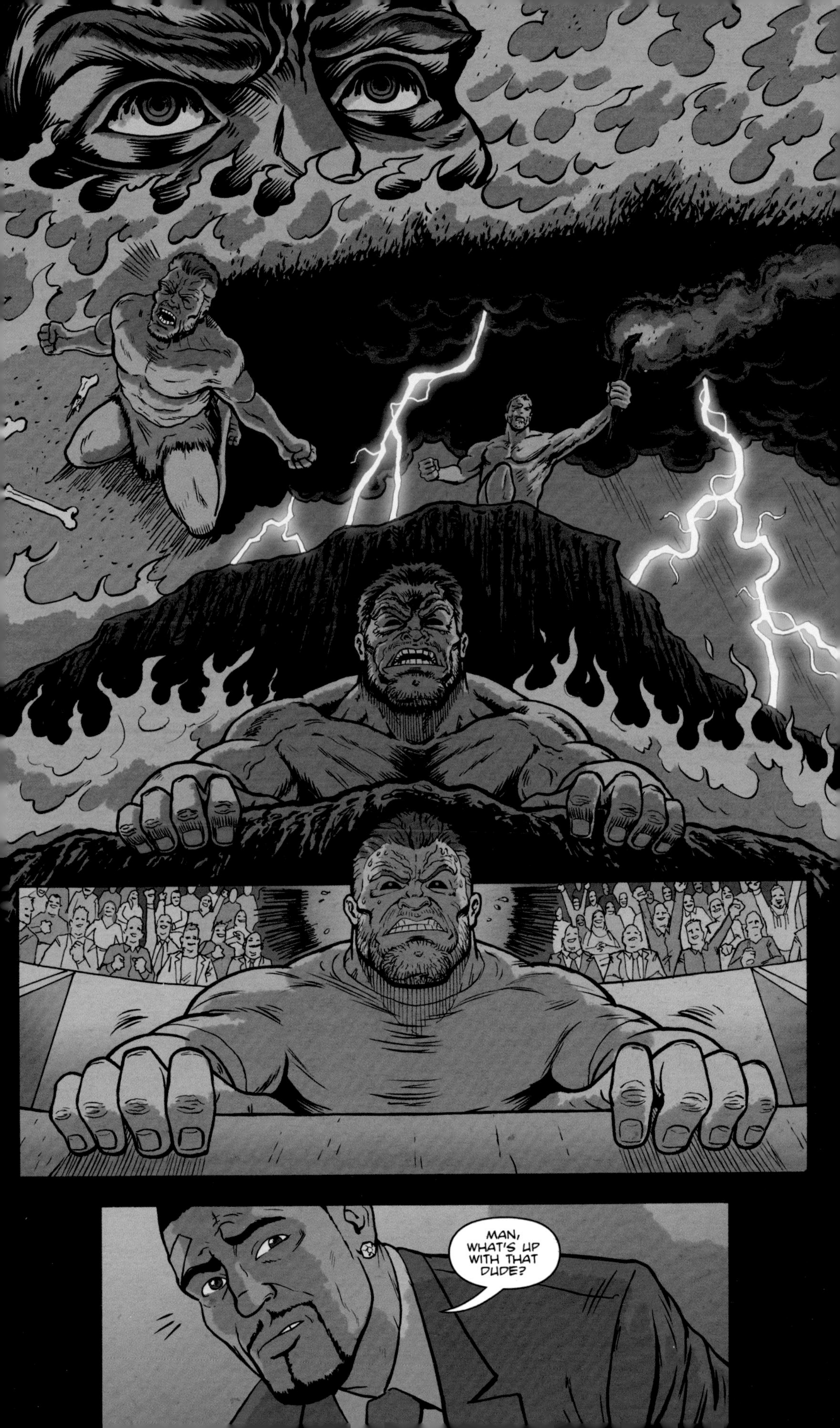
MAN, WHAT'S UP WITH THAT DUDE?

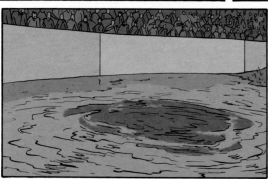

HHSSSSSSSSSSSS

WRRRRAAAW! GRAAAAWWWW!!

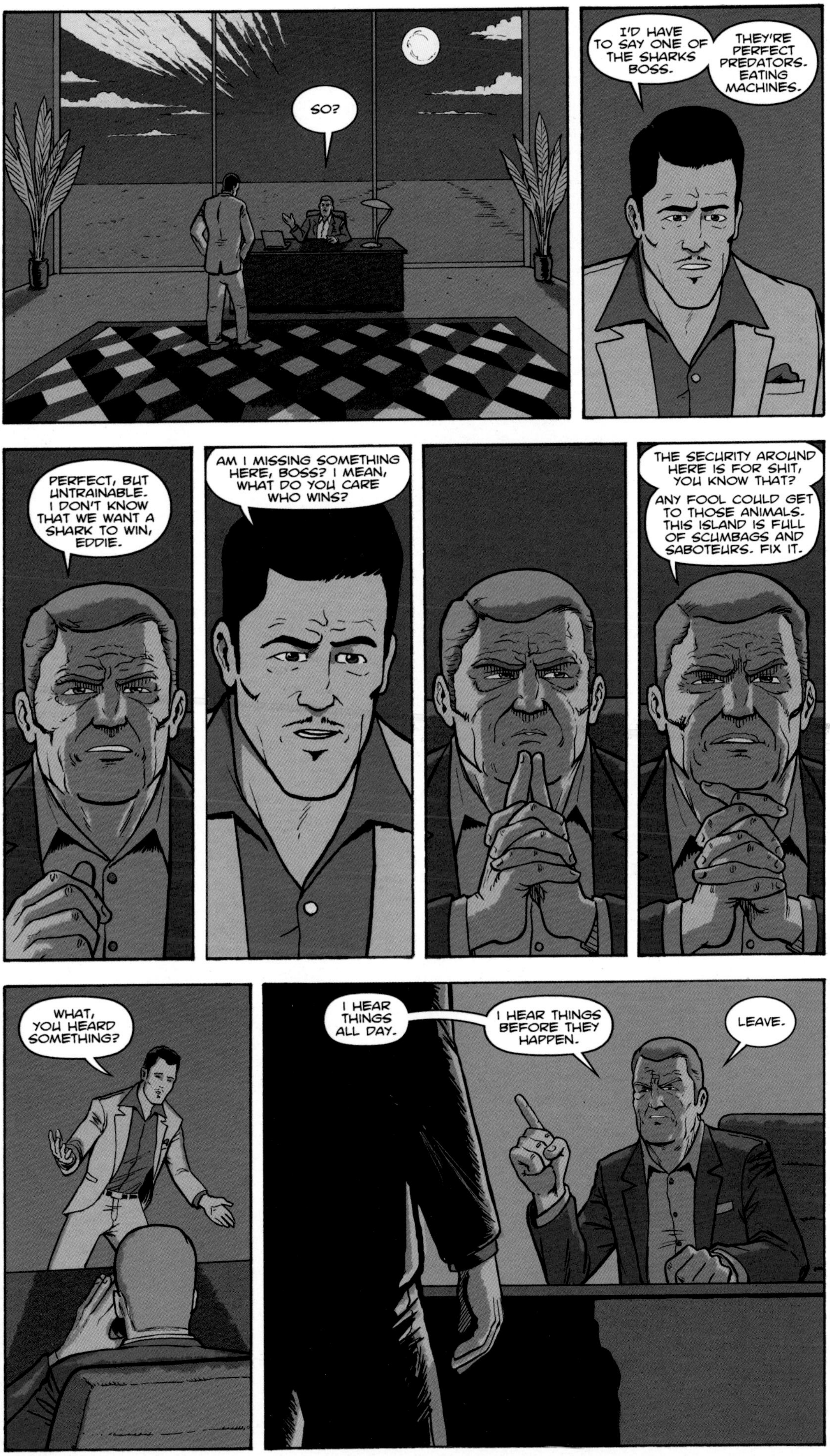
SO?
I'D HAVE TO SAY ONE OF THE SHARKS BOSS.
THEY'RE PERFECT PREDATORS. EATING MACHINES.
PERFECT, BUT UNTRAINABLE. I DON'T KNOW THAT WE WANT A SHARK TO WIN, EDDIE.
AM I MISSING SOMETHING HERE, BOSS? I MEAN, WHAT DO YOU CARE WHO WINS?
THE SECURITY AROUND HERE IS FOR SHIT, YOU KNOW THAT?
ANY FOOL COULD GET TO THOSE ANIMALS. THIS ISLAND IS FULL OF SCUMBAGS AND SABOTEURS. FIX IT.
WHAT, YOU HEARD SOMETHING?
I HEAR THINGS ALL DAY.
I HEAR THINGS BEFORE THEY HAPPEN.
LEAVE.

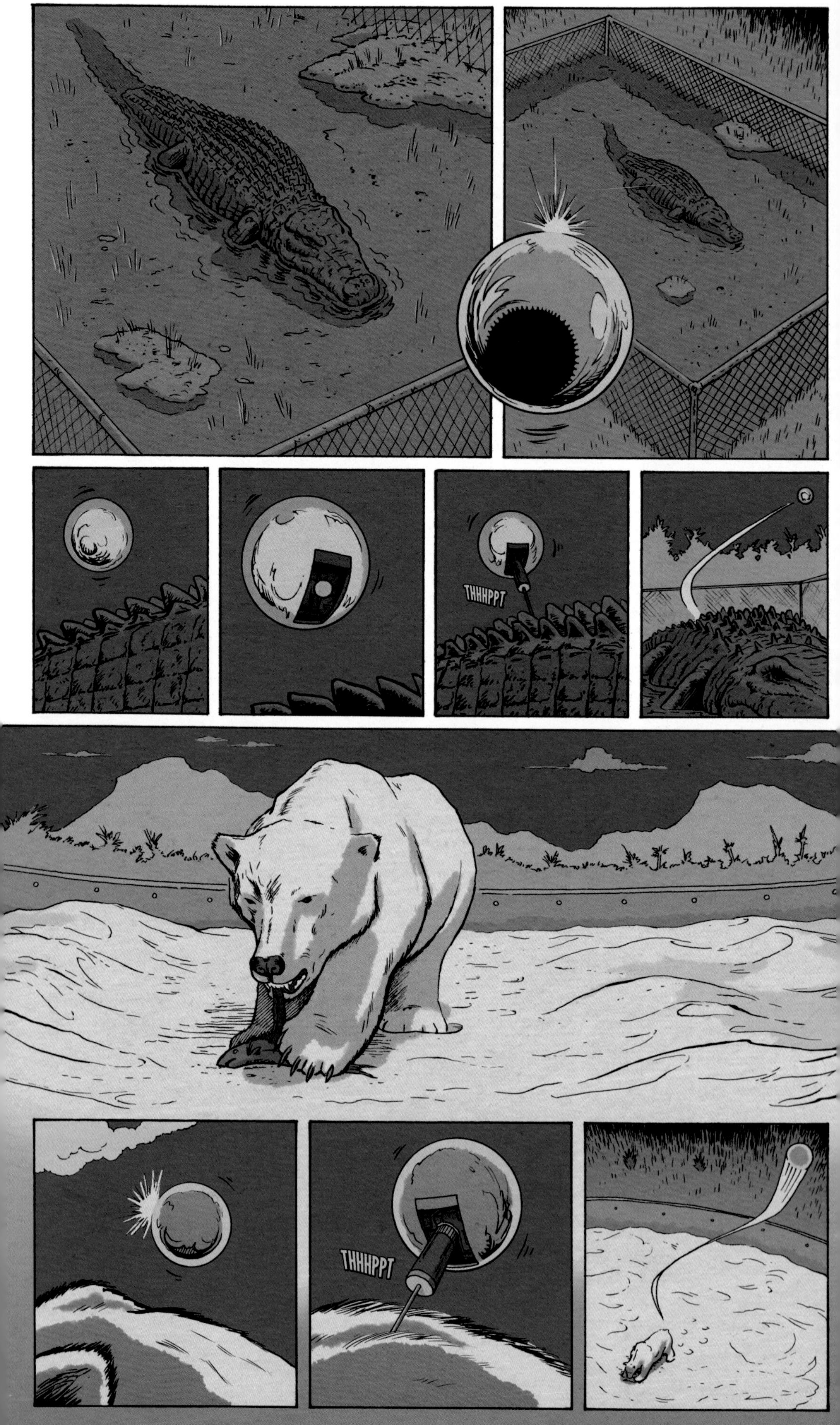
THHHPPT
THHHPPT

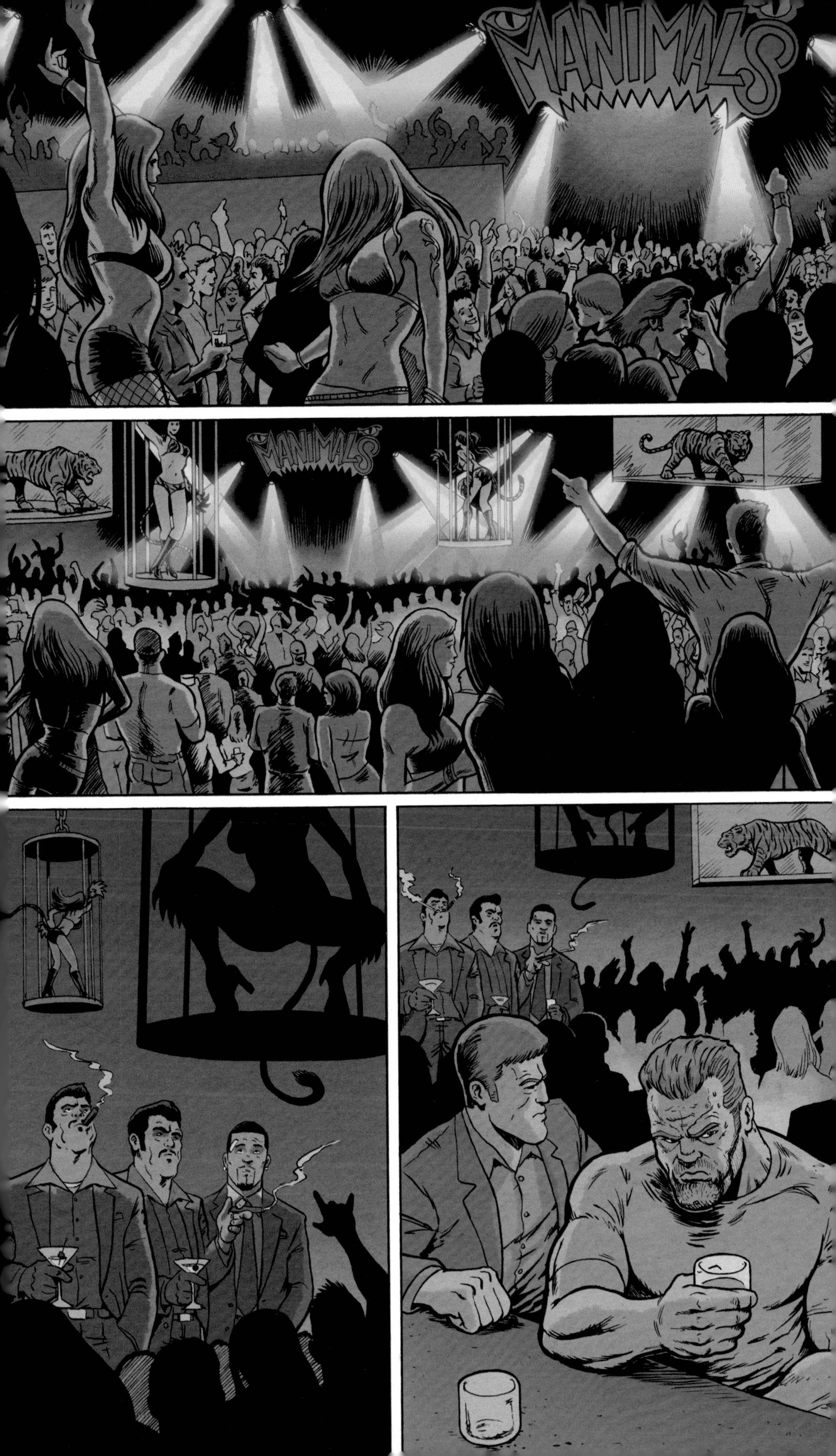
MANIMALS
MANIMALS

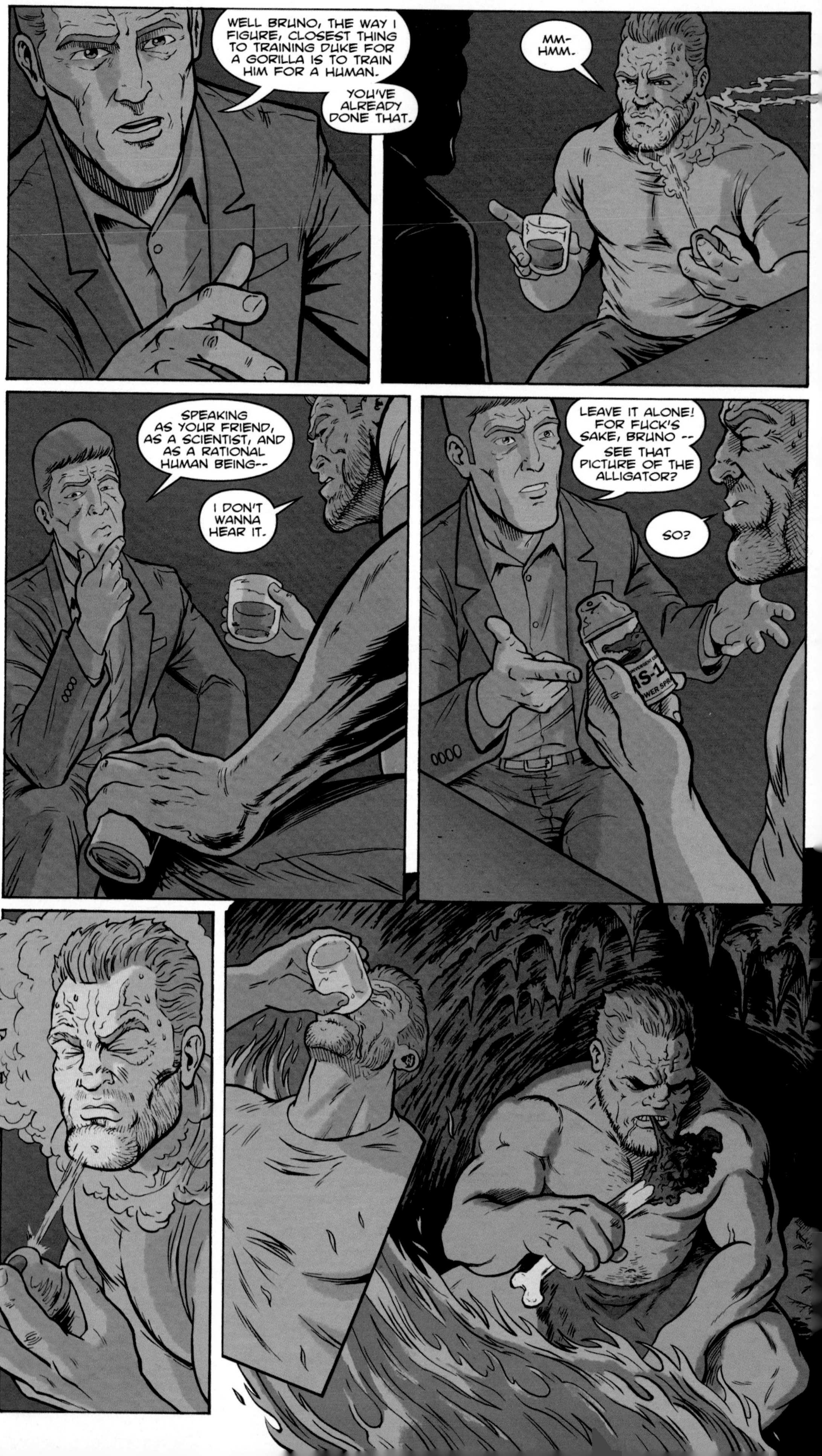
WELL BRUNO, THE WAY I FIGURE, CLOSEST THING TO TRAINING DUKE FOR A GORILLA IS TO TRAIN HIM FOR A HUMAN.
YOU'VE ALREADY DONE THAT.
MM-HMM.
SPEAKING AS YOUR FRIEND, AS A SCIENTIST, AND AS A RATIONAL HUMAN BEING--
I DON'T WANNA HEAR IT.
LEAVE IT ALONE! FOR FUCK'S SAKE, BRUNO -- SEE THAT PICTURE OF THE ALLIGATOR?
SO?

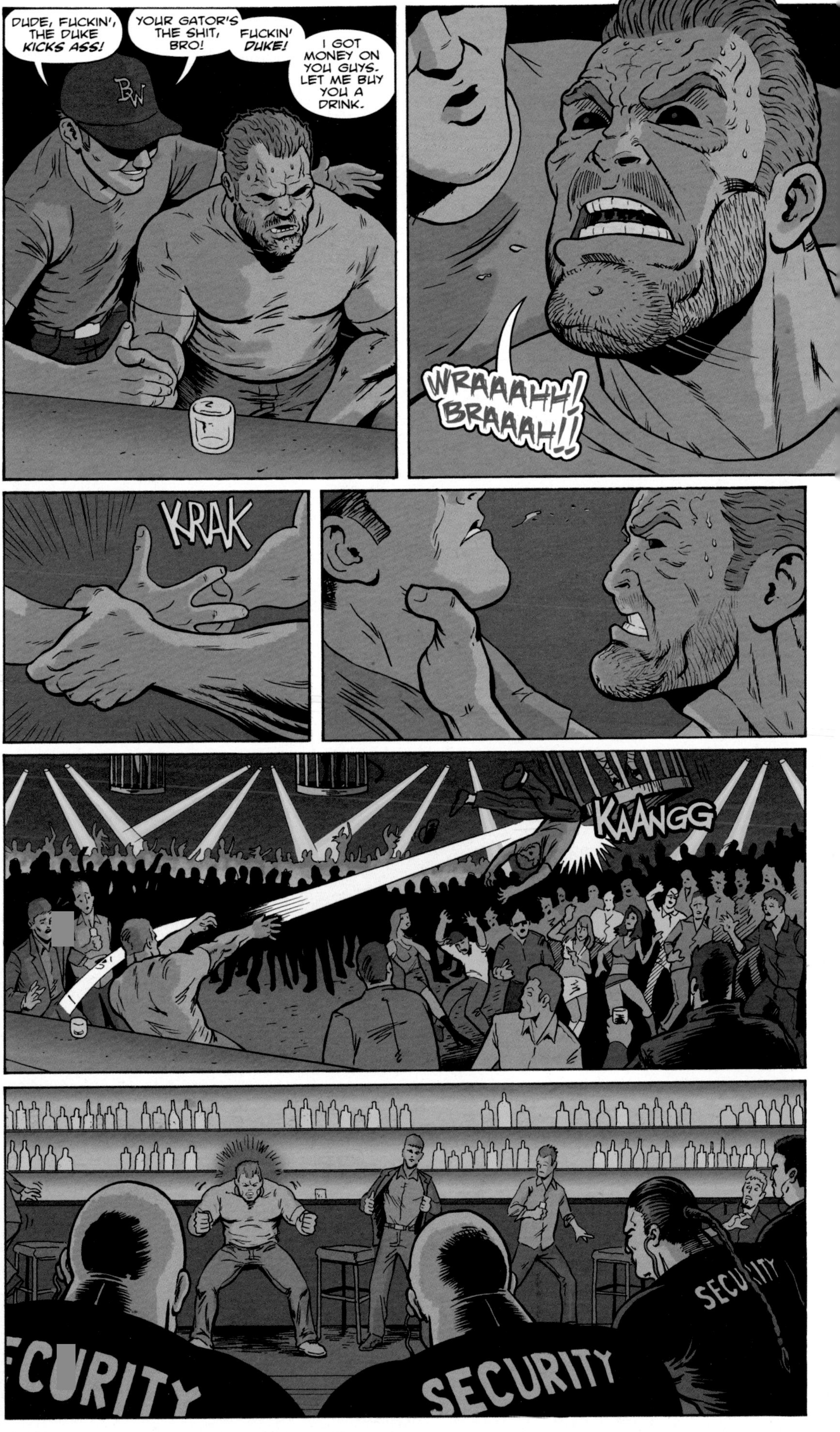

DUDE, FUCKIN', THE DUKE KICKS ASS!
YOUR GATOR'S THE SHIT, BRO!
FUCKIN' DUKE!
I GOT MONEY ON YOU GUYS. LET ME BUY YOU A DRINK.
WRAAAHH! BRAAAH!!
KRAK
KAANGG
SECURITY
SECURITY
SECURITY

SEE? TWELVE STITCHES.

GUY'S A FUCKIN' MENACE.

WE SHOULD PICK ANOTHER MATCH.

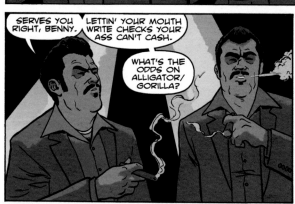

SERVES YOU RIGHT, BENNY.

LETTIN' YOUR MOUTH WRITE CHECKS YOUR ASS CAN'T CASH.

WHAT'S THE ODDS ON ALLIGATOR/GORILLA?

SIX TO ONE.

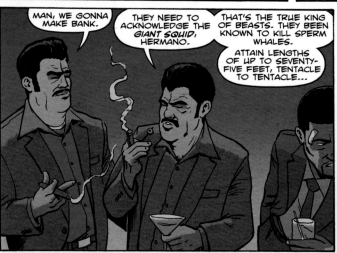

MAN, WE GONNA MAKE BANK.

THEY NEED TO ACKNOWLEDGE THE GIANT SQUID, HERMANO.

THAT'S THE TRUE KING OF BEASTS. THEY BEEN KNOWN TO KILL SPERM WHALES.

ATTAIN LENGTHS OF UP TO SEVENTY-FIVE FEET, TENTACLE TO TENTACLE...

IF YOU COULD CALIBRATE THEIR HEADS NOT TO EXPLODE AT THIS LEVEL OF ATMOSPHERIC PRESSURE...

YOU'D HAVE A CHAMP, CABRON.

FUCK A SHARK.

WHAT'S GOIN' ON, PENDEJOS?

WELL LOOK WHO'S HERE. IT'S EDDIE MOTHERFUCKIN' KLEM.

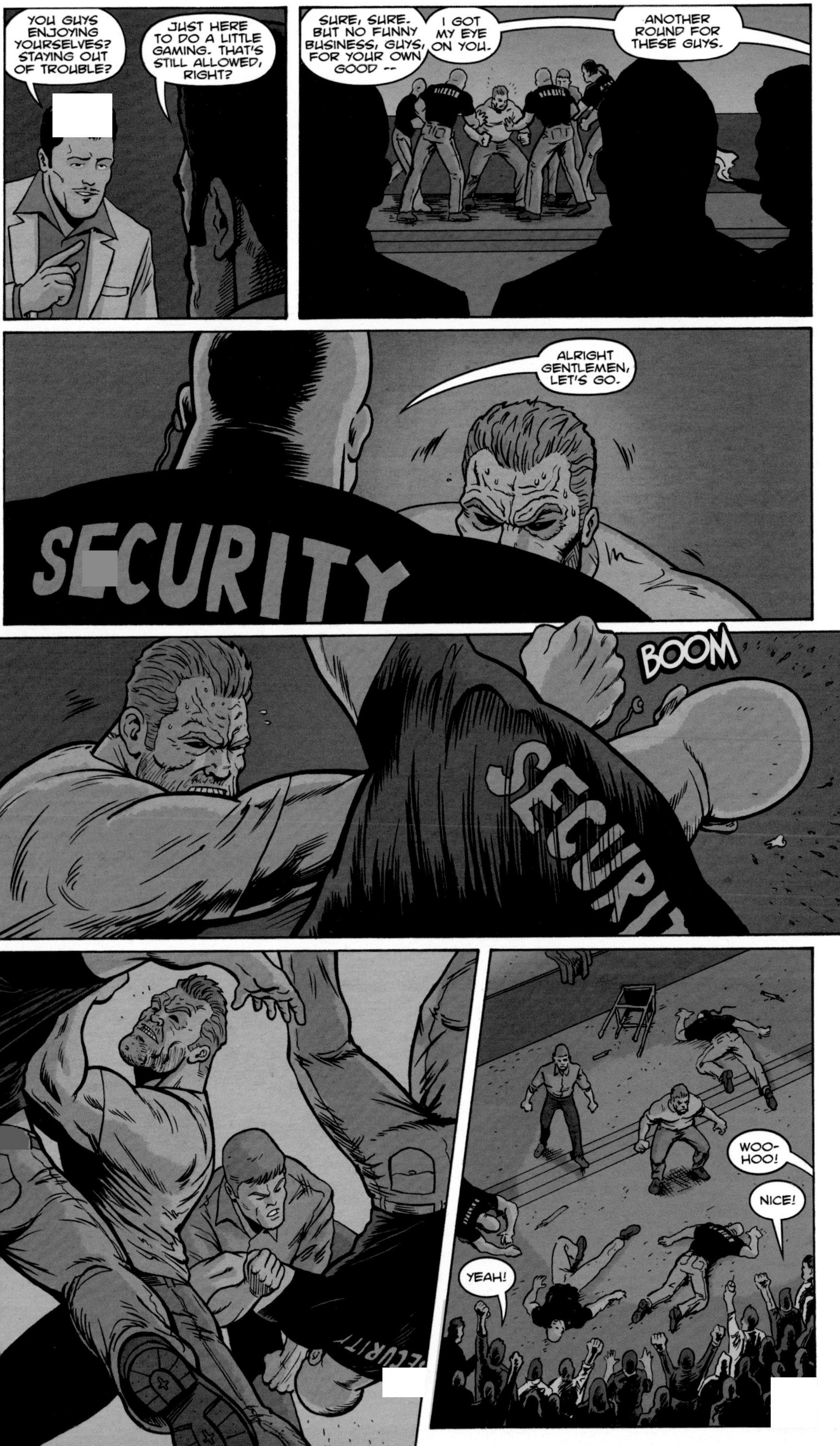
YOU GUYS ENJOYING YOURSELVES? STAYING OUT OF TROUBLE?
JUST HERE TO DO A LITTLE GAMING. THAT'S STILL ALLOWED, RIGHT?
SURE, SURE. BUT NO FUNNY BUSINESS, GUYS, FOR YOUR OWN GOOD --
I GOT MY EYE ON YOU.
ANOTHER ROUND FOR THESE GUYS.
ALRIGHT GENTLEMEN, LET'S GO.
SECURITY
BOOM
WOO-HOO!
NICE!
YEAH!

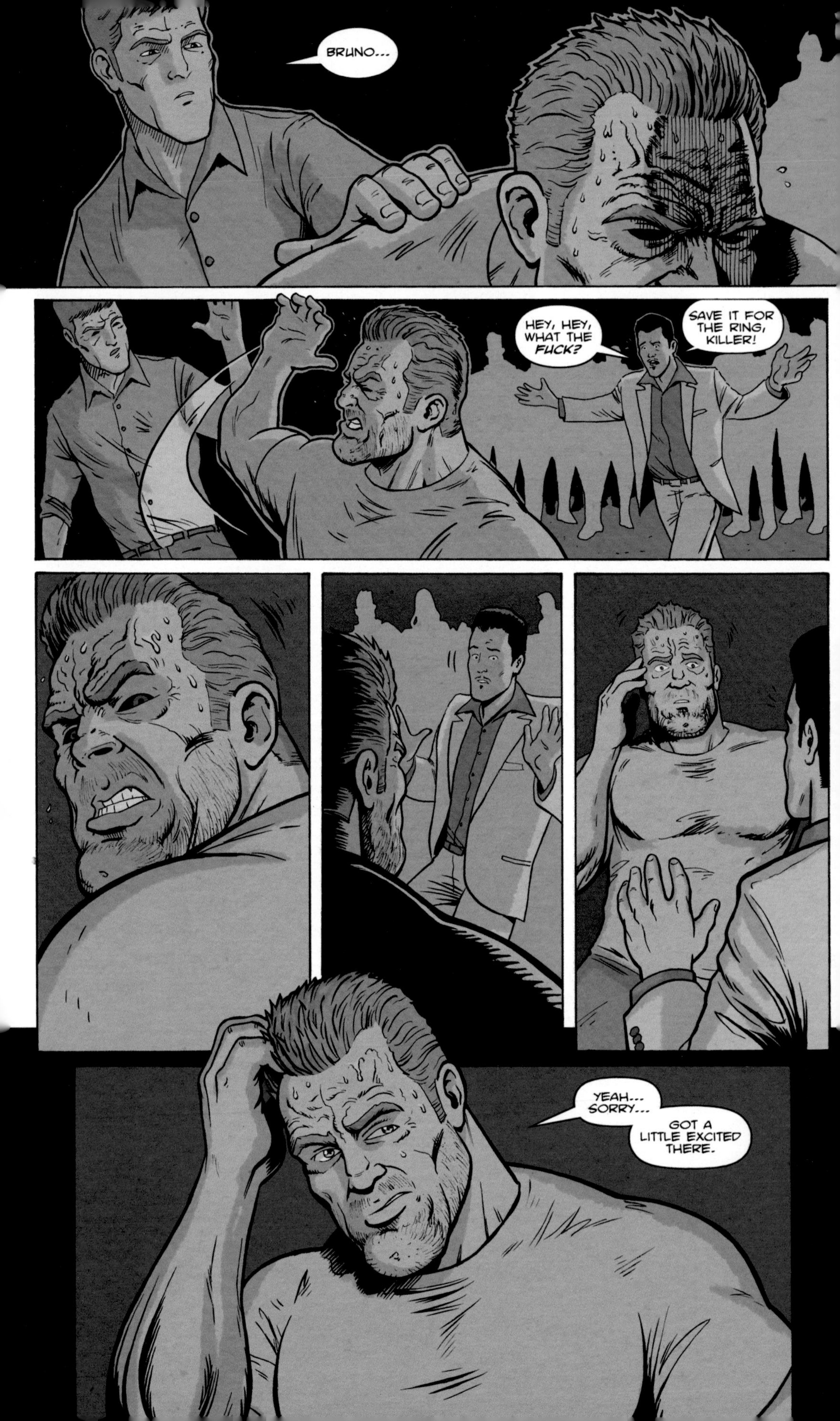
BRUNO...
HEY, HEY, WHAT THE *FUCK?*
SAVE IT FOR THE RING, KILLER!
YEAH... SORRY...
GOT A LITTLE EXCITED THERE.

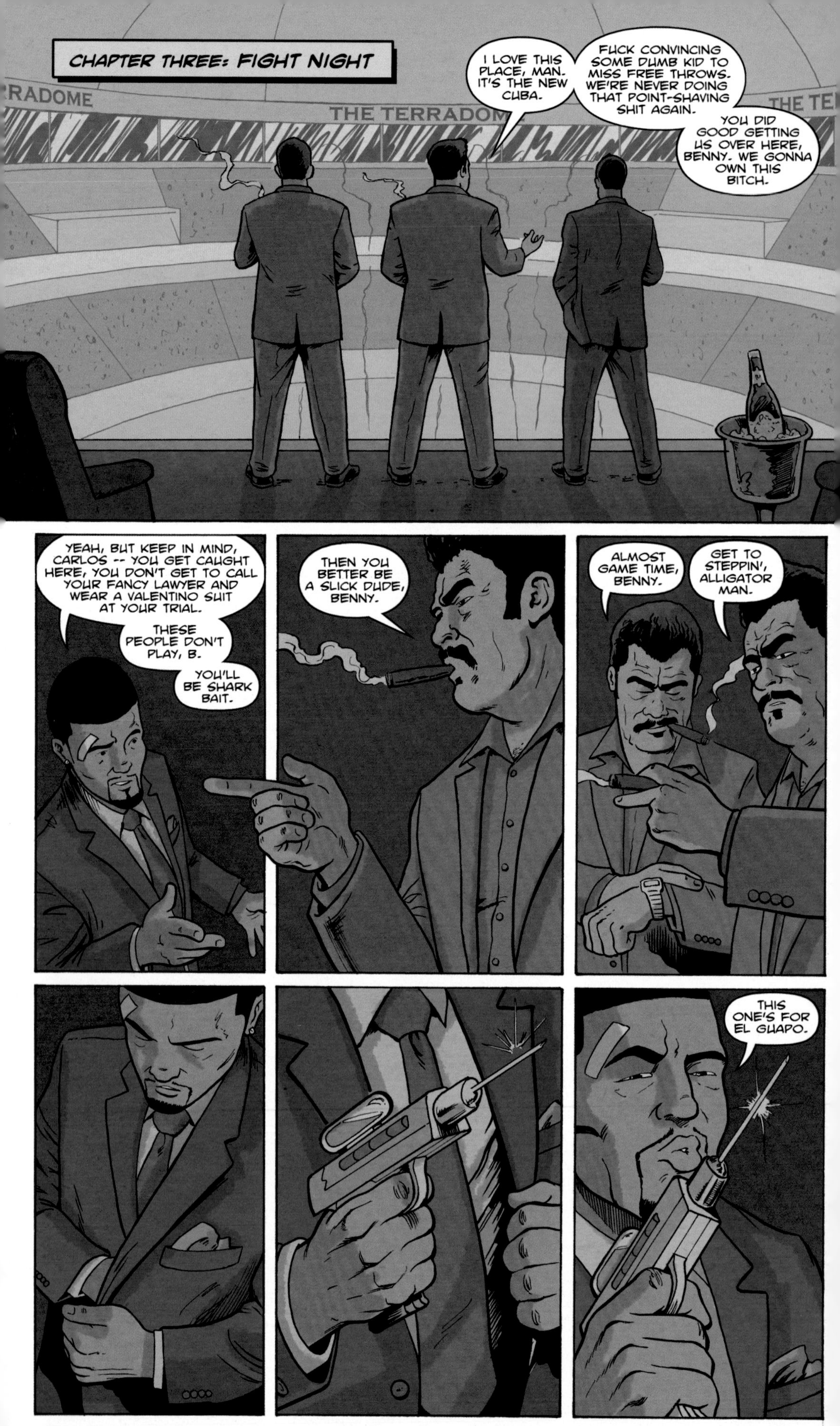
CHAPTER THREE: FIGHT NIGHT
THE TERRADOME
I LOVE THIS PLACE, MAN. IT'S THE NEW CUBA.
FUCK CONVINCING SOME DUMB KID TO MISS FREE THROWS. WE'RE NEVER DOING THAT POINT-SHAVING SHIT AGAIN.
YOU DID GOOD GETTING US OVER HERE, BENNY. WE GONNA OWN THIS BITCH.
YEAH, BUT KEEP IN MIND, CARLOS -- YOU GET CAUGHT HERE, YOU DON'T GET TO CALL YOUR FANCY LAWYER AND WEAR A VALENTINO SUIT AT YOUR TRIAL.
THESE PEOPLE DON'T PLAY, B.
YOU'LL BE SHARK BAIT.
THEN YOU BETTER BE A SLICK DUDE, BENNY.
ALMOST GAME TIME, BENNY.
GET TO STEPPIN', ALLIGATOR MAN.
THIS ONE'S FOR EL GUAPO.

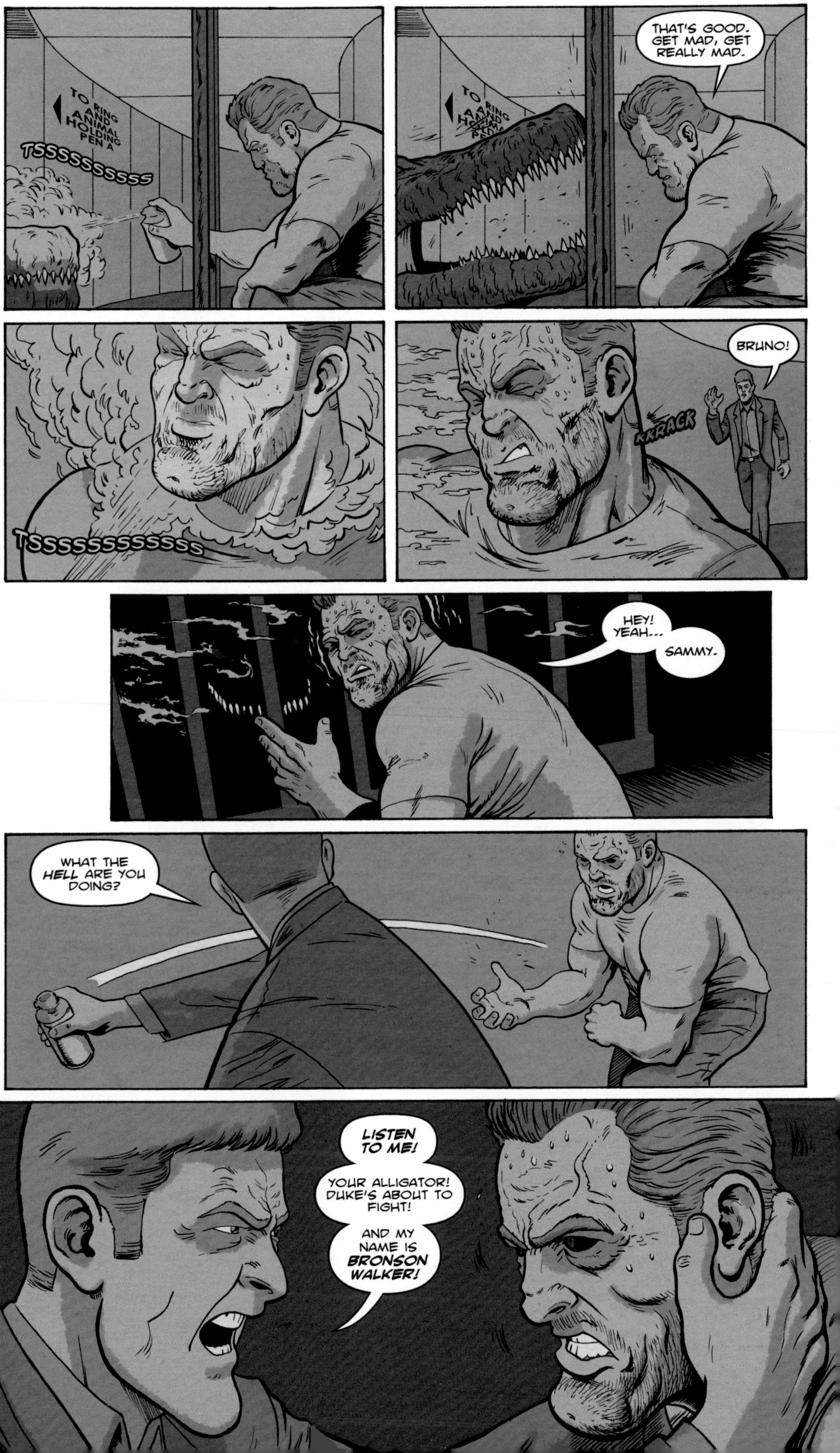
TO RING AND ANIMAL HOLDING PEN A
TSSSSSSSSSSS
THAT'S GOOD. GET MAD, GET REALLY MAD.
TSSSSSSSSSSSSS
BRUNO!
KKRACK
HEY! YEAH...
SAMMY.
WHAT THE HELL ARE YOU DOING?
LISTEN TO ME!
YOUR ALLIGATOR! DUKE'S ABOUT TO FIGHT!
AND MY NAME IS BRONSON WALKER!

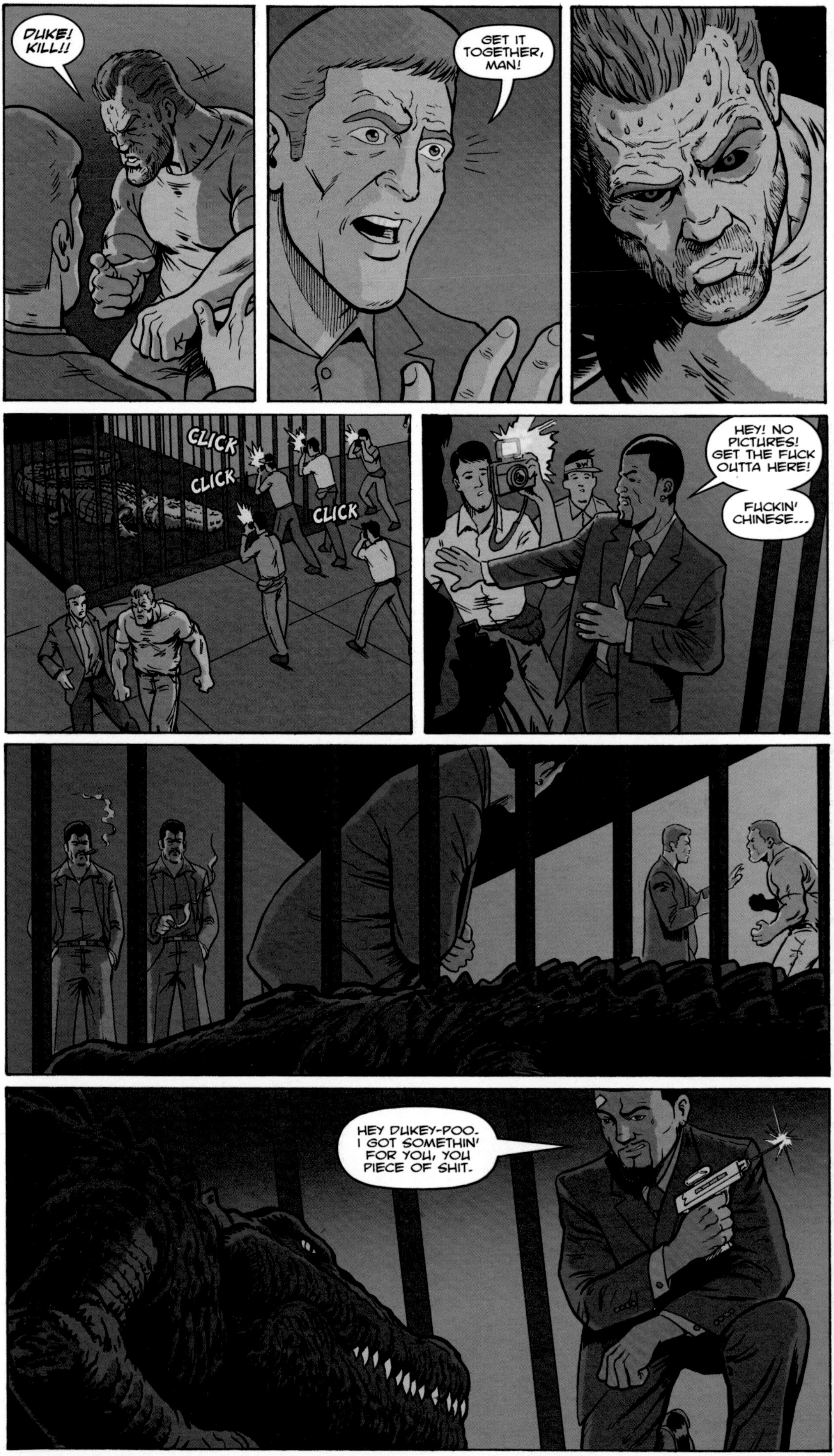
DUKE! KILL!!
GET IT TOGETHER, MAN!
CLICK
CLICK
CLICK
HEY! NO PICTURES! GET THE FUCK OUTTA HERE!
FUCKIN' CHINESE...
HEY DUKEY-POO. I GOT SOMETHIN' FOR YOU, YOU PIECE OF SHIT.

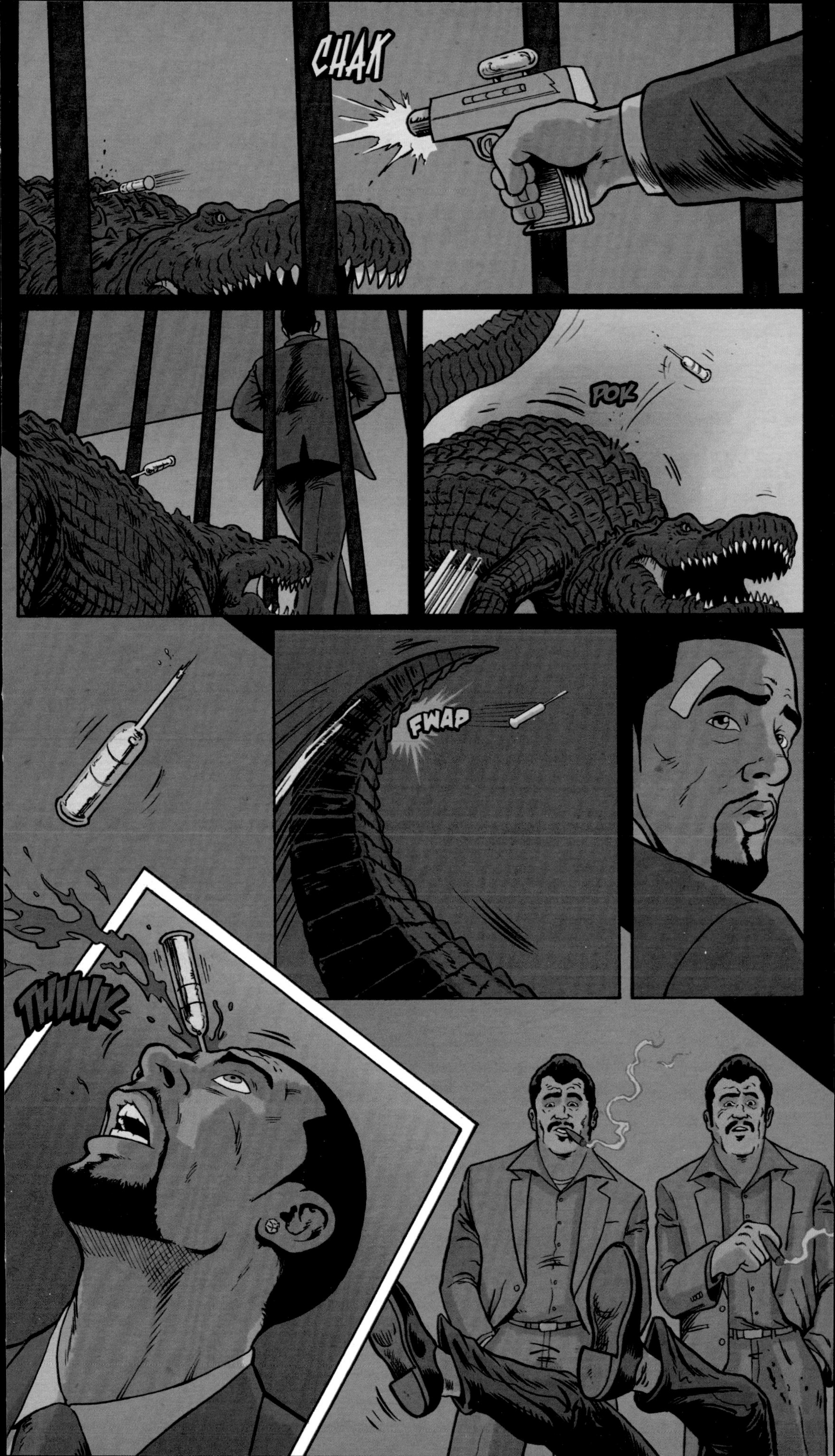
CHAK
POK
FWAP
THUNK

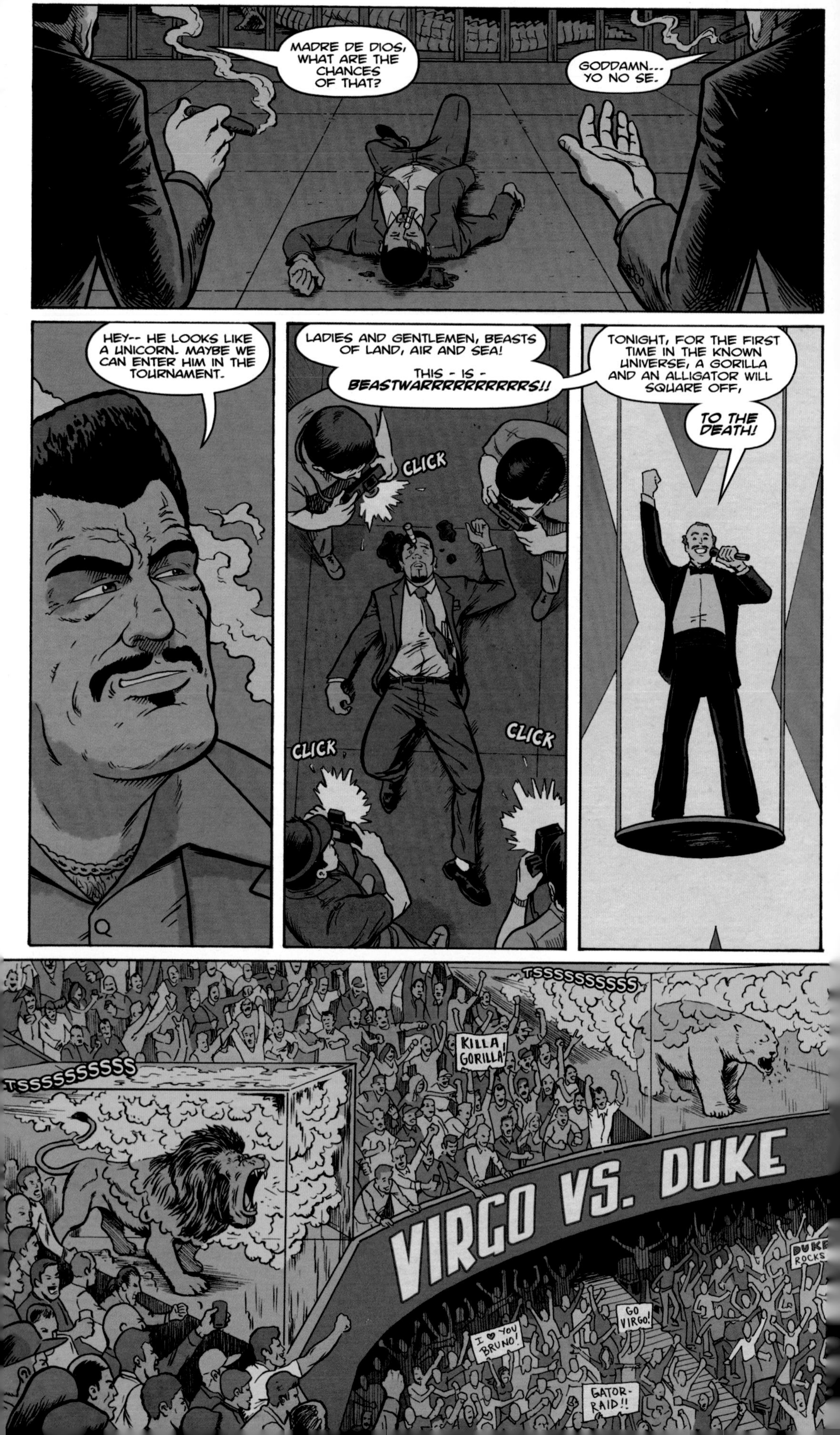
MADRE DE DIOS, WHAT ARE THE CHANCES OF THAT?
GODDAMN... YO NO SE.
HEY-- HE LOOKS LIKE A UNICORN. MAYBE WE CAN ENTER HIM IN THE TOURNAMENT.
LADIES AND GENTLEMEN, BEASTS OF LAND, AIR AND SEA!
THIS - IS - BEASTWARRRRRRRRRRS!!
CLICK
CLICK
CLICK
TONIGHT, FOR THE FIRST TIME IN THE KNOWN UNIVERSE, A GORILLA AND AN ALLIGATOR WILL SQUARE OFF,
TO THE DEATH!
TSSSSSSSSSS
TSSSSSSSSSS
KILLA GORILLA!
VIRGO VS. DUKE
DUKE ROCKS
GO VIRGO!
I ♥ YOU BRUNO!
GATOR-RAID!!

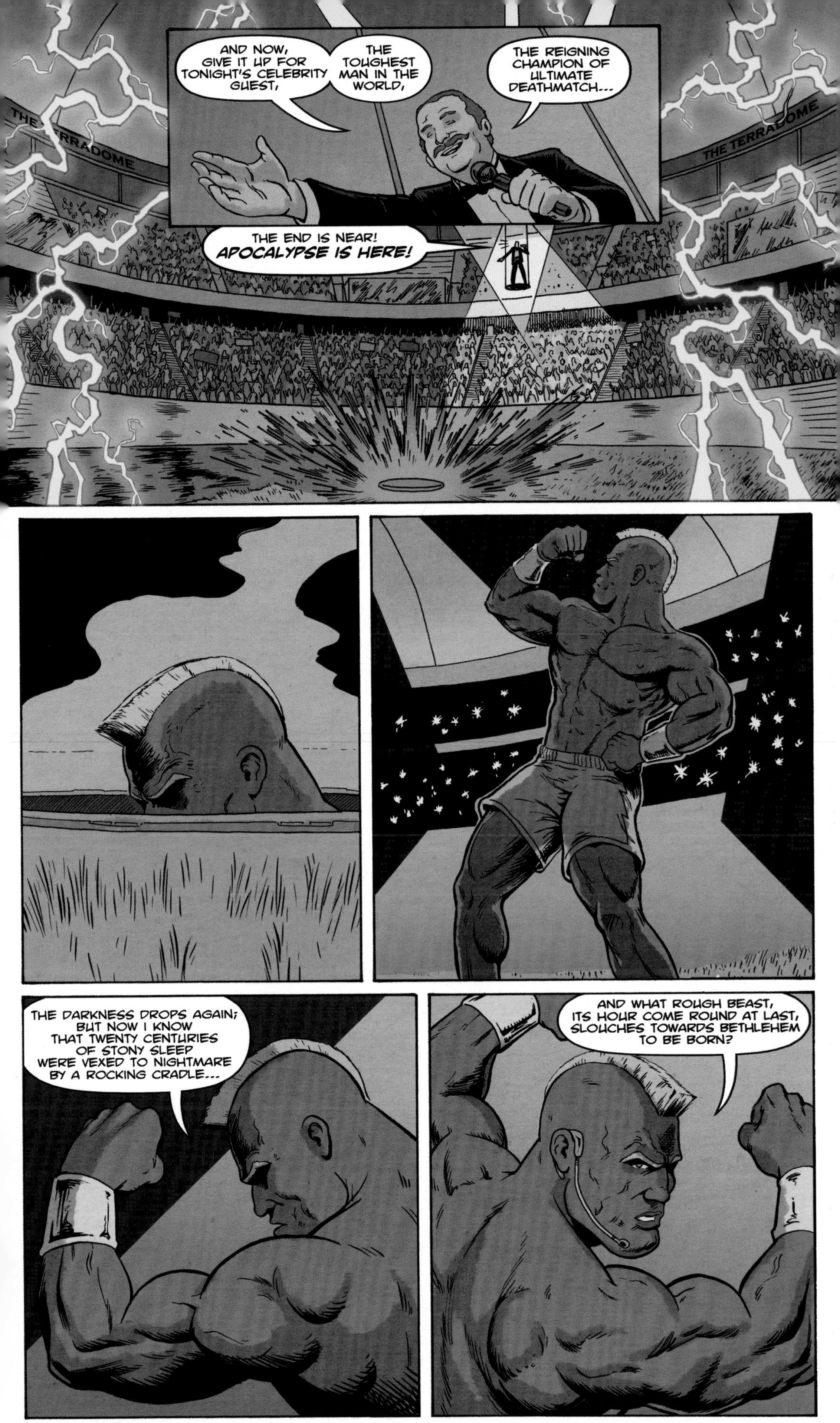
AND NOW, GIVE IT UP FOR TONIGHT'S CELEBRITY GUEST,
THE TOUGHEST MAN IN THE WORLD,
THE REIGNING CHAMPION OF ULTIMATE DEATHMATCH...
THE TERRADOME
THE TERRADOME
THE END IS NEAR! APOCALYPSE IS HERE!
THE DARKNESS DROPS AGAIN; BUT NOW I KNOW THAT TWENTY CENTURIES OF STONY SLEEP WERE VEXED TO NIGHTMARE BY A ROCKING CRADLE...
AND WHAT ROUGH BEAST, ITS HOUR COME ROUND AT LAST, SLOUCHES TOWARDS BETHLEHEM TO BE BORN?

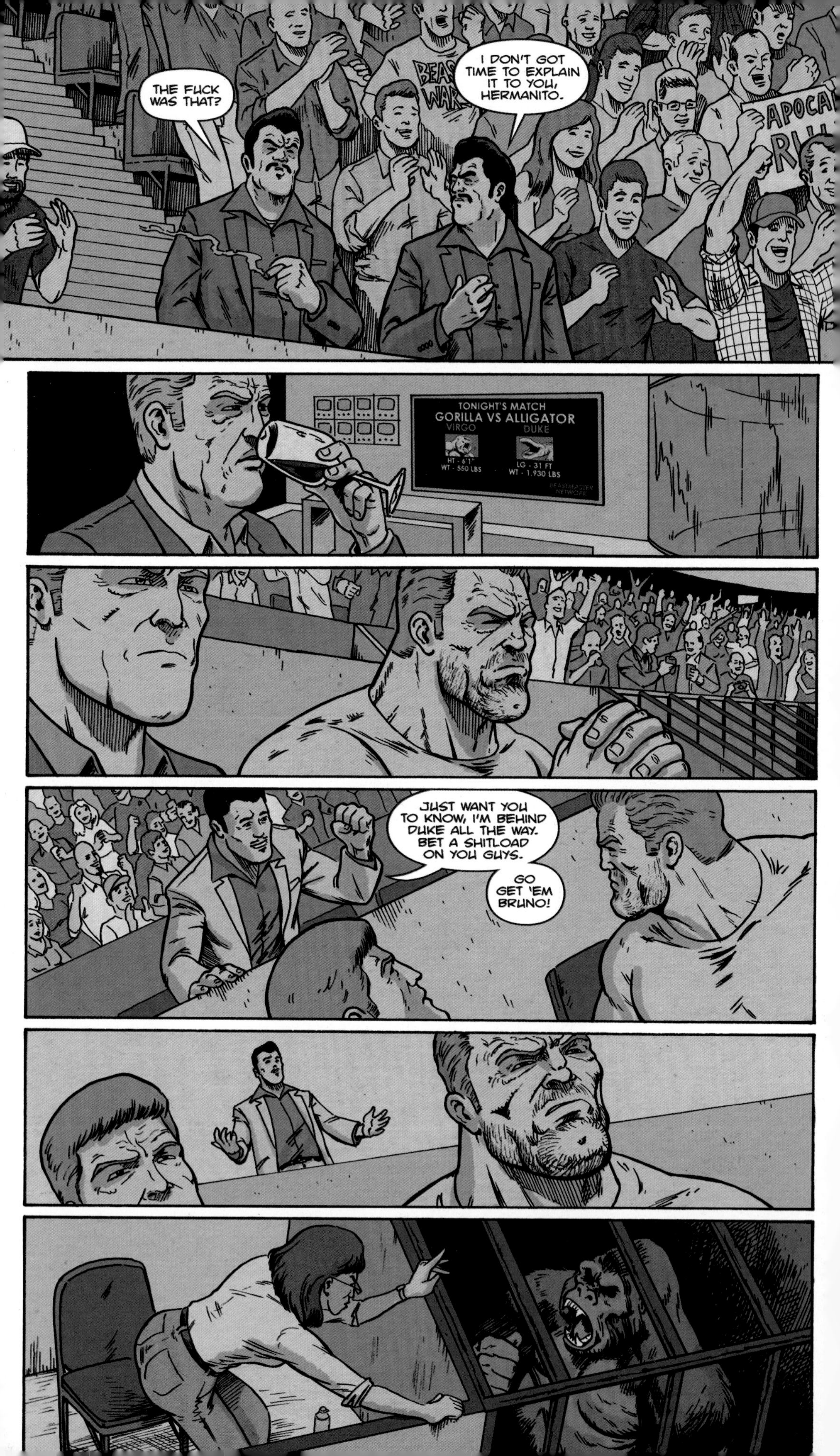
THE FUCK WAS THAT?
I DON'T GOT TIME TO EXPLAIN IT TO YOU, HERMANITO.
TONIGHT'S MATCH
GORILLA VS ALLIGATOR
VIRGO
DUKE
HT - 6'1"
WT - 550 LBS
LG - 31 FT
WT - 1,930 LBS
JUST WANT YOU TO KNOW, I'M BEHIND DUKE ALL THE WAY. BET A SHITLOAD ON YOU GUYS.
GO GET 'EM BRUNO!

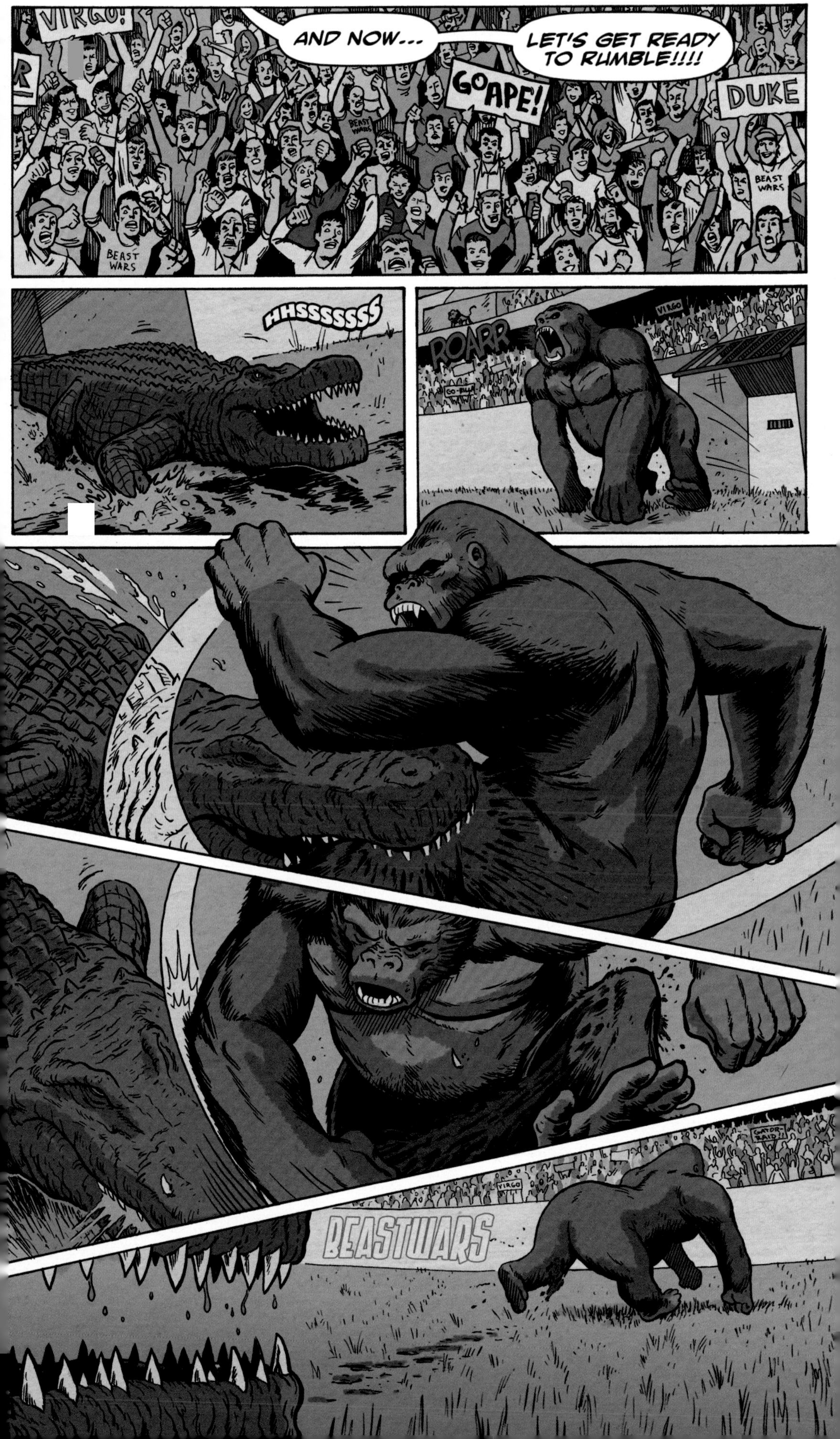

VIRGO!
AND NOW...
LET'S GET READY TO RUMBLE!!!!
GO APE!
DUKE
BEAST WARS
BEAST WARS
BEAST WARS
HHSSSSSSSS
ROARR
VIRGO
BEASTWARS

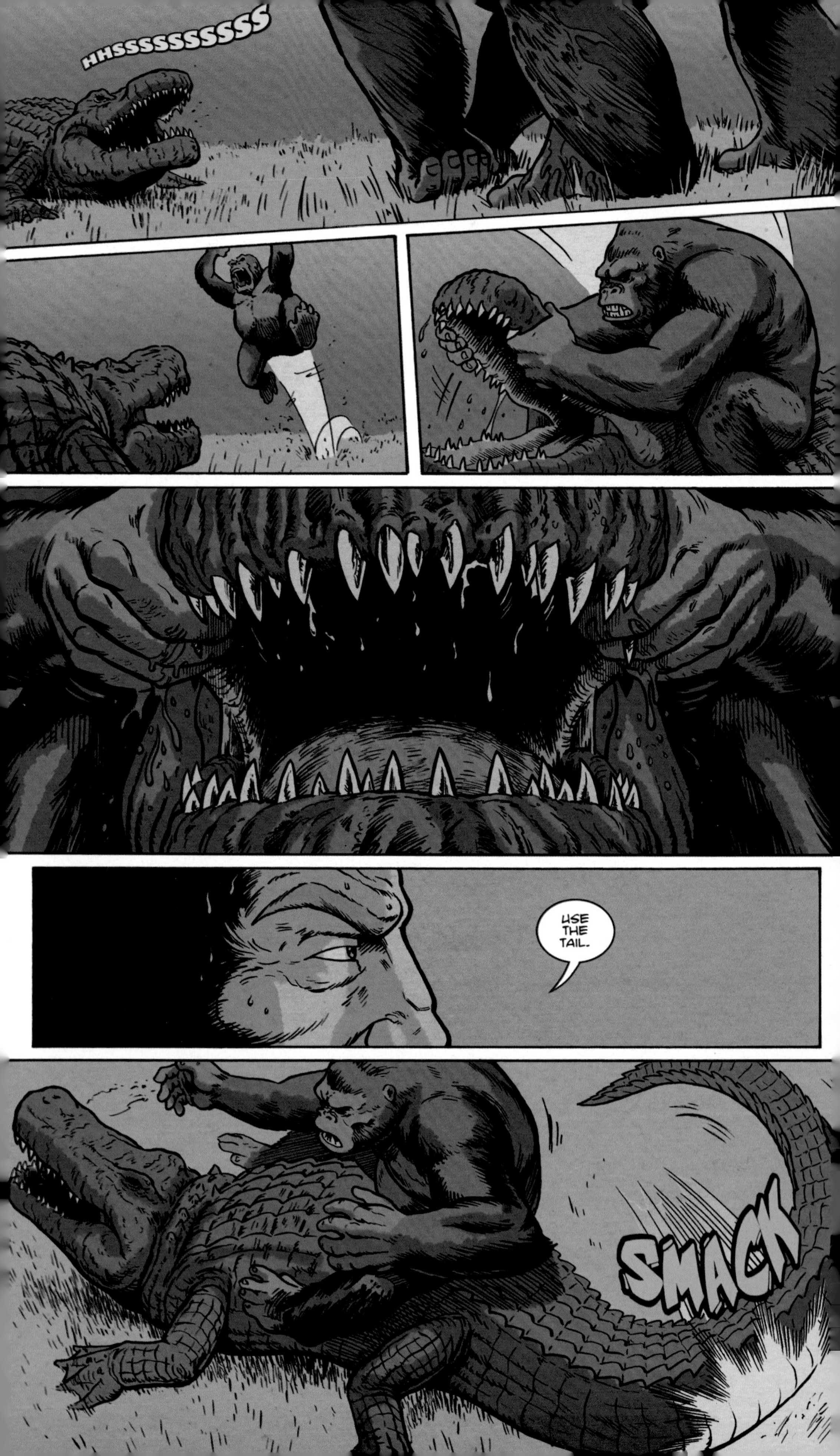
HHSSSSSSSSSS
USE THE TAIL.
SMACK

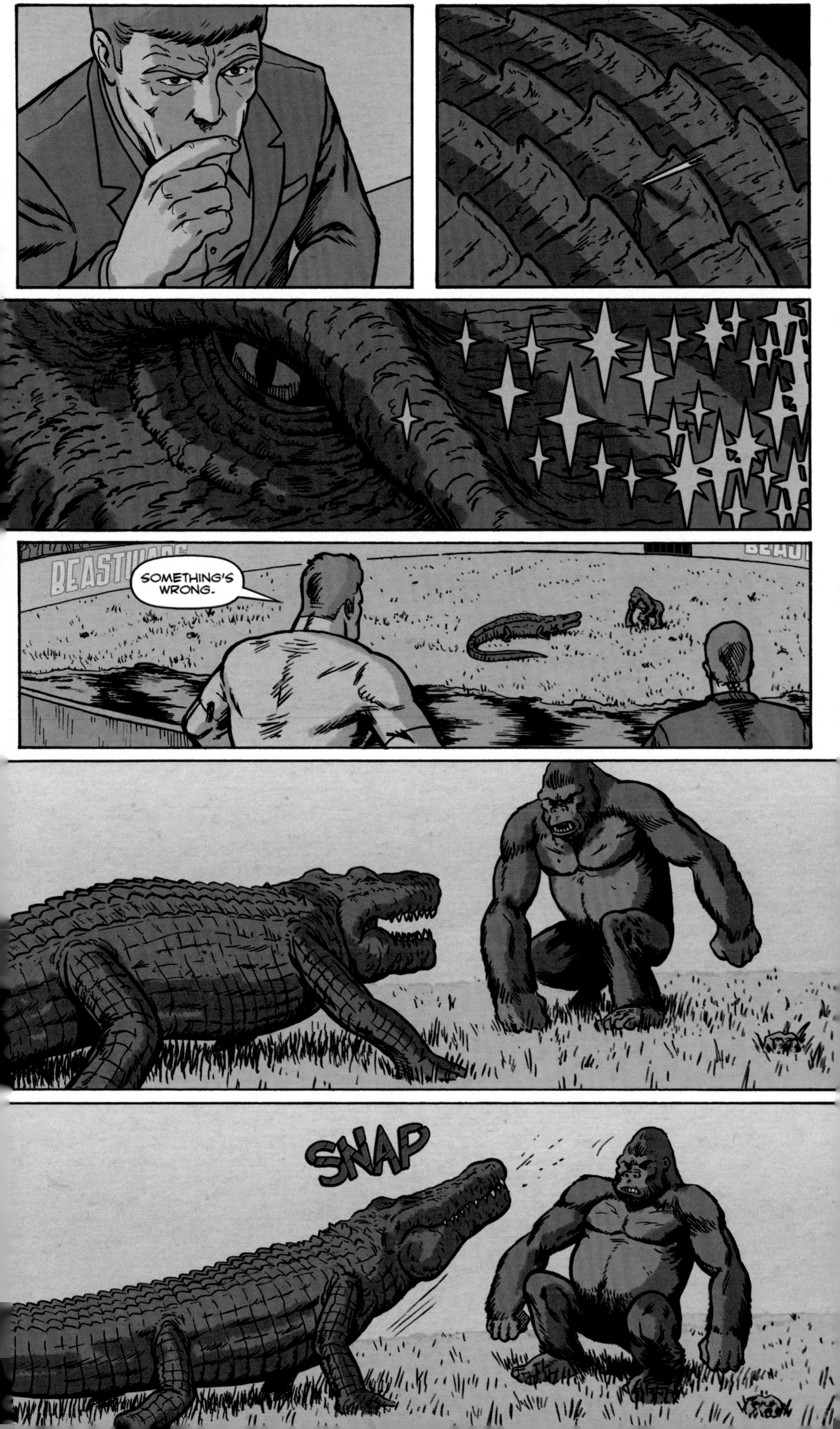
SOMETHING'S WRONG.
SNAP

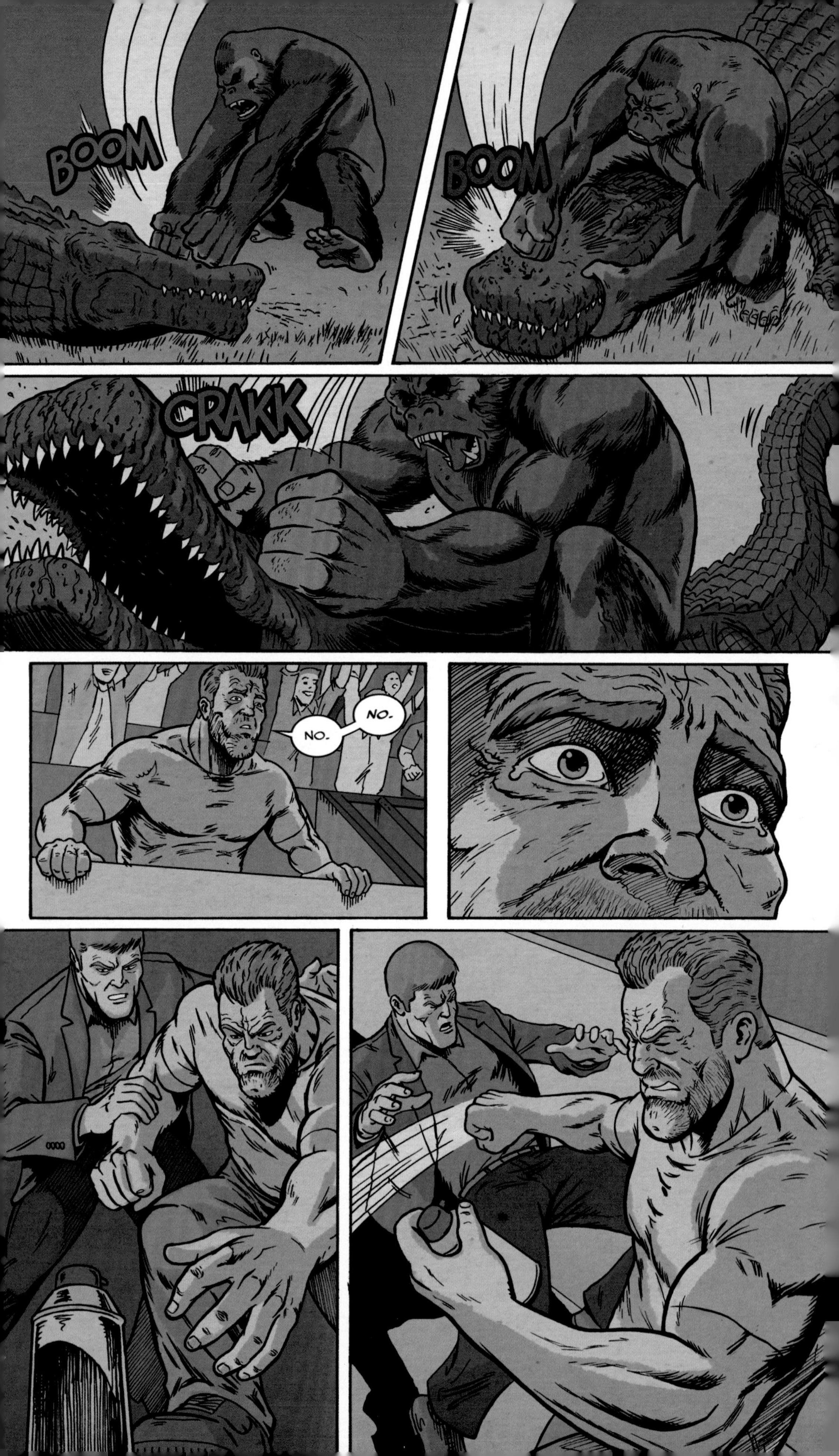
BOOM
BOOM
CRAKK
NO-
NO-

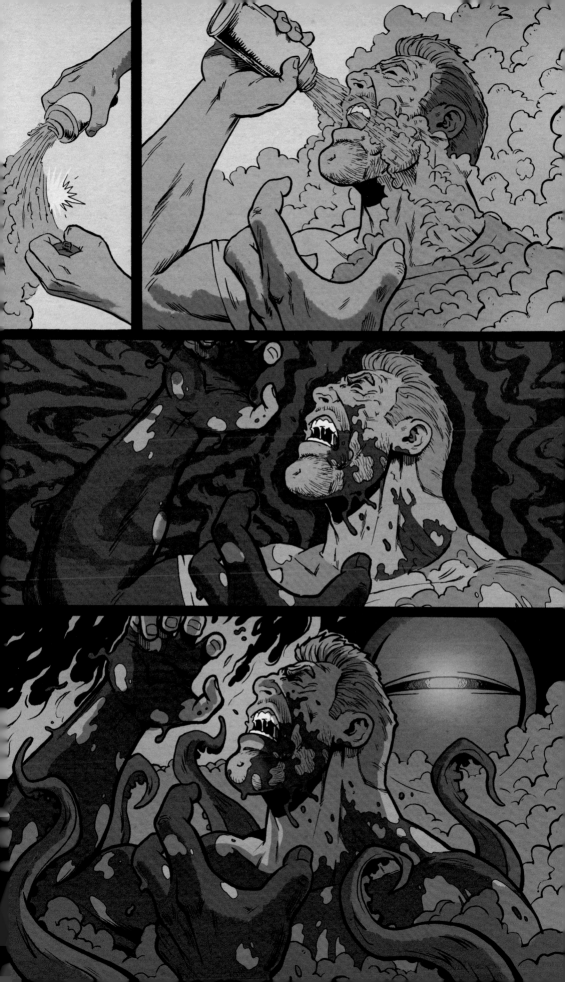

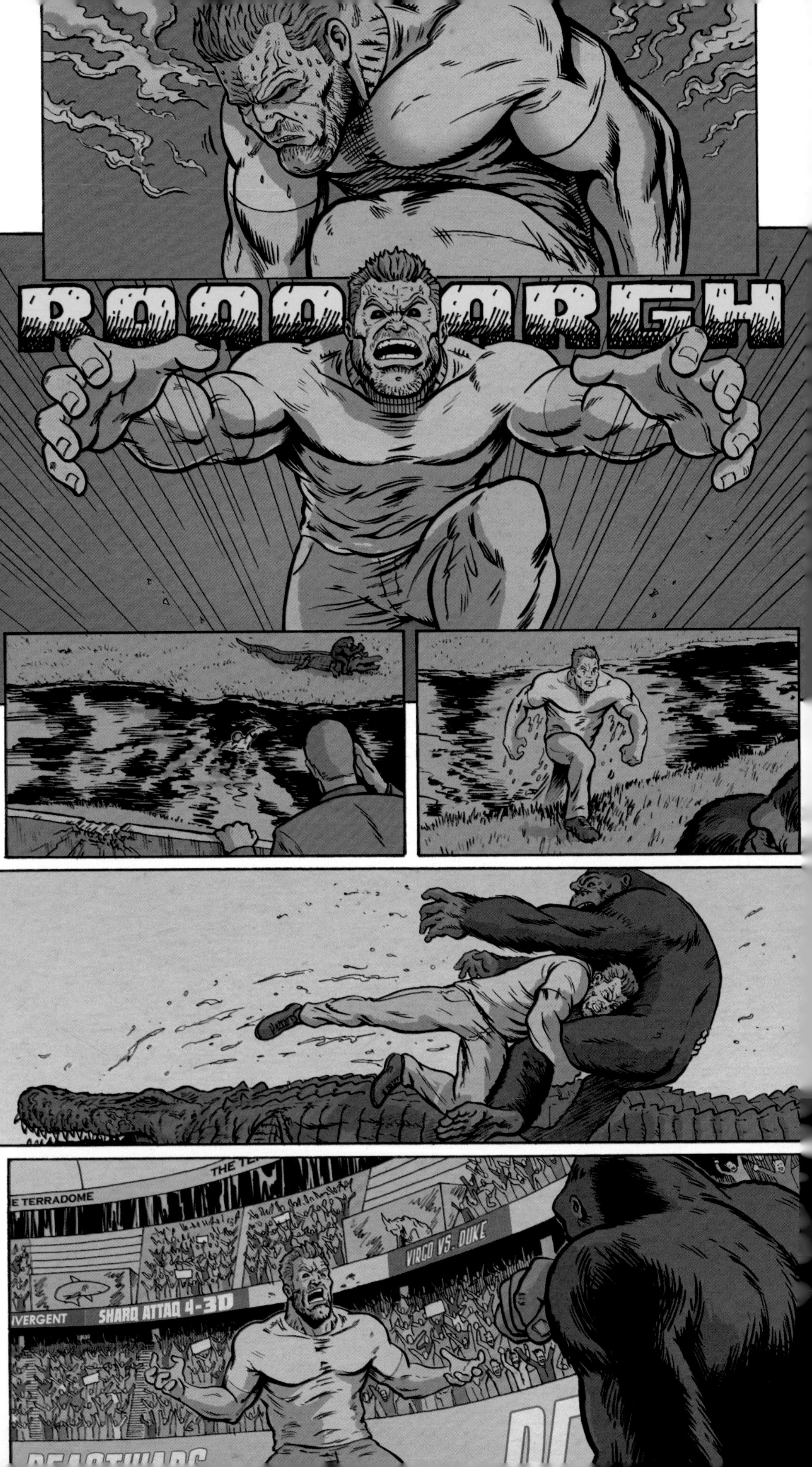

ROOO ARGH
THE TE
E TERRADOME
VIRGO VS. DUKE
IVERGENT
SHARQ ATTAQ 4-3D

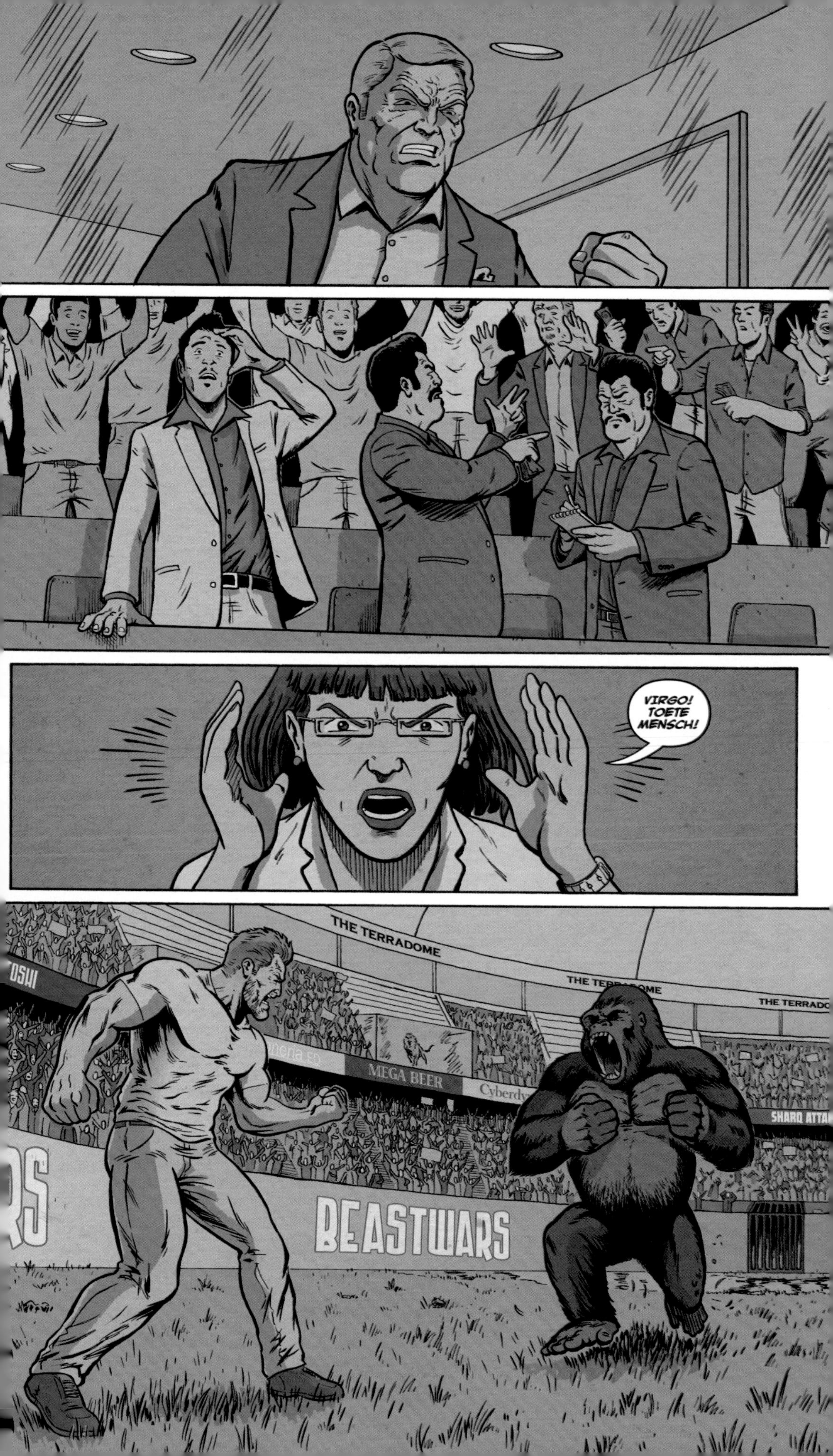
VIRGO! TOETE MENSCH!
THE TERRADOME
THE TERRADOME
THE TERRADO
MEGA BEER
Cyberdy
SHARQ ATTA
BEASTWARS

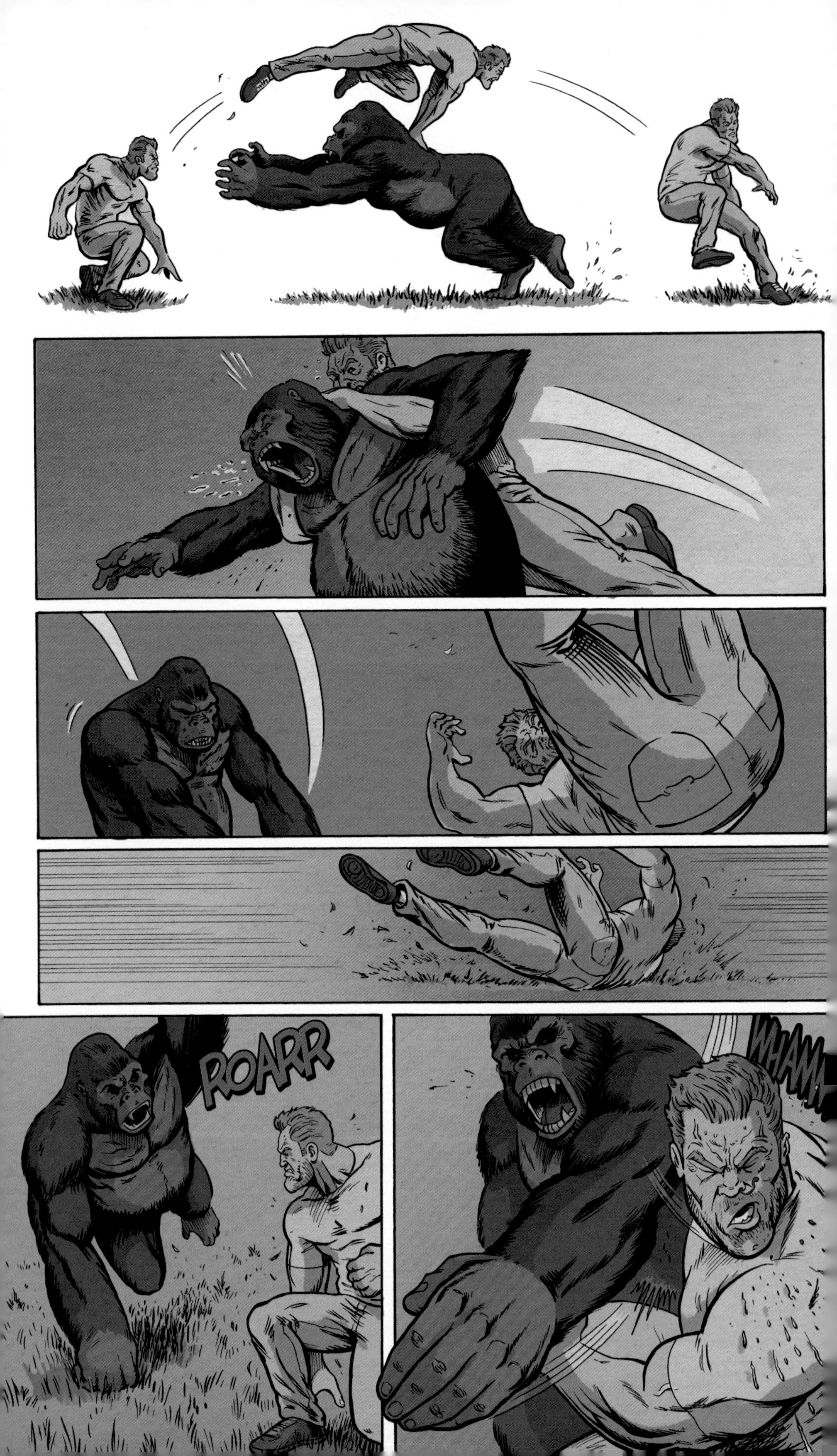
ROARR
WHAMM

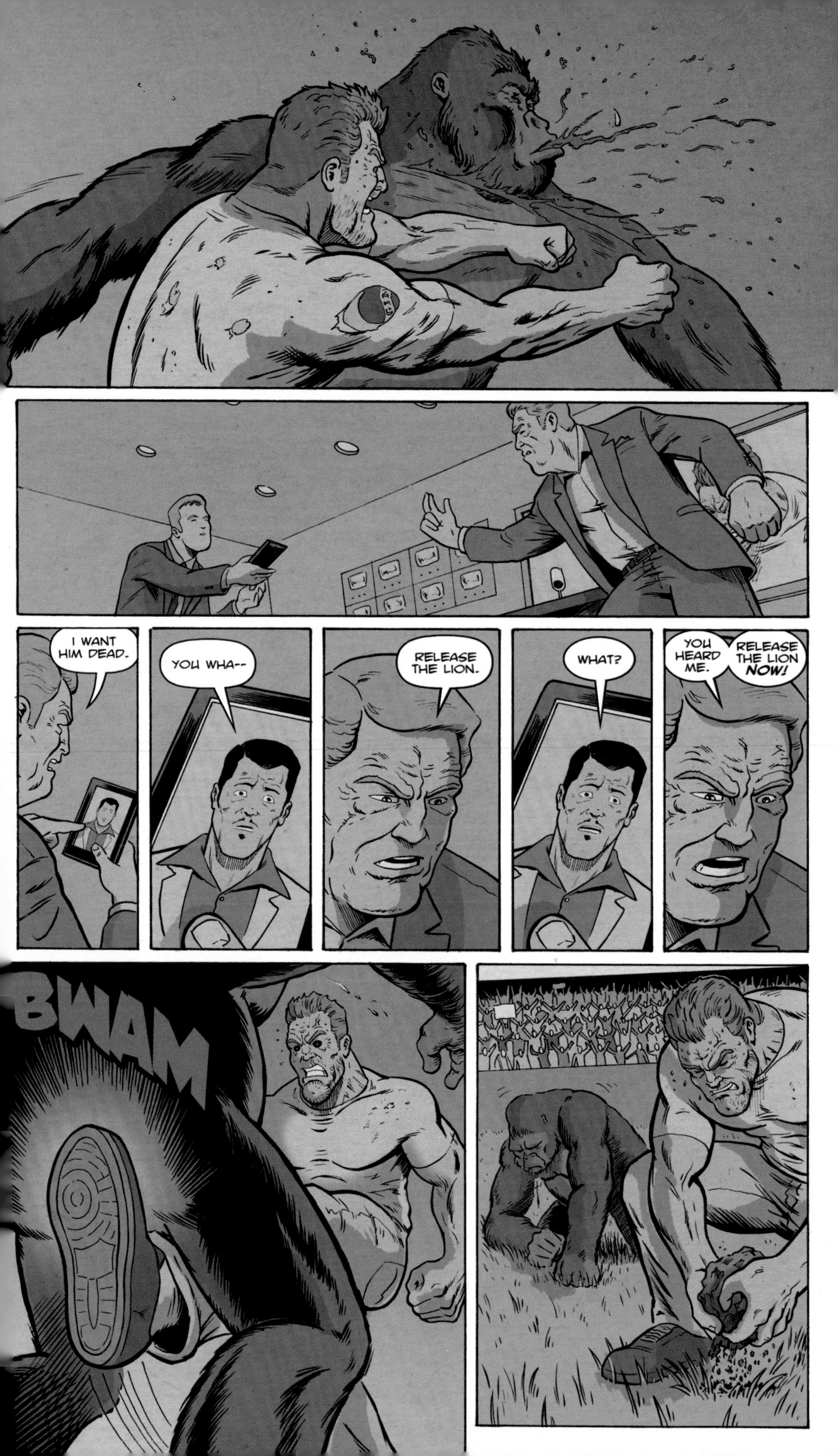
I WANT HIM DEAD.
YOU WHA--
RELEASE THE LION.
WHAT?
YOU HEARD ME.
RELEASE THE LION NOW!
BWAM

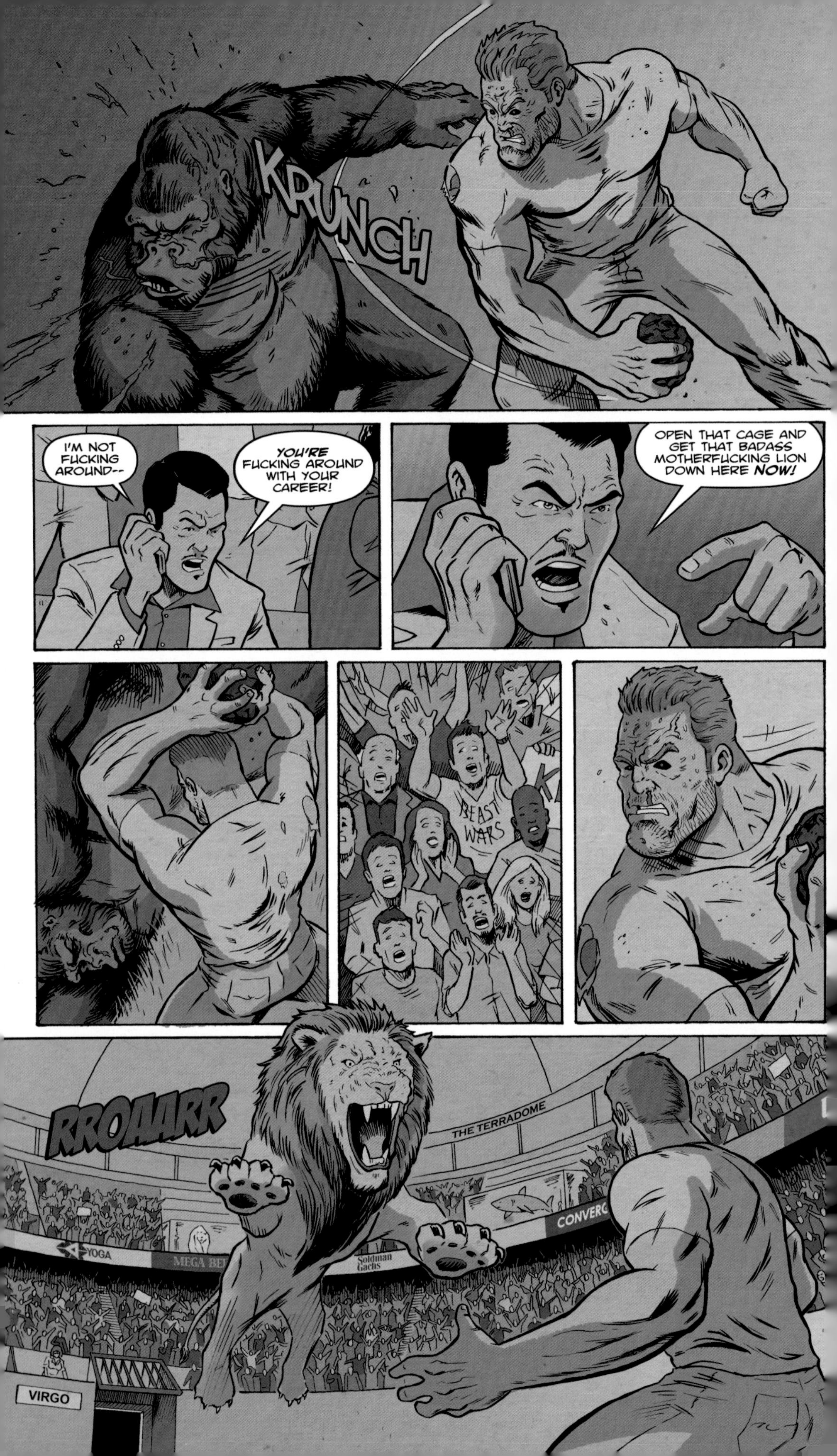
KRUNCH
I'M NOT FUCKING AROUND--
YOU'RE FUCKING AROUND WITH YOUR CAREER!
OPEN THAT CAGE AND GET THAT BADASS MOTHERFUCKING LION DOWN HERE NOW!
BEAST WARS
RROAARR
THE TERRADOME
YOGA
MEGA BE
Soldman Gachs
CONVERG
VIRGO

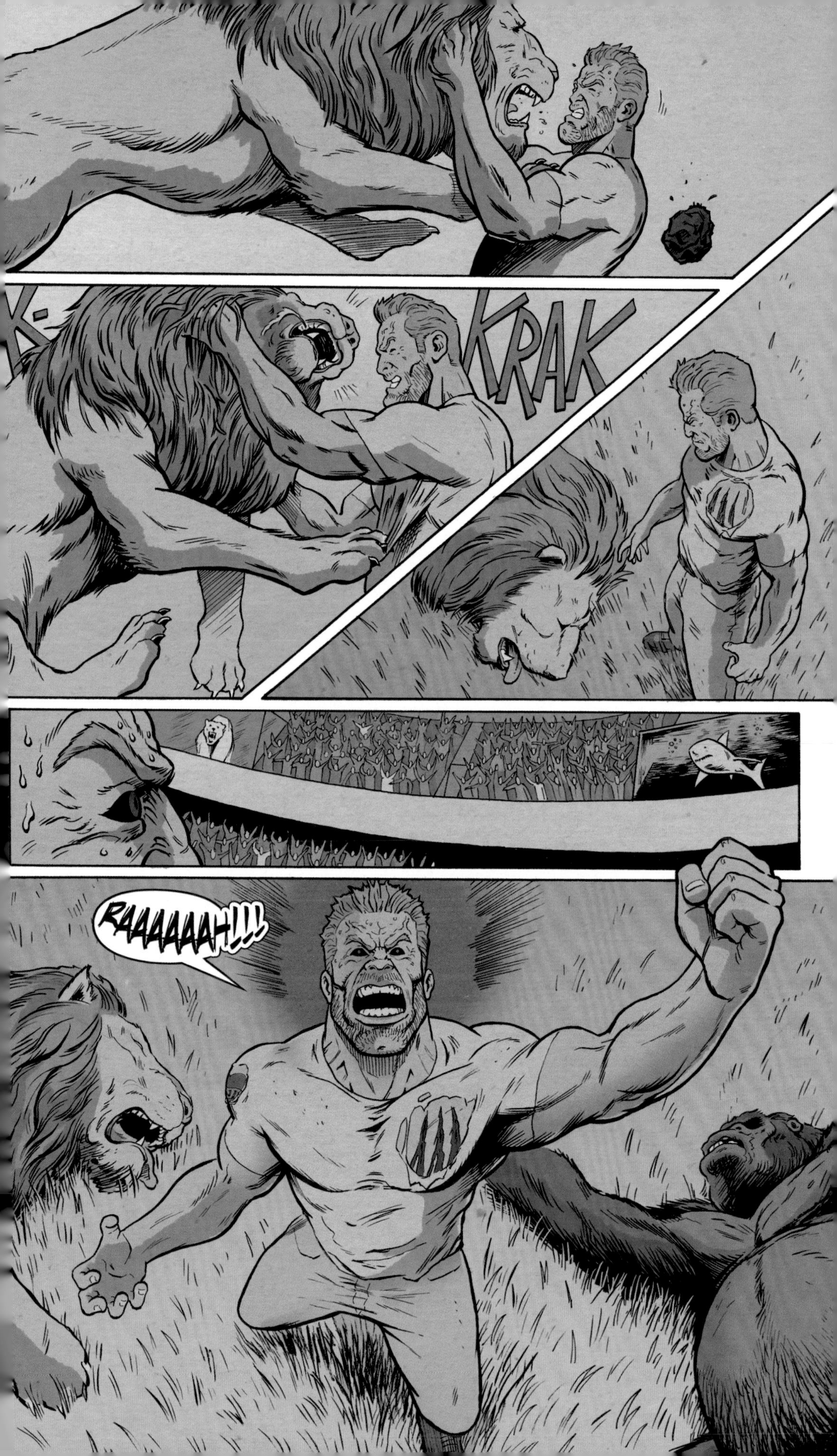

K-
KRAK
RAAAAAAH!!!

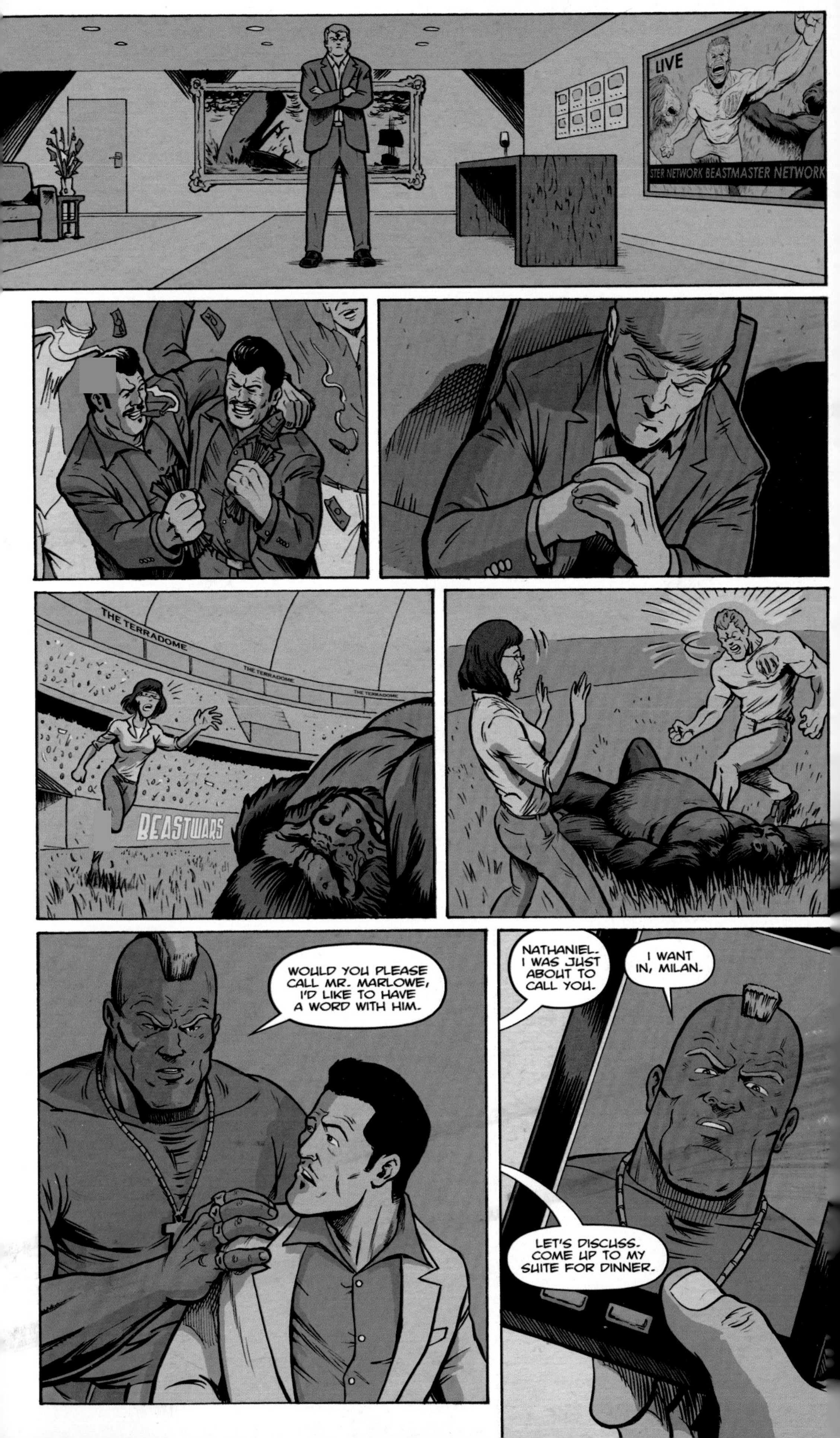
LIVE
STER NETWORK BEASTMASTER NETWORK
THE TERRADOME
THE TERRADOME
THE TERRADOME
BEASTWARS
WOULD YOU PLEASE CALL MR. MARLOWE, I'D LIKE TO HAVE A WORD WITH HIM.
NATHANIEL. I WAS JUST ABOUT TO CALL YOU.
I WANT IN, MILAN.
LET'S DISCUSS. COME UP TO MY SUITE FOR DINNER.

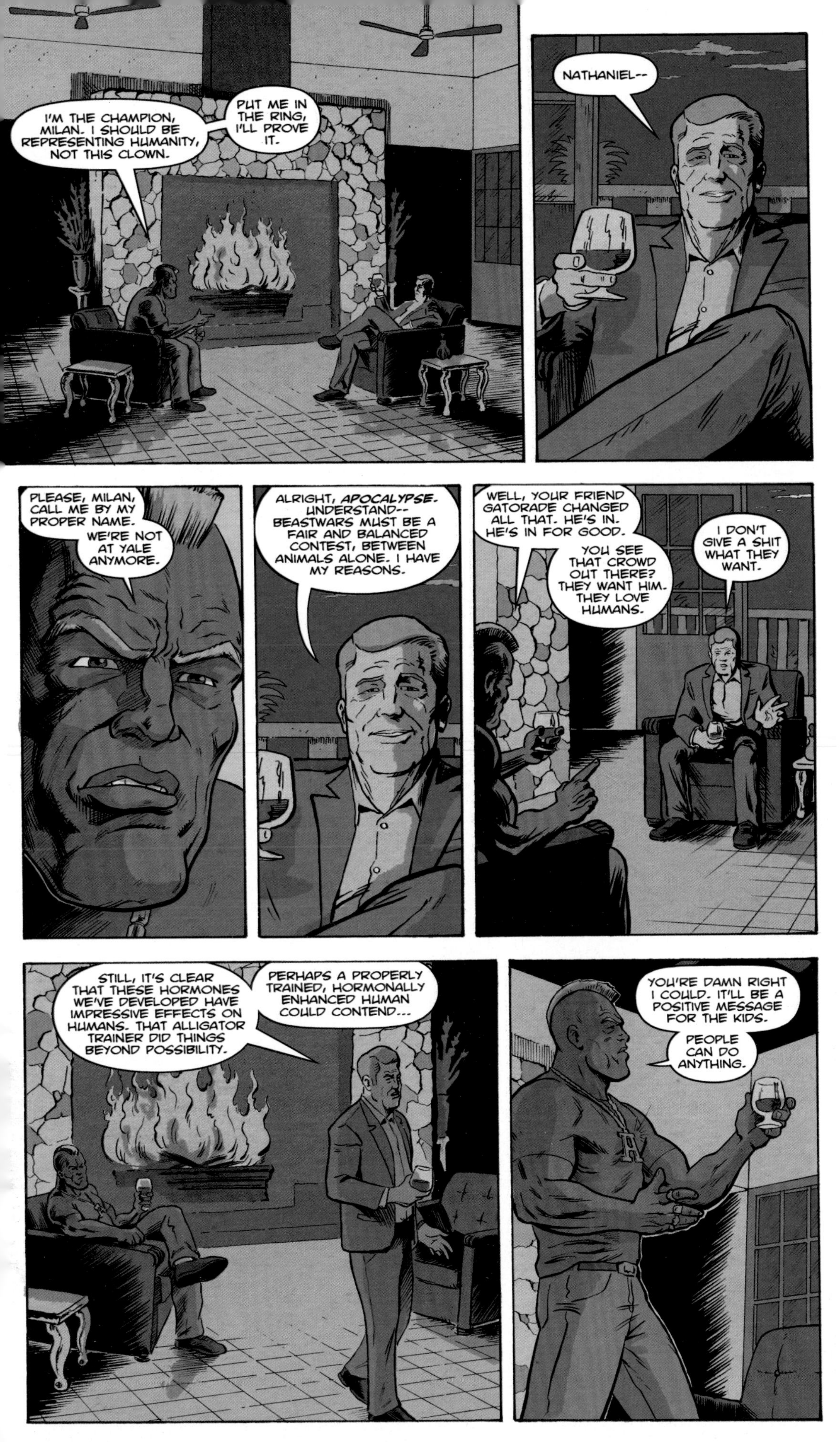
I'M THE CHAMPION, MILAN. I SHOULD BE REPRESENTING HUMANITY, NOT THIS CLOWN.
PUT ME IN THE RING, I'LL PROVE IT.
NATHANIEL--
PLEASE, MILAN, CALL ME BY MY PROPER NAME.
WE'RE NOT AT YALE ANYMORE.
ALRIGHT, *APOCALYPSE.* UNDERSTAND-- BEASTWARS MUST BE A FAIR AND BALANCED CONTEST, BETWEEN ANIMALS ALONE. I HAVE MY REASONS.
WELL, YOUR FRIEND GATORADE CHANGED ALL THAT. HE'S IN. HE'S IN FOR GOOD.
YOU SEE THAT CROWD OUT THERE? THEY WANT HIM. THEY LOVE HUMANS.
I DON'T GIVE A SHIT WHAT THEY WANT.
STILL, IT'S CLEAR THAT THESE HORMONES WE'VE DEVELOPED HAVE IMPRESSIVE EFFECTS ON HUMANS. THAT ALLIGATOR TRAINER DID THINGS BEYOND POSSIBILITY.
PERHAPS A PROPERLY TRAINED, HORMONALLY ENHANCED HUMAN COULD CONTEND...
YOU'RE DAMN RIGHT I COULD. IT'LL BE A POSITIVE MESSAGE FOR THE KIDS.
PEOPLE CAN DO ANYTHING.

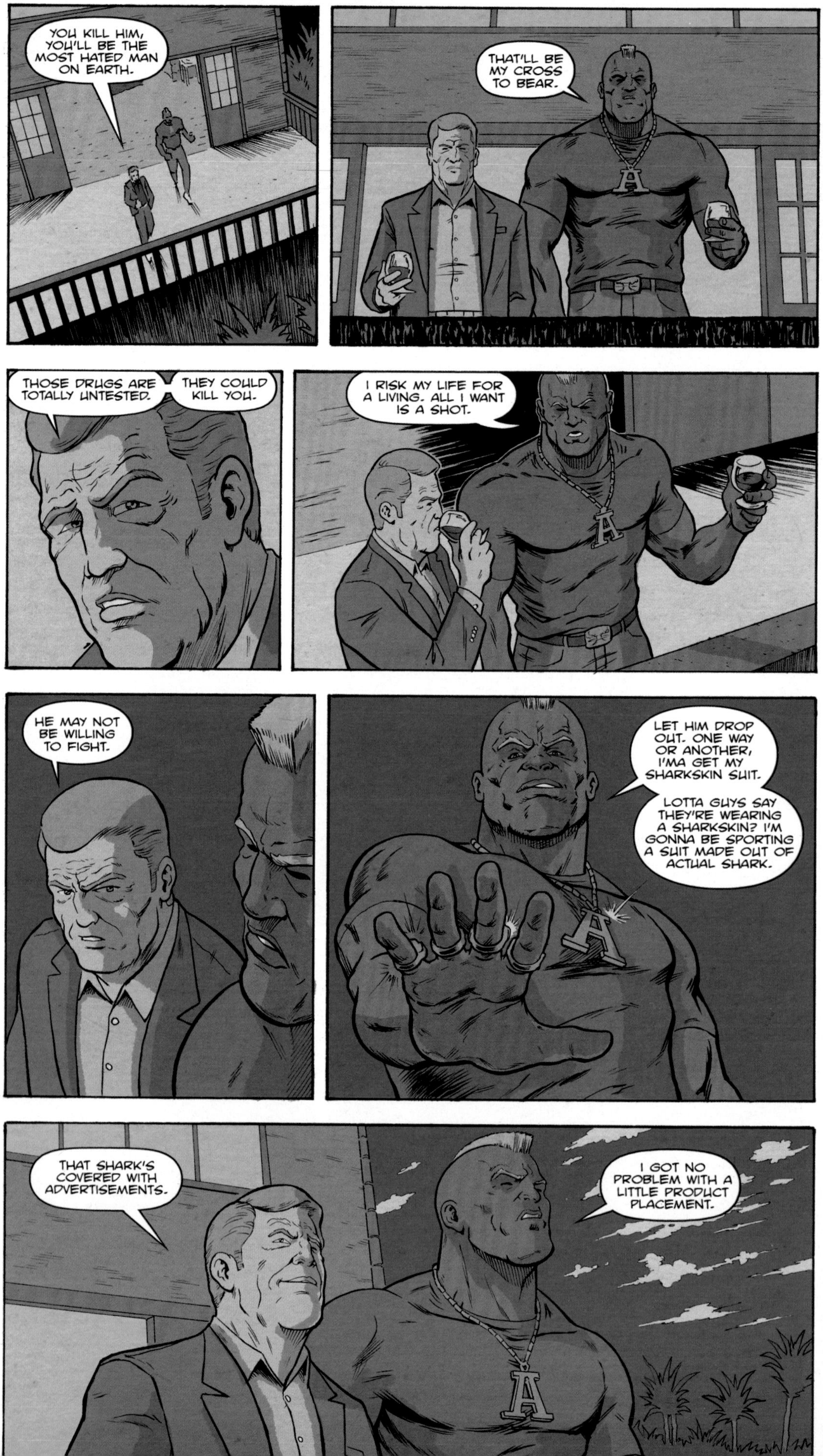
YOU KILL HIM, YOU'LL BE THE MOST HATED MAN ON EARTH.
THAT'LL BE MY CROSS TO BEAR.
THOSE DRUGS ARE TOTALLY UNTESTED.
THEY COULD KILL YOU.
I RISK MY LIFE FOR A LIVING. ALL I WANT IS A SHOT.
HE MAY NOT BE WILLING TO FIGHT.
LET HIM DROP OUT. ONE WAY OR ANOTHER, I'MA GET MY SHARKSKIN SUIT.
LOTTA GUYS SAY THEY'RE WEARING A SHARKSKIN? I'M GONNA BE SPORTING A SUIT MADE OUT OF ACTUAL SHARK.
THAT SHARK'S COVERED WITH ADVERTISEMENTS.
I GOT NO PROBLEM WITH A LITTLE PRODUCT PLACEMENT.

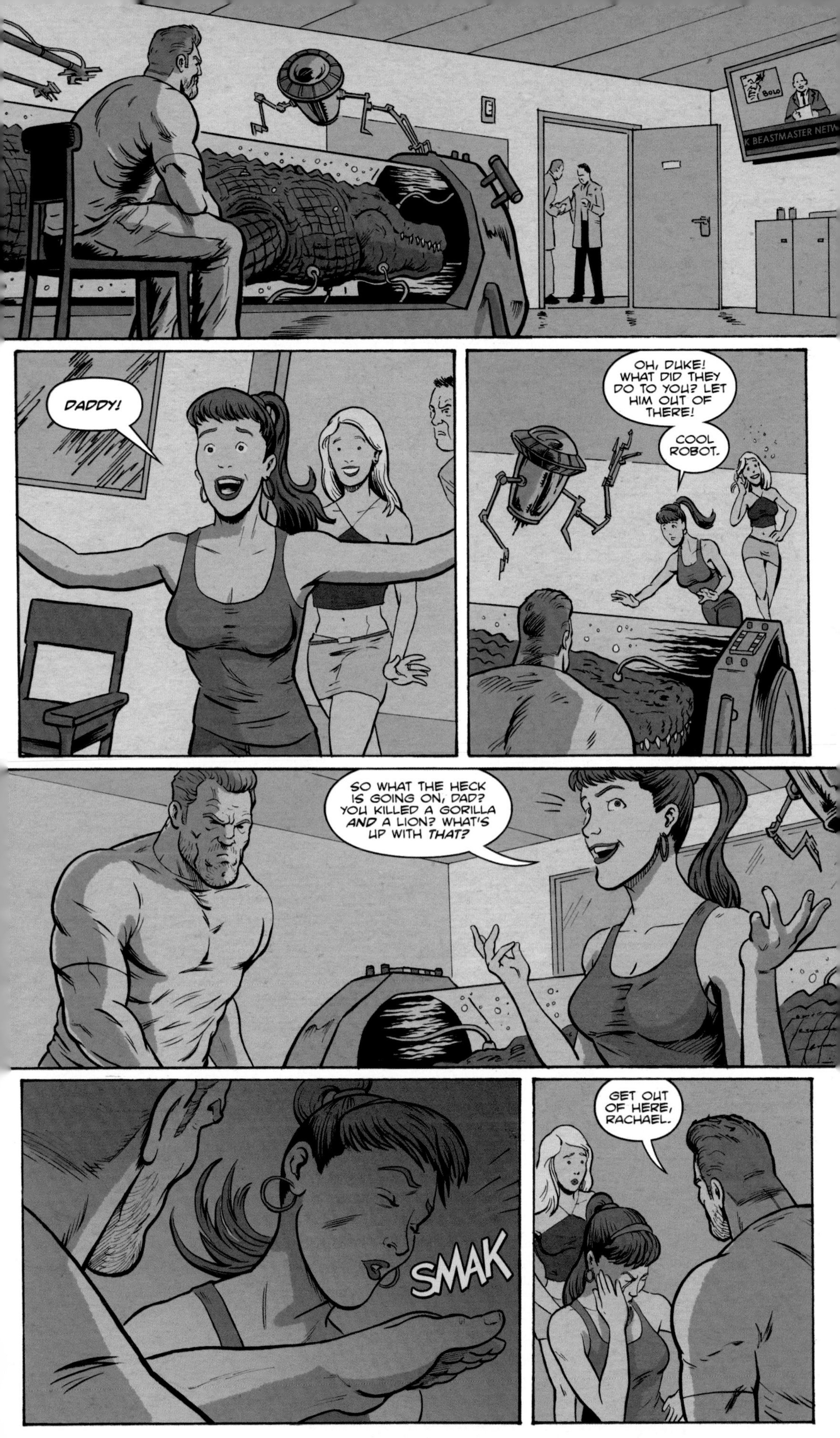
BOLO
K BEASTMASTER NETW
DADDY!
OH, DUKE! WHAT DID THEY DO TO YOU? LET HIM OUT OF THERE!
COOL ROBOT.
SO WHAT THE HECK IS GOING ON, DAD? YOU KILLED A GORILLA AND A LION? WHAT'S UP WITH THAT?
SMAK
GET OUT OF HERE, RACHAEL.

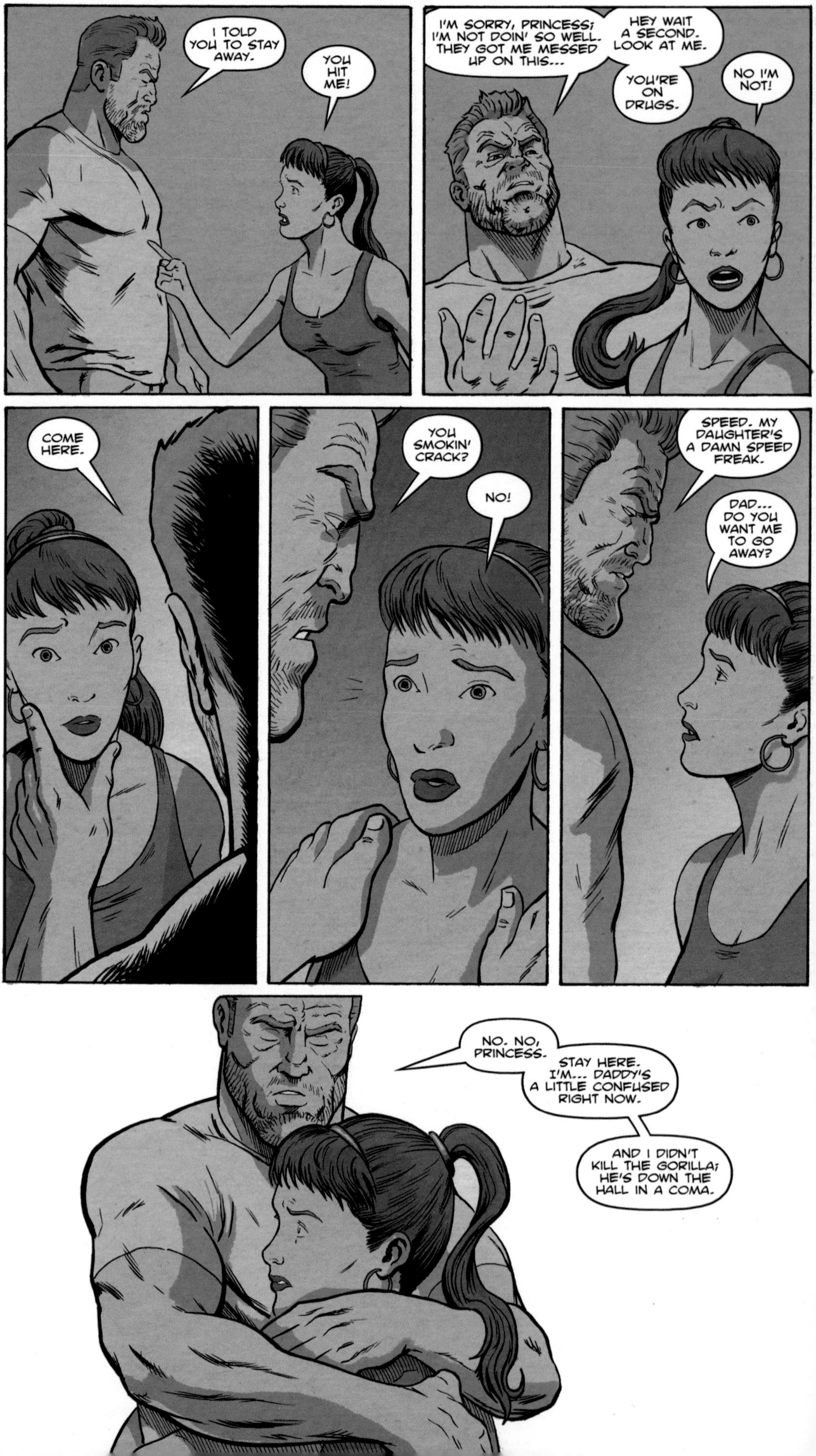
I TOLD YOU TO STAY AWAY.
YOU HIT ME!
I'M SORRY, PRINCESS; I'M NOT DOIN' SO WELL. THEY GOT ME MESSED UP ON THIS...
HEY WAIT A SECOND. LOOK AT ME.
YOU'RE ON DRUGS.
NO I'M NOT!
COME HERE.
YOU SMOKIN' CRACK?
NO!
SPEED. MY DAUGHTER'S A DAMN SPEED FREAK.
DAD... DO YOU WANT ME TO GO AWAY?
NO. NO, PRINCESS.
STAY HERE. I'M... DADDY'S A LITTLE CONFUSED RIGHT NOW.
AND I DIDN'T KILL THE GORILLA; HE'S DOWN THE HALL IN A COMA.

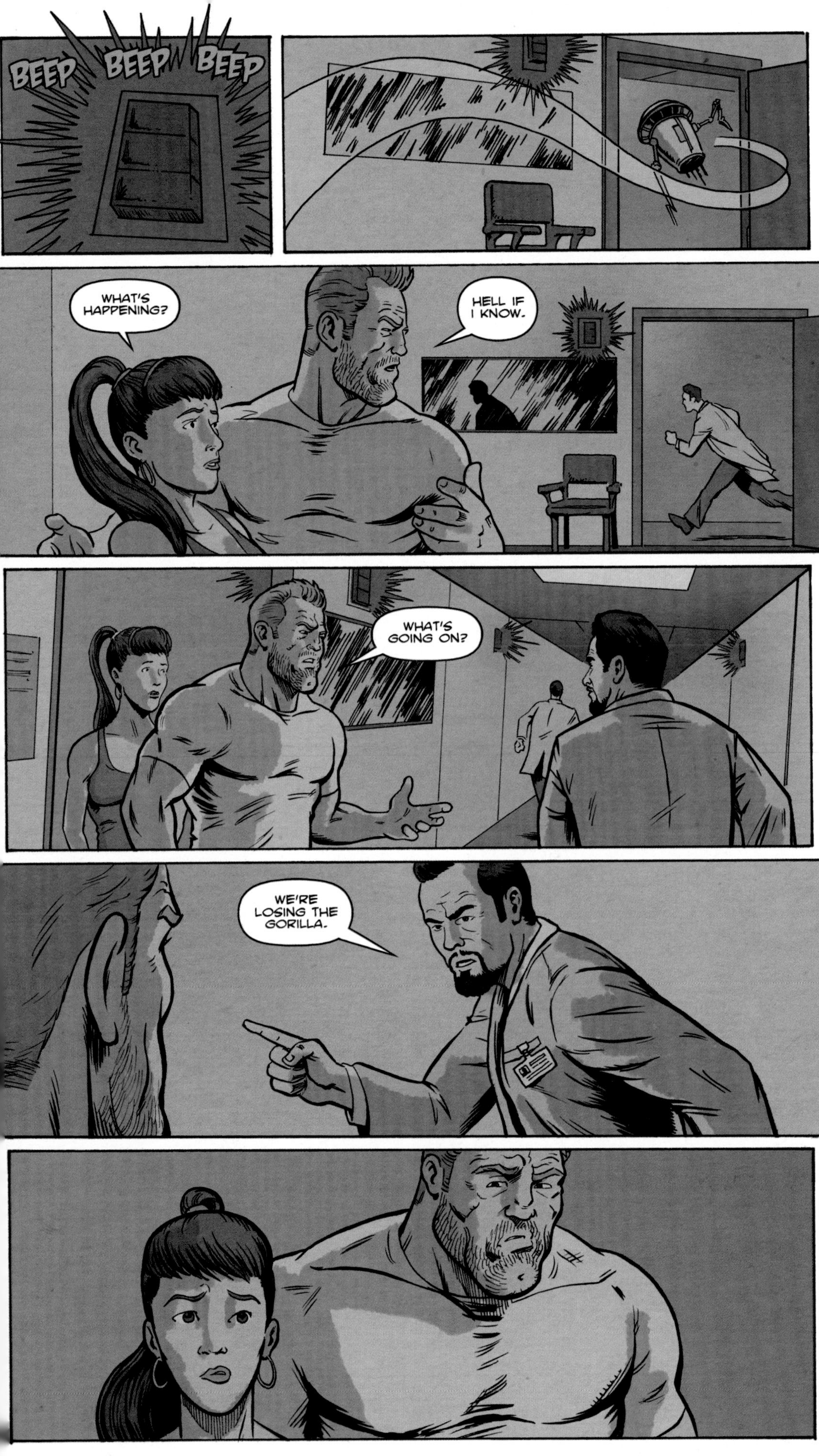
BEEP BEEP BEEP
WHAT'S HAPPENING?
HELL IF I KNOW.
32
WHAT'S GOING ON?
WE'RE LOSING THE GORILLA.

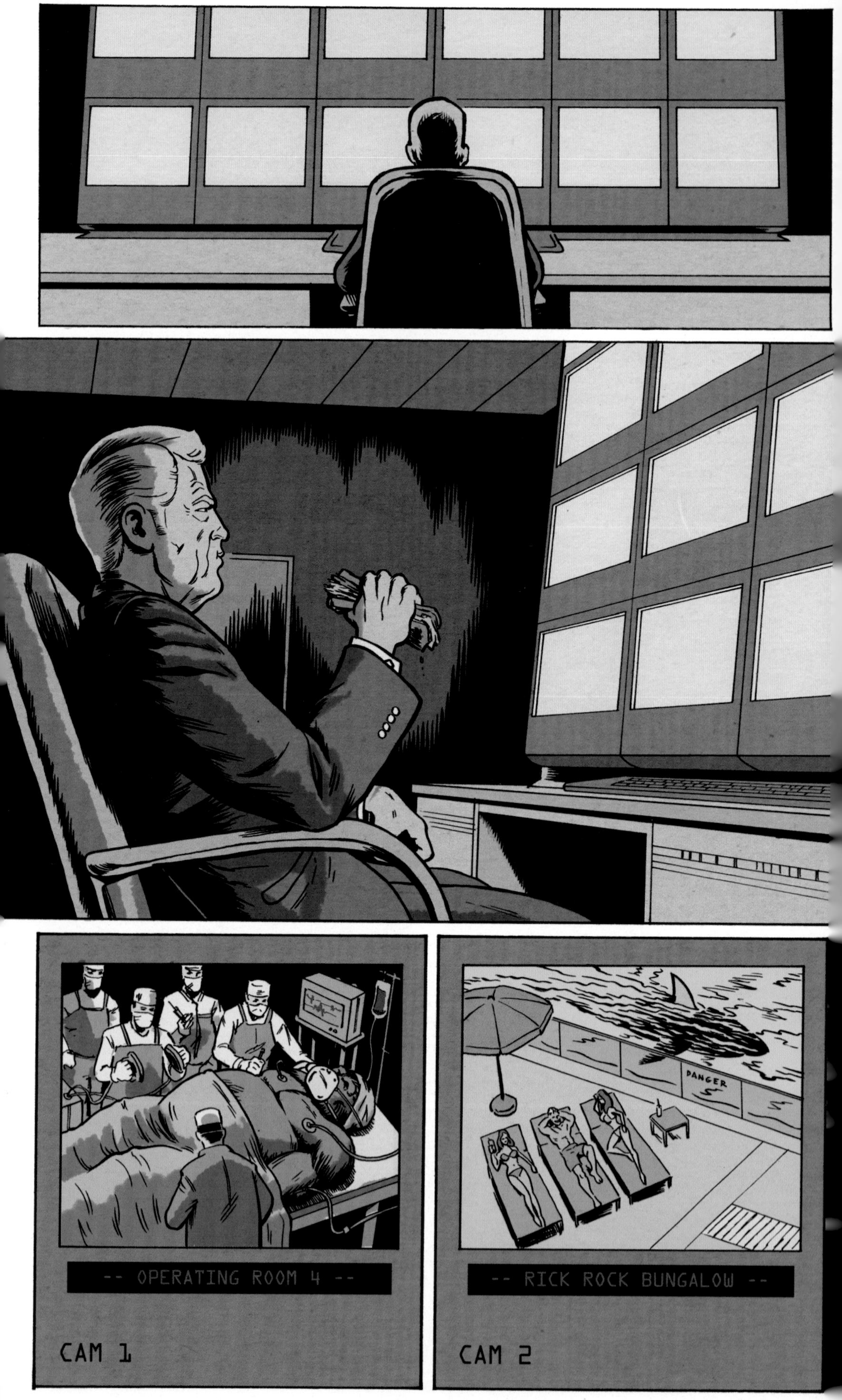
-- OPERATING ROOM 4 --
CAM 1
DANGER
-- RICK ROCK BUNGALOW --
CAM 2

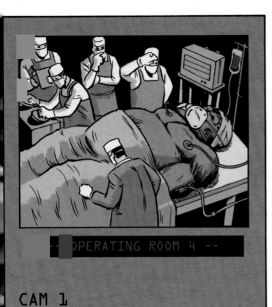

-- OPERATING ROOM 4 --

CAM 1

-- RICK ROCK BUNGLALOW --

CAM 3

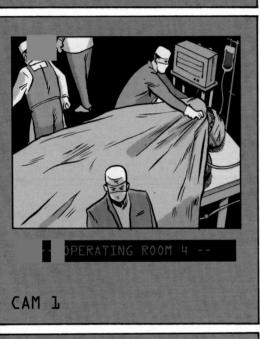

-- OPERATING ROOM 4 --

CAM 1

-- RICK ROCK BUNGALOW --

CAM 2

-- HANGAR 12 --

CAM 7

-- RICK ROCK BUNGALOW --

CAM 2

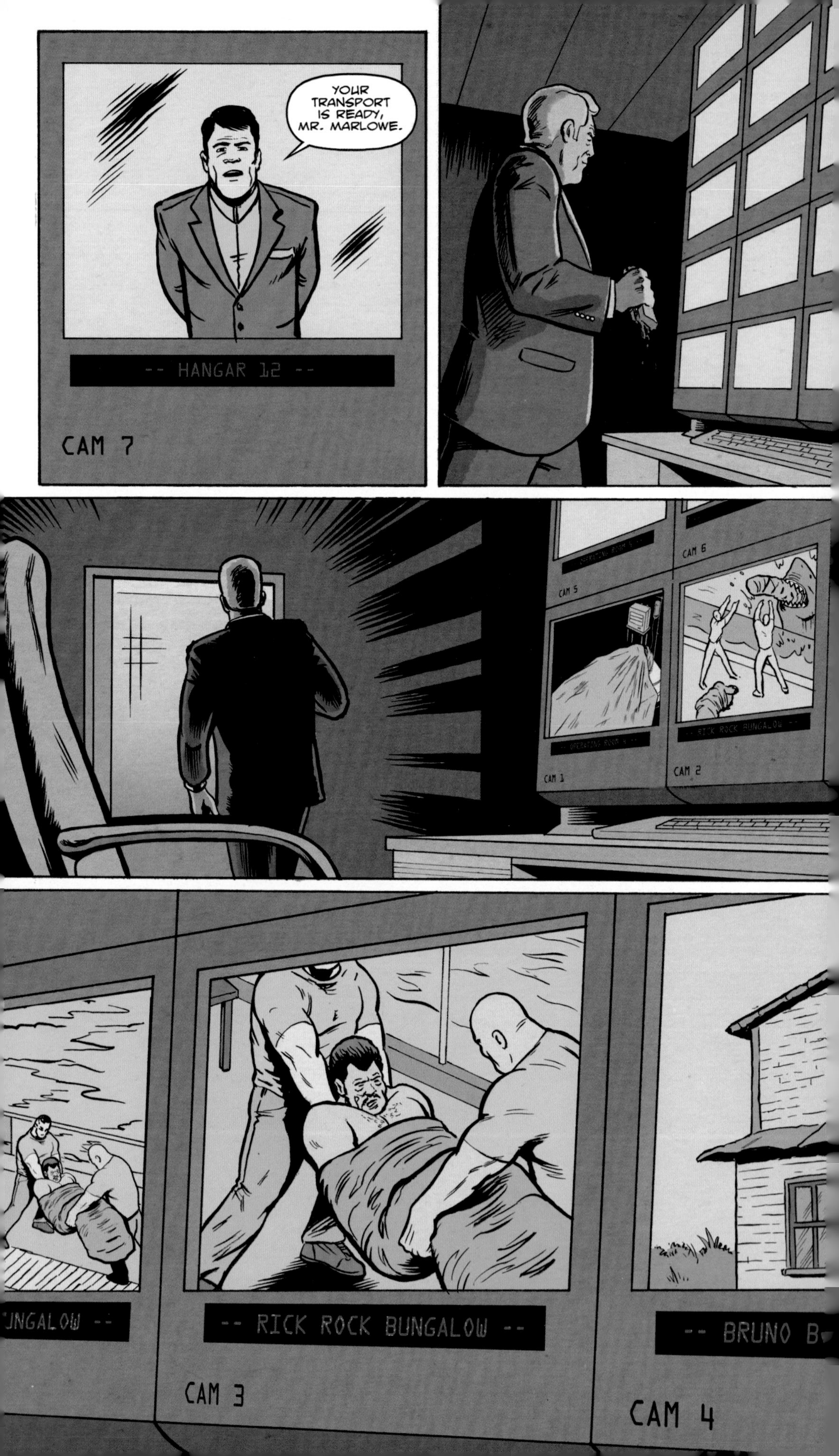
YOUR TRANSPORT IS READY, MR. MARLOWE.
-- HANGAR 12 --
CAM 7
CAM 6
CAM 5
-- OPERATING ROOM 4 --
-- RICK ROCK BUNGALOW --
CAM 1
CAM 2
UNGALOW --
-- RICK ROCK BUNGALOW --
CAM 3
-- BRUNO B
CAM 4

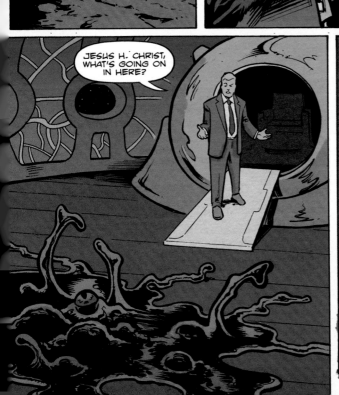

JESUS H. CHRIST, WHAT'S GOING ON IN HERE?

GREETINGS, MR. MARLOWE.

WHAT WERE YOU DOING?

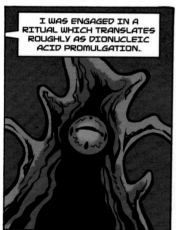

I WAS ENGAGED IN A RITUAL WHICH TRANSLATES ROUGHLY AS DIONUCLEIC ACID PROMULGATION.

YOU MEAN YOU WERE FUCKING YOURSELF? KYLE PLEASE. WHILE YOU'VE BEEN UP HERE SCREWING AROUND I'VE BEEN BUSY FINDING US A CHAMPION TO DEFEND EARTH.

I HAVE OBSERVED. ARE YOU GOING TO ALLOW THE HUMAN TO CONTINUE IN THE COMPETITION?

WHY?

SHOULD I?

MR. MARLOWE, IT MAKES LITTLE DIFFERENCE, ANY EARTH CREATURE WILL BE DESTROYED IN THE CHALLENGE OF THE HERETIC.

SO WHAT ABOUT IT? DID YOU CHALLENGE THEM?

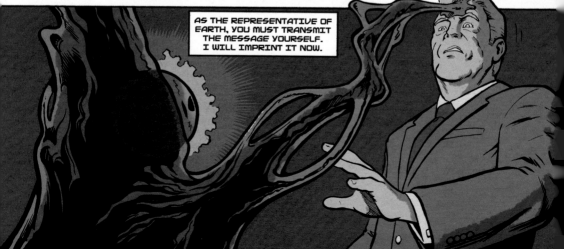

AS THE REPRESENTATIVE OF EARTH, YOU MUST TRANSMIT THE MESSAGE YOURSELF. I WILL IMPRINT IT NOW.

HOLY SHIT.

DO THAT AGAIN.

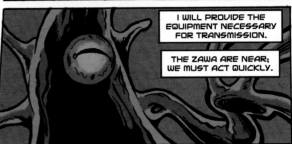

I WILL PROVIDE THE EQUIPMENT NECESSARY FOR TRANSMISSION.

THE ZAWA ARE NEAR; WE MUST ACT QUICKLY.

HEY, HOW ABOUT YOU IMPRINT WHAT YOU HAVE TO TELL ME INSTEAD OF TALKING?

I HAVE OBSERVED THAT YOU HAVE NOT BEEN MAKING ADEQUATE PREPARATIONS FOR THE PRESERVATION OF YOUR CULTURE, MR. MARLOWE.

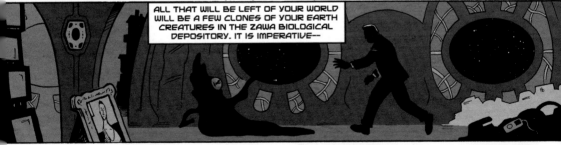

ALL THAT WILL BE LEFT OF YOUR WORLD WILL BE A FEW CLONES OF YOUR EARTH CREATURES IN THE ZAWA BIOLOGICAL DEPOSITORY. IT IS IMPERATIVE--

STOP RIGHT THERE, KYLE. I DON'T COME TO YOUR HOUSE AND TELL YOU WHAT TO DO, DO I?

I DO NOT UNDERSTAND THE QUESTION.

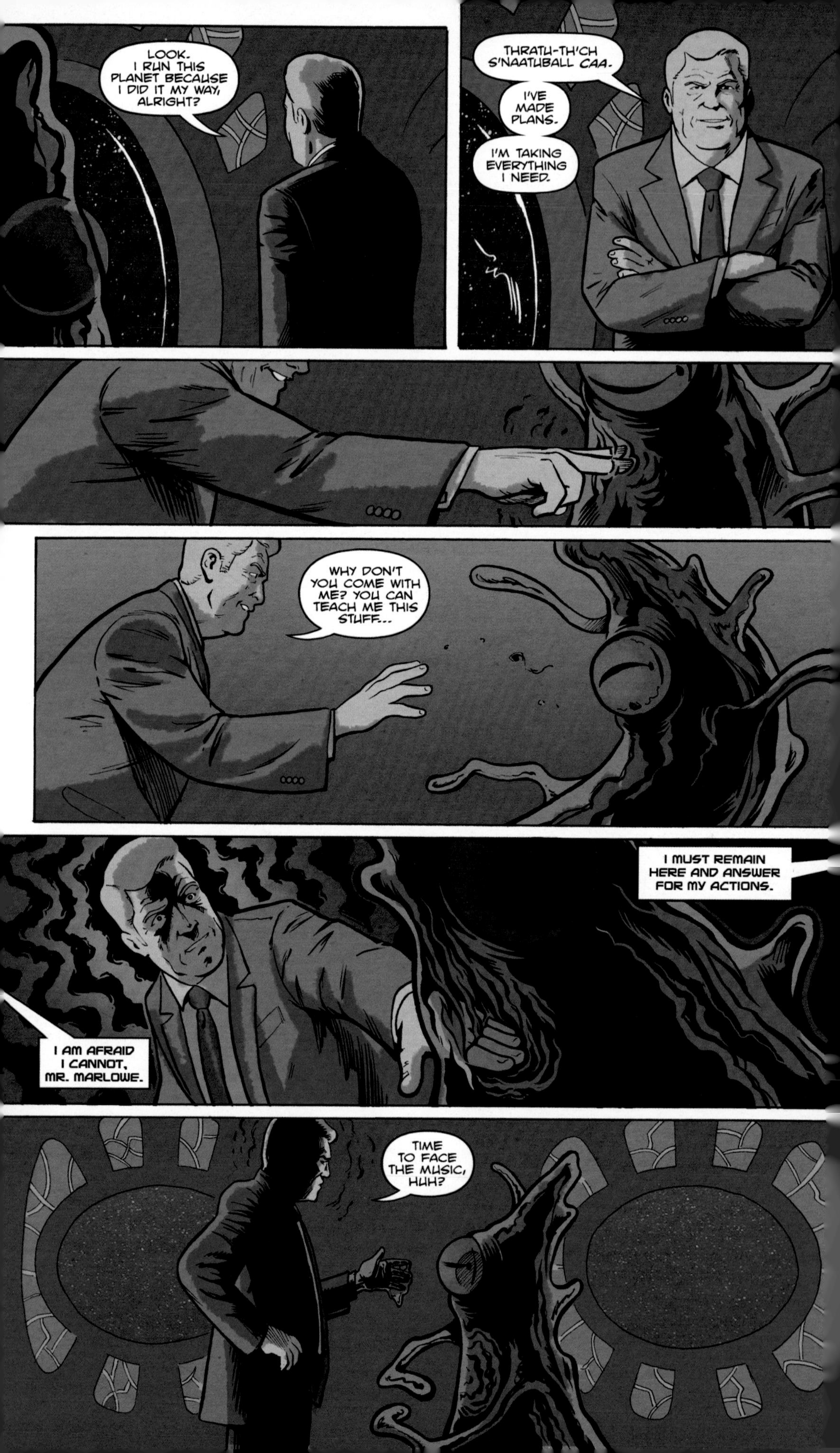
LOOK. I RUN THIS PLANET BECAUSE I DID IT MY WAY, ALRIGHT?
THRATU-TH'CH S'NAATUBALL CAA.
I'VE MADE PLANS.
I'M TAKING EVERYTHING I NEED.
WHY DON'T YOU COME WITH ME? YOU CAN TEACH ME THIS STUFF...
I MUST REMAIN HERE AND ANSWER FOR MY ACTIONS.
I AM AFRAID I CANNOT, MR. MARLOWE.
TIME TO FACE THE MUSIC, HUH?

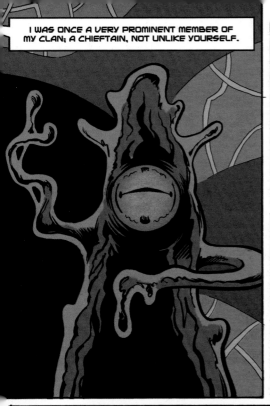

I WAS ONCE A VERY PROMINENT MEMBER OF MY CLAN; A CHIEFTAIN, NOT UNLIKE YOURSELF.

ONLY MY CLAN'S INFLUENCE HAS POSTPONED MY CAPTURE.

BUT NO LONGER.

SO WHAT THE HELL ARE YOU WAITING FOR?

HAUL ASS OUTTA HERE.

THEY ARE ALREADY TOO CLOSE NOW. THERE CAN BE NO ESCAPE.

I DON'T GET IT, KYLE.

WHY WOULD YOU SACRIFICE YOURSELF FOR US?

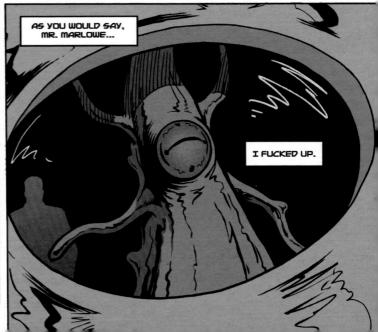

AS YOU WOULD SAY, MR. MARLOWE...

I FUCKED UP.

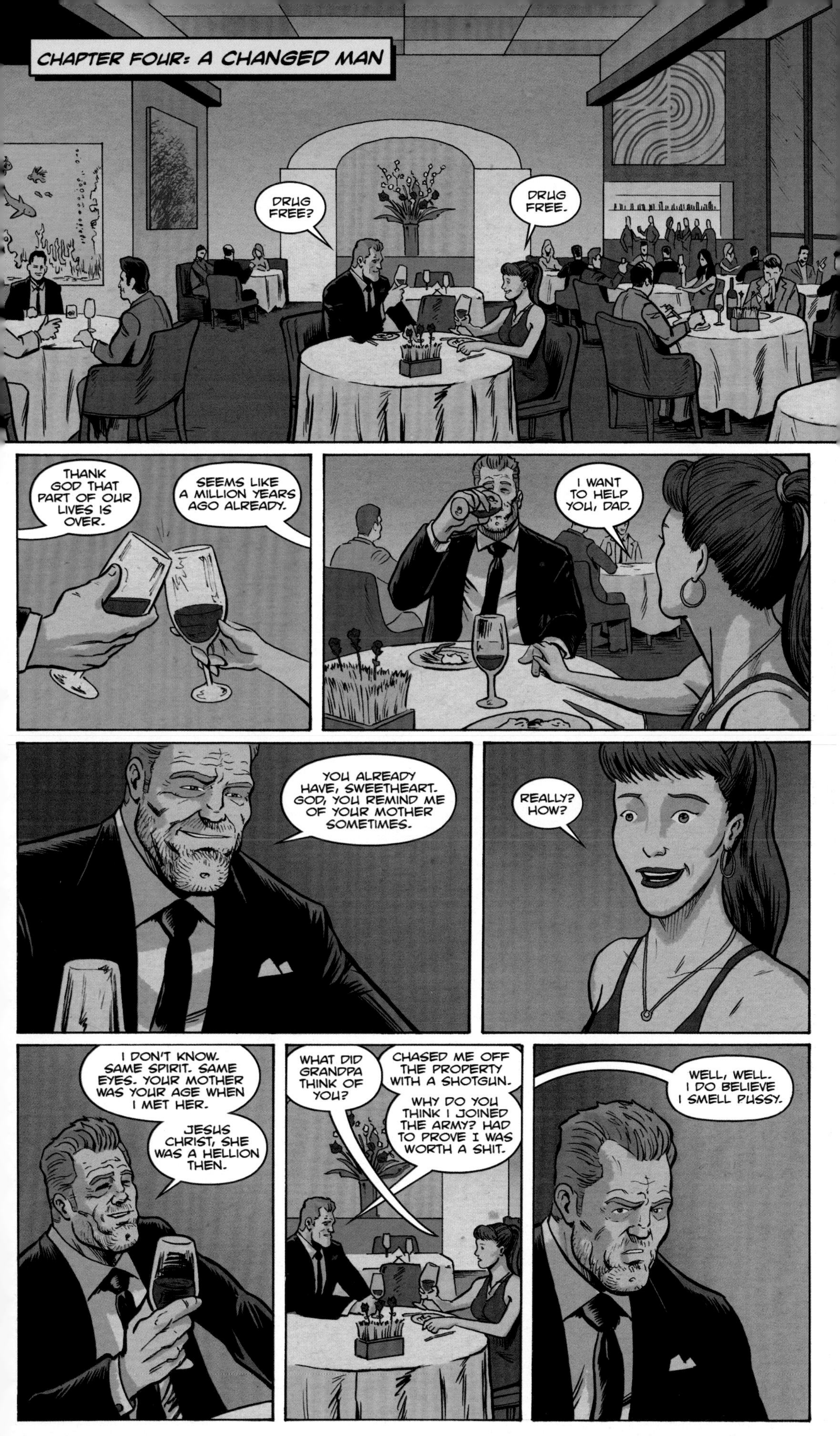
CHAPTER FOUR: A CHANGED MAN
DRUG FREE?
DRUG FREE.
THANK GOD THAT PART OF OUR LIVES IS OVER.
SEEMS LIKE A MILLION YEARS AGO ALREADY.
I WANT TO HELP YOU, DAD.
YOU ALREADY HAVE, SWEETHEART. GOD, YOU REMIND ME OF YOUR MOTHER SOMETIMES.
REALLY? HOW?
I DON'T KNOW. SAME SPIRIT. SAME EYES. YOUR MOTHER WAS YOUR AGE WHEN I MET HER.
JESUS CHRIST, SHE WAS A HELLION THEN.
WHAT DID GRANDPA THINK OF YOU?
CHASED ME OFF THE PROPERTY WITH A SHOTGUN.
WHY DO YOU THINK I JOINED THE ARMY? HAD TO PROVE I WAS WORTH A SHIT.
WELL, WELL. I DO BELIEVE I SMELL PUSSY.

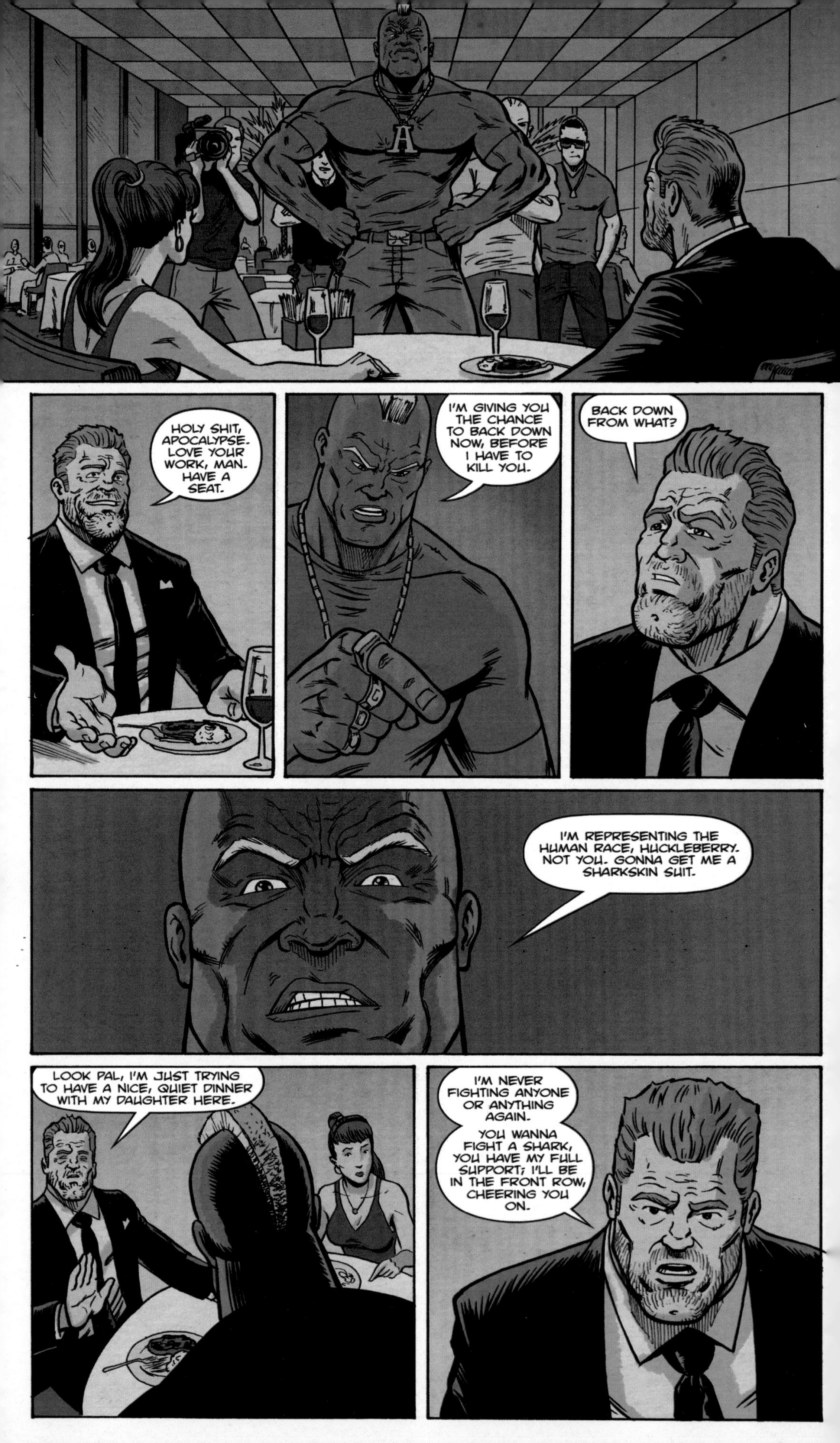
HOLY SHIT, APOCALYPSE. LOVE YOUR WORK, MAN. HAVE A SEAT.
I'M GIVING YOU THE CHANCE TO BACK DOWN NOW, BEFORE I HAVE TO KILL YOU.
BACK DOWN FROM WHAT?
I'M REPRESENTING THE HUMAN RACE, HUCKLEBERRY. NOT YOU. GONNA GET ME A SHARKSKIN SUIT.
LOOK PAL, I'M JUST TRYING TO HAVE A NICE, QUIET DINNER WITH MY DAUGHTER HERE.
I'M NEVER FIGHTING ANYONE OR ANYTHING AGAIN.
YOU WANNA FIGHT A SHARK, YOU HAVE MY FULL SUPPORT; I'LL BE IN THE FRONT ROW, CHEERING YOU ON.

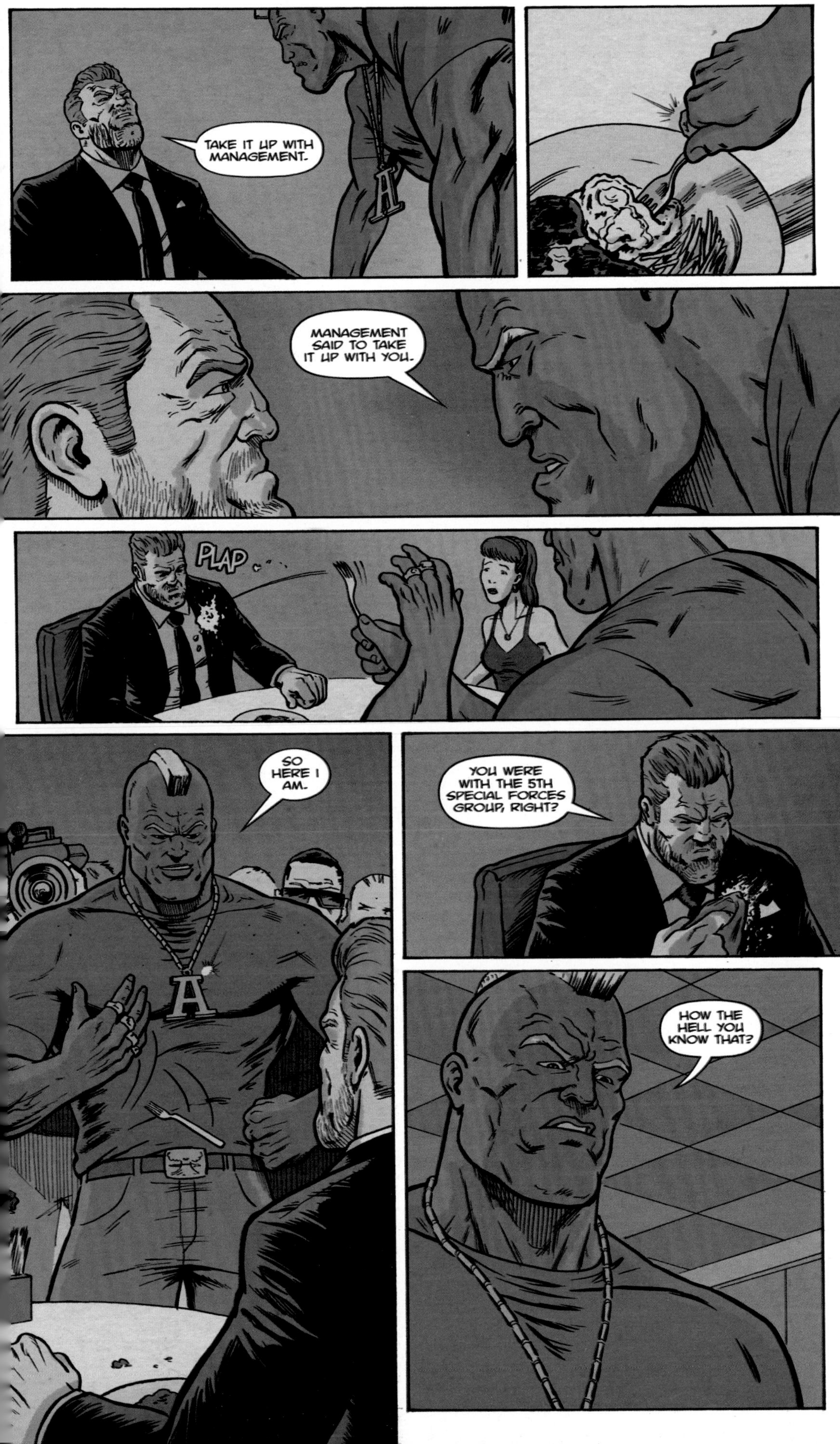

TAKE IT UP WITH MANAGEMENT.
MANAGEMENT SAID TO TAKE IT UP WITH YOU.
PLAP
SO HERE I AM.
YOU WERE WITH THE 5TH SPECIAL FORCES GROUP, RIGHT?
HOW THE HELL YOU KNOW THAT?

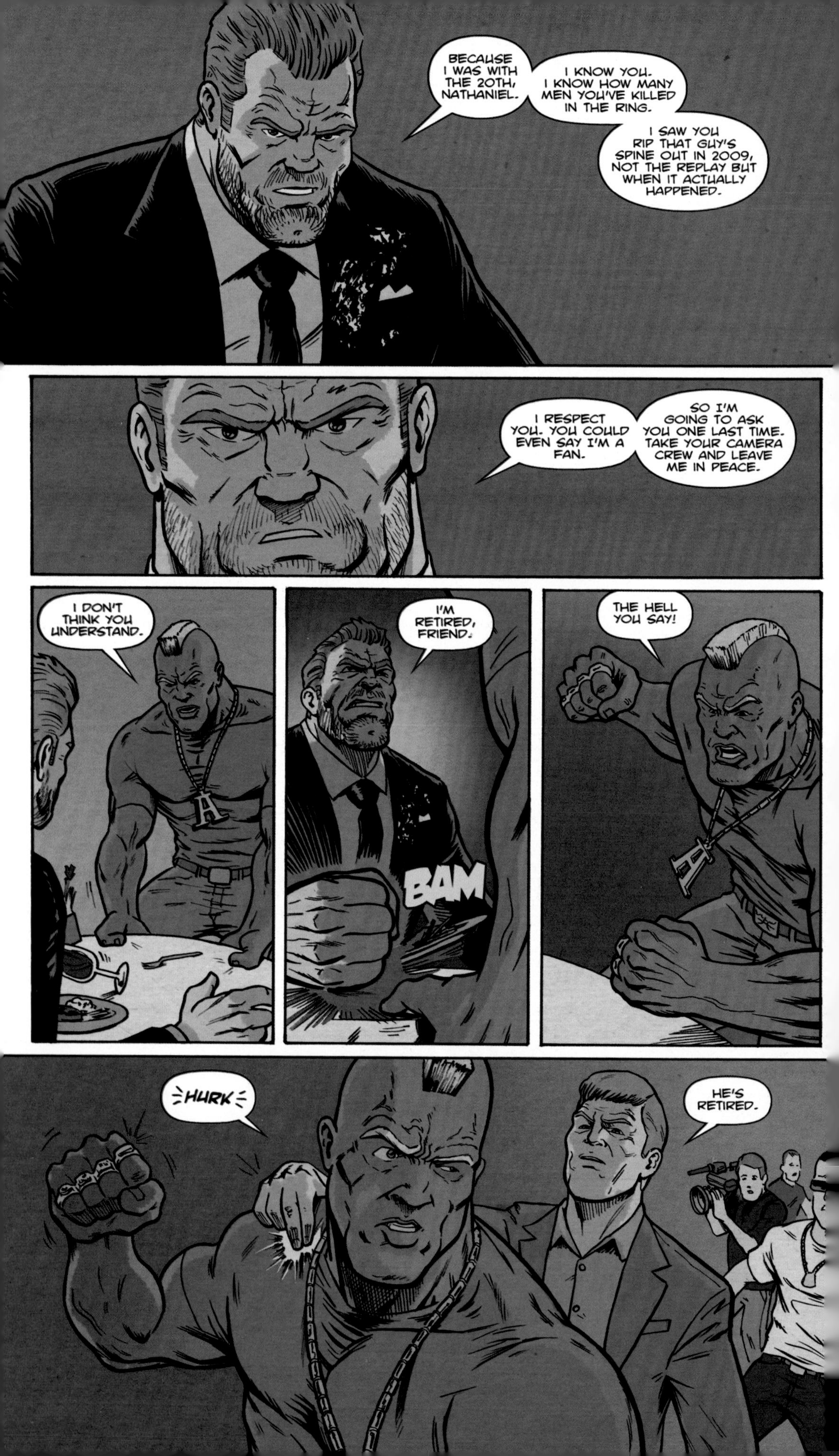
BECAUSE I WAS WITH THE 20TH, NATHANIEL.
I KNOW YOU. I KNOW HOW MANY MEN YOU'VE KILLED IN THE RING.
I SAW YOU RIP THAT GUY'S SPINE OUT IN 2009, NOT THE REPLAY BUT WHEN IT ACTUALLY HAPPENED.
I RESPECT YOU. YOU COULD EVEN SAY I'M A FAN.
SO I'M GOING TO ASK YOU ONE LAST TIME. TAKE YOUR CAMERA CREW AND LEAVE ME IN PEACE.
I DON'T THINK YOU UNDERSTAND.
I'M RETIRED, FRIEND.
BAM
THE HELL YOU SAY!
HURK
HE'S RETIRED.

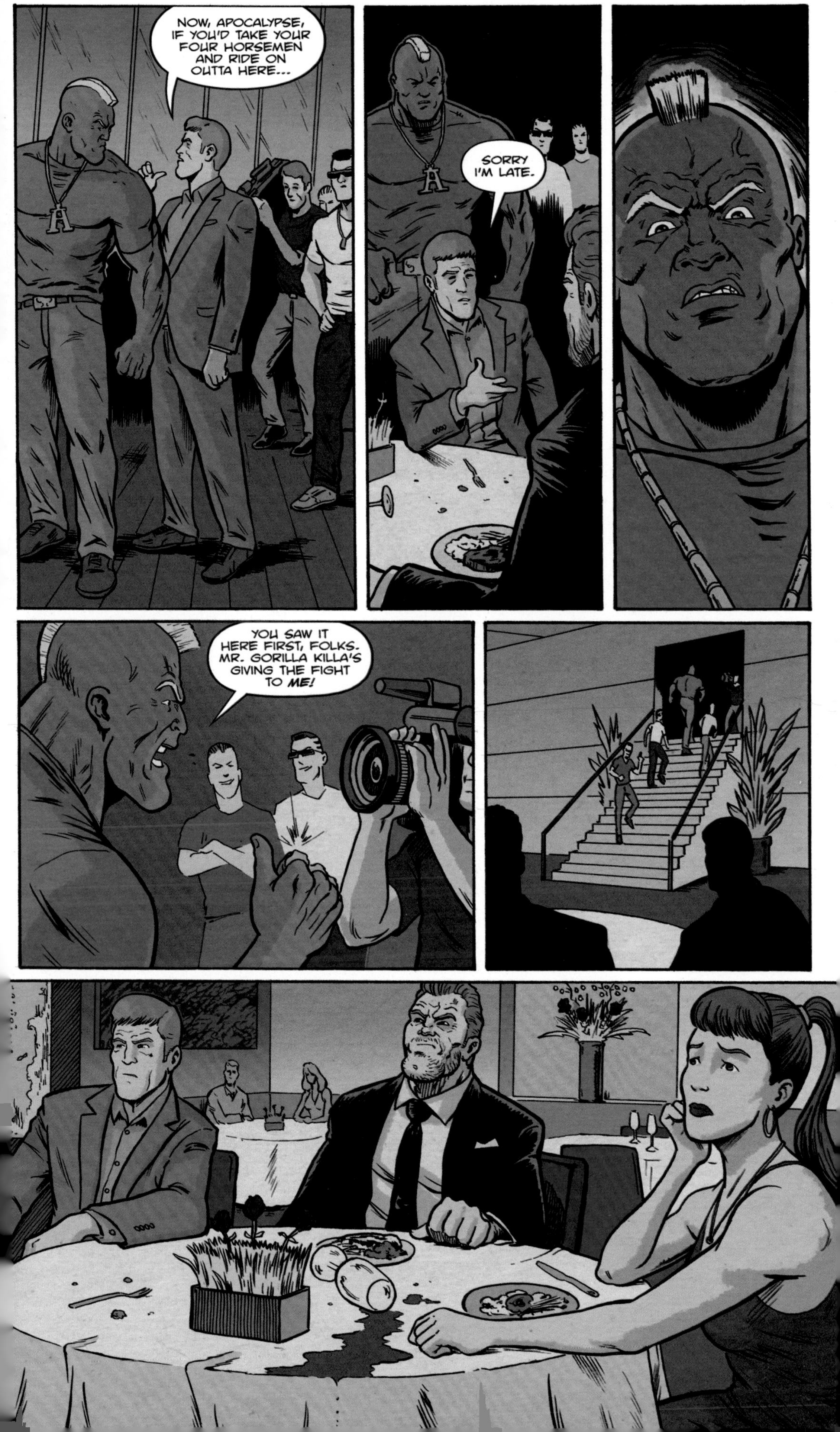
NOW, APOCALYPSE, IF YOU'D TAKE YOUR FOUR HORSEMEN AND RIDE ON OUTTA HERE...
SORRY I'M LATE.
YOU SAW IT HERE FIRST, FOLKS. MR. GORILLA KILLA'S GIVING THE FIGHT TO *ME!*

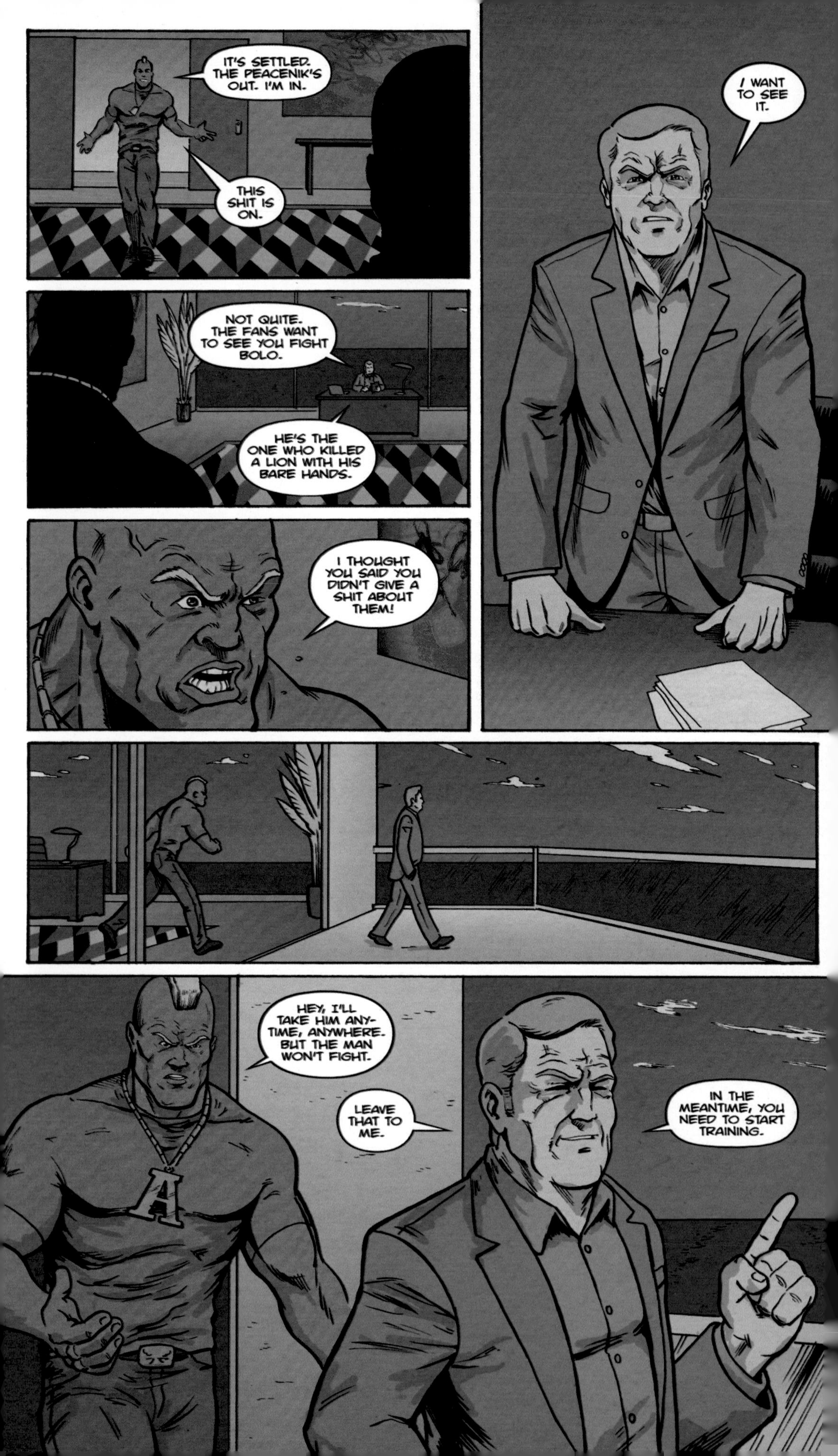
IT'S SETTLED. THE PEACENIK'S OUT. I'M IN.
THIS SHIT IS ON.
NOT QUITE. THE FANS WANT TO SEE YOU FIGHT BOLO.
HE'S THE ONE WHO KILLED A LION WITH HIS BARE HANDS.
I THOUGHT YOU SAID YOU DIDN'T GIVE A SHIT ABOUT THEM!
I WANT TO SEE IT.
HEY, I'LL TAKE HIM ANY-TIME, ANYWHERE. BUT THE MAN WON'T FIGHT.
LEAVE THAT TO ME.
IN THE MEANTIME, YOU NEED TO START TRAINING.

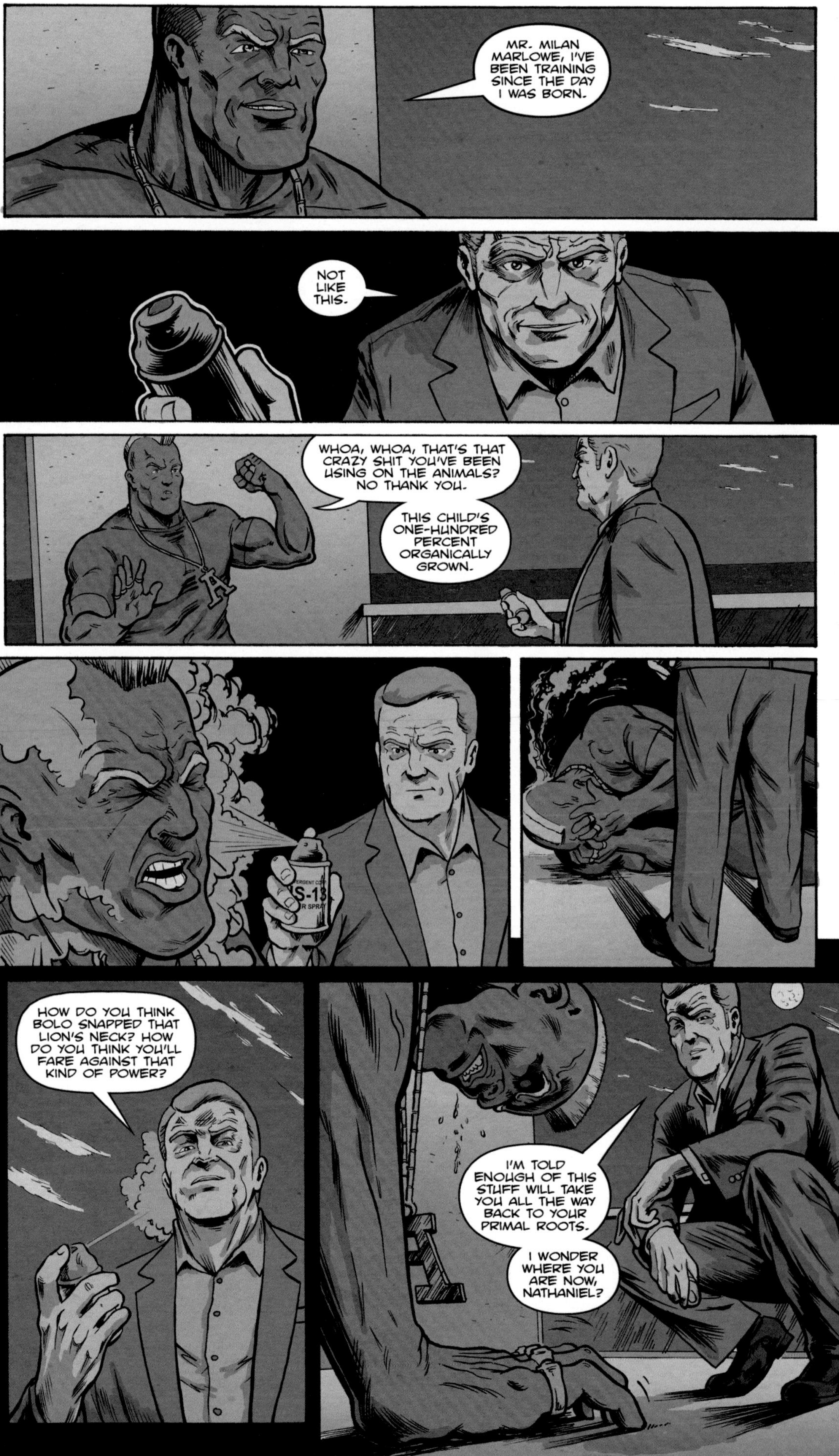
MR. MILAN MARLOWE, I'VE BEEN TRAINING SINCE THE DAY I WAS BORN.
NOT LIKE THIS.
WHOA, WHOA, THAT'S THAT CRAZY SHIT YOU'VE BEEN USING ON THE ANIMALS? NO THANK YOU.
THIS CHILD'S ONE-HUNDRED PERCENT ORGANICALLY GROWN.
HOW DO YOU THINK BOLO SNAPPED THAT LION'S NECK? HOW DO YOU THINK YOU'LL FARE AGAINST THAT KIND OF POWER?
I'M TOLD ENOUGH OF THIS STUFF WILL TAKE YOU ALL THE WAY BACK TO YOUR PRIMAL ROOTS.
I WONDER WHERE YOU ARE NOW, NATHANIEL?

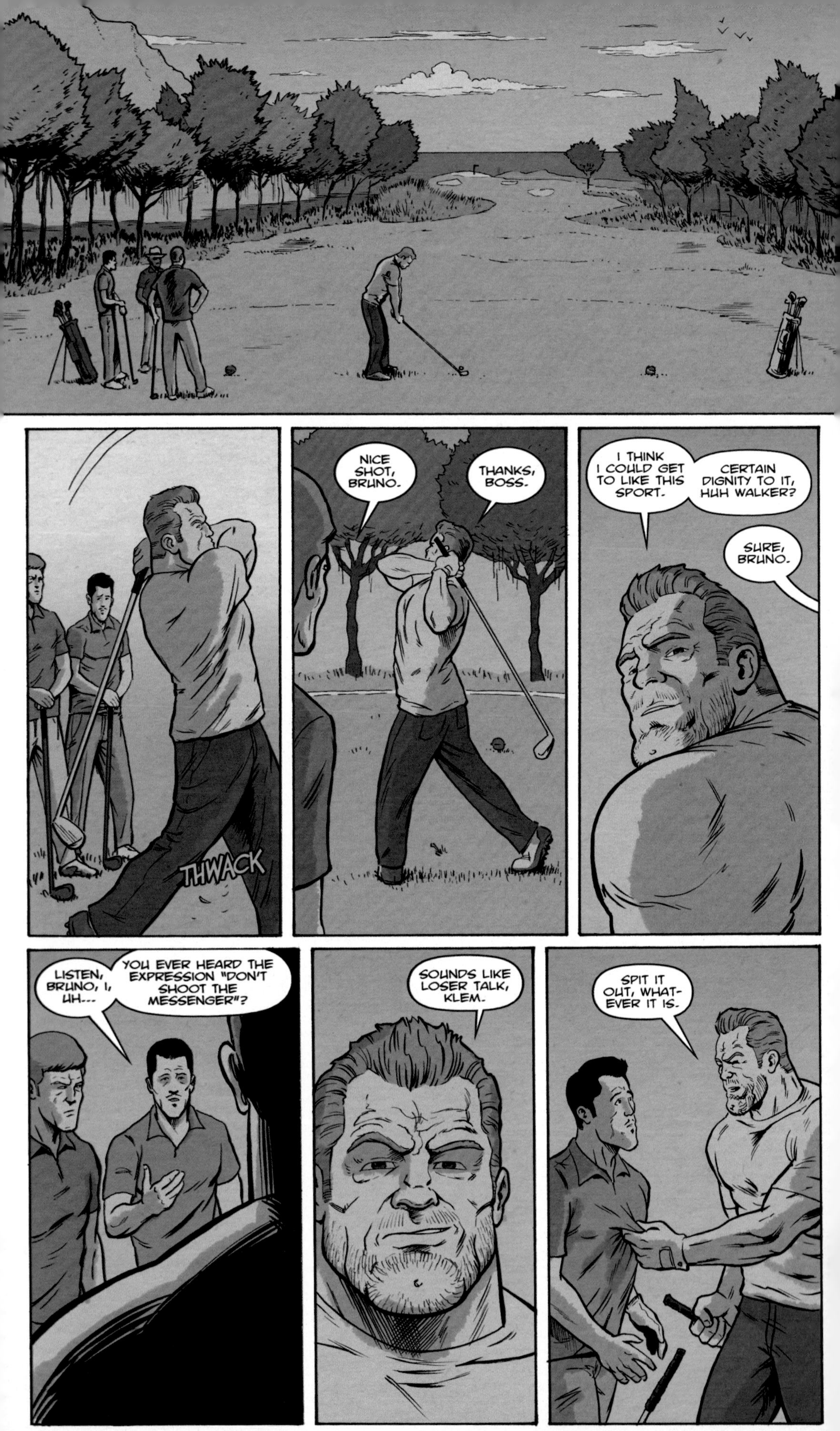
THWACK
NICE SHOT, BRUNO.
THANKS, BOSS.
I THINK I COULD GET TO LIKE THIS SPORT.
CERTAIN DIGNITY TO IT, HUH WALKER?
SURE, BRUNO.
LISTEN, BRUNO, I, UH...
YOU EVER HEARD THE EXPRESSION "DON'T SHOOT THE MESSENGER"?
SOUNDS LIKE LOSER TALK, KLEM.
SPIT IT OUT, WHAT-EVER IT IS.

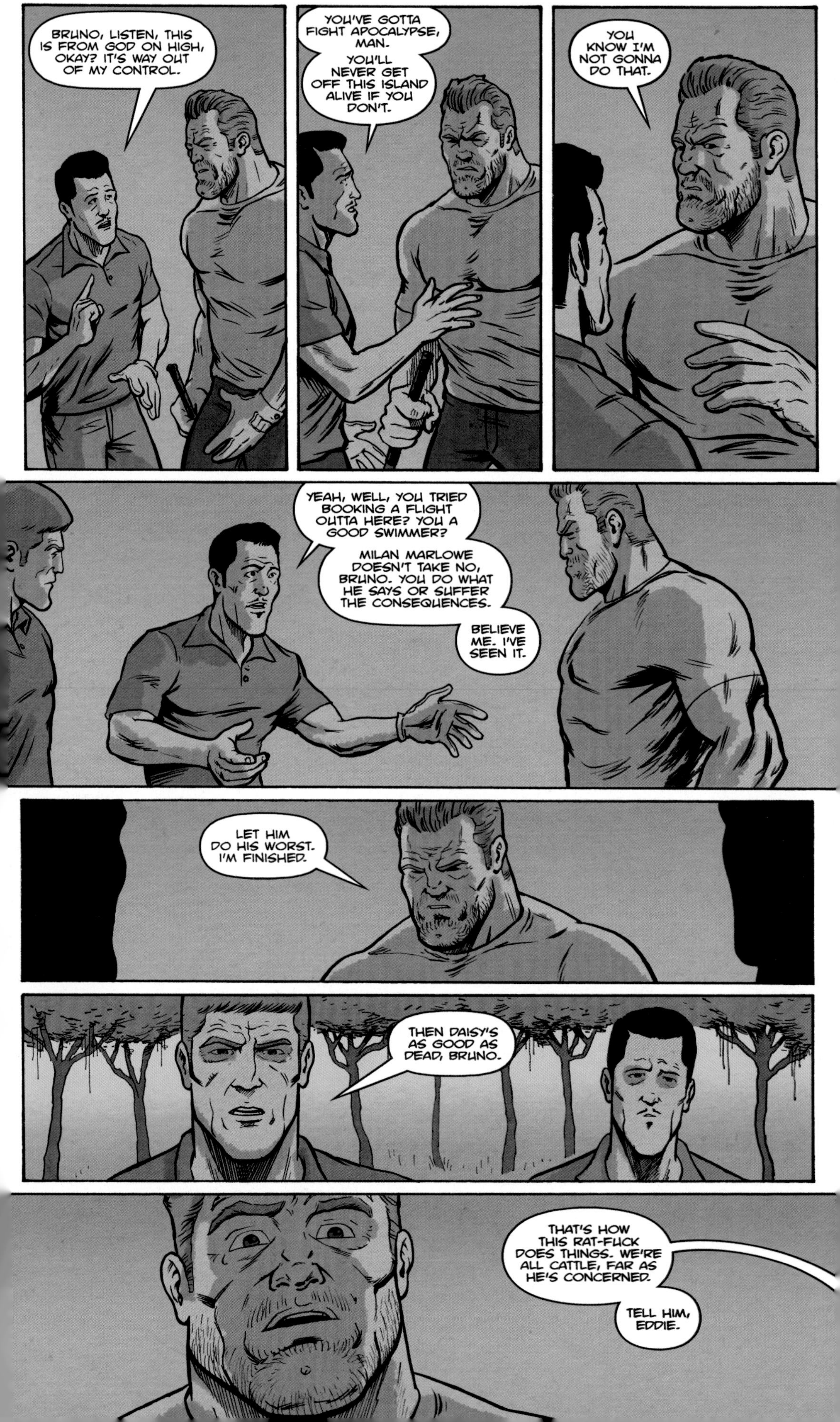
BRUNO, LISTEN, THIS IS FROM GOD ON HIGH, OKAY? IT'S WAY OUT OF MY CONTROL.
YOU'VE GOTTA FIGHT APOCALYPSE, MAN.
YOU'LL NEVER GET OFF THIS ISLAND ALIVE IF YOU DON'T.
YOU KNOW I'M NOT GONNA DO THAT.
YEAH, WELL, YOU TRIED BOOKING A FLIGHT OUTTA HERE? YOU A GOOD SWIMMER?
MILAN MARLOWE DOESN'T TAKE NO, BRUNO. YOU DO WHAT HE SAYS OR SUFFER THE CONSEQUENCES.
BELIEVE ME. I'VE SEEN IT.
LET HIM DO HIS WORST. I'M FINISHED.
THEN DAISY'S AS GOOD AS DEAD, BRUNO.
THAT'S HOW THIS RAT-FUCK DOES THINGS. WE'RE ALL CATTLE, FAR AS HE'S CONCERNED.
TELL HIM, EDDIE.

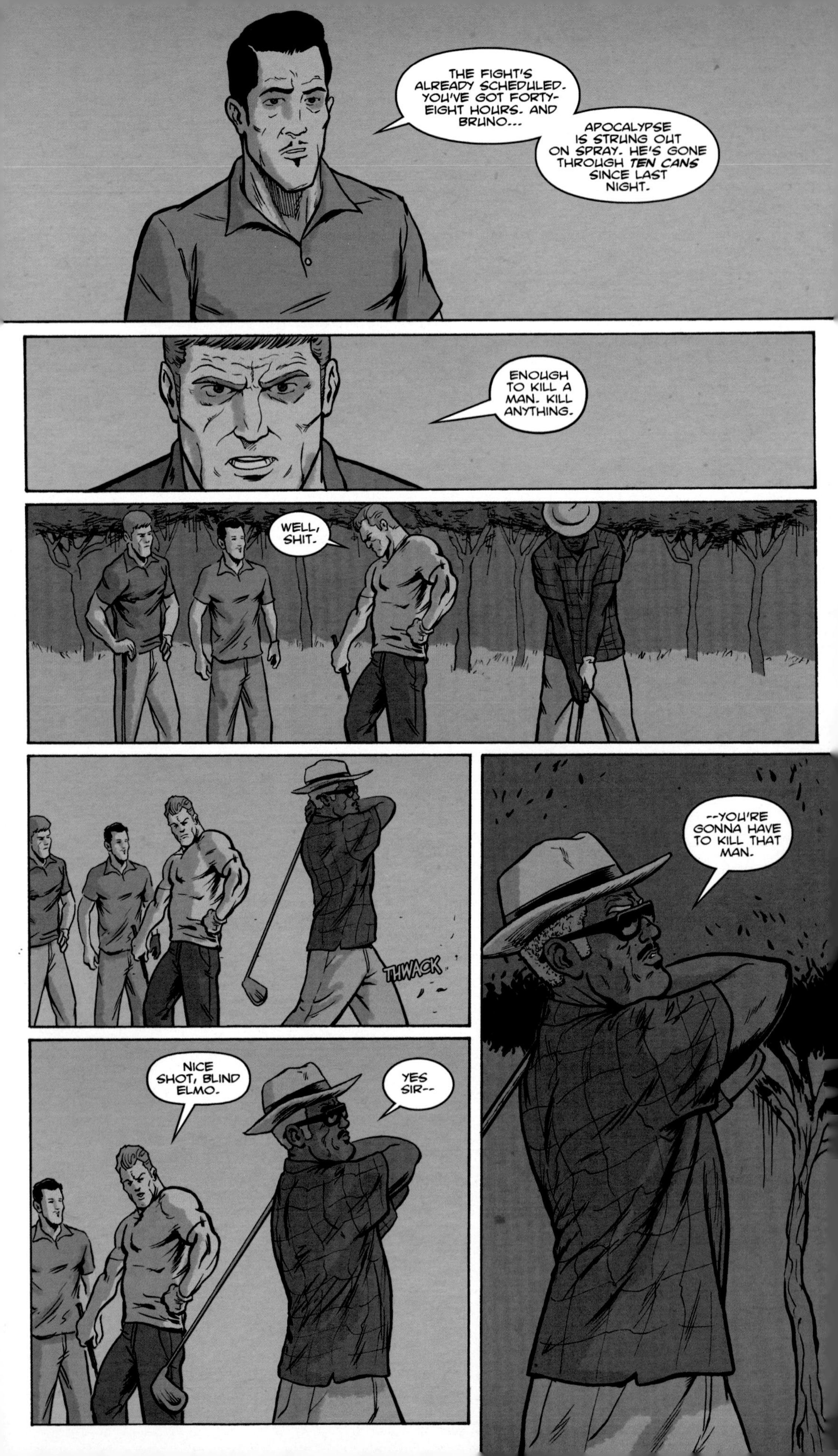
THE FIGHT'S ALREADY SCHEDULED. YOU'VE GOT FORTY-EIGHT HOURS. AND BRUNO...
APOCALYPSE IS STRUNG OUT ON SPRAY. HE'S GONE THROUGH *TEN CANS* SINCE LAST NIGHT.
ENOUGH TO KILL A MAN. KILL ANYTHING.
WELL, SHIT.
THWACK
NICE SHOT, BLIND ELMO.
YES SIR--
--YOU'RE GONNA HAVE TO KILL THAT MAN.

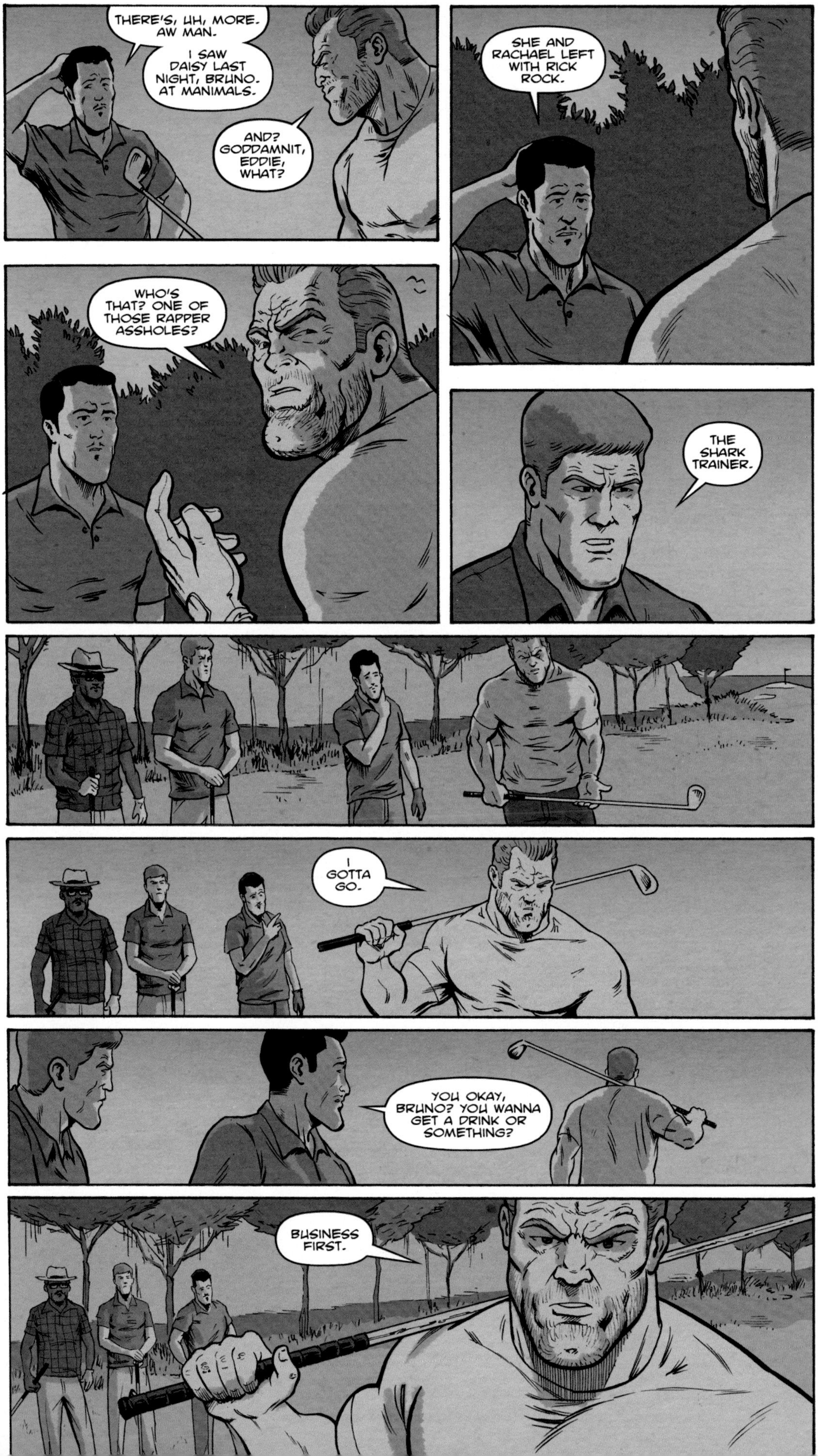
THERE'S, UH, MORE. AW MAN.
I SAW DAISY LAST NIGHT, BRUNO. AT MANIMALS.
AND? GODDAMNIT, EDDIE, WHAT?
SHE AND RACHAEL LEFT WITH RICK ROCK.
WHO'S THAT? ONE OF THOSE RAPPER ASSHOLES?
THE SHARK TRAINER.
I GOTTA GO.
YOU OKAY, BRUNO? YOU WANNA GET A DRINK OR SOMETHING?
BUSINESS FIRST.

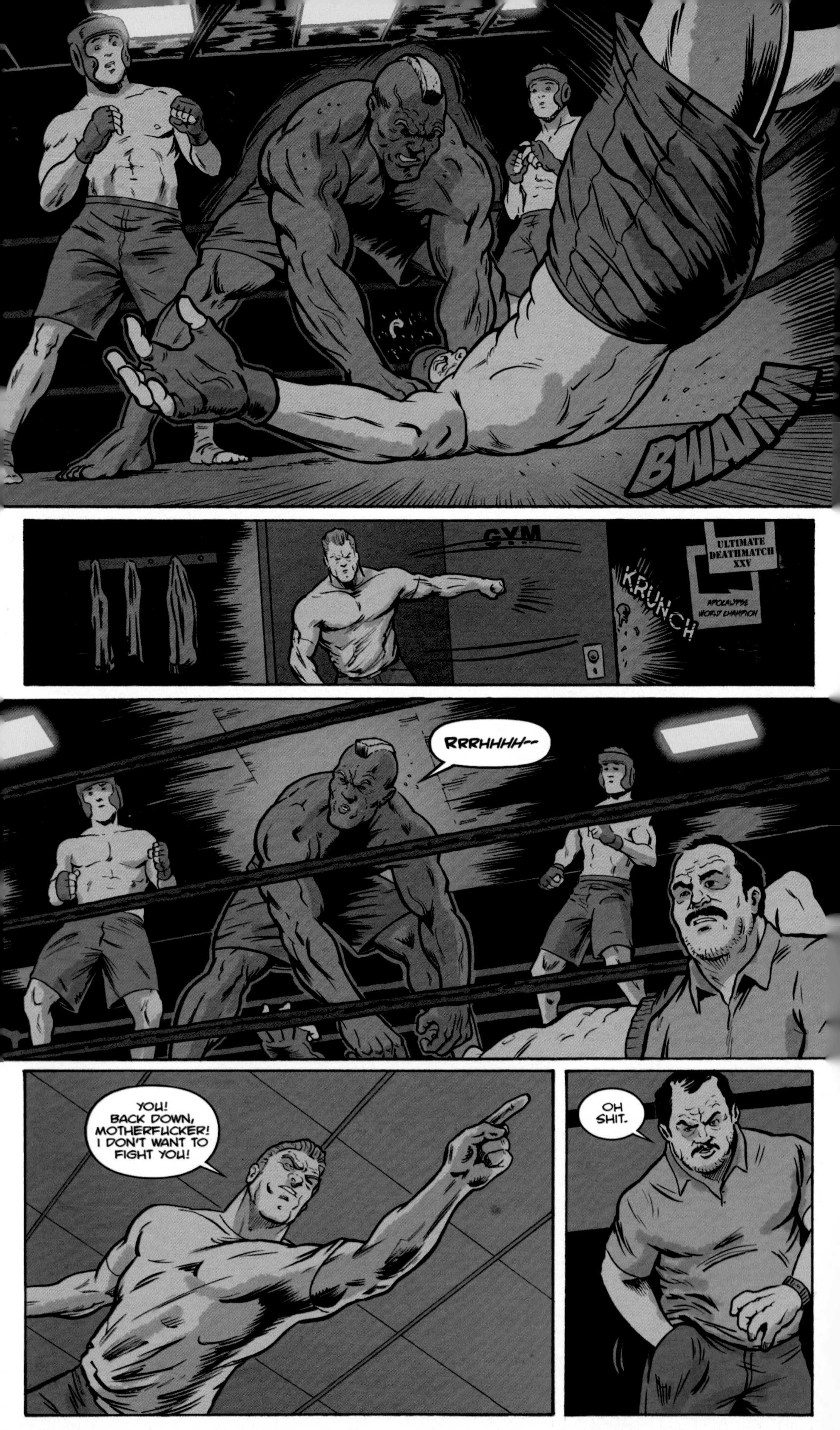
BWAM
GYM
ULTIMATE DEATHMATCH XXV
APOCALYPSE WORLD CHAMPION
KRUNCH!
RRRHHHH--
YOU! BACK DOWN, MOTHERFUCKER! I DON'T WANT TO FIGHT YOU!
OH SHIT.

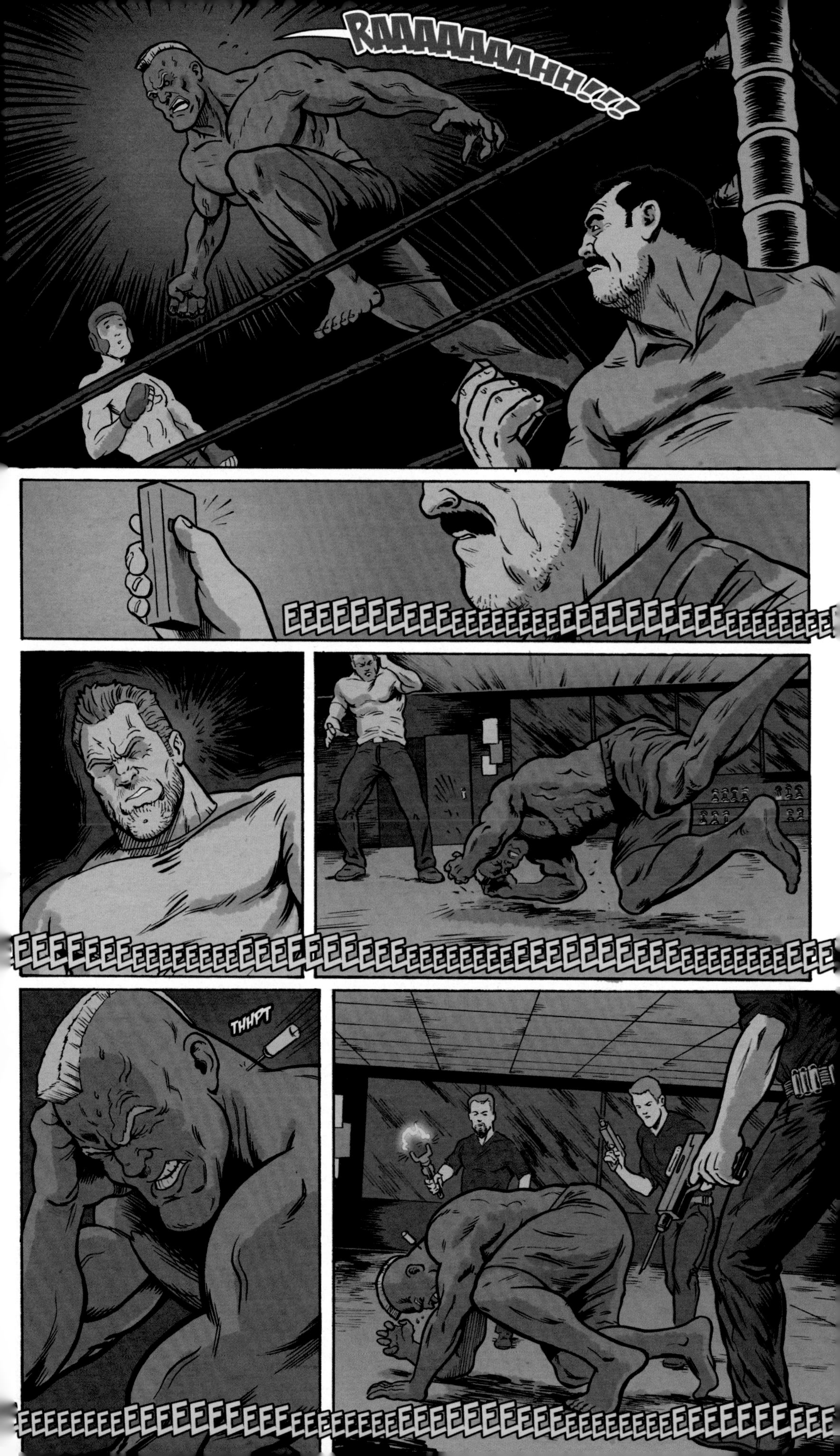
RAAAAAAAAHH!!!!
EEEEEEEEEEEEeeeeeeeeeEEEEEEEEEEEEeeeeeeeee
EEEEeeeeeeeeeeeeeEEEEEEEEEEEeeeeeeeeeeeEEEEEEEEEEEeeeeeeeeeeeEEE
THHPT
EEEEEEEEEEEEEEEEEEEEEeeeeeeeeEEEEEEEEEEEEeeeeeeeeeeeEEEEEEEEEEE

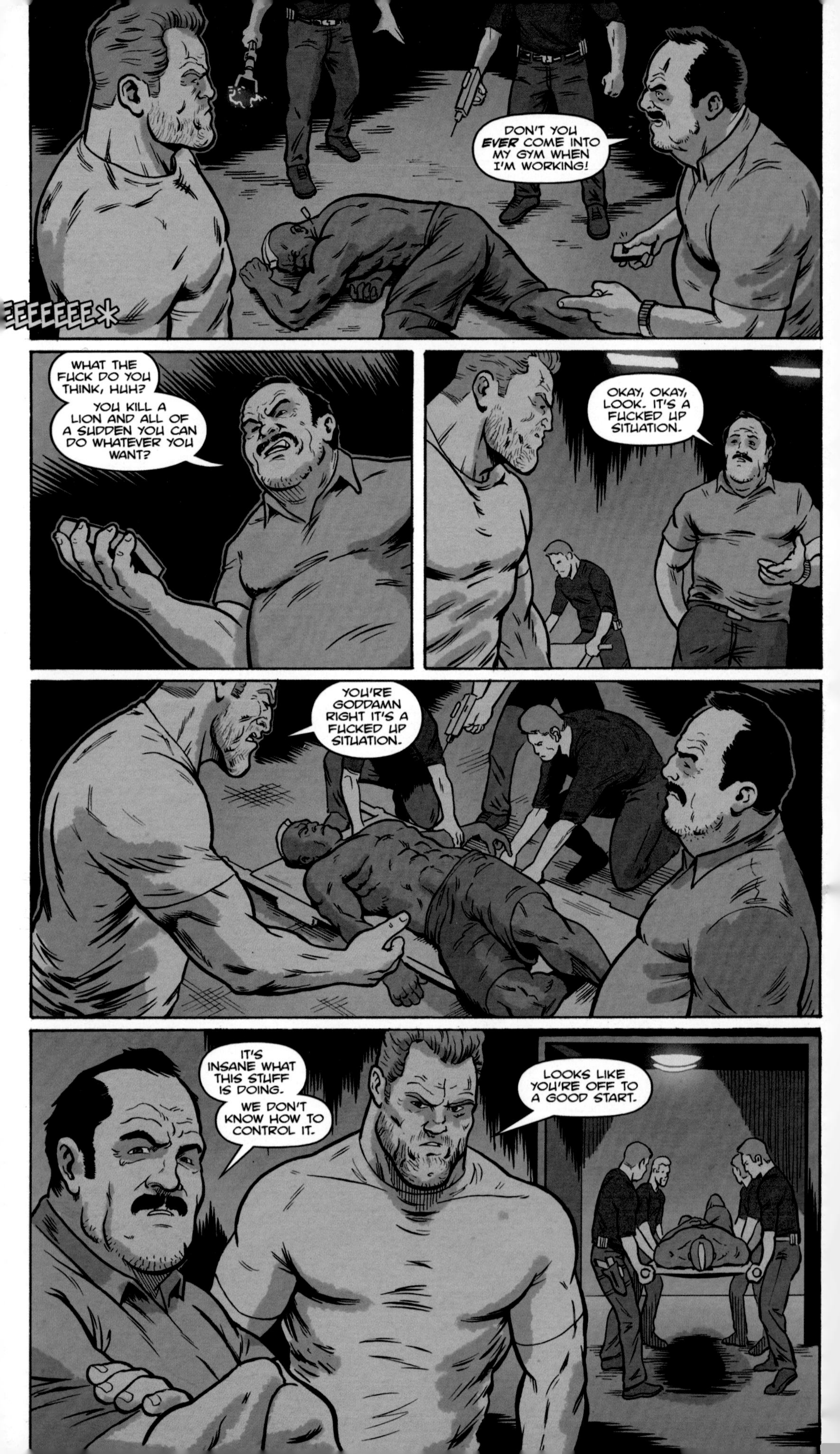
EEEEEEEE*
DON'T YOU EVER COME INTO MY GYM WHEN I'M WORKING!
WHAT THE FUCK DO YOU THINK, HUH?
YOU KILL A LION AND ALL OF A SUDDEN YOU CAN DO WHATEVER YOU WANT?
OKAY, OKAY, LOOK. IT'S A FUCKED UP SITUATION.
YOU'RE GODDAMN RIGHT IT'S A FUCKED UP SITUATION.
IT'S INSANE WHAT THIS STUFF IS DOING.
WE DON'T KNOW HOW TO CONTROL IT.
LOOKS LIKE YOU'RE OFF TO A GOOD START.

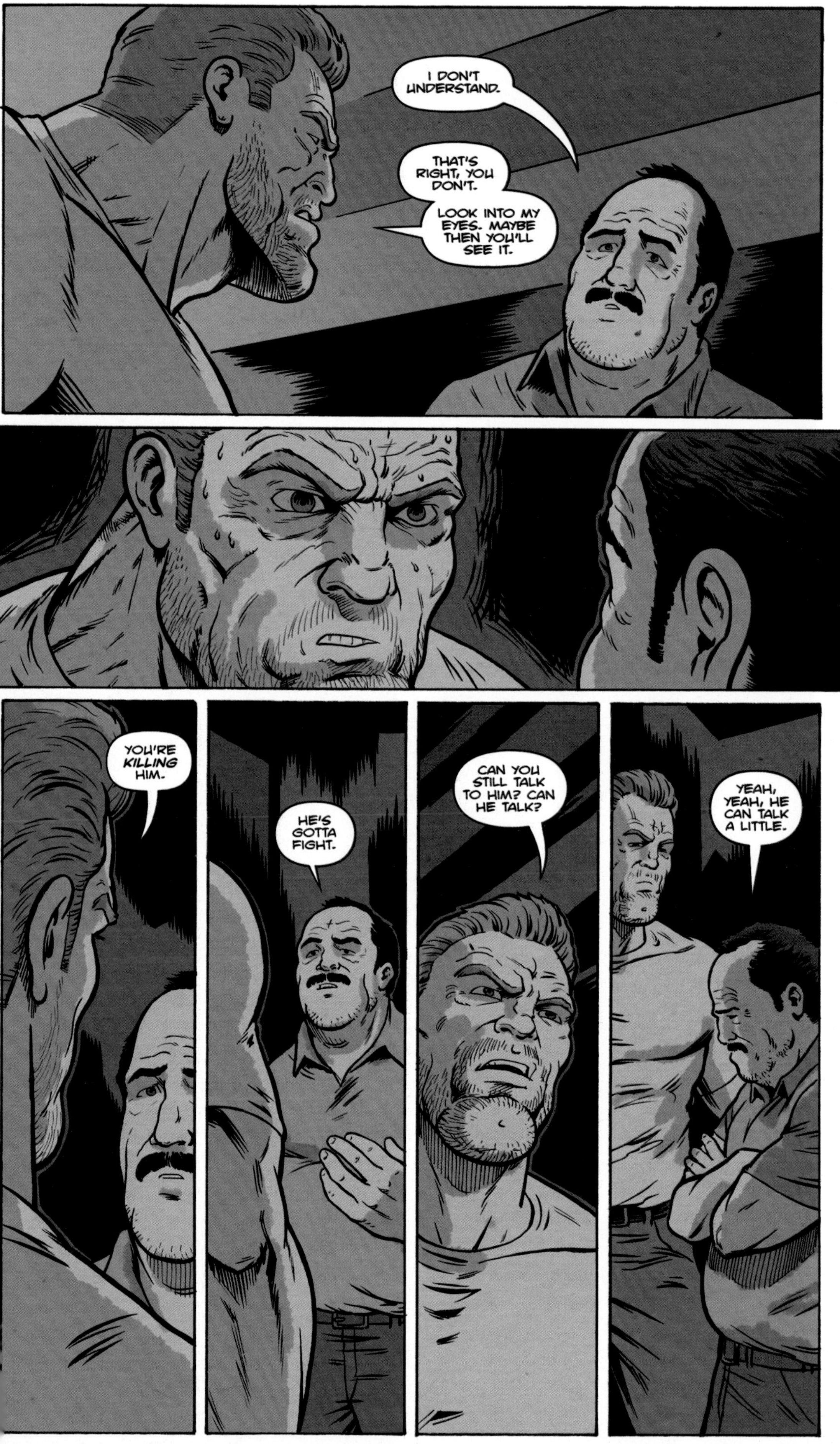
I DON'T UNDERSTAND.
THAT'S RIGHT, YOU DON'T.
LOOK INTO MY EYES. MAYBE THEN YOU'LL SEE IT.
YOU'RE KILLING HIM.
HE'S GOTTA FIGHT.
CAN YOU STILL TALK TO HIM? CAN HE TALK?
YEAH, YEAH, HE CAN TALK A LITTLE.

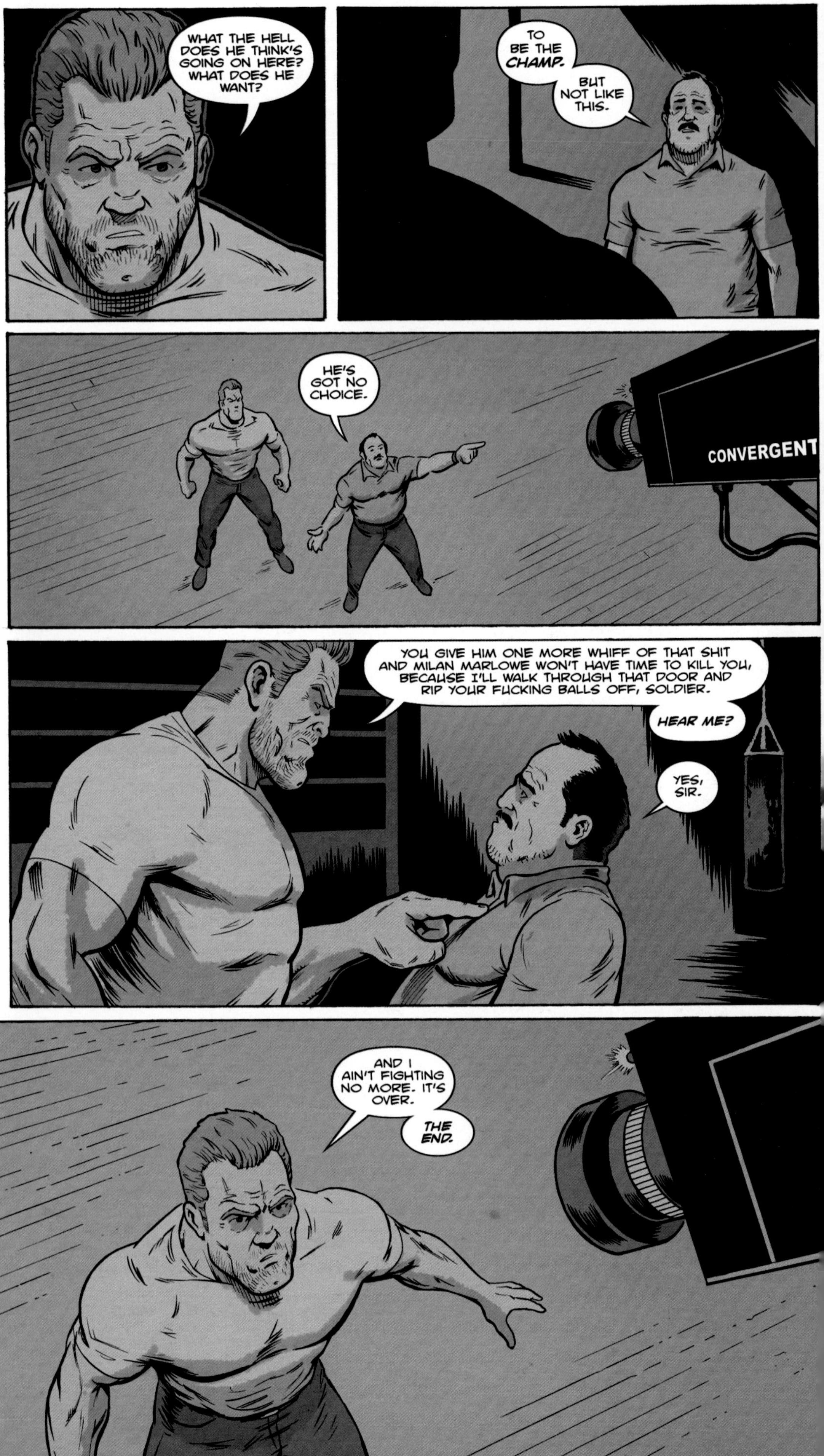

WHAT THE HELL DOES HE THINK'S GOING ON HERE? WHAT DOES HE WANT?
TO BE THE CHAMP.
BUT NOT LIKE THIS.
HE'S GOT NO CHOICE.
CONVERGENT
YOU GIVE HIM ONE MORE WHIFF OF THAT SHIT AND MILAN MARLOWE WON'T HAVE TIME TO KILL YOU, BECAUSE I'LL WALK THROUGH THAT DOOR AND RIP YOUR FUCKING BALLS OFF, SOLDIER.
HEAR ME?
YES, SIR.
AND I AIN'T FIGHTING NO MORE. IT'S OVER.
THE END.

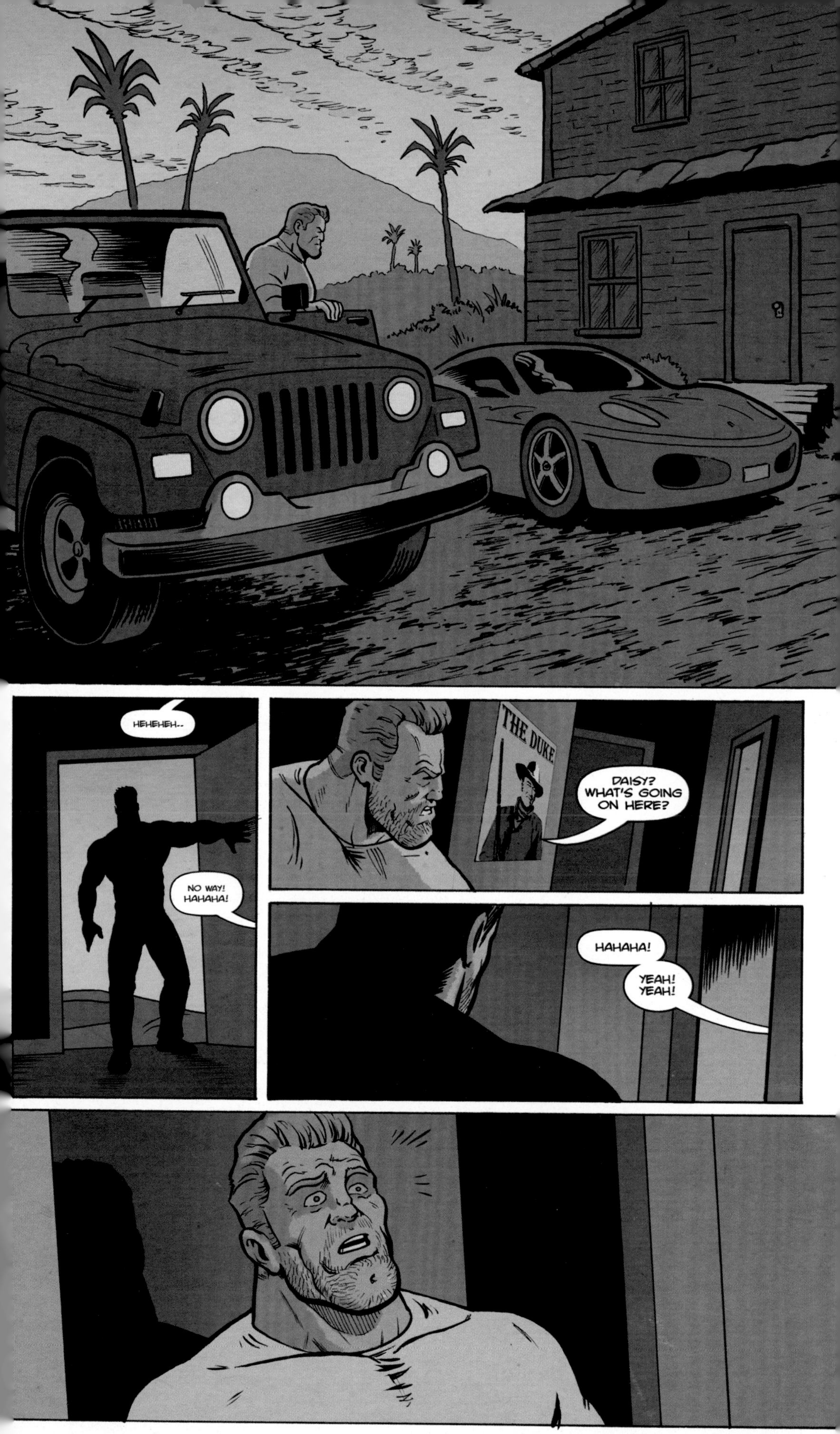
HEHEHEH--
NO WAY! HAHAHA!
THE DUKE
DAISY? WHAT'S GOING ON HERE?
HAHAHA!
YEAH! YEAH!

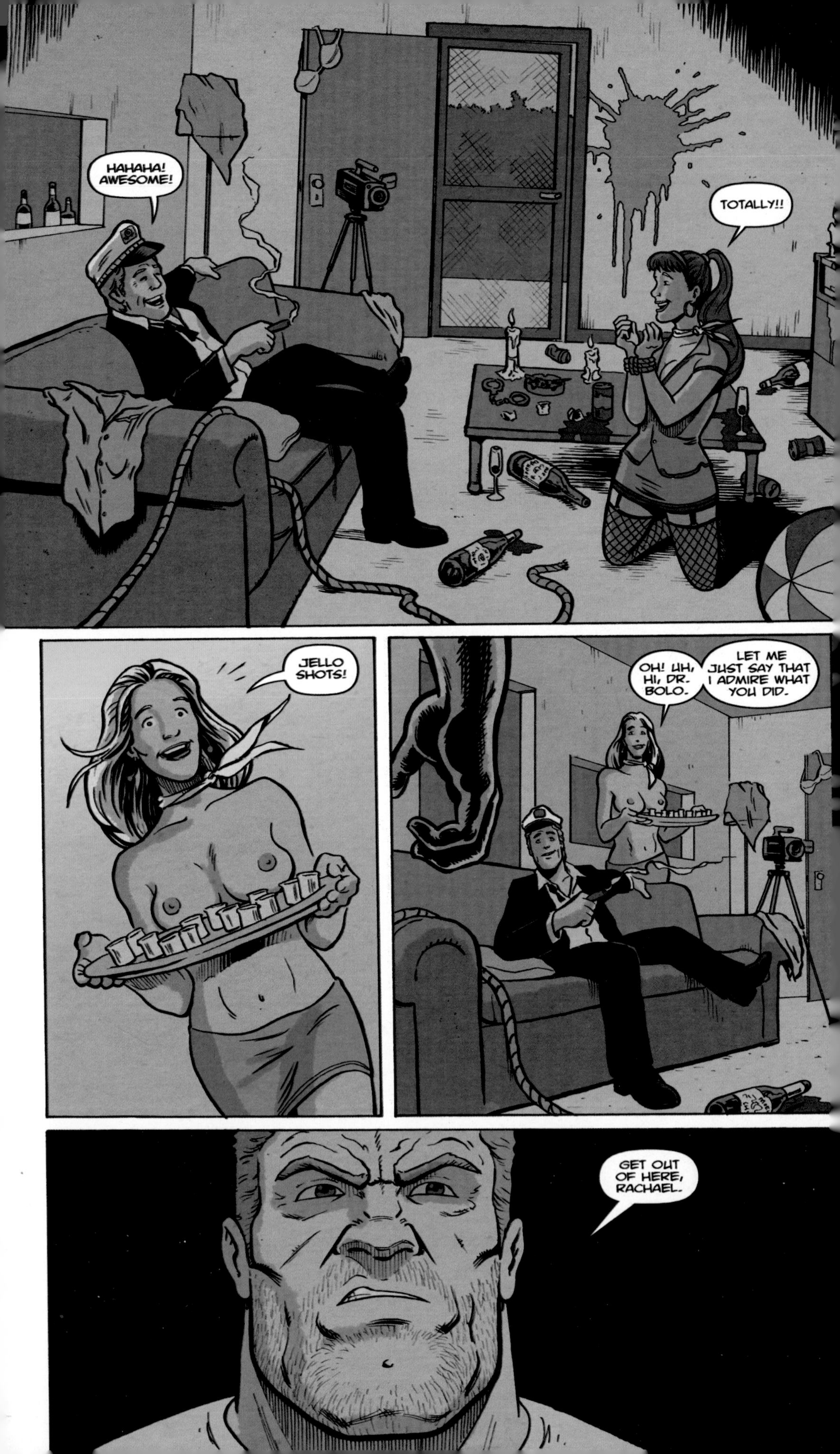

HAHAHA! AWESOME!
TOTALLY!!
JELLO SHOTS!
OH! UH, HI, DR. BOLO.
LET ME JUST SAY THAT I ADMIRE WHAT YOU DID.
GET OUT OF HERE, RACHAEL.

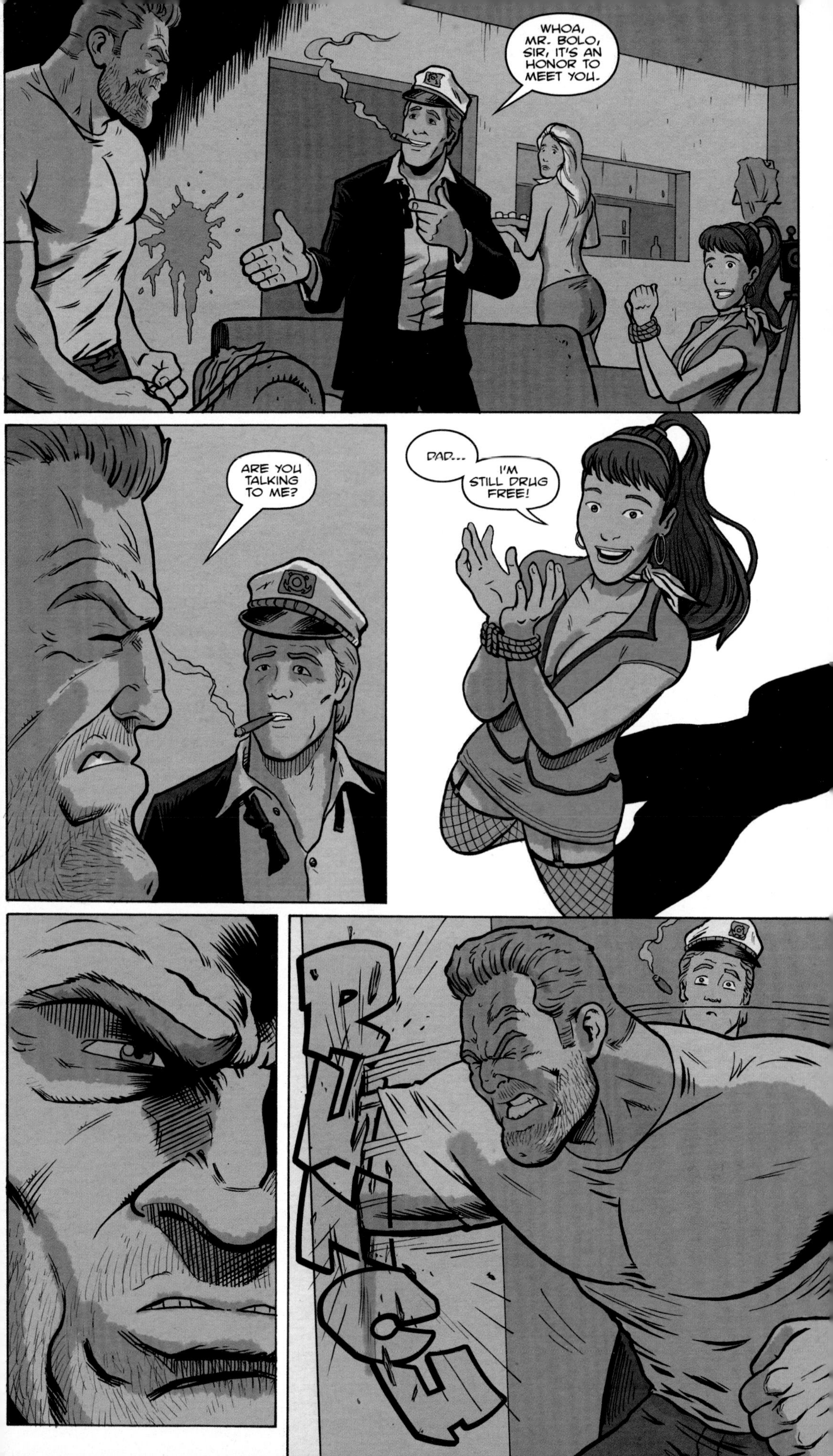
WHOA, MR. BOLO, SIR, IT'S AN HONOR TO MEET YOU.
ARE YOU TALKING TO ME?
DAD...
I'M STILL DRUG FREE!

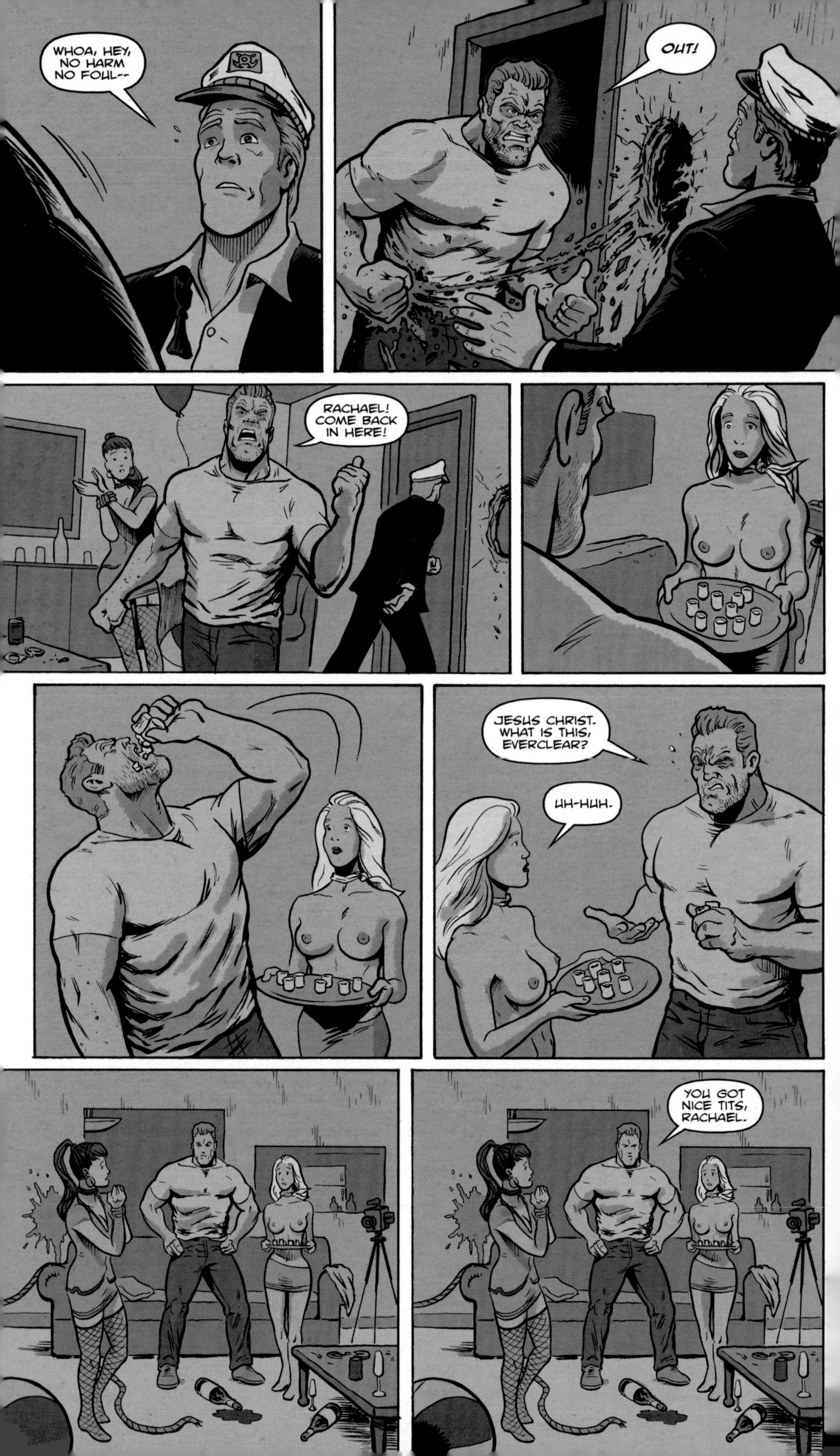
WHOA, HEY, NO HARM NO FOUL--
OUT!
RACHAEL! COME BACK IN HERE!
JESUS CHRIST. WHAT IS THIS, EVERCLEAR?
UH-HUH.
YOU GOT NICE TITS, RACHAEL.

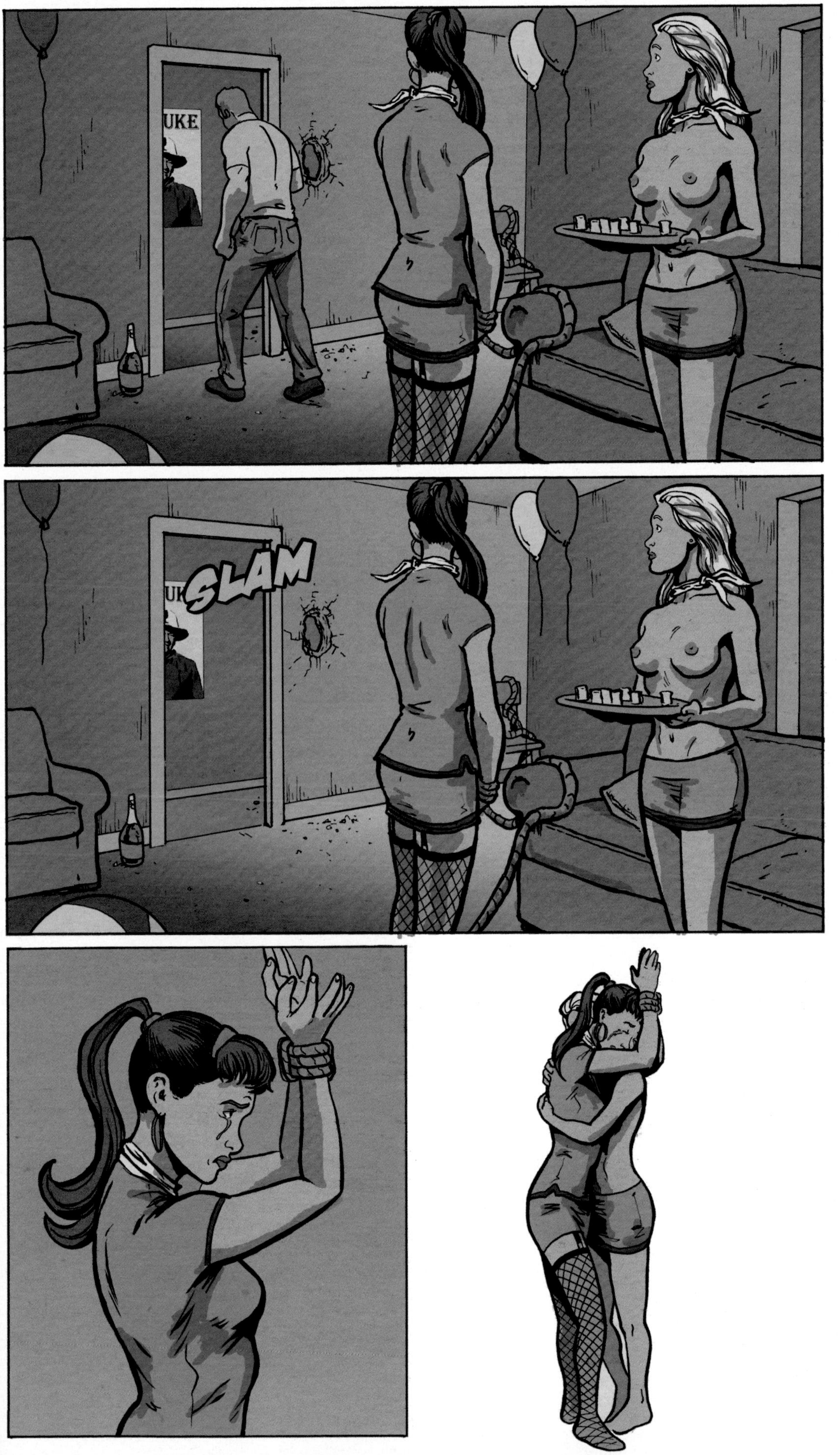
UKE
SLAM

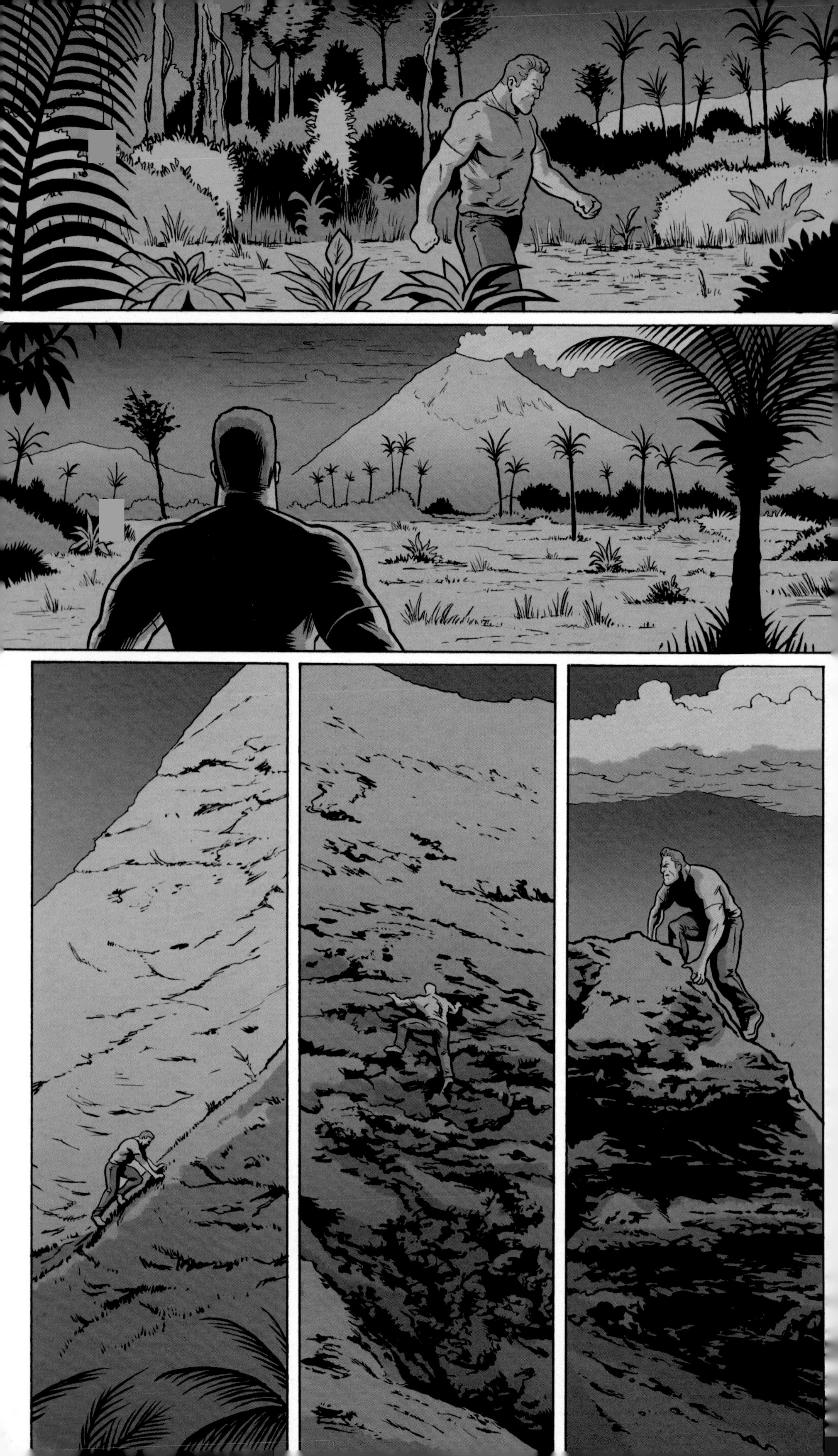

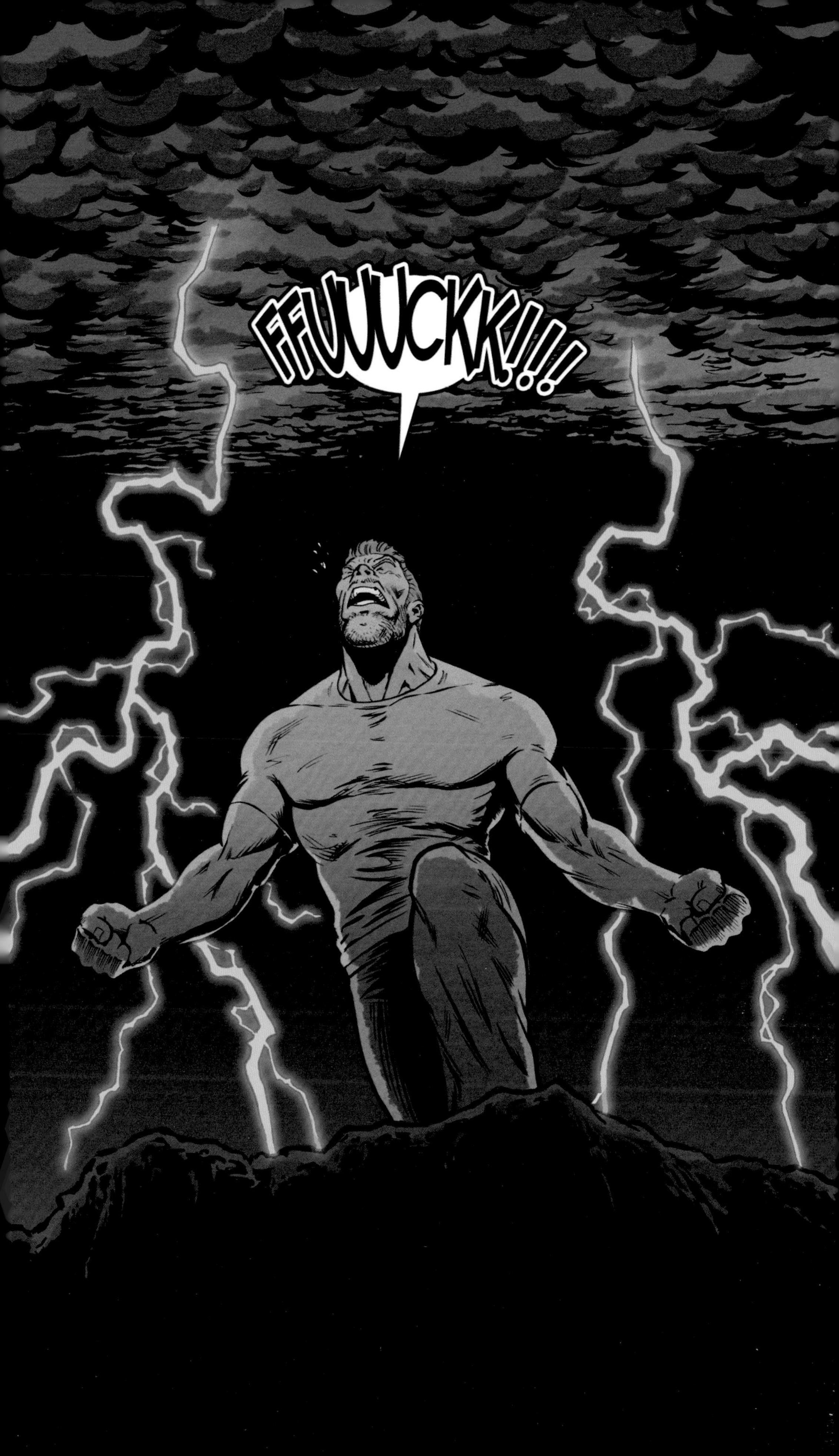
FFUUUCKK!!!

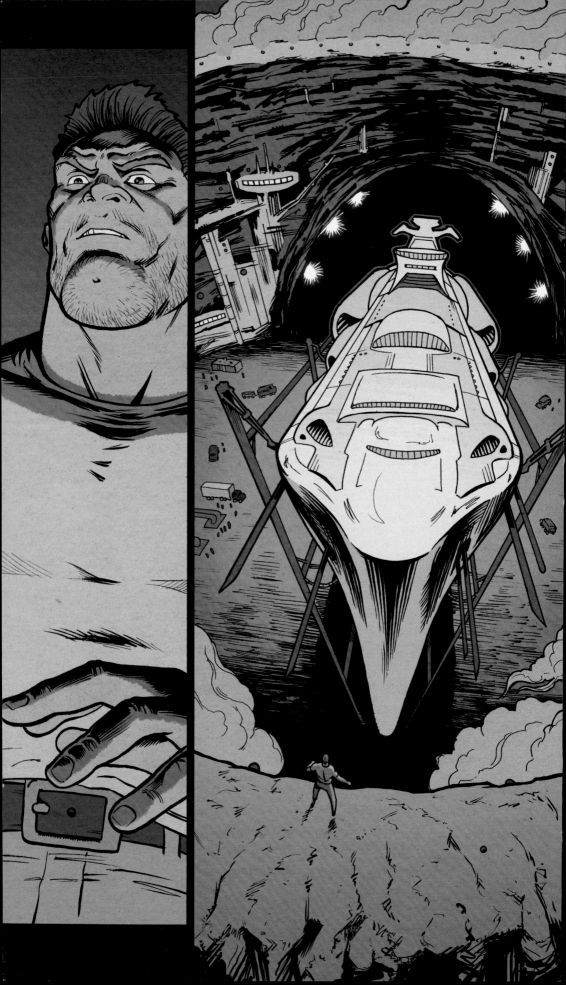

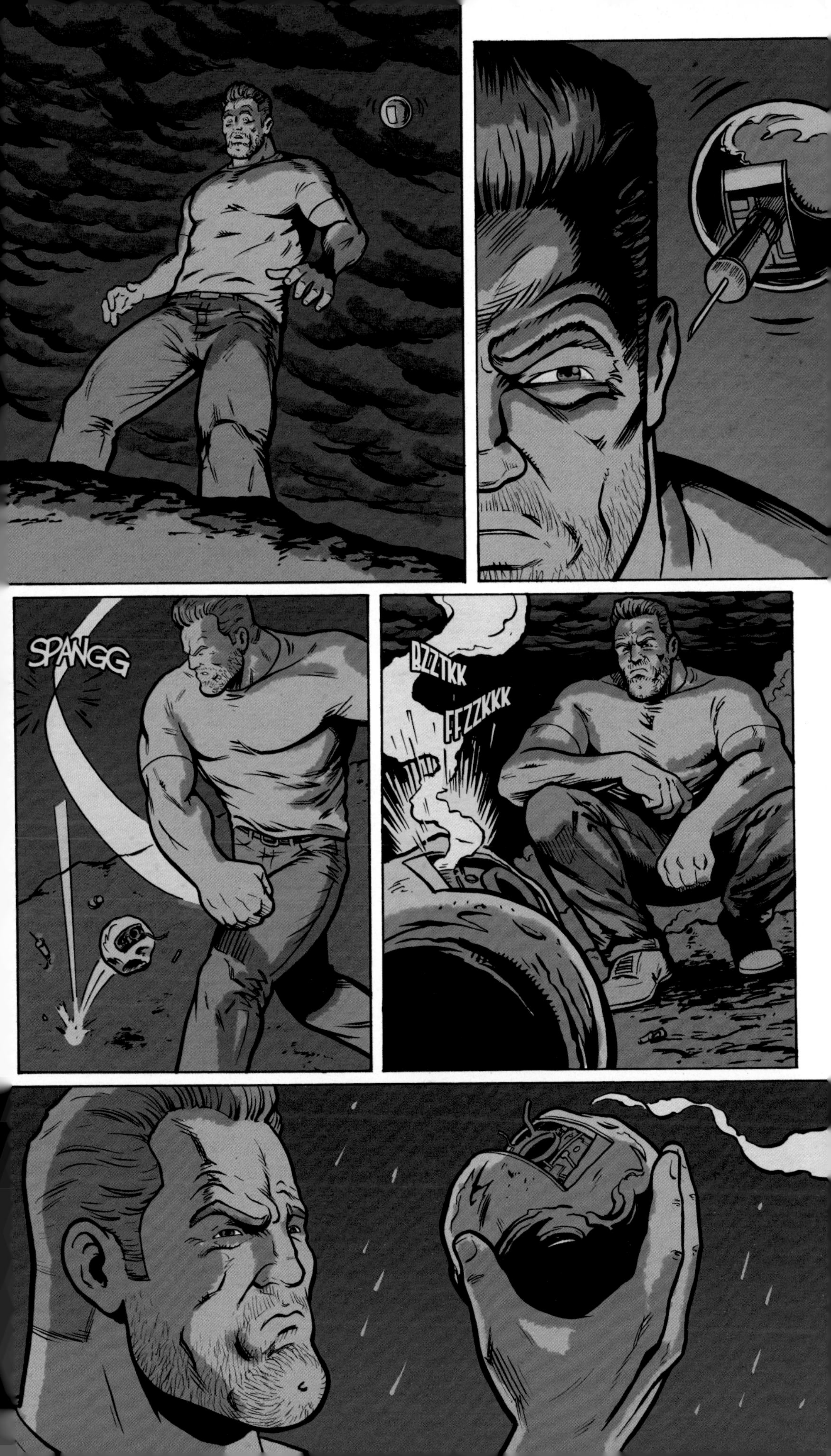

SPANGG
BZZTKK
FFZZKKK

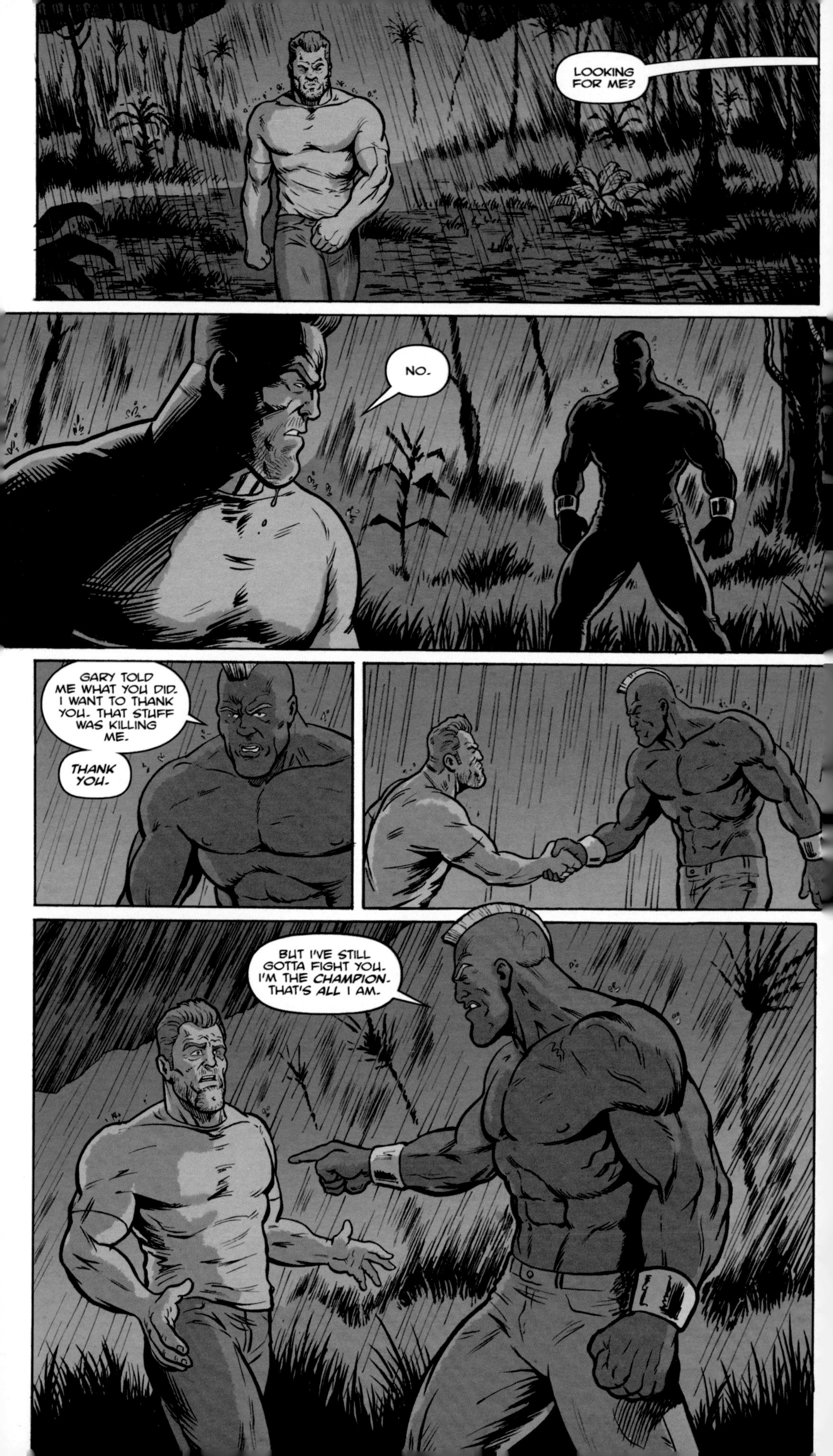
LOOKING FOR ME?
NO.
GARY TOLD ME WHAT YOU DID. I WANT TO THANK YOU. THAT STUFF WAS KILLING ME.
THANK YOU.
BUT I'VE STILL GOTTA FIGHT YOU. I'M THE *CHAMPION*. THAT'S *ALL* I AM.

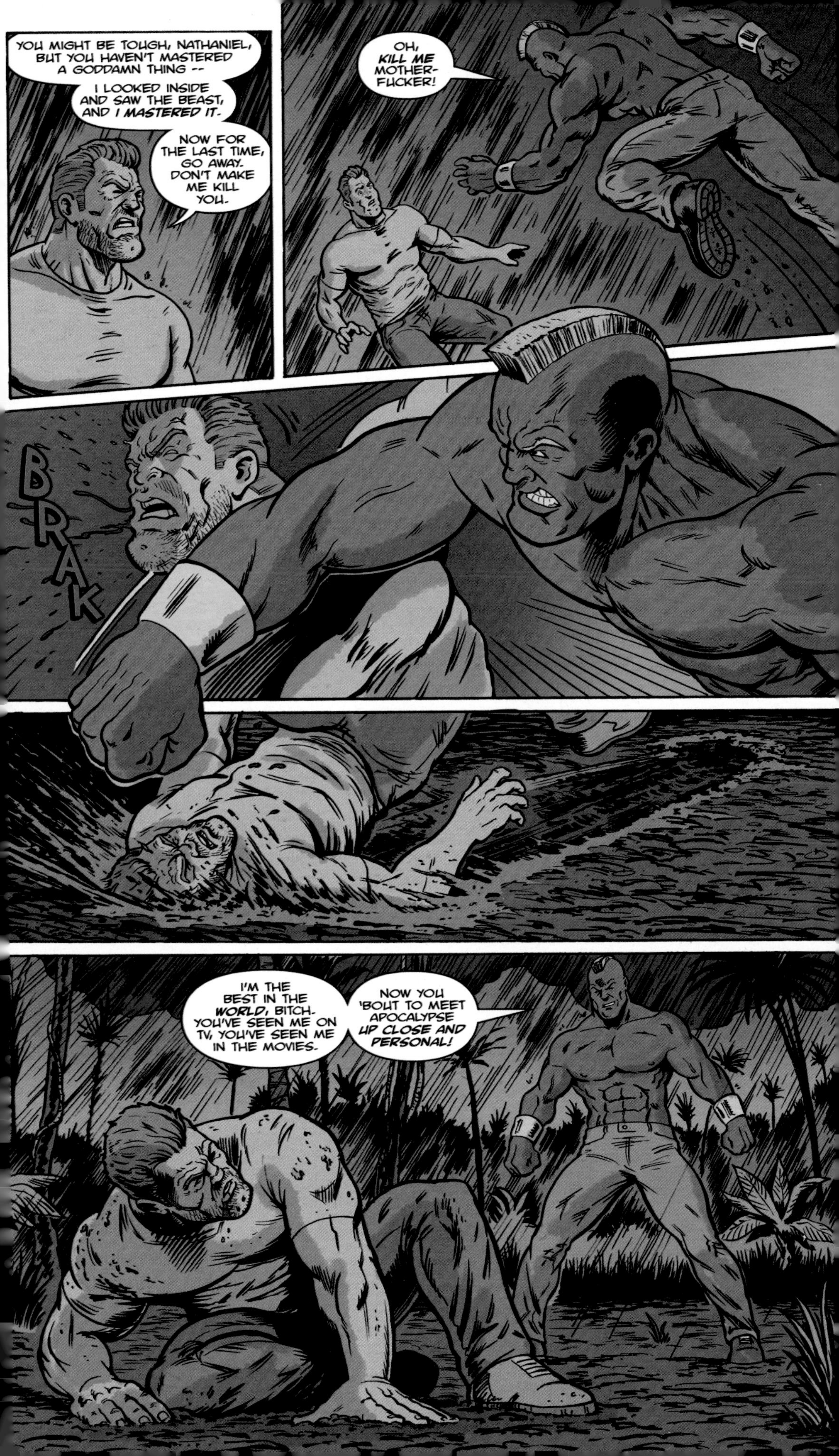
YOU MIGHT BE TOUGH, NATHANIEL, BUT YOU HAVEN'T MASTERED A GODDAMN THING --
I LOOKED INSIDE AND SAW THE BEAST, AND I MASTERED IT.
NOW FOR THE LAST TIME, GO AWAY. DON'T MAKE ME KILL YOU.
OH, KILL ME MOTHER-FUCKER!
BRAK
I'M THE BEST IN THE WORLD, BITCH. YOU'VE SEEN ME ON TV, YOU'VE SEEN ME IN THE MOVIES.
NOW YOU 'BOUT TO MEET APOCALYPSE UP CLOSE AND PERSONAL!

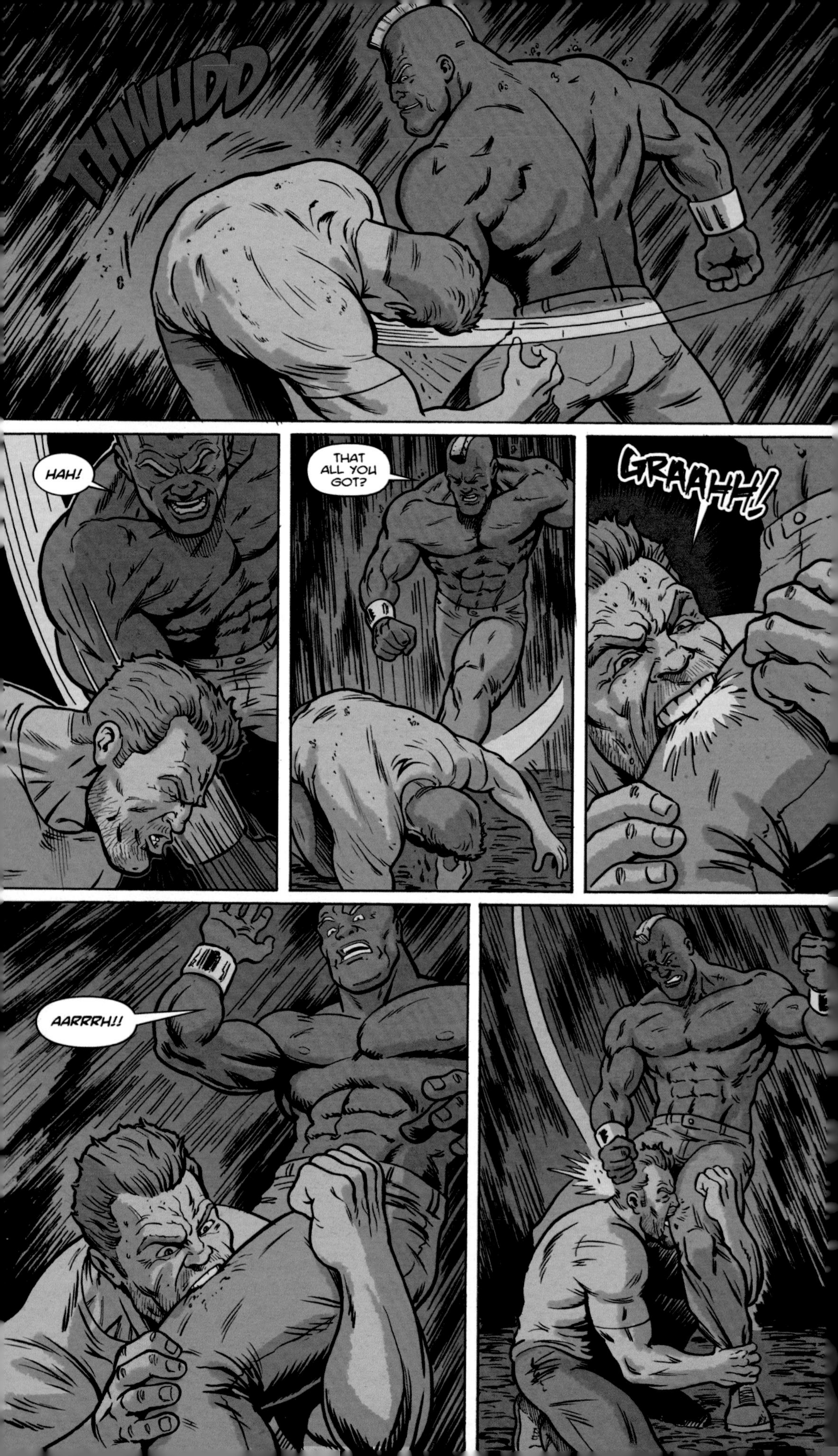
THWUDD
HAH!
THAT ALL YOU GOT?
GRAAHH!
AARRRH!!

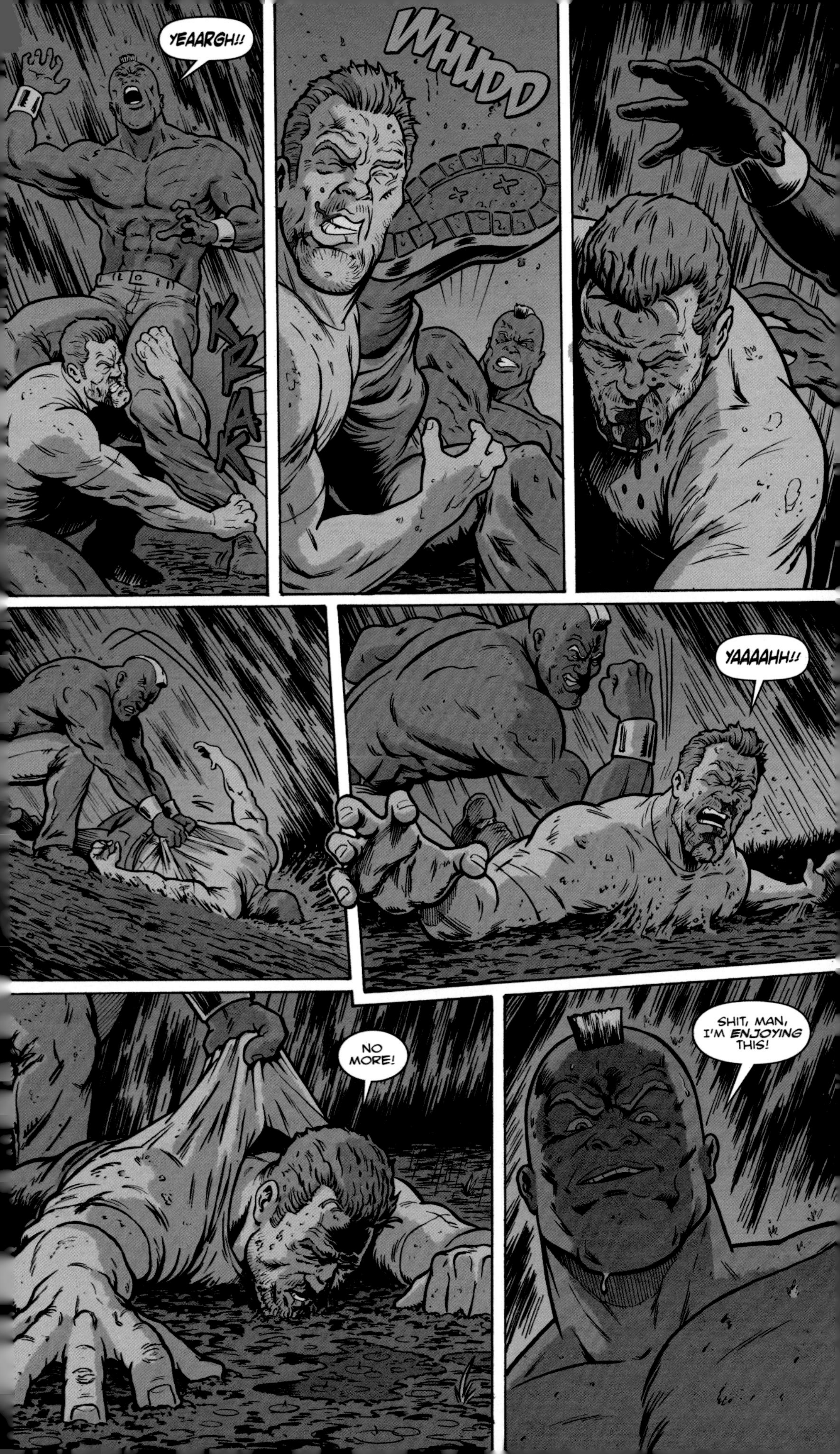
YEAARGH!!
KRAK
WHUDD
YAAAAHH!!
NO MORE!
SHIT, MAN, I'M ENJOYING THIS!

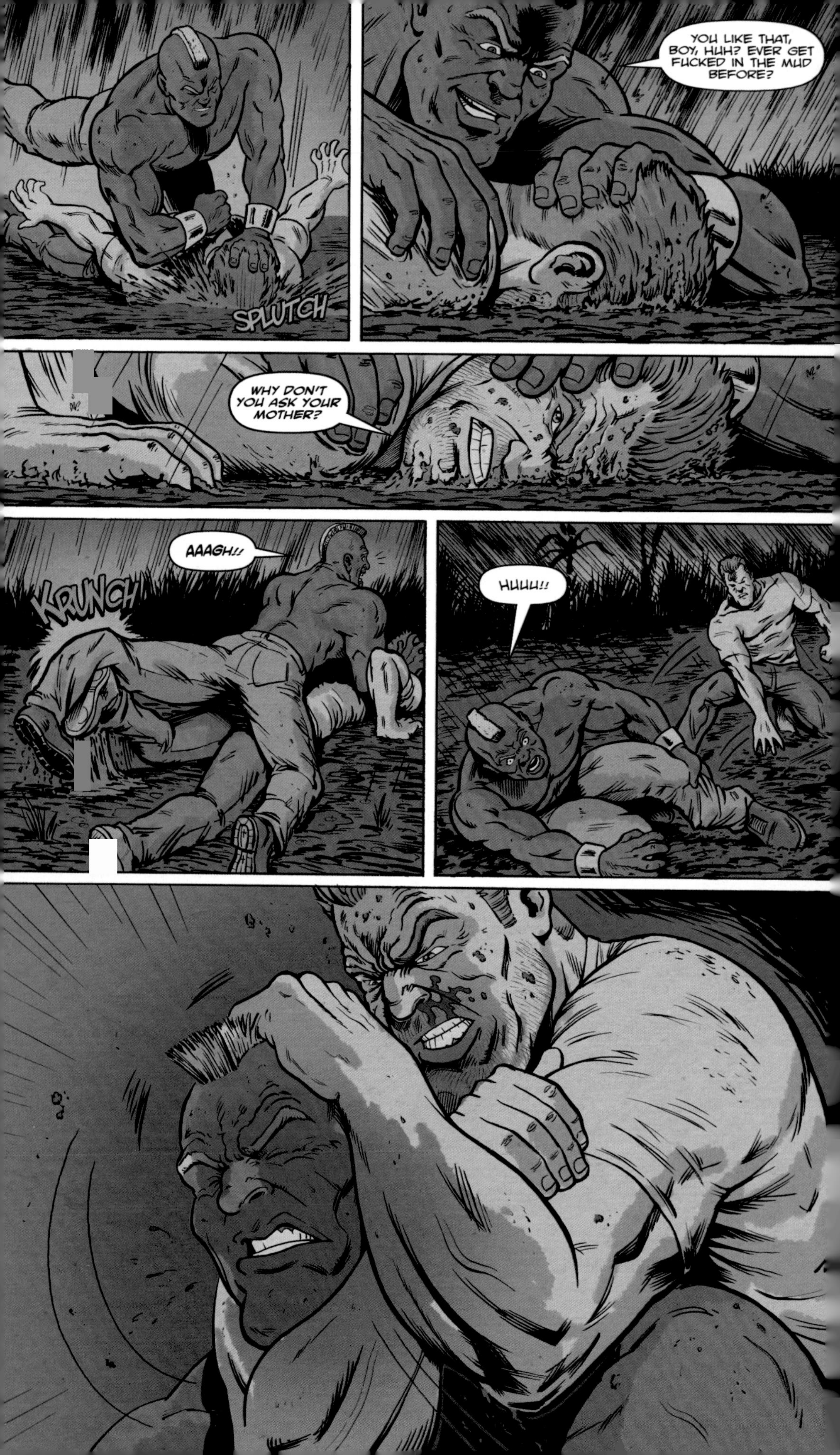
SPLUTCH
YOU LIKE THAT, BOY, HUH? EVER GET FUCKED IN THE MUD BEFORE?
WHY DON'T YOU ASK YOUR MOTHER?
KRUNCH
AAAGH!!
HUUU!!

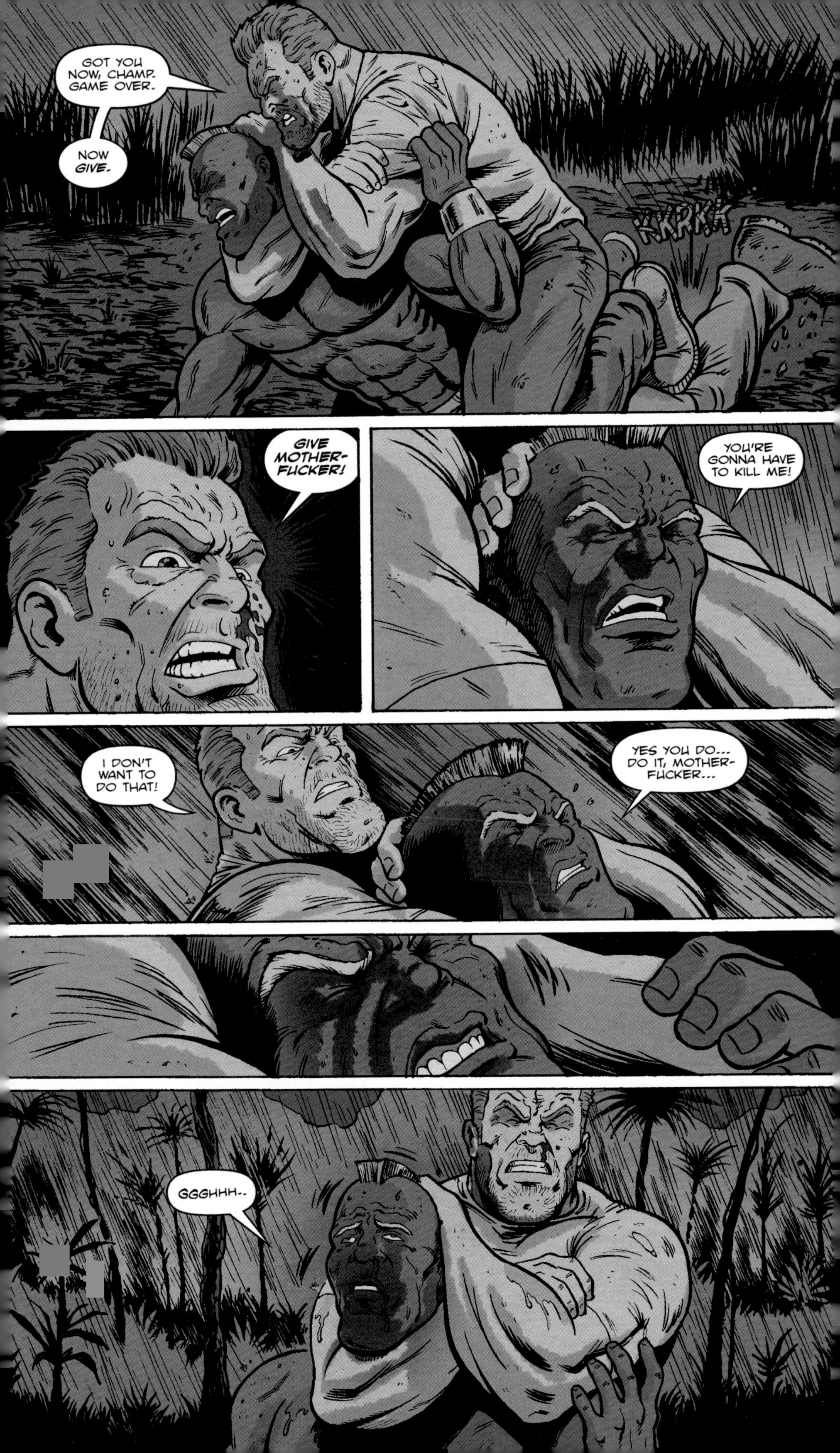
GOT YOU NOW, CHAMP. GAME OVER.
NOW GIVE.
KKRRK!
GIVE MOTHER-FUCKER!
YOU'RE GONNA HAVE TO KILL ME!
I DON'T WANT TO DO THAT!
YES YOU DO... DO IT, MOTHER-FUCKER...
GGGHHH..

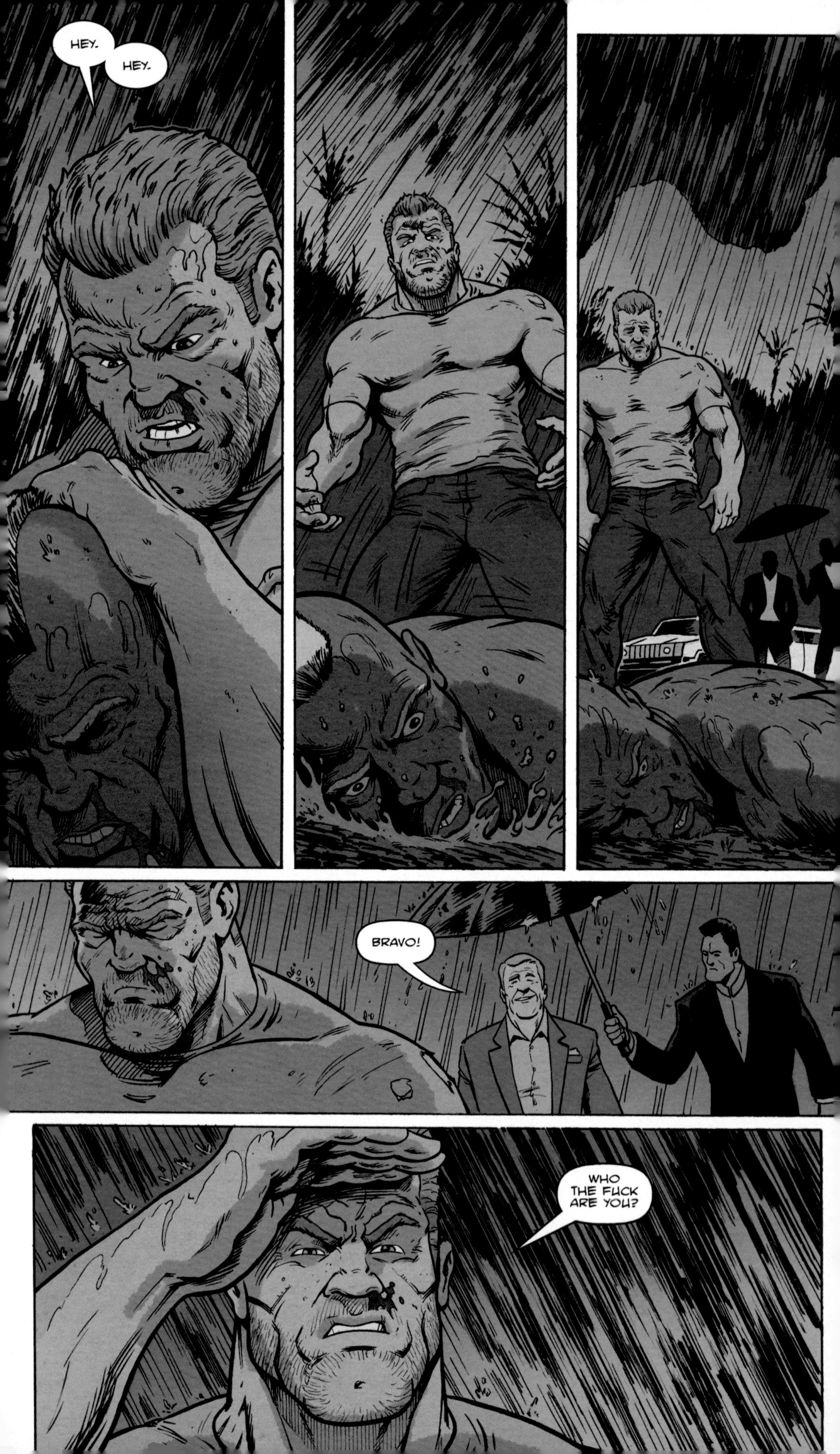
HEY.
HEY.
BRAVO!
WHO THE FUCK ARE YOU?

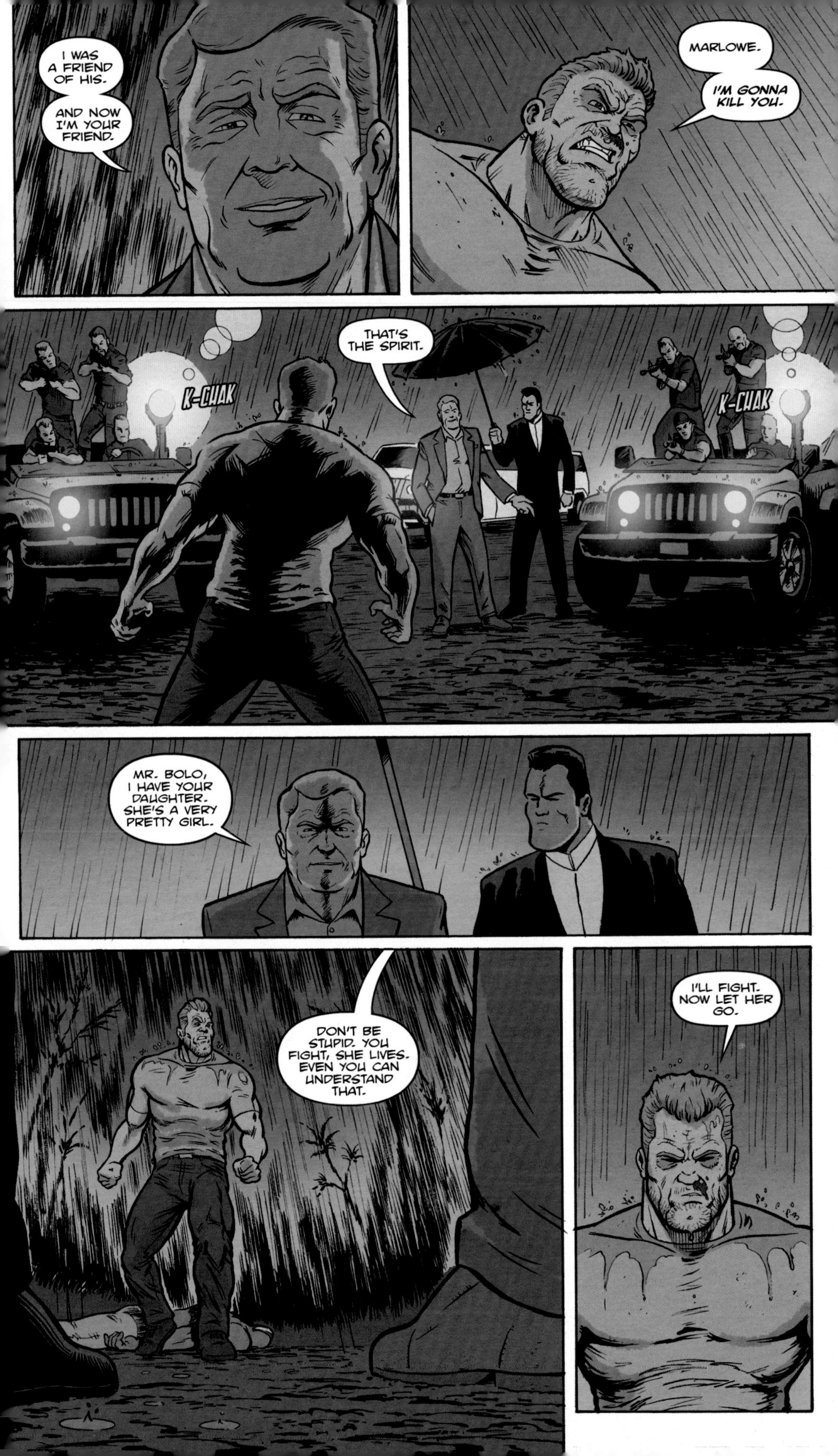
I WAS A FRIEND OF HIS.
AND NOW I'M YOUR FRIEND.
MARLOWE.
I'M GONNA KILL YOU.
K-CHAK
THAT'S THE SPIRIT.
K-CHAK
MR. BOLO, I HAVE YOUR DAUGHTER. SHE'S A VERY PRETTY GIRL.
DON'T BE STUPID. YOU FIGHT, SHE LIVES. EVEN YOU CAN UNDERSTAND THAT.
I'LL FIGHT. NOW LET HER GO.

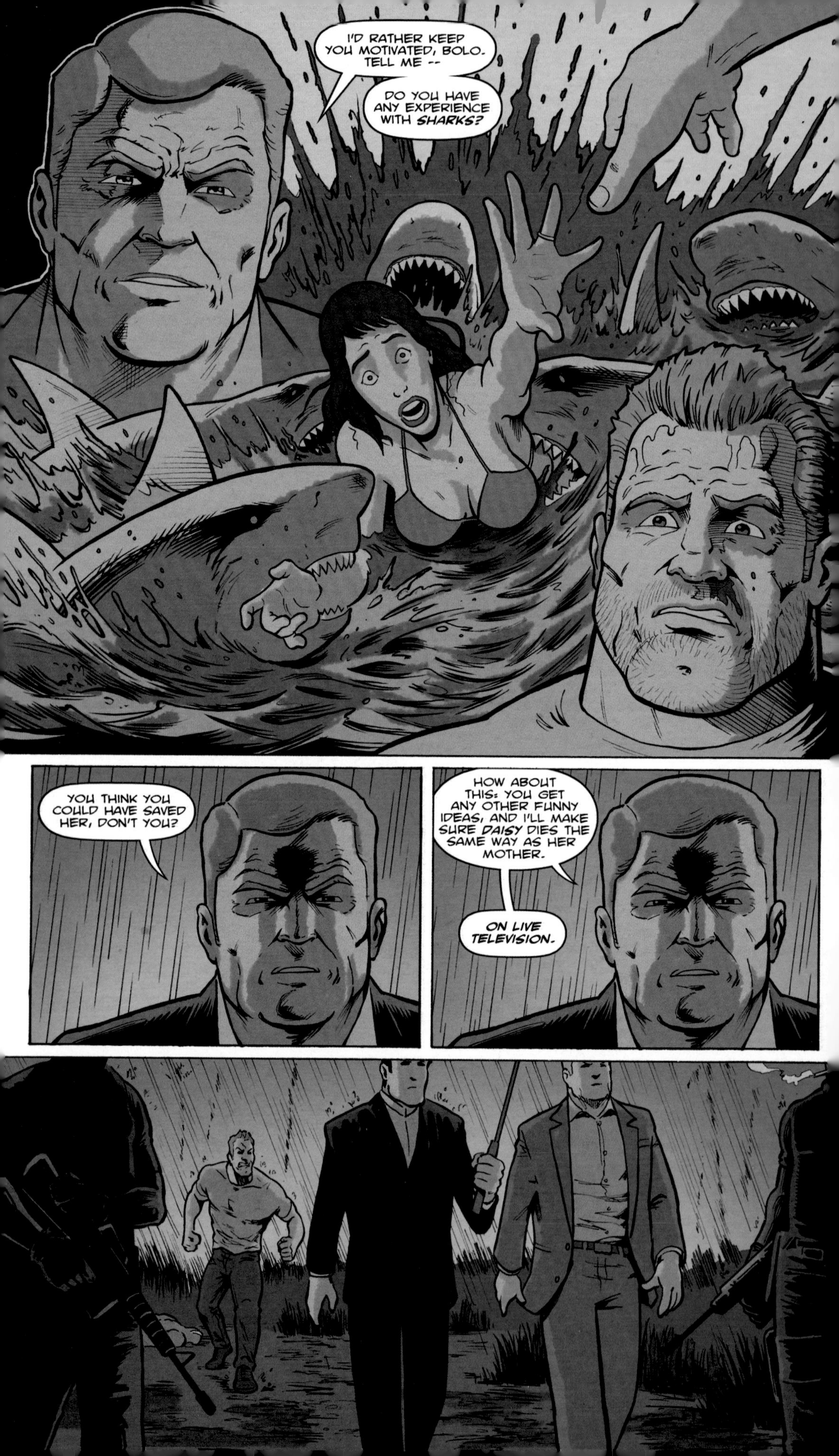
I'D RATHER KEEP YOU MOTIVATED, BOLO. TELL ME --
DO YOU HAVE ANY EXPERIENCE WITH SHARKS?
YOU THINK YOU COULD HAVE SAVED HER, DON'T YOU?
HOW ABOUT THIS: YOU GET ANY OTHER FUNNY IDEAS, AND I'LL MAKE SURE DAISY DIES THE SAME WAY AS HER MOTHER.
ON LIVE TELEVISION.

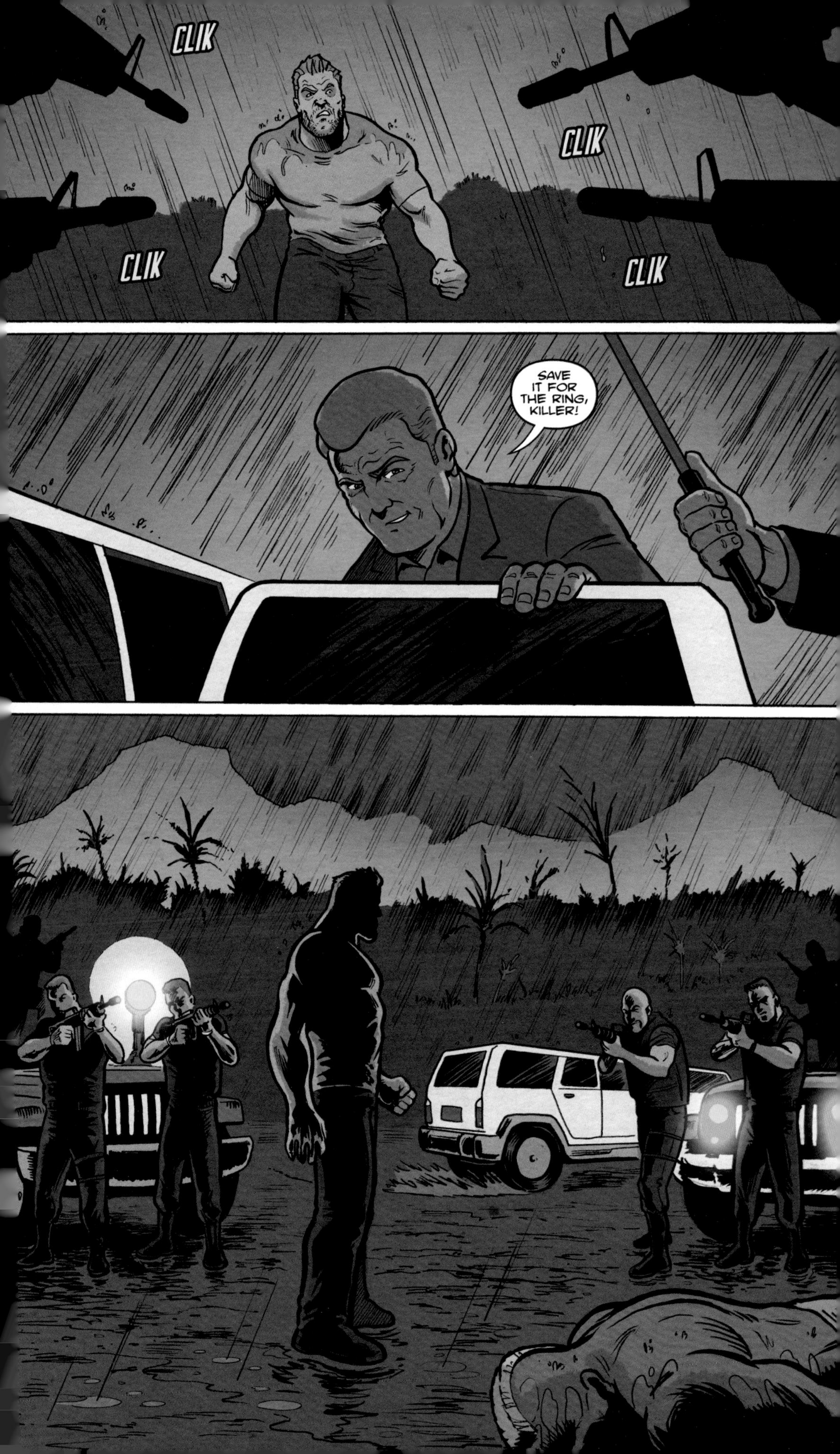
CLIK
CLIK
CLIK
CLIK
SAVE IT FOR THE RING, KILLER!

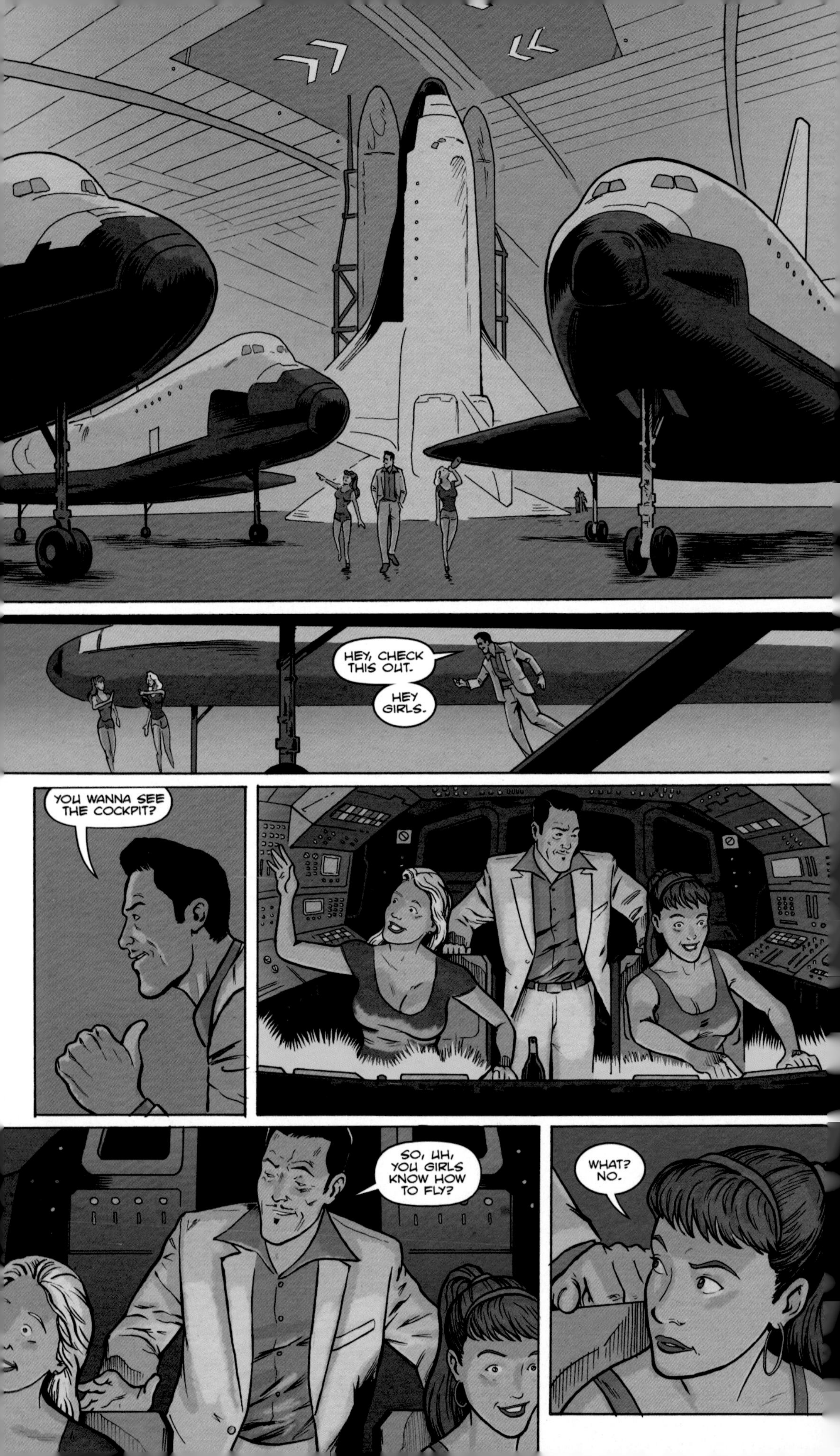
HEY, CHECK THIS OUT.
HEY GIRLS.
YOU WANNA SEE THE COCKPIT?
SO, UH, YOU GIRLS KNOW HOW TO FLY?
WHAT? NO.

I DO.

I HAD TO LAND THIS PLANE ONCE WHEN THESE TERRORISTS KILLED THE PILOT.

IT WAS COOL.

THIS ISN'T A PLANE, SWEETHEART. IT'S A SPACESHIP.

I'M GOING TO THE MOON.

YOU GIRLS ARE COMING, RIGHT?

YEAH, SURE EDDIE.

CAN WE GO SEE MY DAD NOW?

CAN YOU FLY THIS PLANE?

YEAH, IN A LITTLE WHILE.

I'M SERIOUS. YOU GUYS ARE ON THE LIST, RIGHT?

WHAT LIST? I'M NOT ON ANY LIST.

REALLY? FUCK, I GOTTA GET YOU ON THE LIST...

I'M NOT SUPPOSED TO TELL YOU THIS, BUT THE COMPANY I WORK FOR? THEY'RE UP ON A LOT OF TOP SECRET SHIT, RIGHT? AND THEY'RE GONNA START EVACUATING PEOPLE TO THE MOON LIKE, REAL SOON.

THIS COMET'S HEADED RIGHT FOR EARTH AND IF WE DON'T GET OUTTA HERE WE'RE FUCKED, KNOW WHAT I MEAN?

DAMN, I SHOULDN'T BE TELLING YOU THIS.

I COULD LOSE MY JOB.

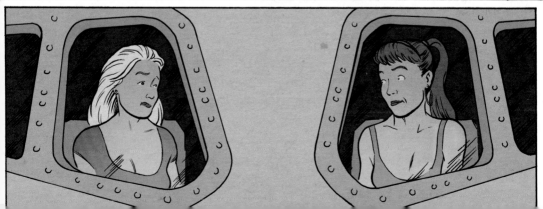

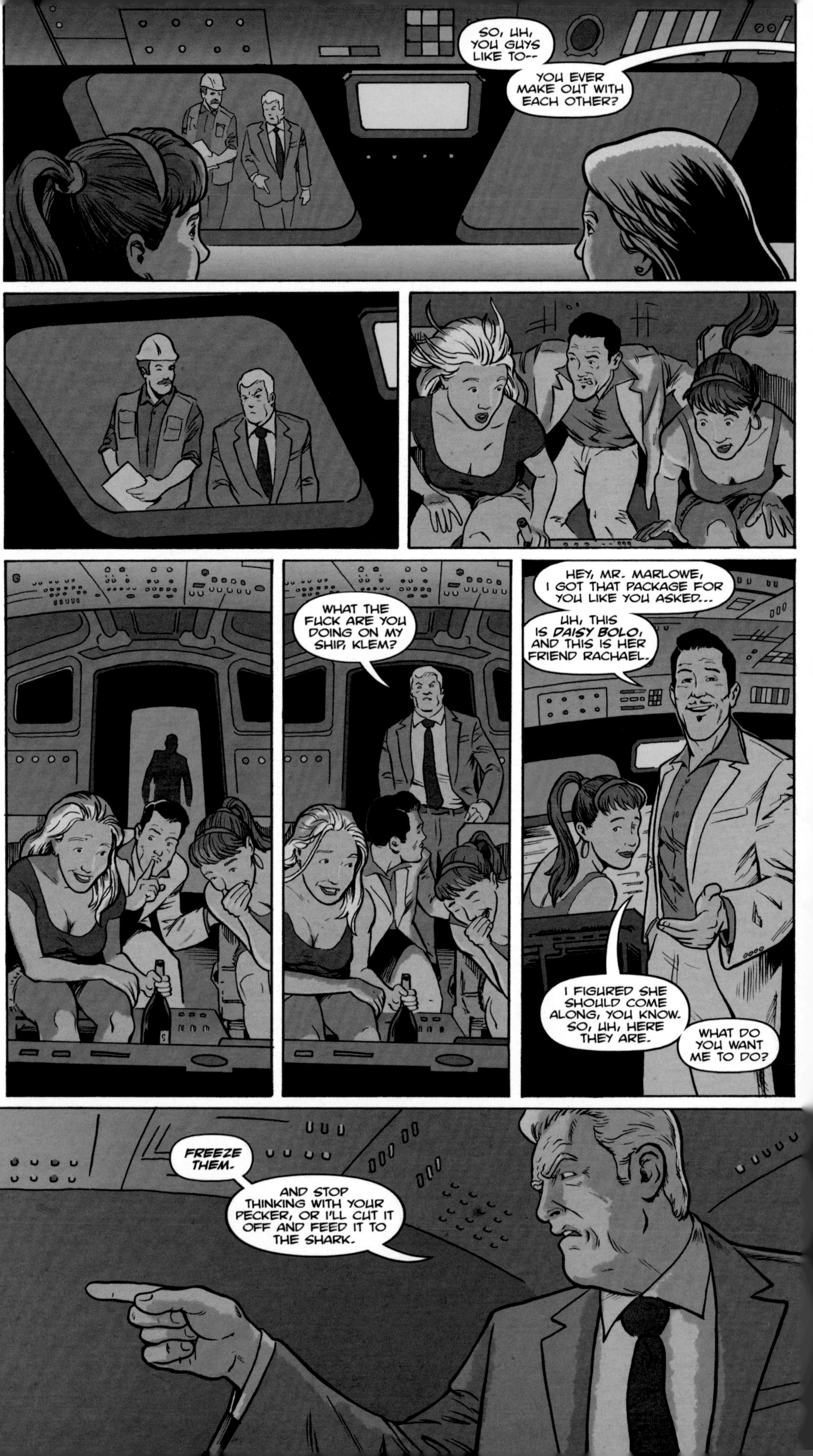
SO, UH, YOU GUYS LIKE TO--
YOU EVER MAKE OUT WITH EACH OTHER?
WHAT THE FUCK ARE YOU DOING ON MY SHIP, KLEM?
HEY, MR. MARLOWE, I GOT THAT PACKAGE FOR YOU LIKE YOU ASKED...
UH, THIS IS DAISY BOLO, AND THIS IS HER FRIEND RACHAEL.
I FIGURED SHE SHOULD COME ALONG, YOU KNOW. SO, UH, HERE THEY ARE.
WHAT DO YOU WANT ME TO DO?
FREEZE THEM.
AND STOP THINKING WITH YOUR PECKER, OR I'LL CUT IT OFF AND FEED IT TO THE SHARK.

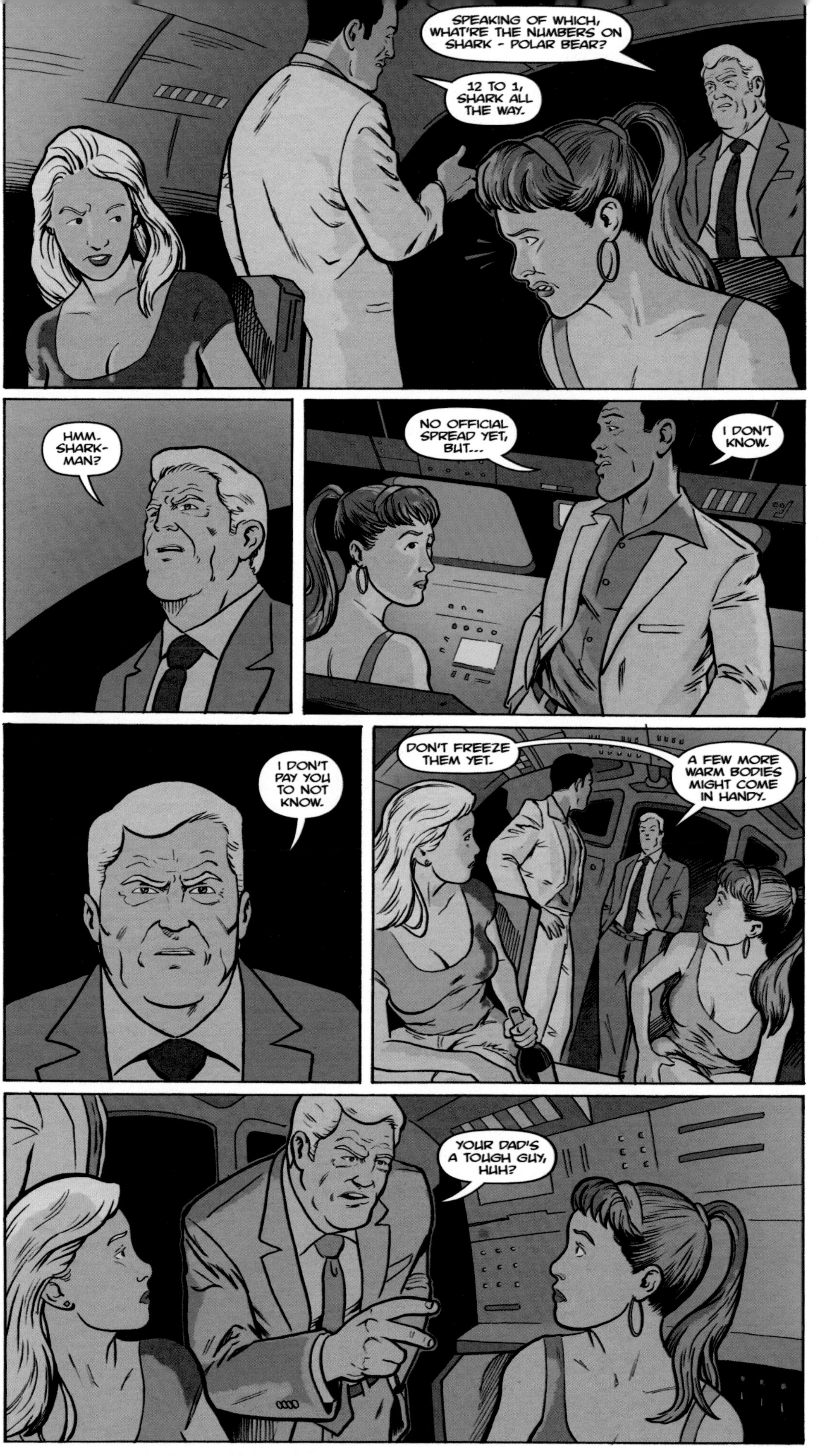
SPEAKING OF WHICH, WHAT'RE THE NUMBERS ON SHARK - POLAR BEAR?
12 TO 1, SHARK ALL THE WAY.
HMM. SHARK-MAN?
NO OFFICIAL SPREAD YET, BUT...
I DON'T KNOW.
I DON'T PAY YOU TO NOT KNOW.
DON'T FREEZE THEM YET.
A FEW MORE WARM BODIES MIGHT COME IN HANDY.
YOUR DAD'S A TOUGH GUY, HUH?

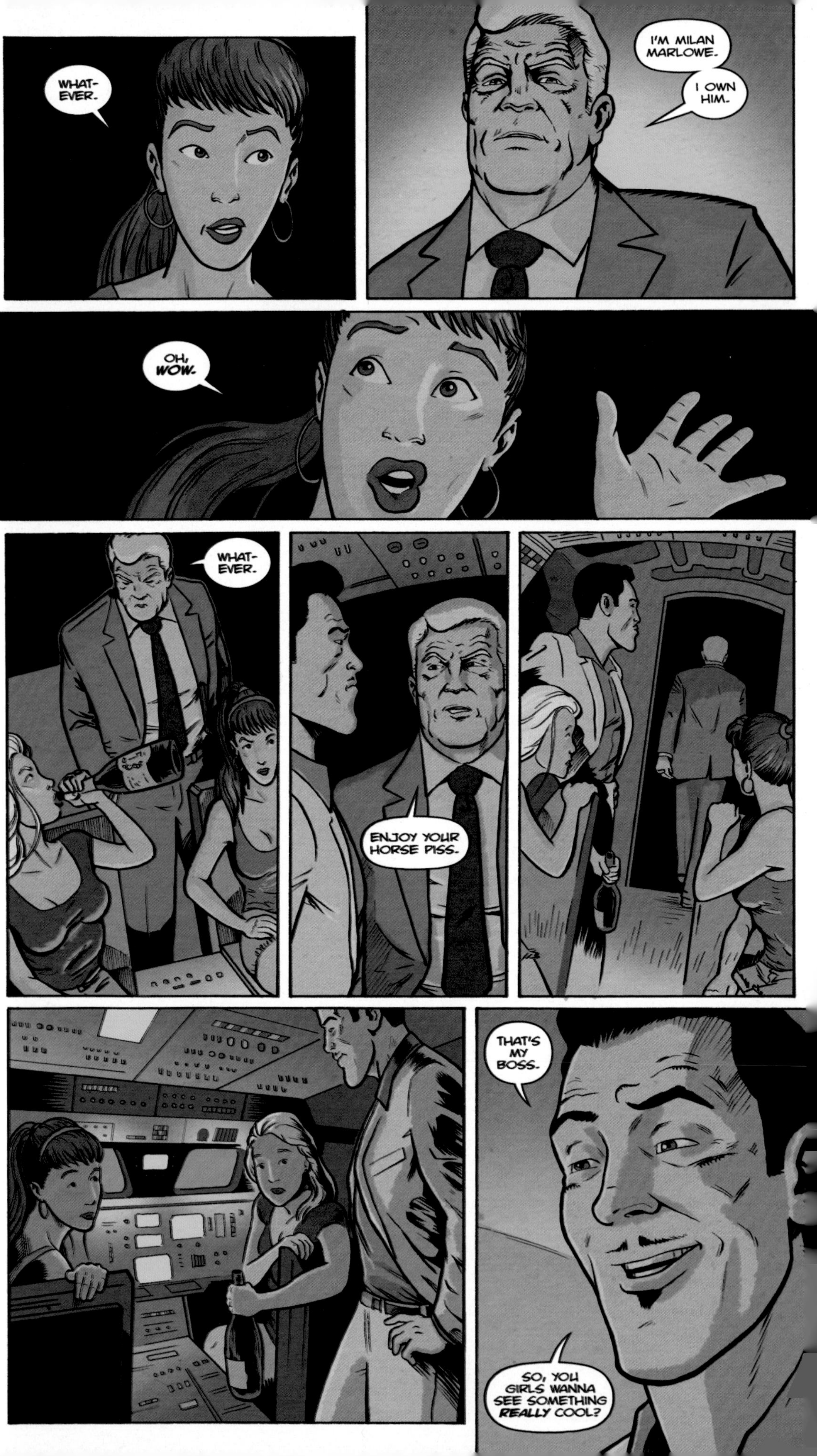
WHAT-EVER.
I'M MILAN MARLOWE.
I OWN HIM.
OH, *WOW.*
WHAT-EVER.
ENJOY YOUR HORSE PISS.
THAT'S MY BOSS.
SO, YOU GIRLS WANNA SEE SOMETHING *REALLY* COOL?

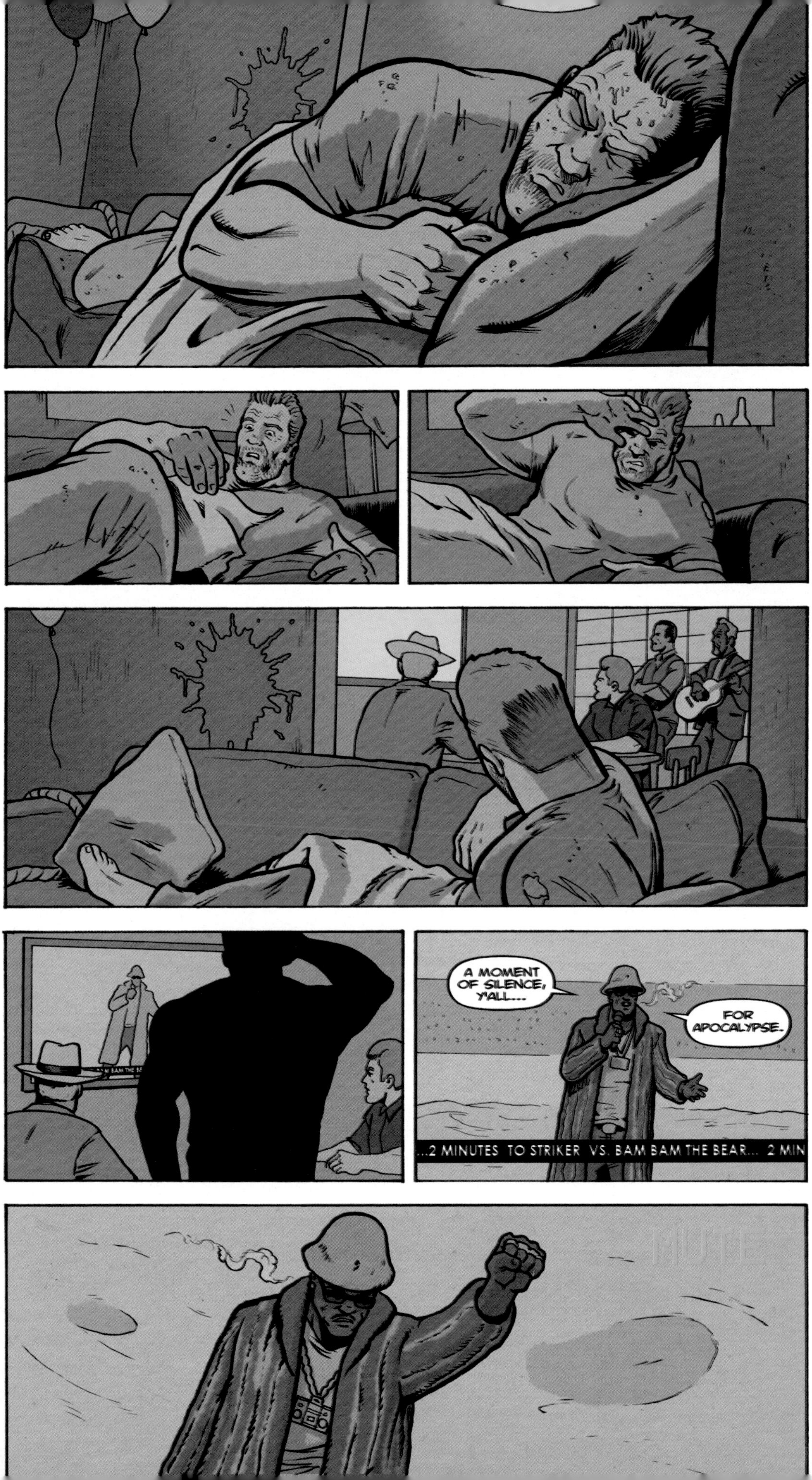
A MOMENT OF SILENCE, Y'ALL...
FOR APOCALYPSE.
...2 MINUTES TO STRIKER VS. BAM BAM THE BEAR... 2 MIN

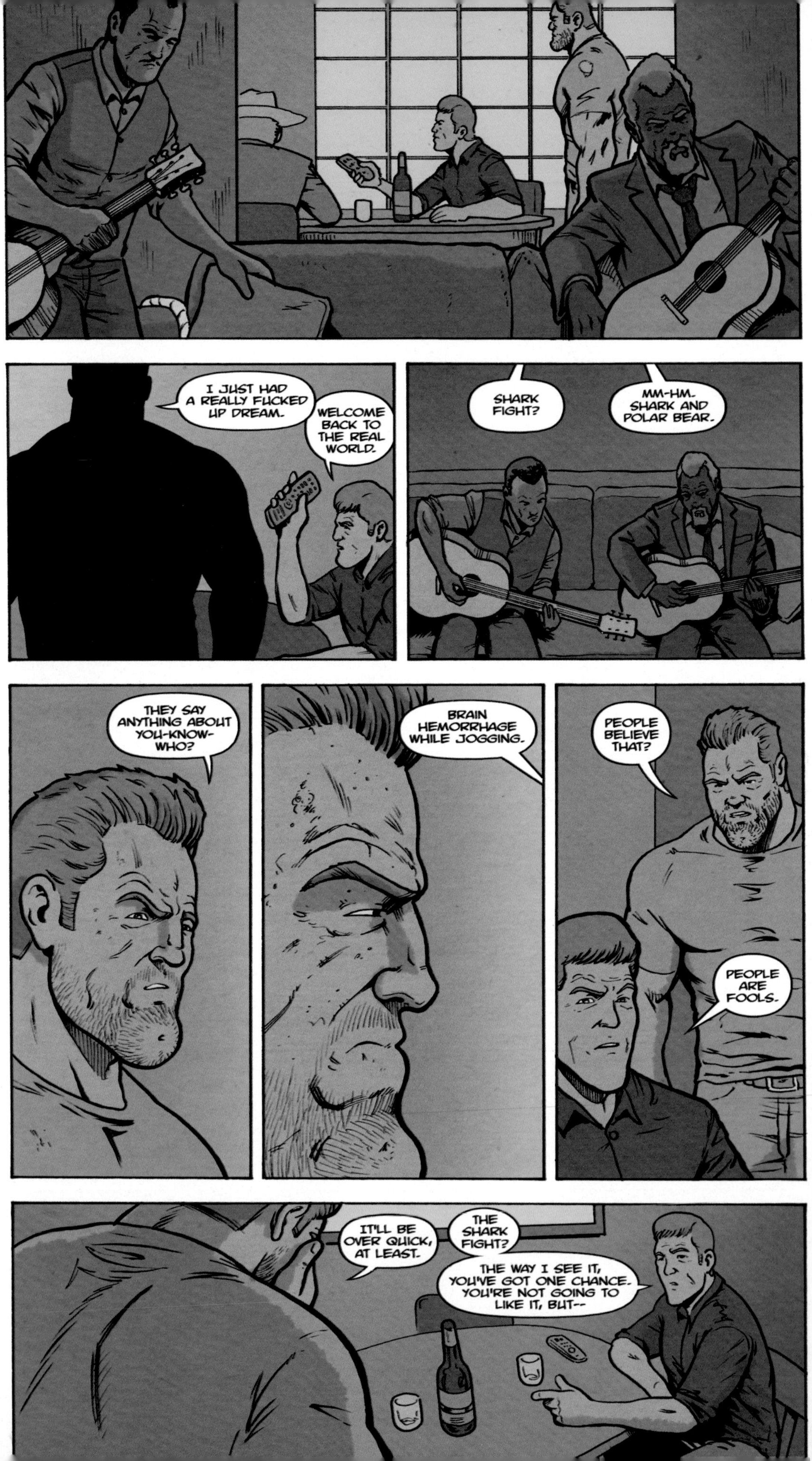
I JUST HAD A REALLY FUCKED UP DREAM.
WELCOME BACK TO THE REAL WORLD.
SHARK FIGHT?
MM-HM. SHARK AND POLAR BEAR.
THEY SAY ANYTHING ABOUT YOU-KNOW-WHO?
BRAIN HEMORRHAGE WHILE JOGGING.
PEOPLE BELIEVE THAT?
PEOPLE ARE FOOLS.
IT'LL BE OVER QUICK, AT LEAST.
THE SHARK FIGHT?
THE WAY I SEE IT, YOU'VE GOT ONE CHANCE. YOU'RE NOT GOING TO LIKE IT, BUT--

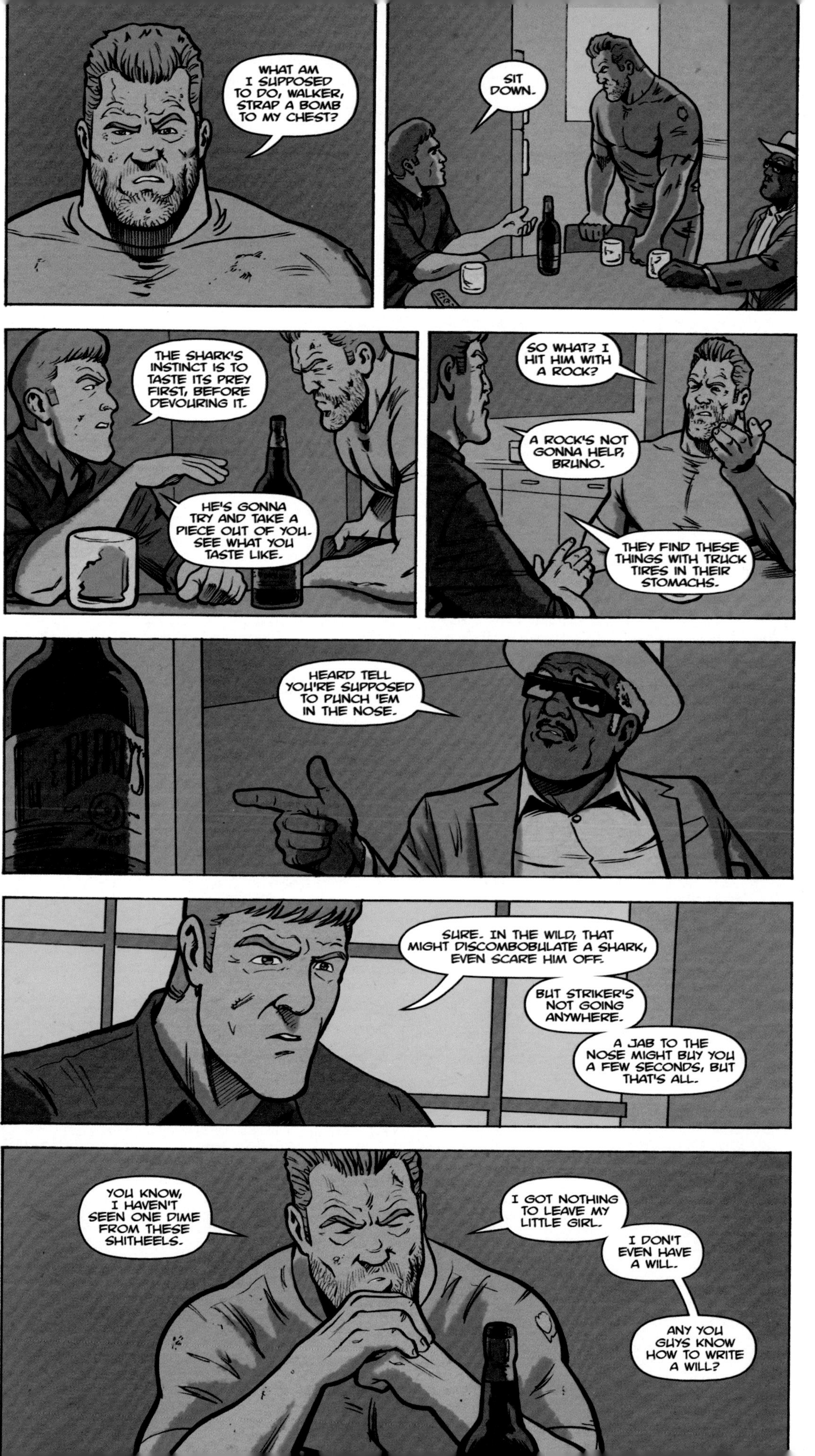
WHAT AM I SUPPOSED TO DO, WALKER, STRAP A BOMB TO MY CHEST?
SIT DOWN.
THE SHARK'S INSTINCT IS TO TASTE ITS PREY FIRST, BEFORE DEVOURING IT.
HE'S GONNA TRY AND TAKE A PIECE OUT OF YOU. SEE WHAT YOU TASTE LIKE.
SO WHAT? I HIT HIM WITH A ROCK?
A ROCK'S NOT GONNA HELP, BRUNO.
THEY FIND THESE THINGS WITH TRUCK TIRES IN THEIR STOMACHS.
HEARD TELL YOU'RE SUPPOSED TO PUNCH 'EM IN THE NOSE.
SURE. IN THE WILD, THAT MIGHT DISCOMBOBULATE A SHARK, EVEN SCARE HIM OFF.
BUT STRIKER'S NOT GOING ANYWHERE.
A JAB TO THE NOSE MIGHT BUY YOU A FEW SECONDS, BUT THAT'S ALL.
YOU KNOW, I HAVEN'T SEEN ONE DIME FROM THESE SHITHEELS.
I GOT NOTHING TO LEAVE MY LITTLE GIRL.
I DON'T EVEN HAVE A WILL.
ANY YOU GUYS KNOW HOW TO WRITE A WILL?

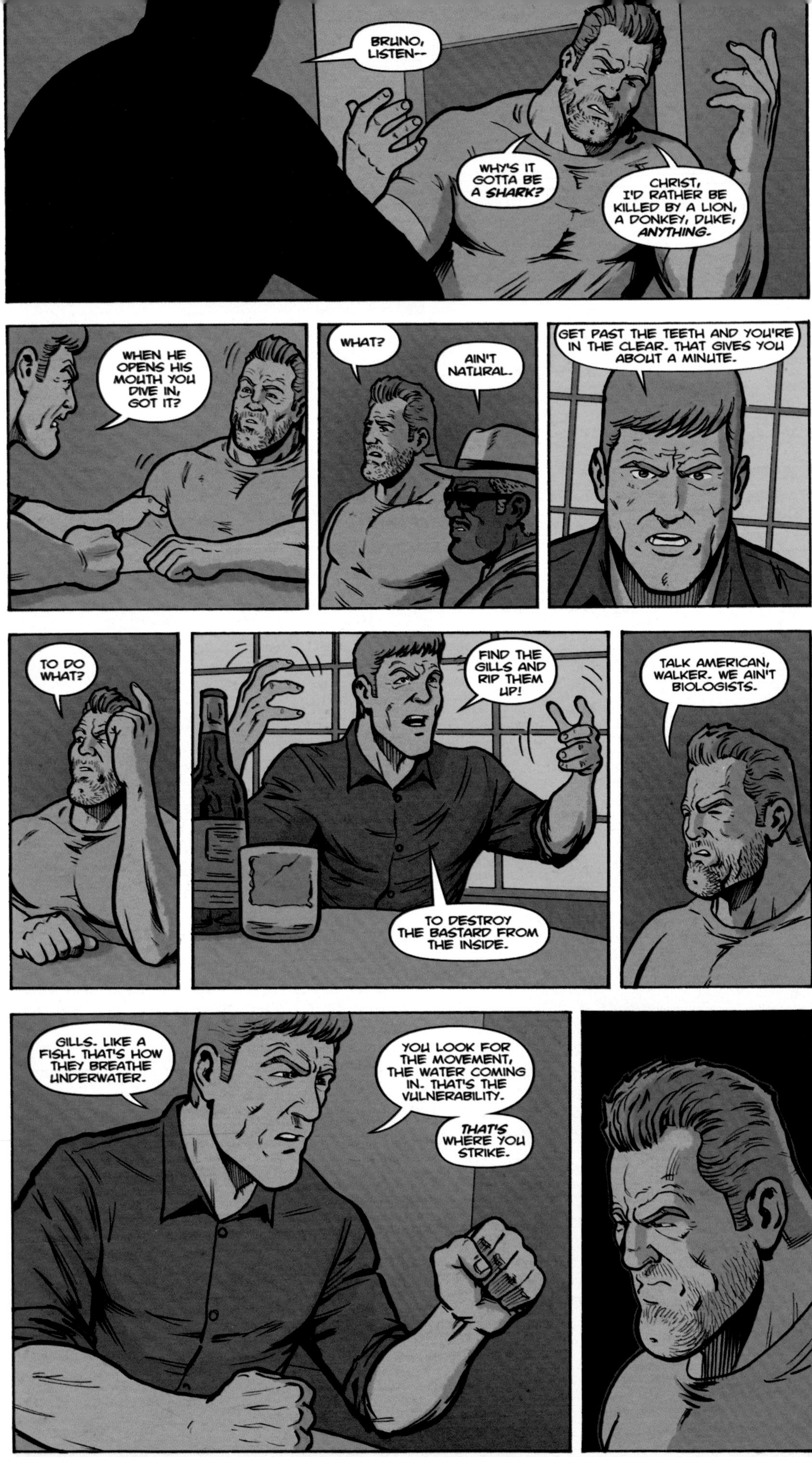
BRUNO, LISTEN--
WHY'S IT GOTTA BE A *SHARK?*
CHRIST, I'D RATHER BE KILLED BY A LION, A DONKEY, DUKE, *ANYTHING.*
WHEN HE OPENS HIS MOUTH YOU DIVE IN, GOT IT?
WHAT?
AIN'T NATURAL.
GET PAST THE TEETH AND YOU'RE IN THE CLEAR. THAT GIVES YOU ABOUT A MINUTE.
TO DO WHAT?
FIND THE GILLS AND RIP THEM UP!
TO DESTROY THE BASTARD FROM THE INSIDE.
TALK AMERICAN, WALKER. WE AIN'T BIOLOGISTS.
GILLS. LIKE A FISH. THAT'S HOW THEY BREATHE UNDERWATER.
YOU LOOK FOR THE MOVEMENT, THE WATER COMING IN. THAT'S THE VULNERABILITY.
THAT'S WHERE YOU STRIKE.

SO WHAT YOU'RE SAYING IS, ALL I HAVE TO DO IS DIVE HEADFIRST INTO THE SUPERSHARK, PAST A MILLION FUCKIN' ROWS OF TEETH, AND THEN I'M INSIDE HIM AND SOMEHOW I FIND THE GILLS AND RIP 'EM OUT. AND I'M GOOD.

EXACTLY.

TIME FOR A DRINK.

HEY, LOOK ON THE BRIGHT SIDE --

IT'S NOT NECESSARILY GOING TO BE THE SHARK...

BEASTMAS. NETWORK

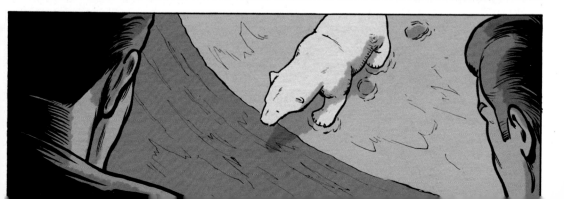

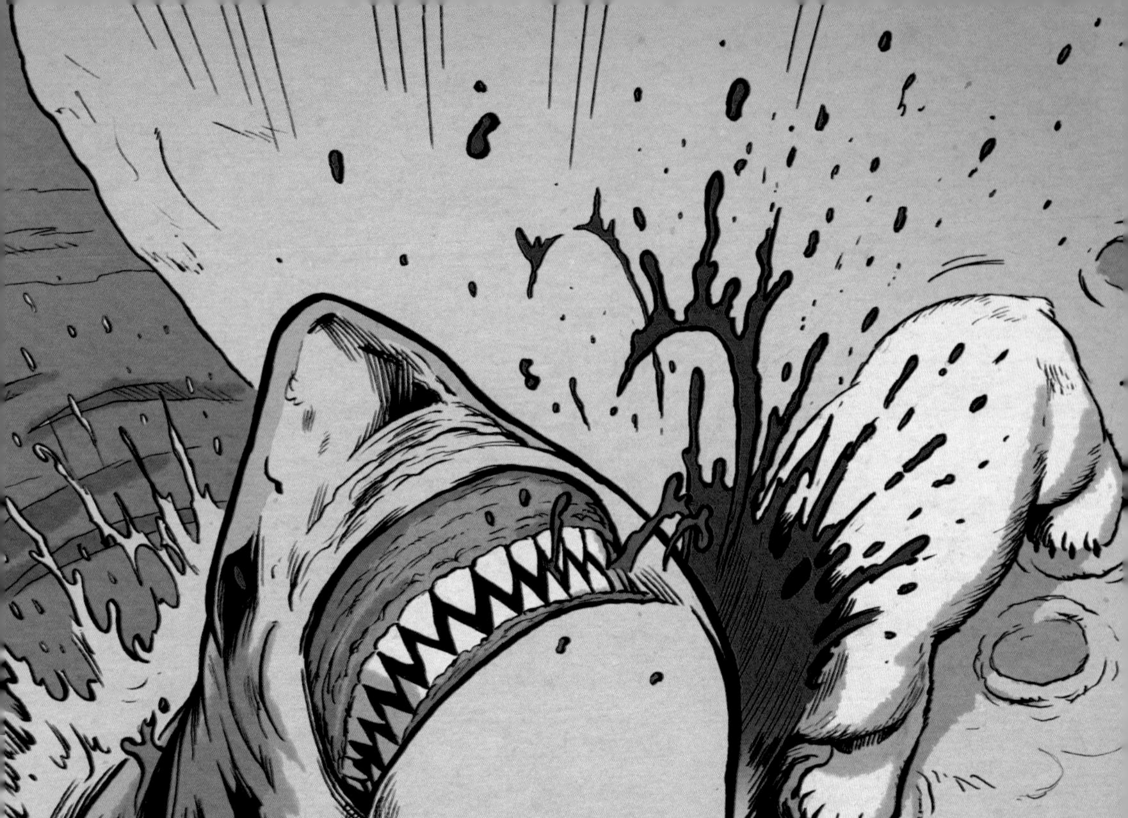
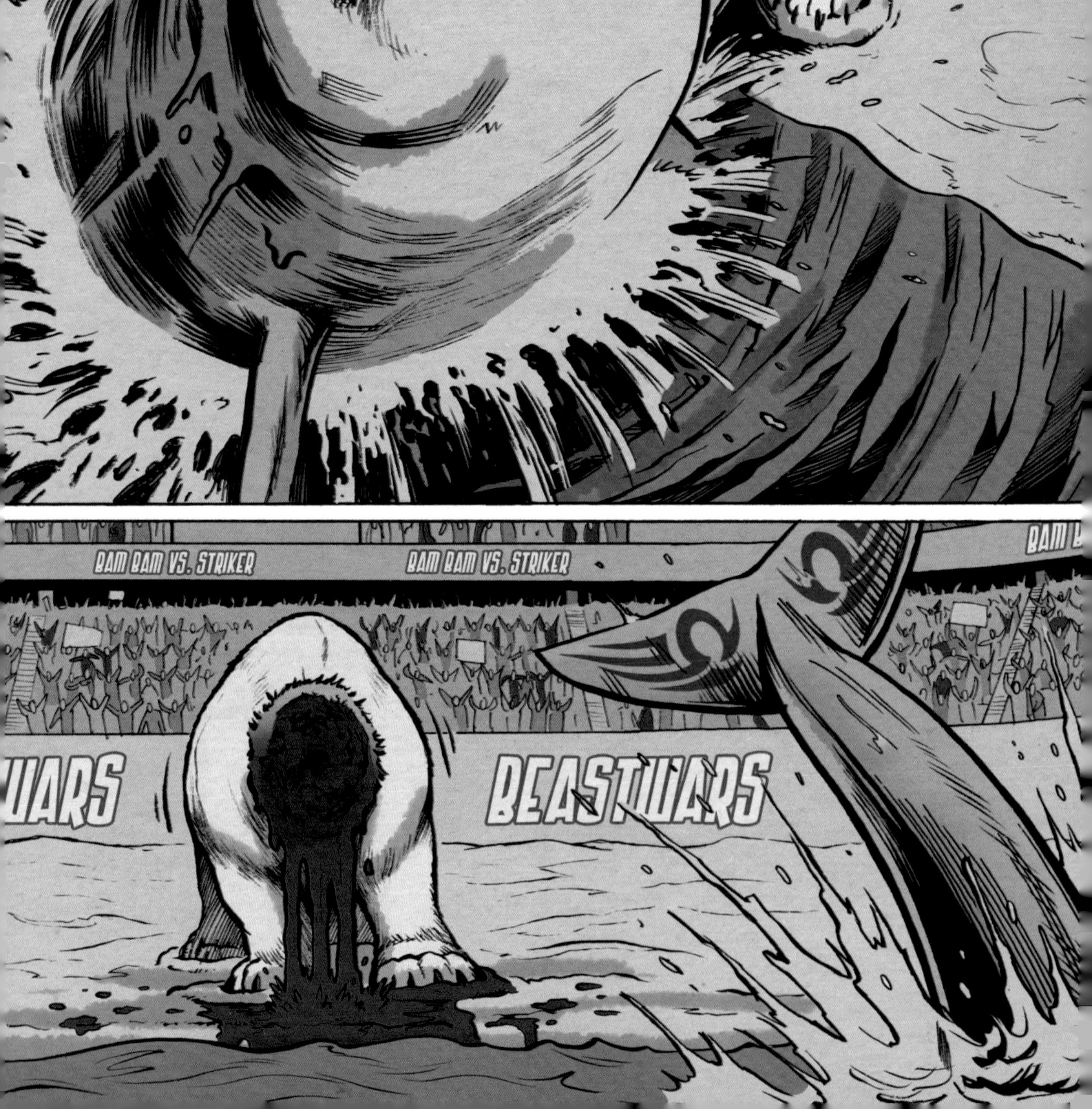
BAM BAM VS. STRIKER
BAM BAM VS. STRIKER
BEASTWARS

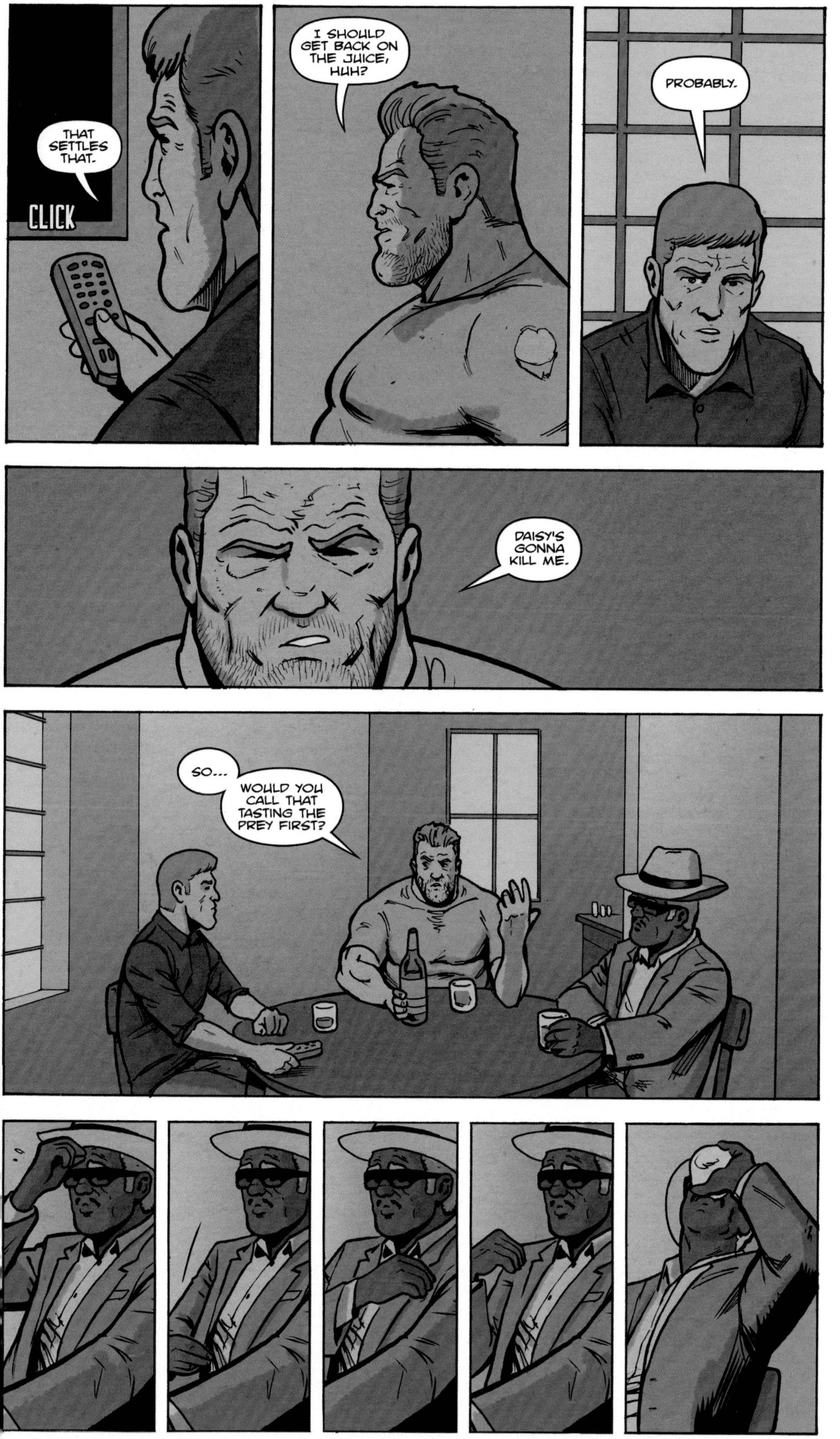
THAT SETTLES THAT.
CLICK
I SHOULD GET BACK ON THE JUICE, HUH?
PROBABLY.
DAISY'S GONNA KILL ME.
SO...
WOULD YOU CALL THAT TASTING THE PREY FIRST?

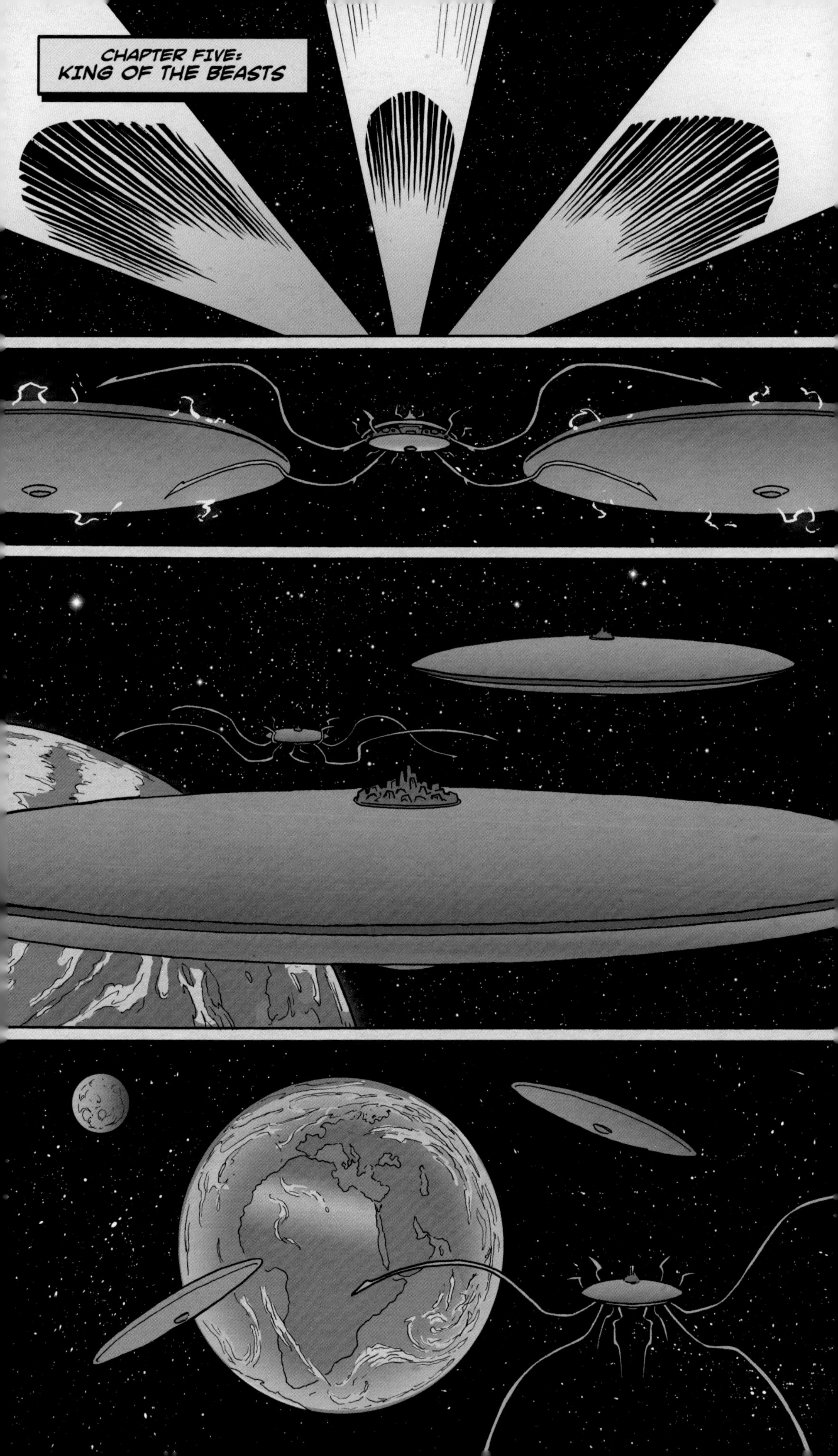
CHAPTER FIVE:
KING OF THE BEASTS

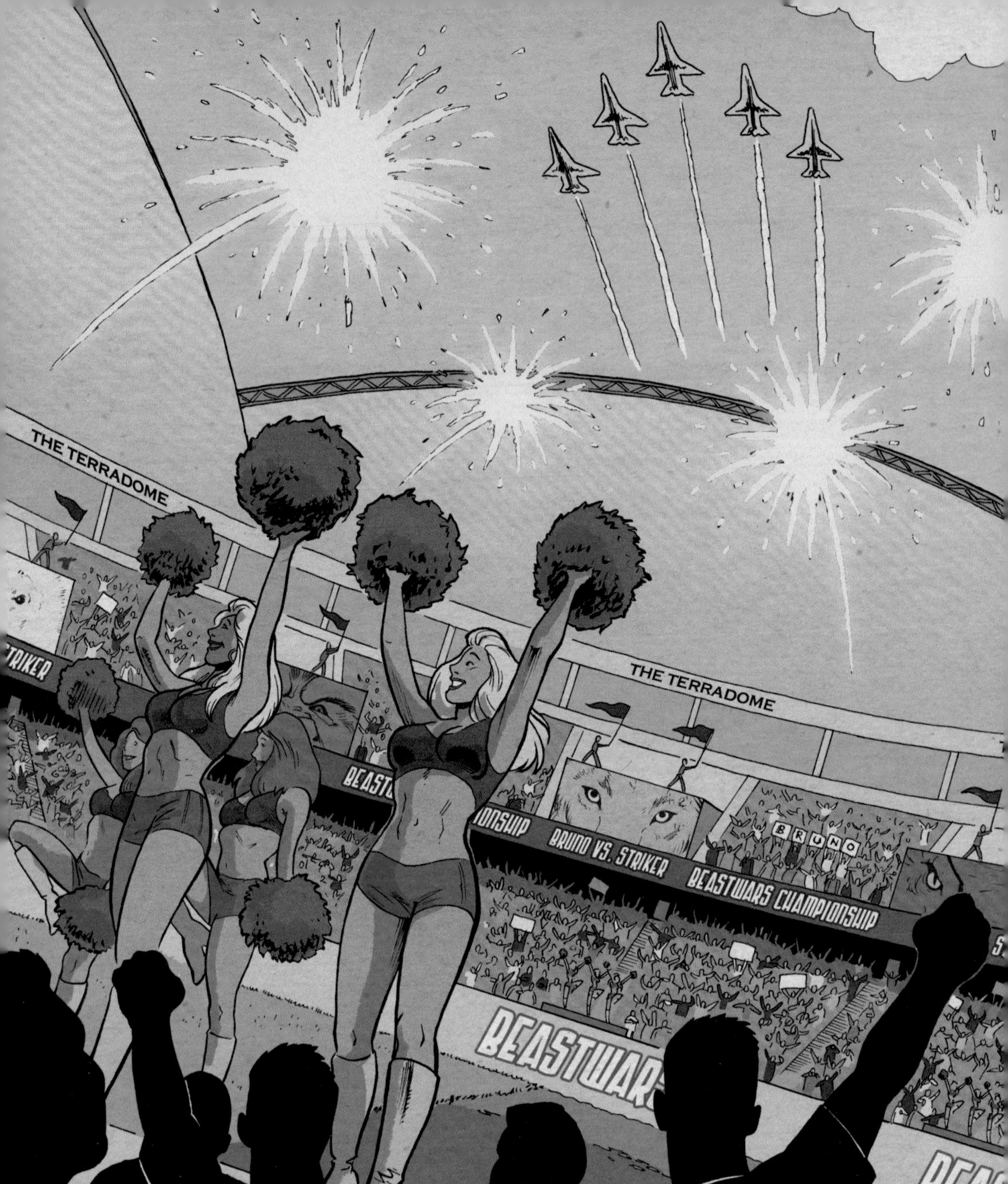
THE TERRADOME
STRIKER
THE TERRADOME
BRUNO VS. STRIKER
BEASTWARS CHAMPIONSHIP
BRUNO
BEASTWARS
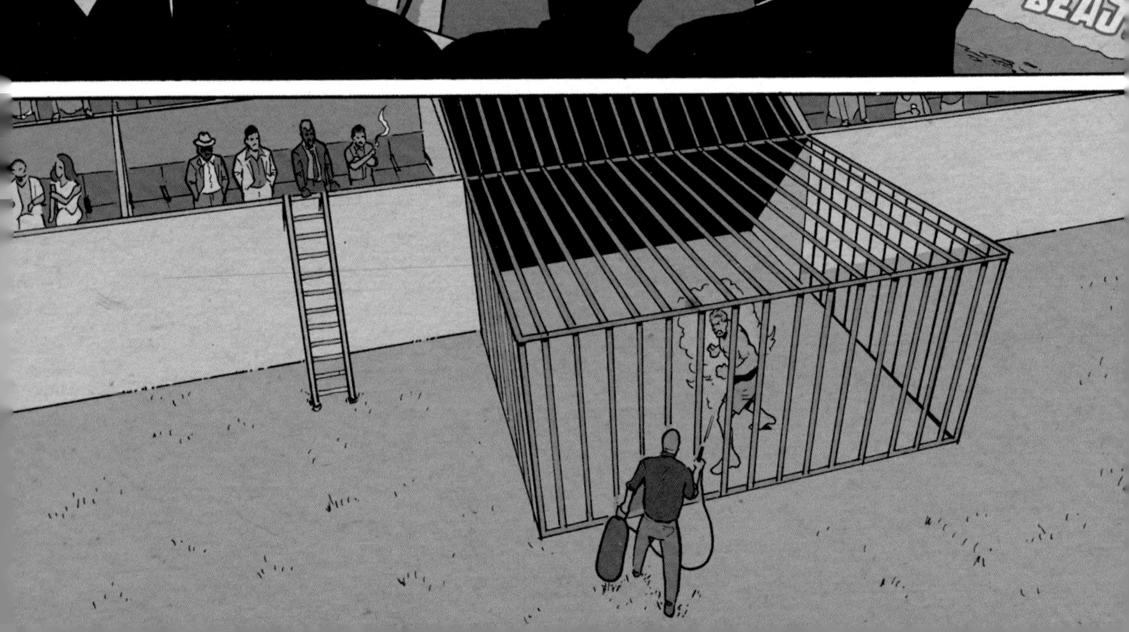

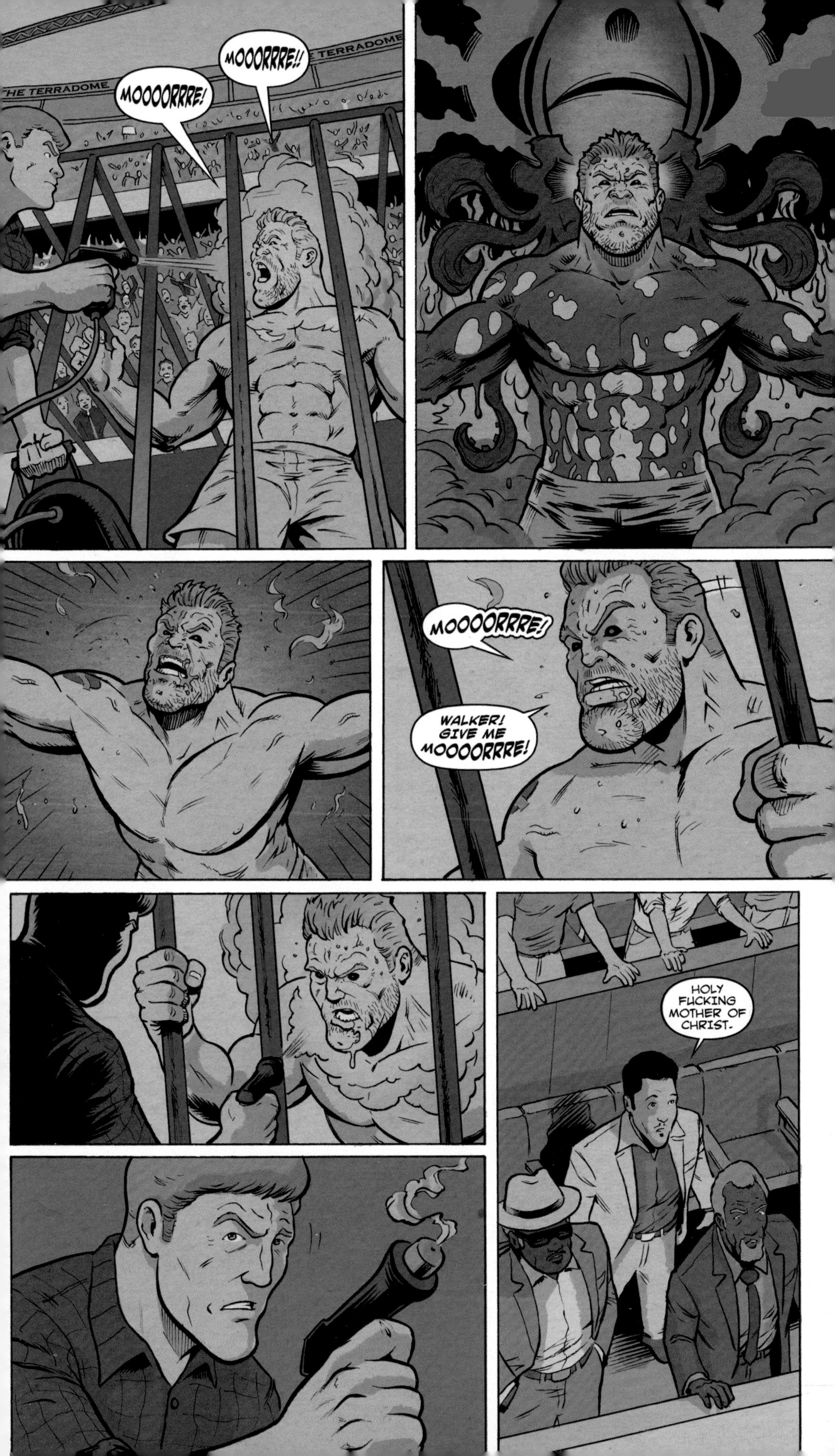
THE TERRADOME
TERRADOME
MOOOORRRE!
MOOORRRE!!
MOOOORRRE!
WALKER! GIVE ME MOOOORRRE!
HOLY FUCKING MOTHER OF CHRIST.

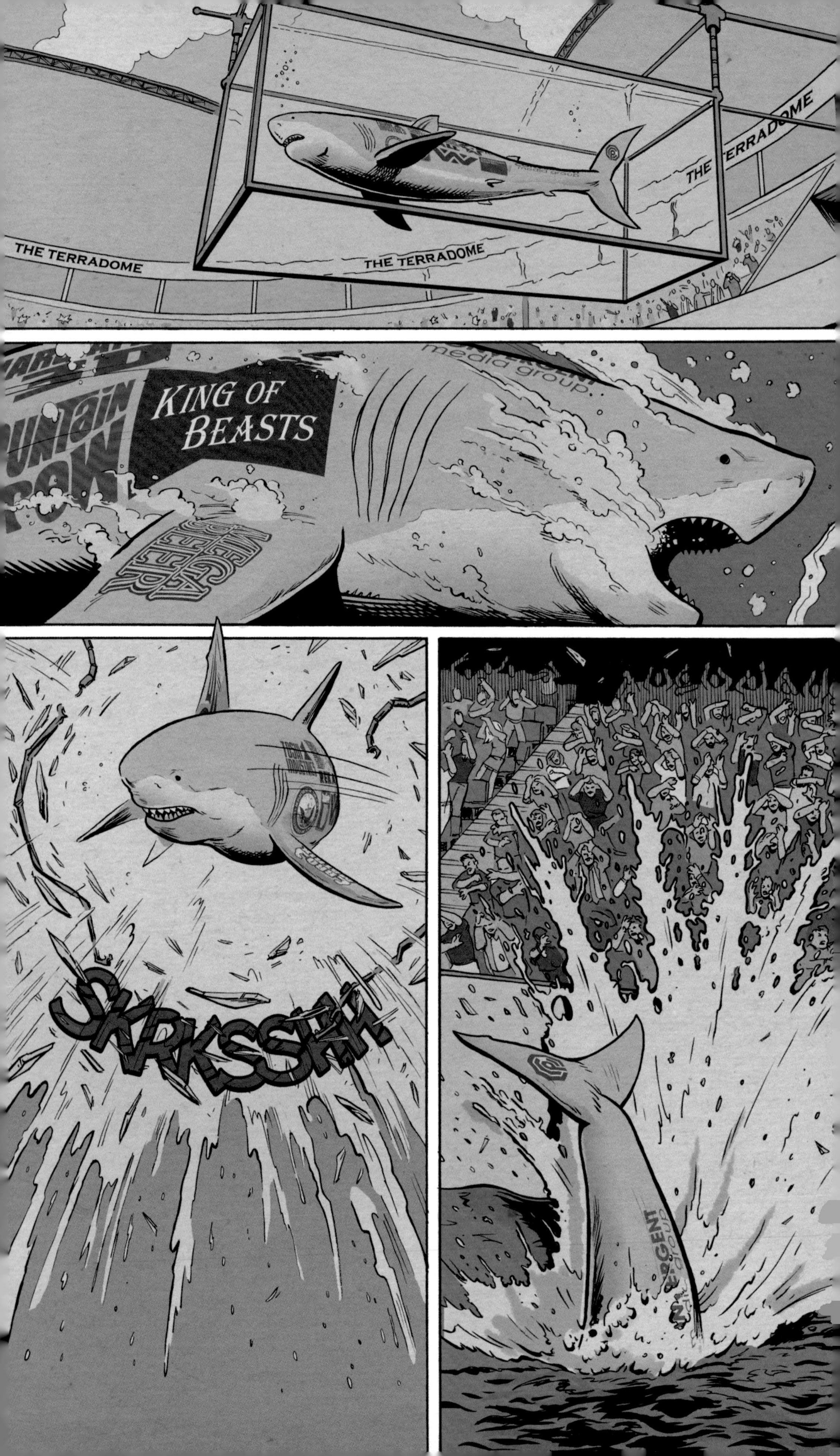
THE TERRADOME
THE TERRADOME
THE TERRADOME
THE TERRADOME
media group
KING OF BEASTS
SKRKSSHH

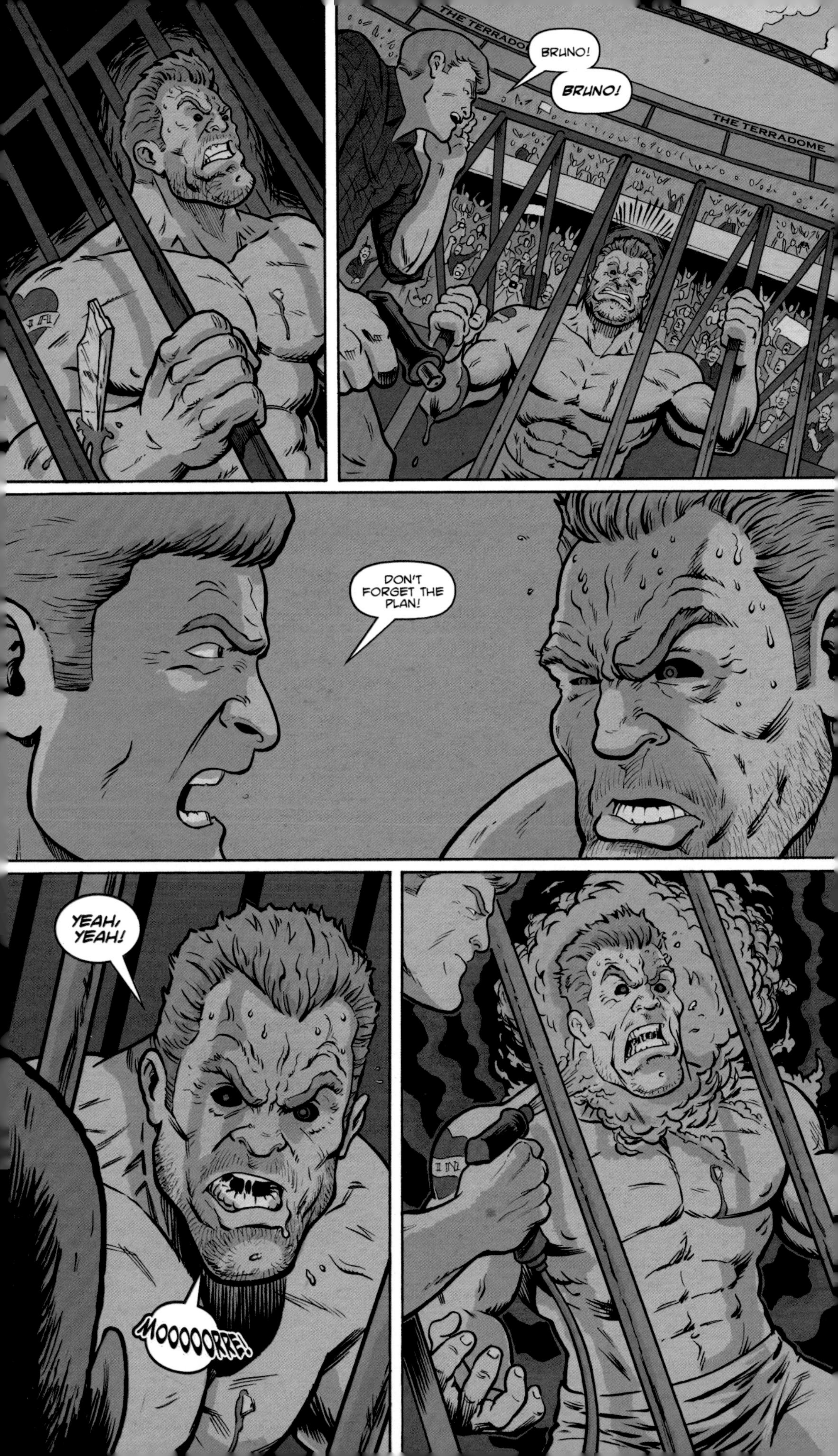
THE TERRADOME
BRUNO!
BRUNO!
THE TERRADOME
DON'T FORGET THE PLAN!
YEAH, YEAH!
MOOOOORRE!

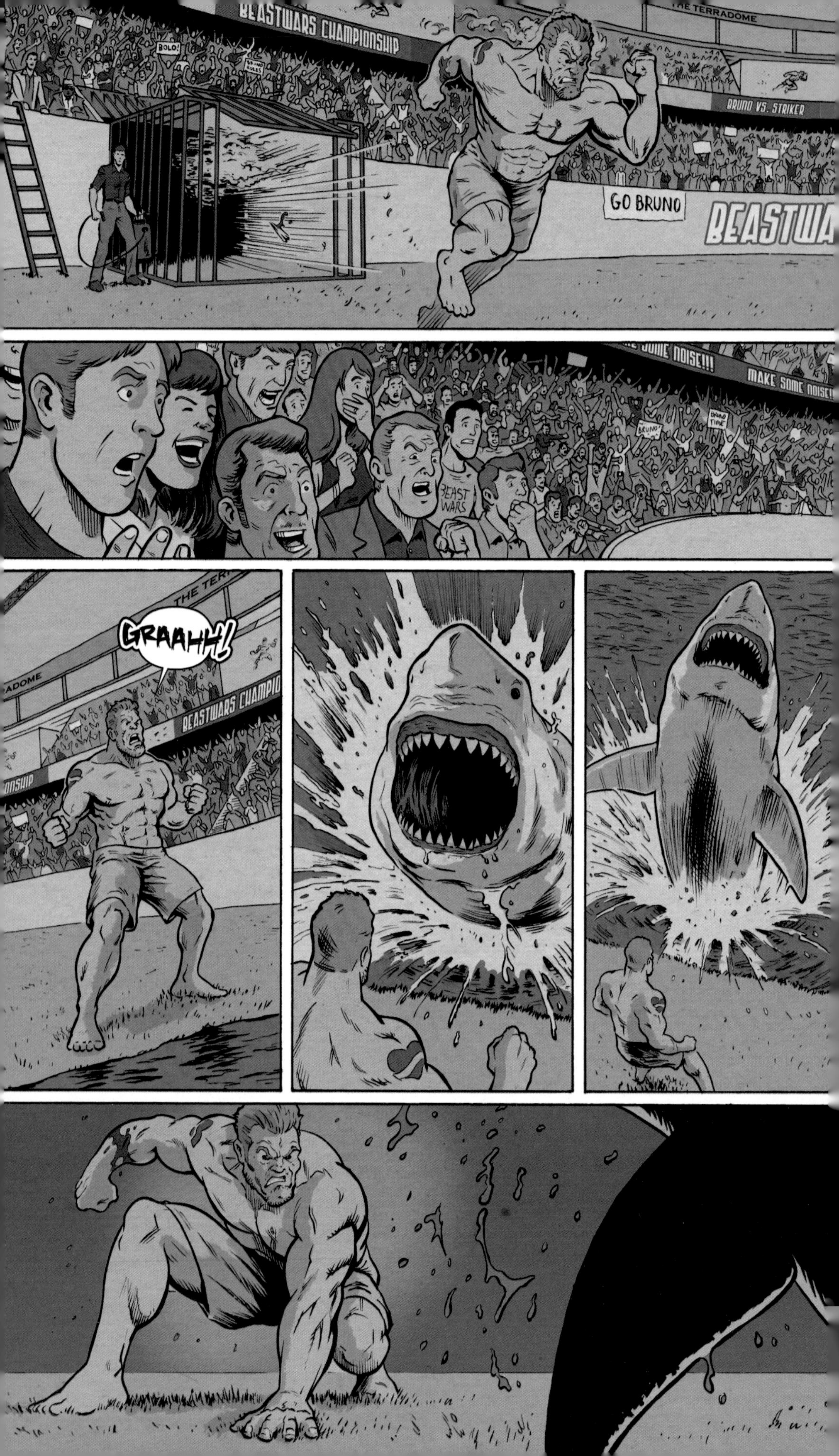
BEASTWARS CHAMPIONSHIP
THE TERRADOME
BRUNO VS. STRIKER
GO BRUNO
BEASTWA
MAKE SOME NOISE!!!
MAKE SOME NOISE!
BRUNO!
BRUNO TIME
BEAST WARS
THE TERR
RADOME
BEASTWARS CHAMPIO
ONSHIP
GRAAHH!

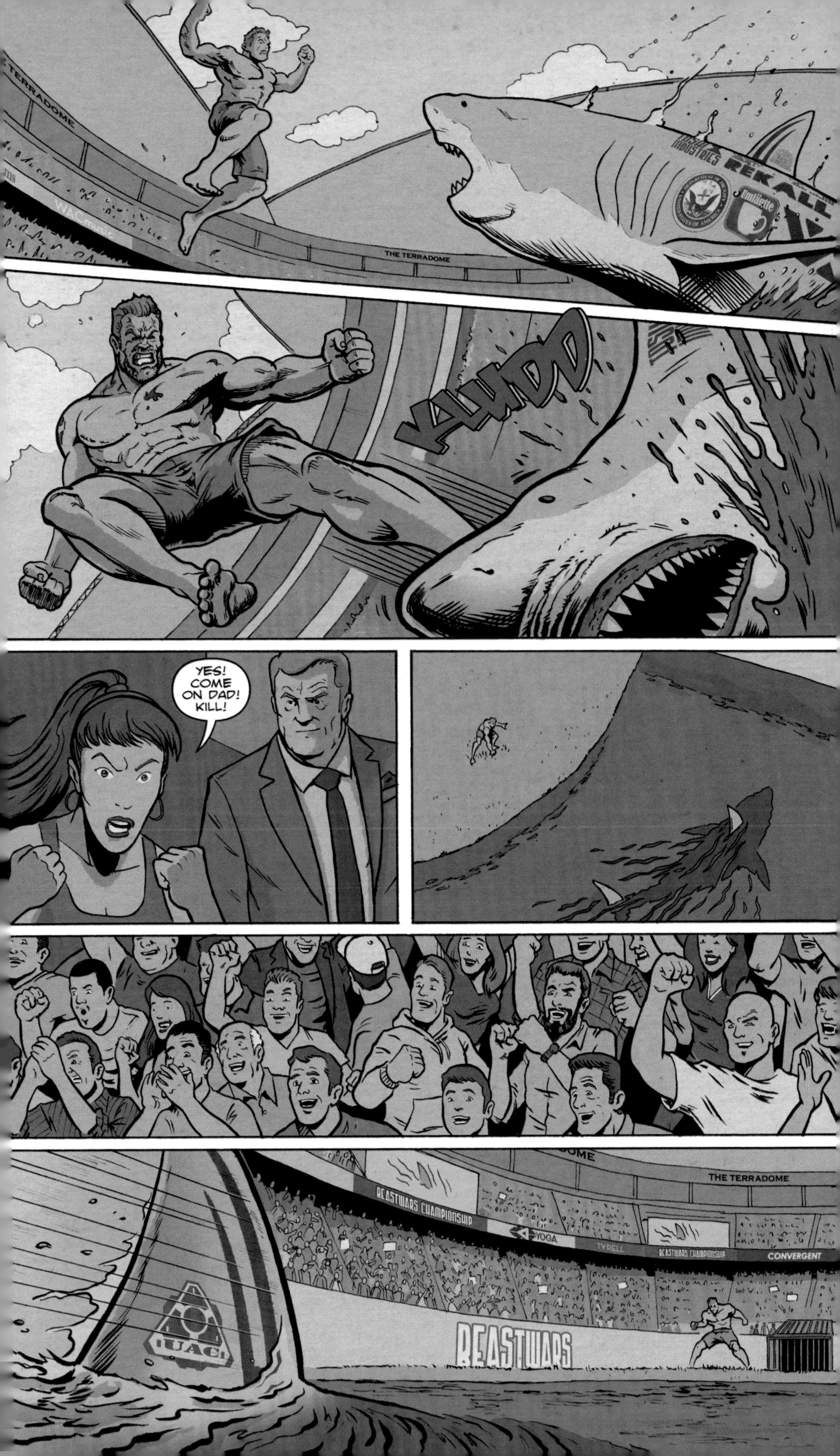

THE TERRADOME
WACmusic
REKALL
THE TERRADOME
KLUDD
YES! COME ON DAD! KILL!
THE TERRADOME
BEASTWARS CHAMPIONSHIP
YOGA
TYRELL
BEASTWARS CHAMPIONSHIP
CONVERGENT
UAC
BEASTWARS

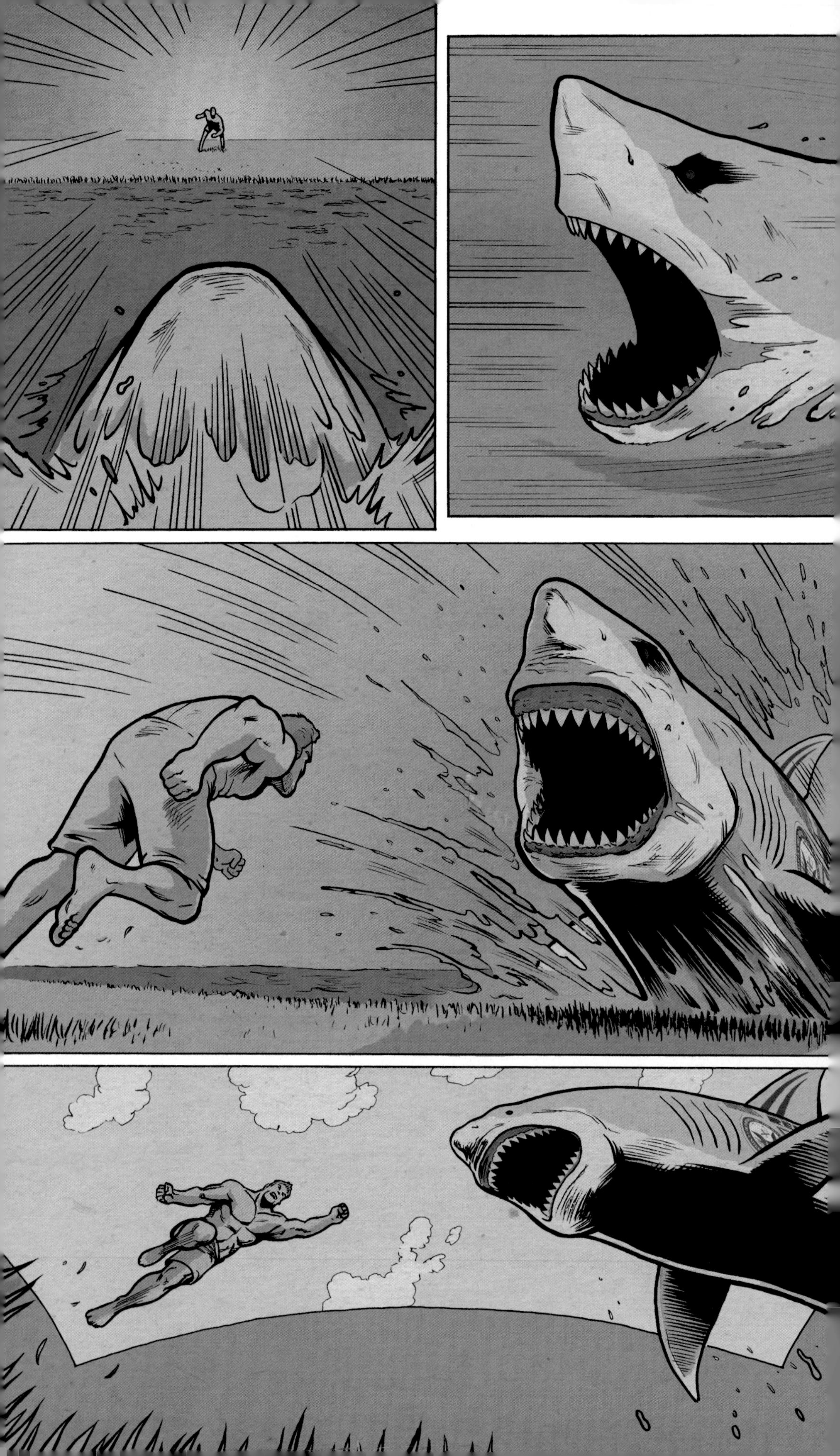

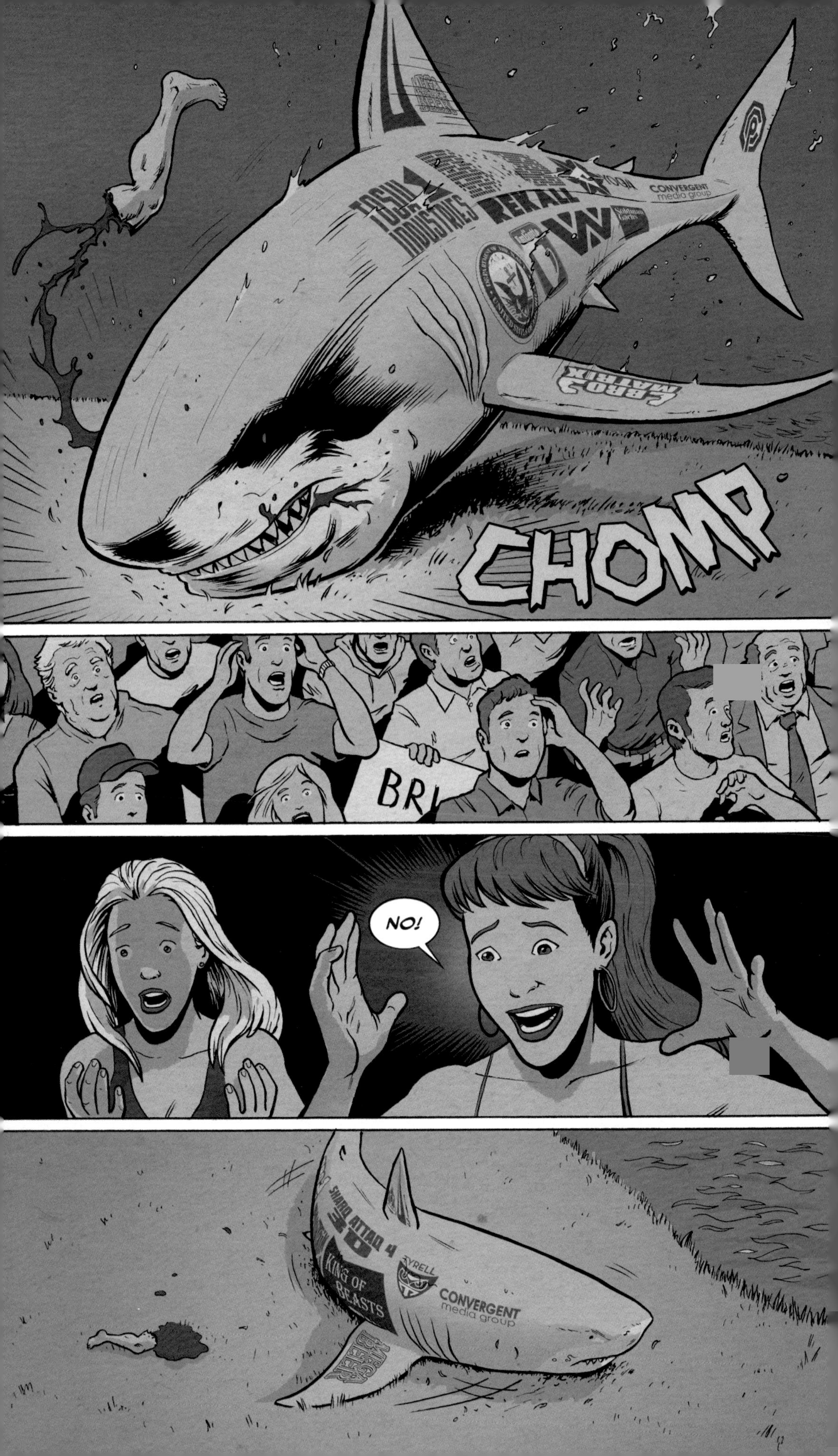
REKALL
CONVERGENT
media group
CHOMP
BR
NO!
KING OF
BEASTS
CONVERGENT
media group

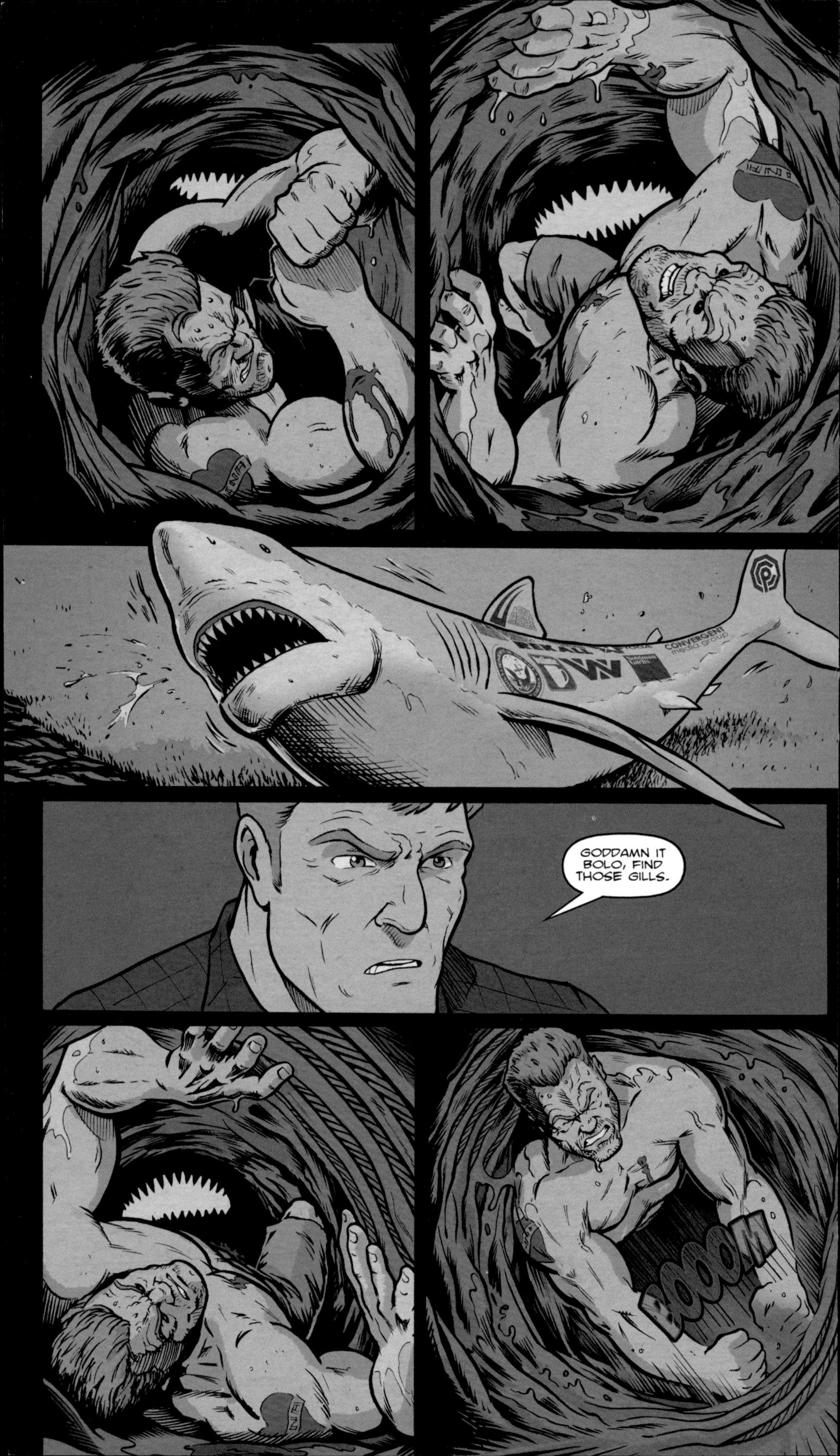
GODDAMN IT BOLO, FIND THOSE GILLS.
BOOOM

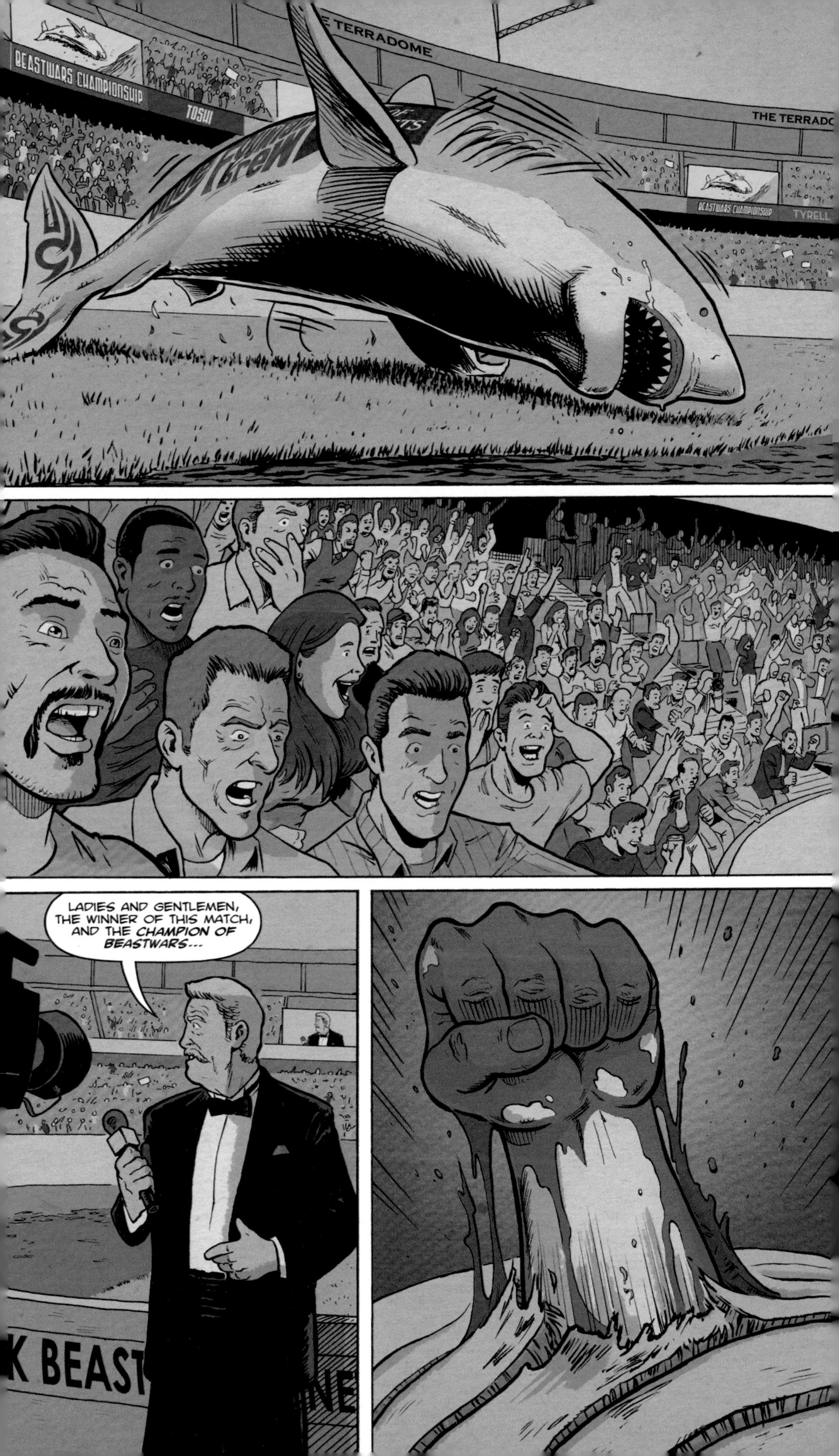
THE TERRADOME
BEASTWARS CHAMPIONSHIP
TYRELL
LADIES AND GENTLEMEN, THE WINNER OF THIS MATCH, AND THE *CHAMPION OF BEASTWARS*...

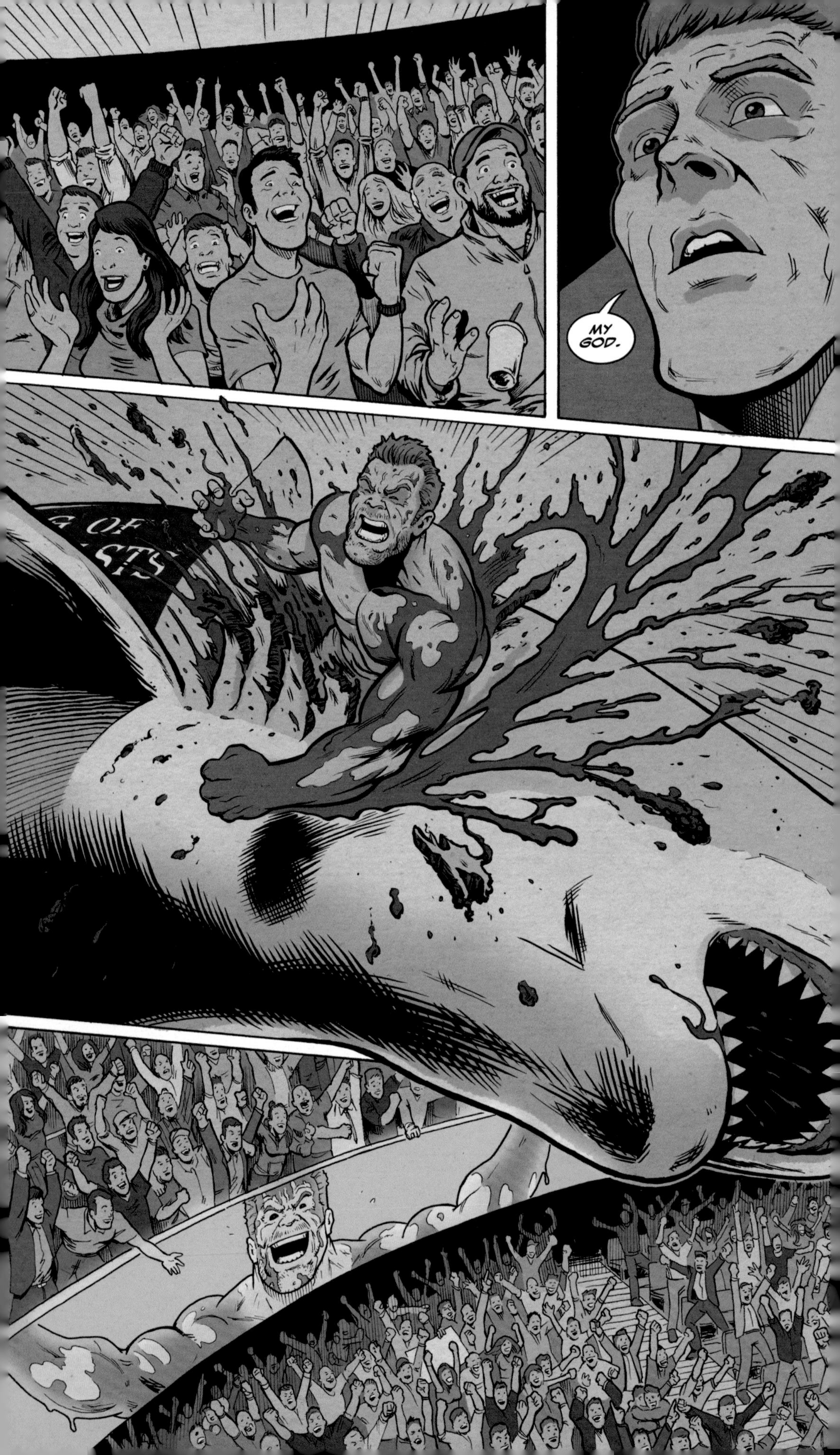
MY GOD.

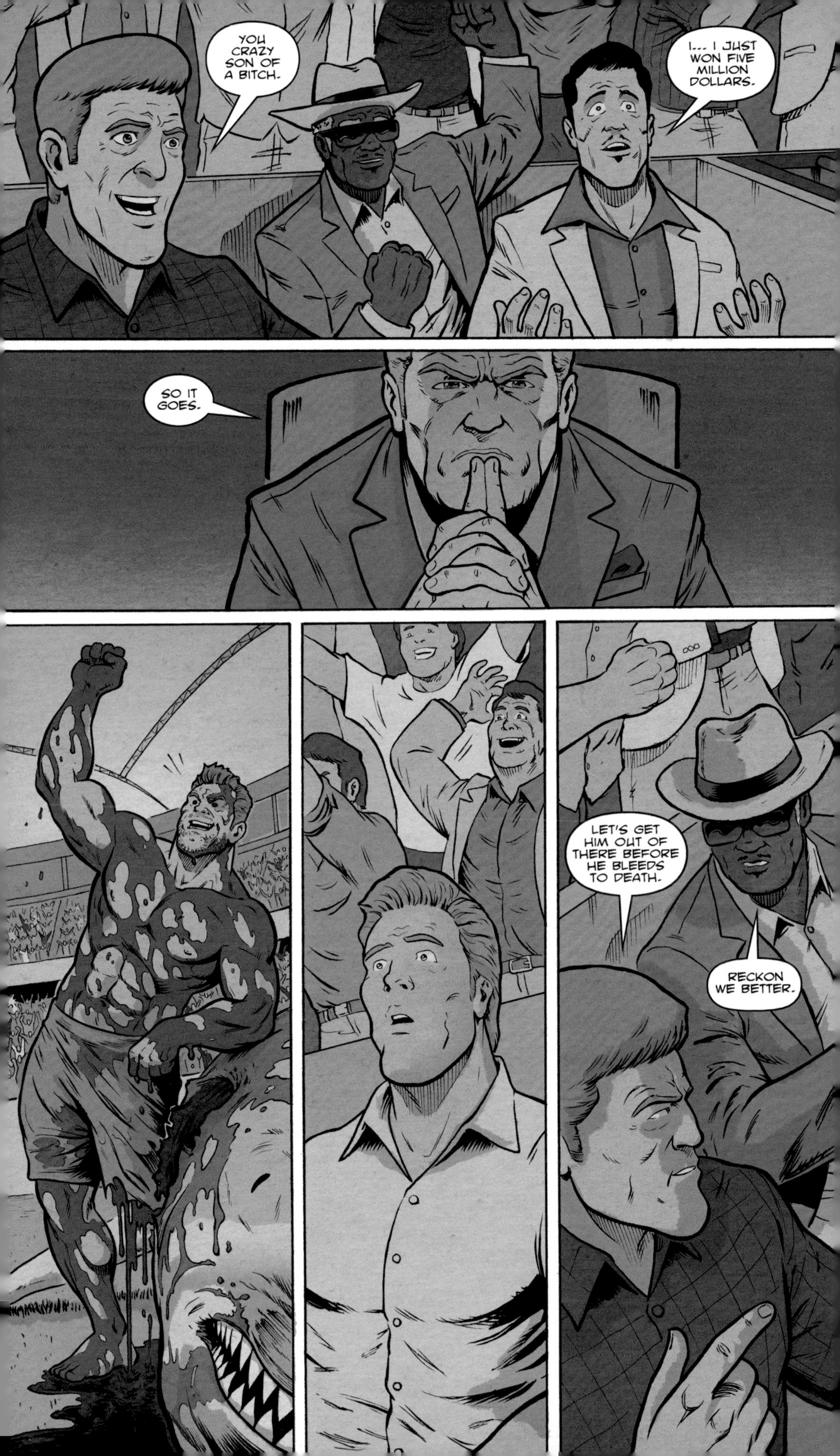
YOU CRAZY SON OF A BITCH.
I... I JUST WON FIVE MILLION DOLLARS.
SO IT GOES.
LET'S GET HIM OUT OF THERE BEFORE HE BLEEDS TO DEATH.
RECKON WE BETTER.

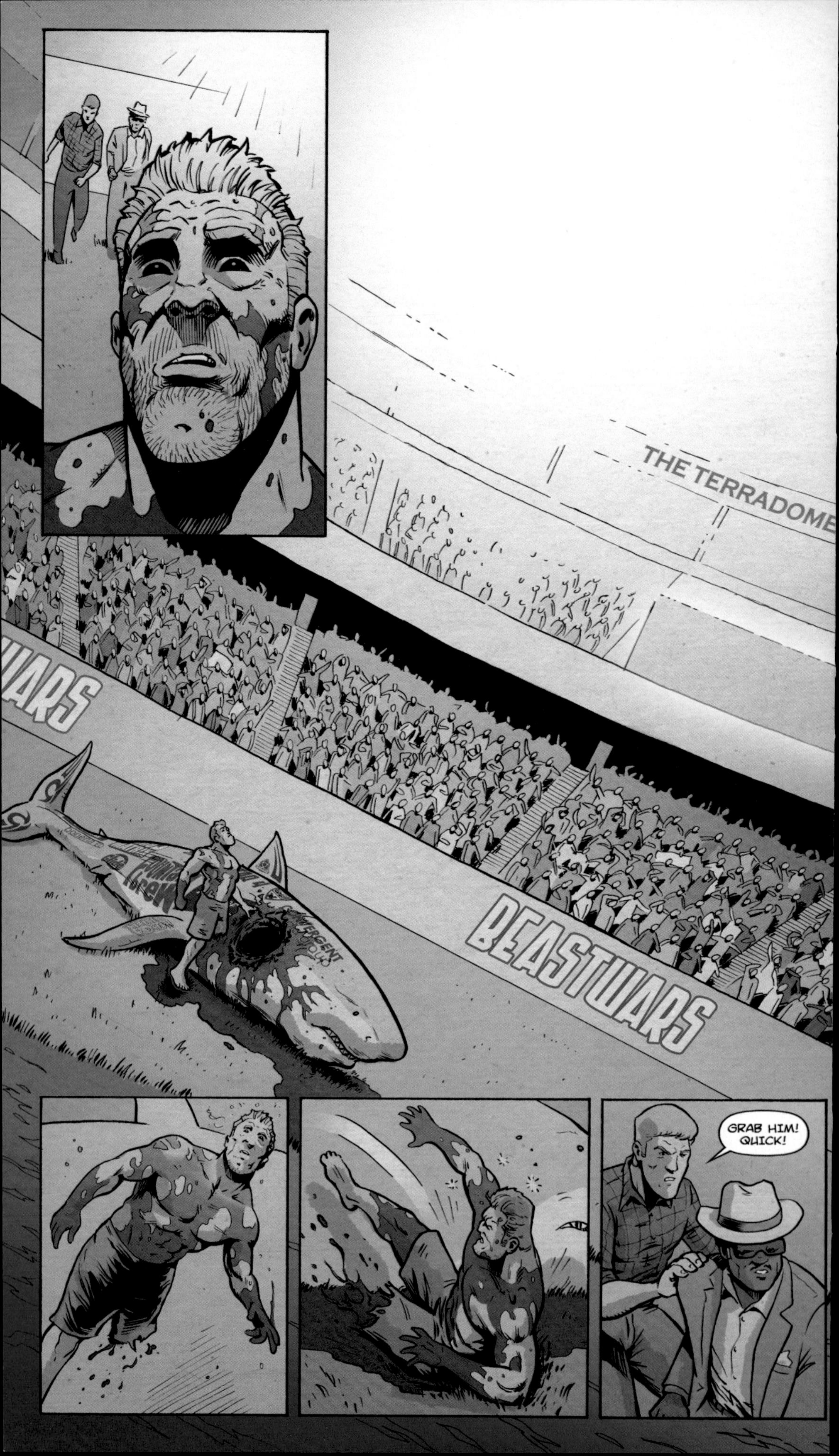
THE TERRADOME
BEASTWARS
GRAB HIM! QUICK!

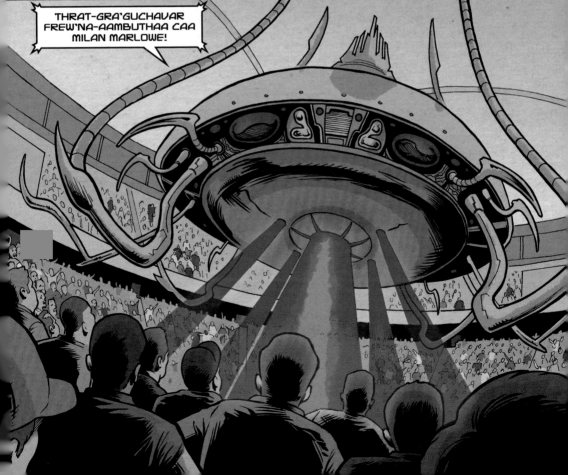

THRAT-GRA'GUCHAVAR FREW'NA-AAMBUTHAA CAA MILAN MARLOWE!

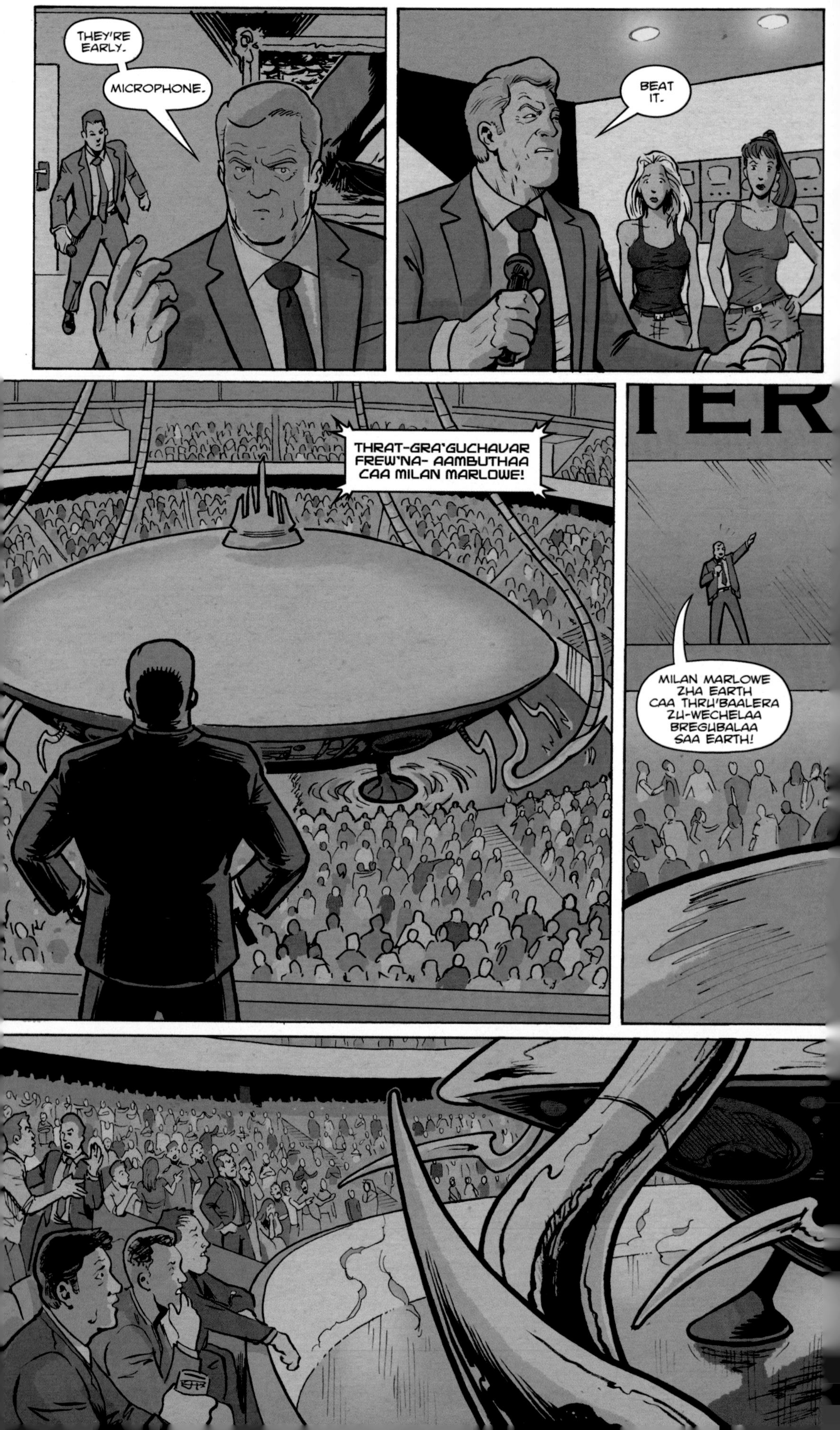
THEY'RE EARLY.
MICROPHONE.
BEAT IT.
THRAT-GRA'GUCHAVAR FREW'NA- AAMBUTHAA CAA MILAN MARLOWE!
TER
MILAN MARLOWE ZHA EARTH CAA THRU'BAALERA ZU-WECHELAA BREGUBALAA SAA EARTH!

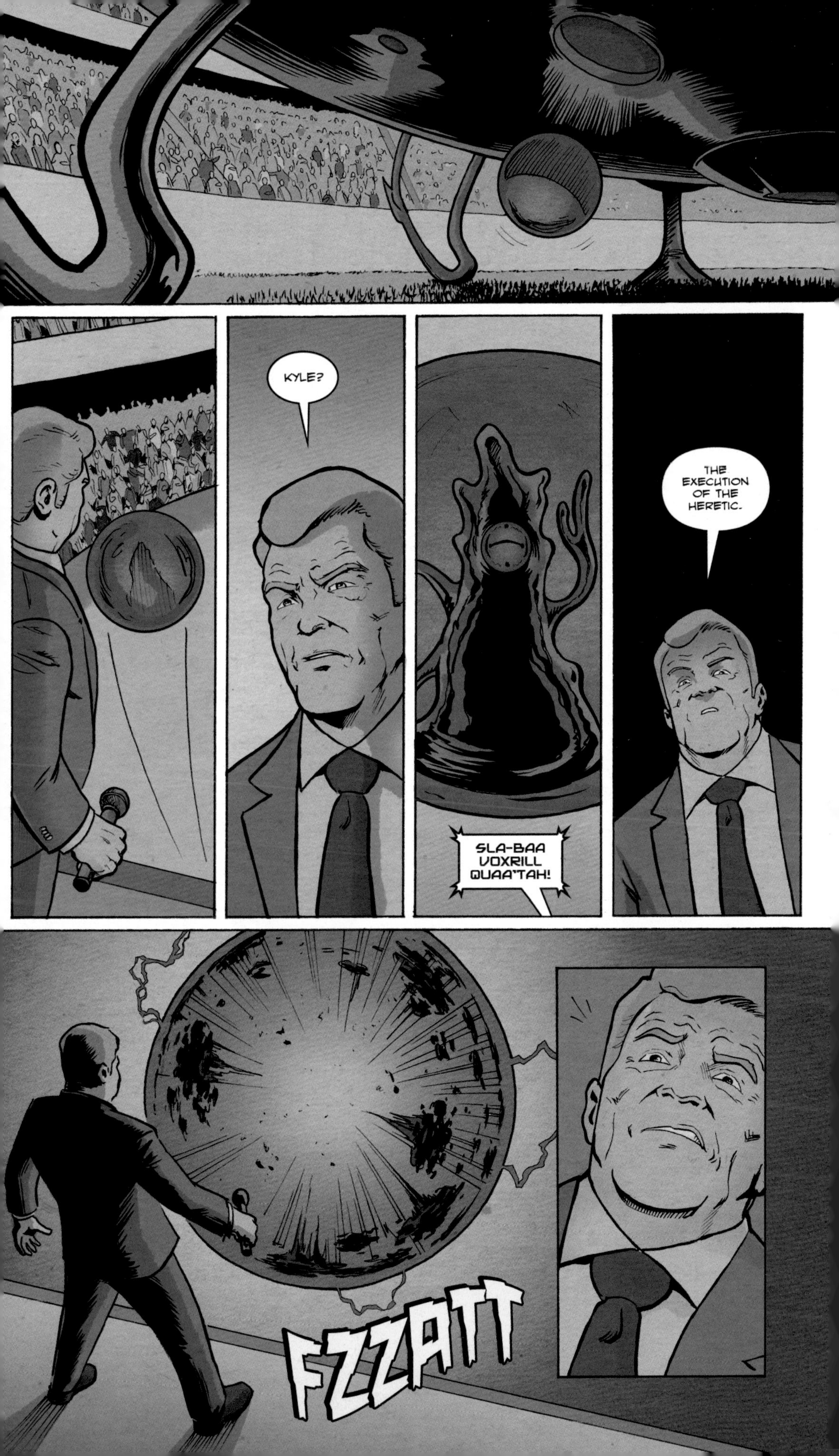
KYLE?
SLA-BAA VOXRILL QUAA'TAH!
THE EXECUTION OF THE HERETIC.
FZZATT

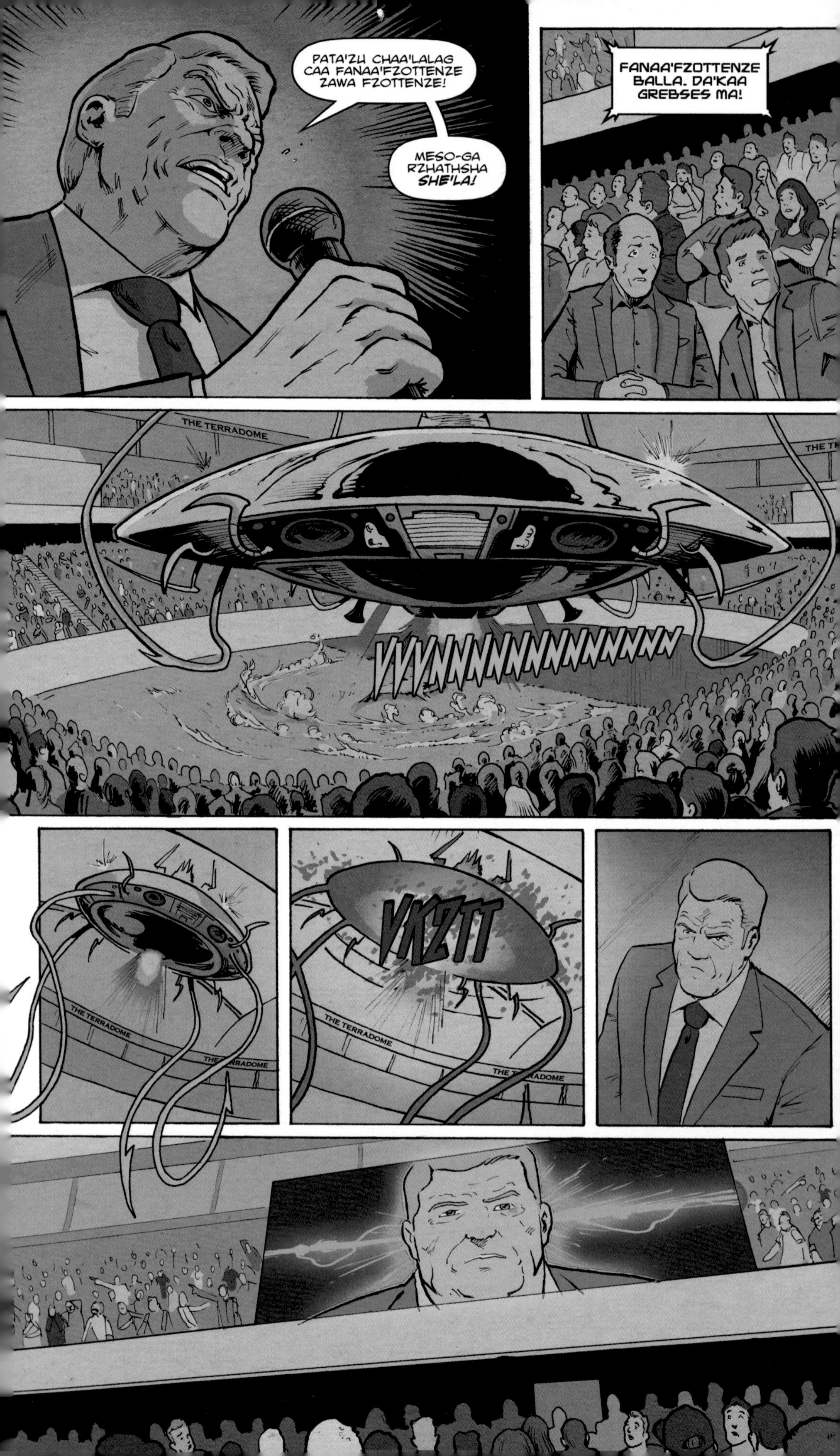
PATA'ZU CHAA'LALAG CAA FANAA'FZOTTENZE ZAWA FZOTTENZE!
MESO-GA RZHATHSHA SHE'LA!
FANAA'FZOTTENZE BALLA. DA'KAA GREBSES MA!
THE TERRADOME
VVVNNNNNNNNNNNNNN
THE TERRADOME
THE TERRADOME
VKZTT
THE TERRADOME
THE TERRADOME

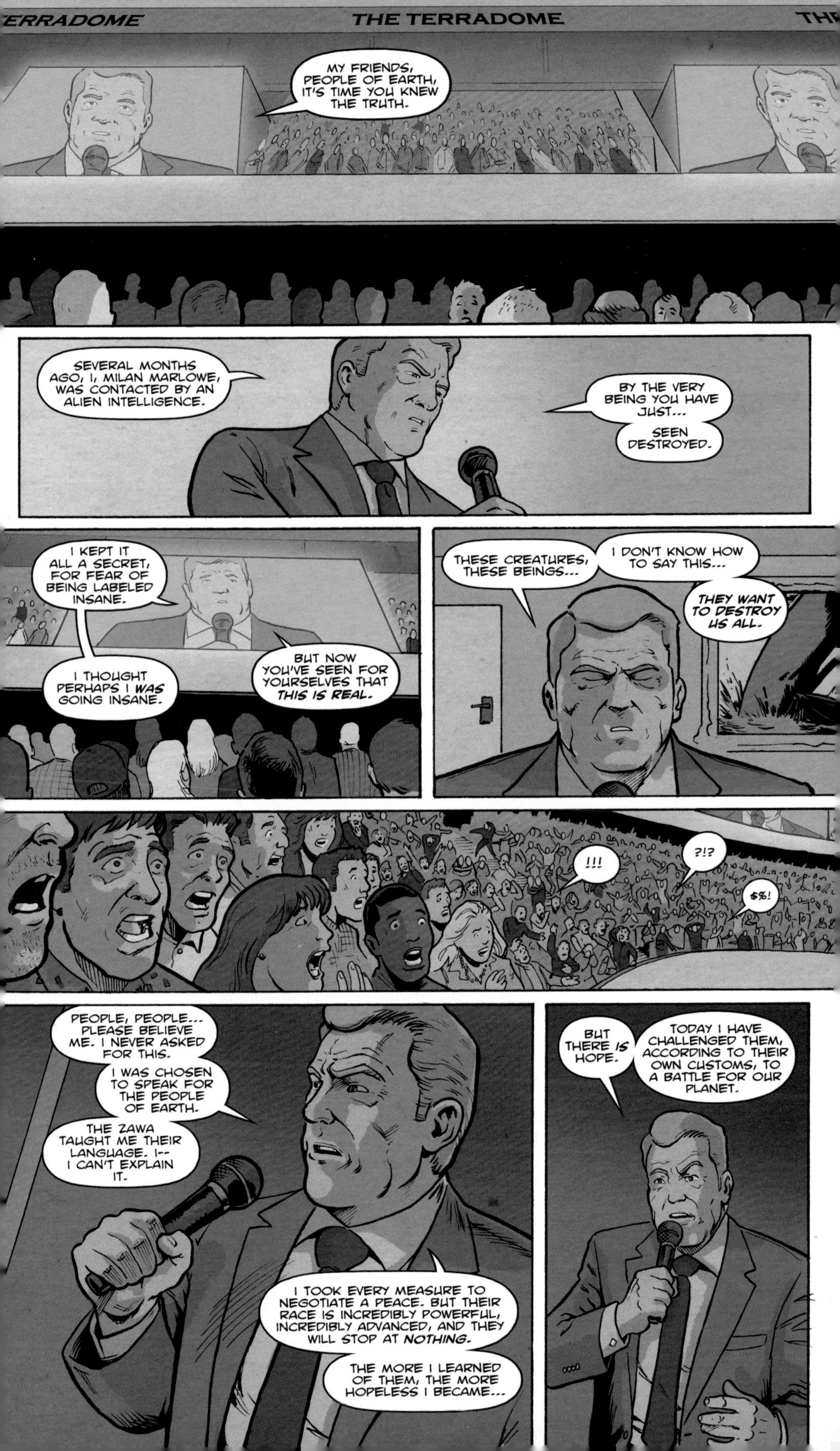

THE TERRADOME
MY FRIENDS, PEOPLE OF EARTH, IT'S TIME YOU KNEW THE TRUTH.
SEVERAL MONTHS AGO, I, MILAN MARLOWE, WAS CONTACTED BY AN ALIEN INTELLIGENCE.
BY THE VERY BEING YOU HAVE JUST...
SEEN DESTROYED.
I KEPT IT ALL A SECRET, FOR FEAR OF BEING LABELED INSANE.
I THOUGHT PERHAPS I *WAS* GOING INSANE.
BUT NOW YOU'VE SEEN FOR YOURSELVES THAT *THIS IS REAL.*
THESE CREATURES, THESE BEINGS...
I DON'T KNOW HOW TO SAY THIS...
THEY WANT TO DESTROY US ALL.
!!!
?!?
$%!
PEOPLE, PEOPLE... PLEASE BELIEVE ME. I NEVER ASKED FOR THIS.
I WAS CHOSEN TO SPEAK FOR THE PEOPLE OF EARTH.
THE ZAWA TAUGHT ME THEIR LANGUAGE. I-- I CAN'T EXPLAIN IT.
I TOOK EVERY MEASURE TO NEGOTIATE A PEACE. BUT THEIR RACE IS INCREDIBLY POWERFUL, INCREDIBLY ADVANCED, AND THEY WILL STOP AT *NOTHING.*
THE MORE I LEARNED OF THEM, THE MORE HOPELESS I BECAME...
BUT THERE *IS* HOPE.
TODAY I HAVE CHALLENGED THEM, ACCORDING TO THEIR OWN CUSTOMS, TO A BATTLE FOR OUR PLANET.

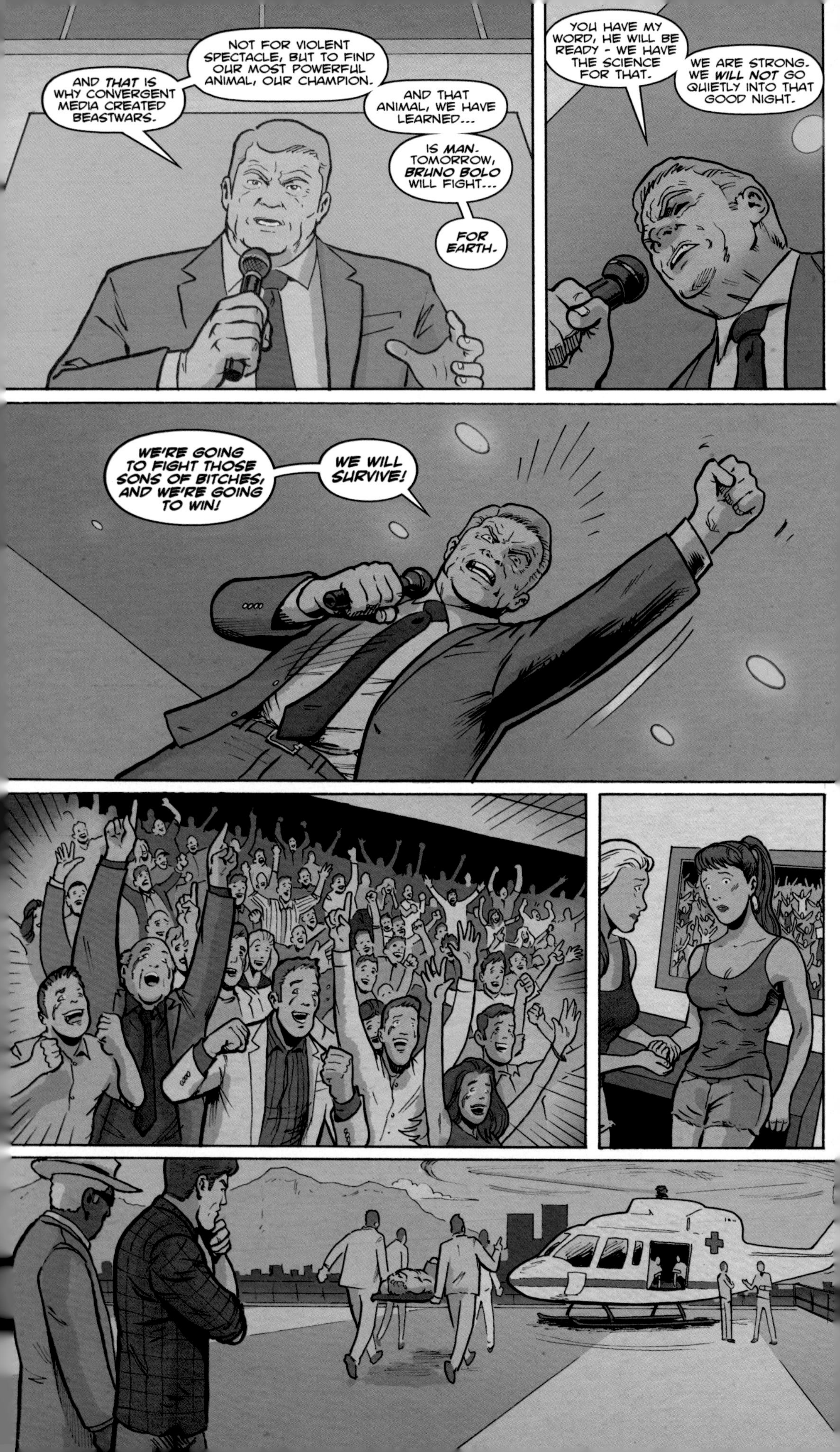
AND *THAT* IS WHY CONVERGENT MEDIA CREATED BEASTWARS.
NOT FOR VIOLENT SPECTACLE, BUT TO FIND OUR MOST POWERFUL ANIMAL, OUR CHAMPION.
AND THAT ANIMAL, WE HAVE LEARNED...
IS *MAN*. TOMORROW, *BRUNO BOLO* WILL FIGHT...
FOR EARTH.
YOU HAVE MY WORD, HE WILL BE READY - WE HAVE THE SCIENCE FOR THAT.
WE ARE STRONG. WE *WILL NOT* GO QUIETLY INTO THAT GOOD NIGHT.
WE'RE GOING TO FIGHT THOSE SONS OF BITCHES, AND WE'RE GOING TO WIN!
WE WILL SURVIVE!

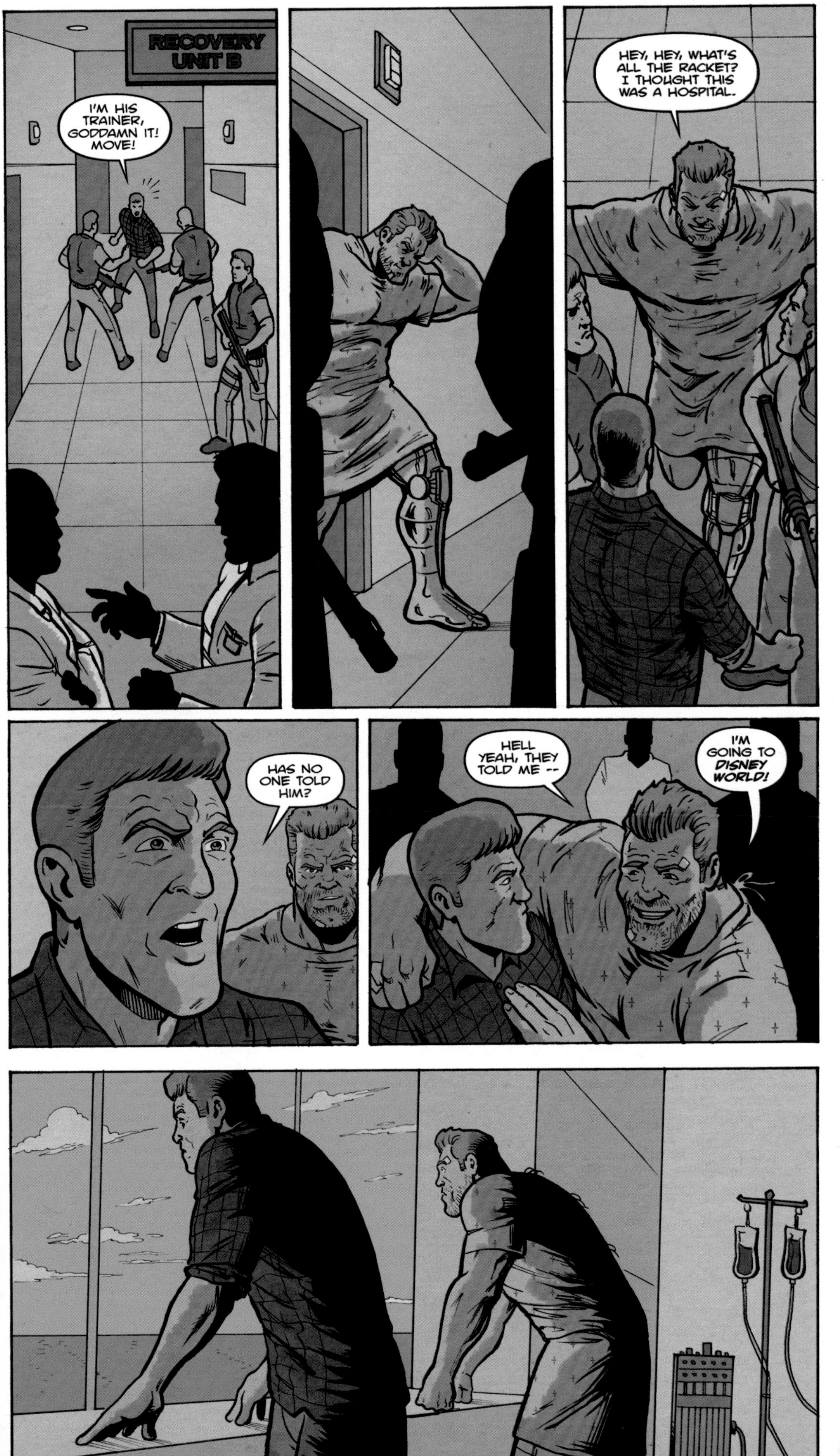
RECOVERY UNIT B
I'M HIS TRAINER, GODDAMN IT! MOVE!
HEY, HEY, WHAT'S ALL THE RACKET? I THOUGHT THIS WAS A HOSPITAL.
HAS NO ONE TOLD HIM?
HELL YEAH, THEY TOLD ME --
I'M GOING TO *DISNEY WORLD!*

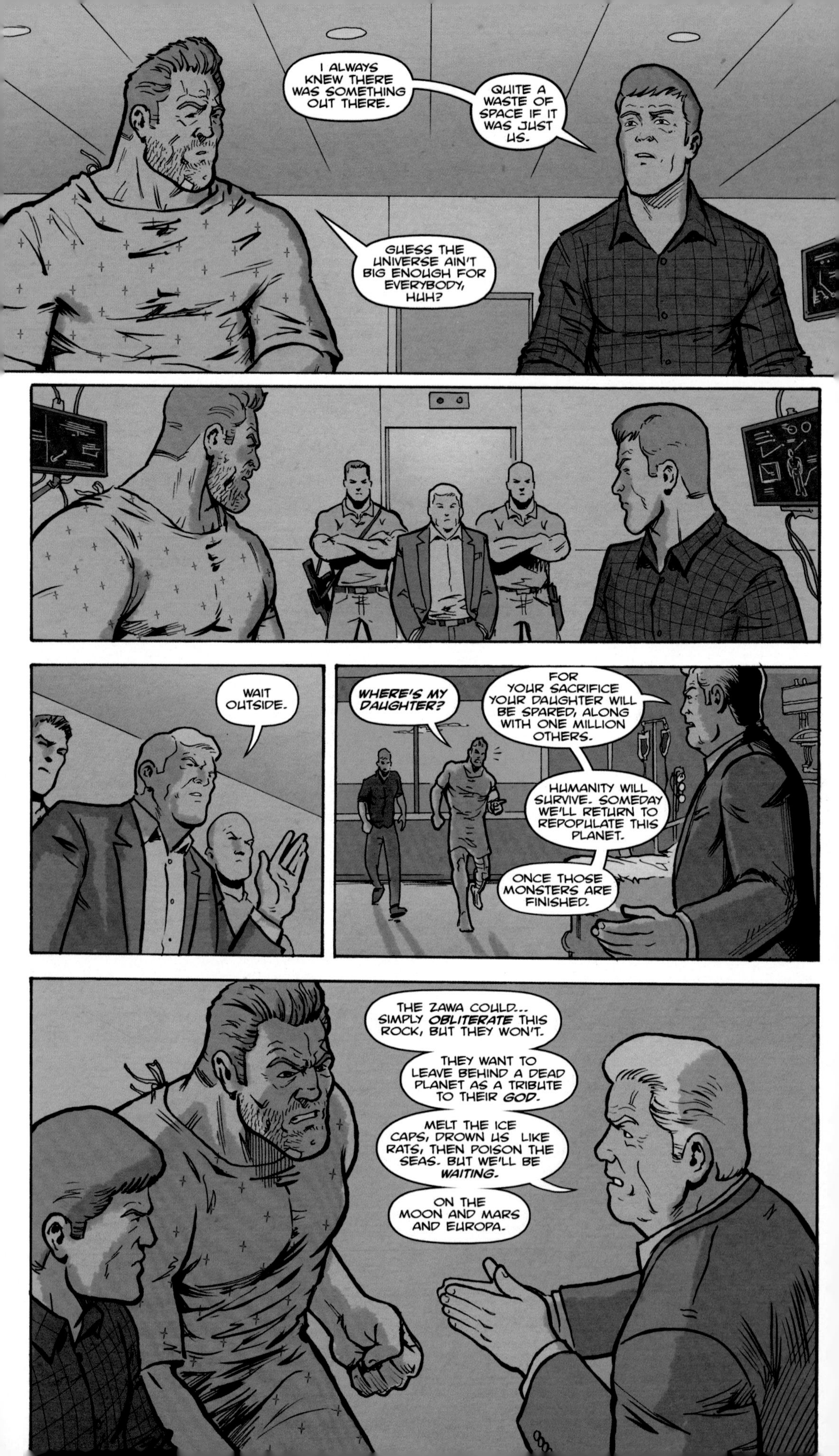

I ALWAYS KNEW THERE WAS SOMETHING OUT THERE.
QUITE A WASTE OF SPACE IF IT WAS JUST US.
GUESS THE UNIVERSE AIN'T BIG ENOUGH FOR EVERYBODY, HUH?
WAIT OUTSIDE.
WHERE'S MY DAUGHTER?
FOR YOUR SACRIFICE YOUR DAUGHTER WILL BE SPARED, ALONG WITH ONE MILLION OTHERS.
HUMANITY WILL SURVIVE. SOMEDAY WE'LL RETURN TO REPOPULATE THIS PLANET.
ONCE THOSE MONSTERS ARE FINISHED.
THE ZAWA COULD... SIMPLY OBLITERATE THIS ROCK, BUT THEY WON'T.
THEY WANT TO LEAVE BEHIND A DEAD PLANET AS A TRIBUTE TO THEIR GOD.
MELT THE ICE CAPS, DROWN US LIKE RATS, THEN POISON THE SEAS. BUT WE'LL BE WAITING.
ON THE MOON AND MARS AND EUROPA.

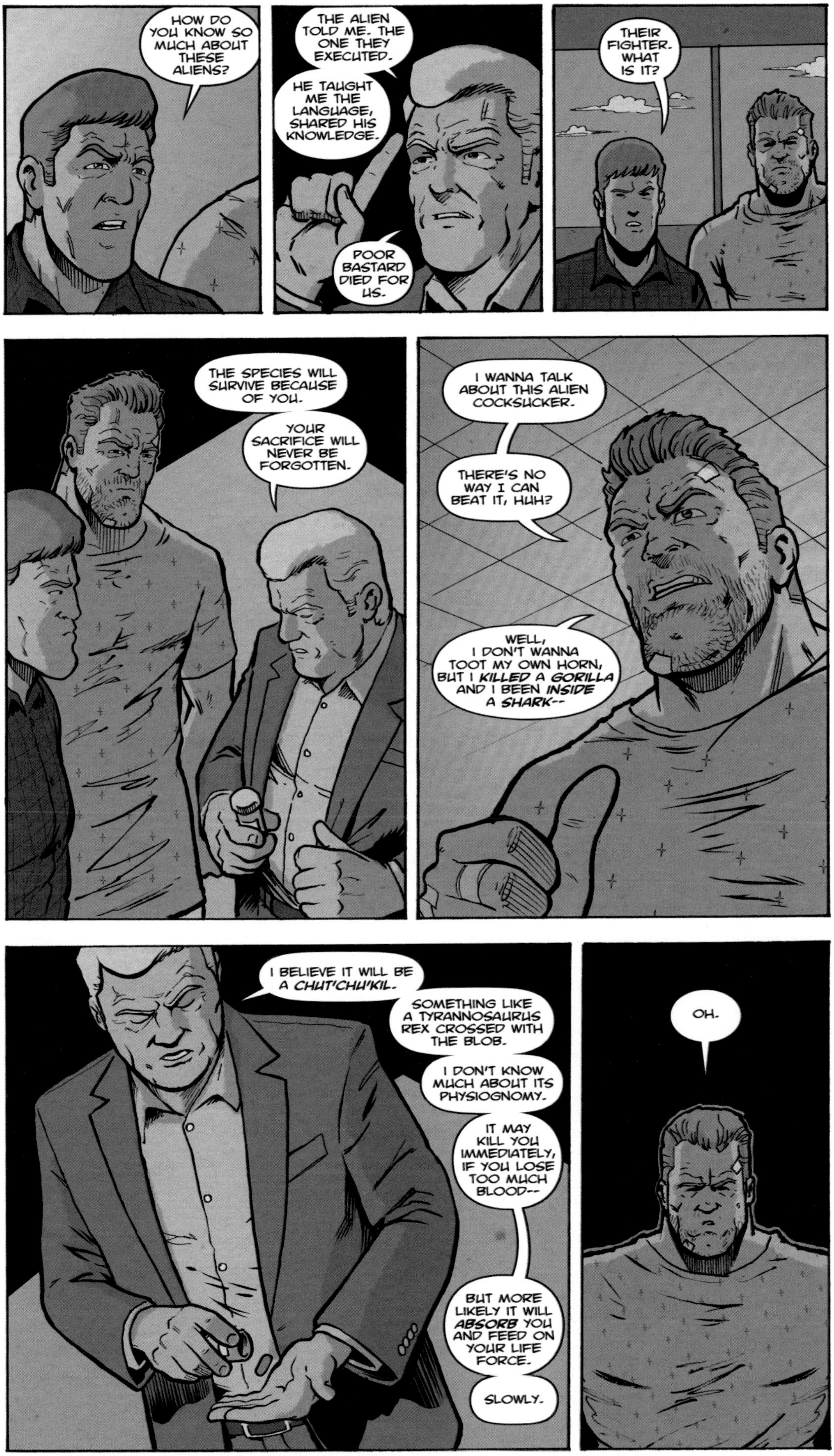
HOW DO YOU KNOW SO MUCH ABOUT THESE ALIENS?
THE ALIEN TOLD ME. THE ONE THEY EXECUTED.
HE TAUGHT ME THE LANGUAGE, SHARED HIS KNOWLEDGE.
POOR BASTARD DIED FOR US.
THEIR FIGHTER. WHAT IS IT?
THE SPECIES WILL SURVIVE BECAUSE OF YOU.
YOUR SACRIFICE WILL NEVER BE FORGOTTEN.
I WANNA TALK ABOUT THIS ALIEN COCKSUCKER.
THERE'S NO WAY I CAN BEAT IT, HUH?
WELL, I DON'T WANNA TOOT MY OWN HORN, BUT I *KILLED A GORILLA* AND I BEEN *INSIDE* A *SHARK*--
I BELIEVE IT WILL BE A *CHUT'CHU'KIL*.
SOMETHING LIKE A TYRANNOSAURUS REX CROSSED WITH THE BLOB.
I DON'T KNOW MUCH ABOUT ITS PHYSIOGNOMY.
IT MAY KILL YOU IMMEDIATELY, IF YOU LOSE TOO MUCH BLOOD--
BUT MORE LIKELY IT WILL *ABSORB* YOU AND FEED ON YOUR LIFE FORCE.
SLOWLY.
OH.

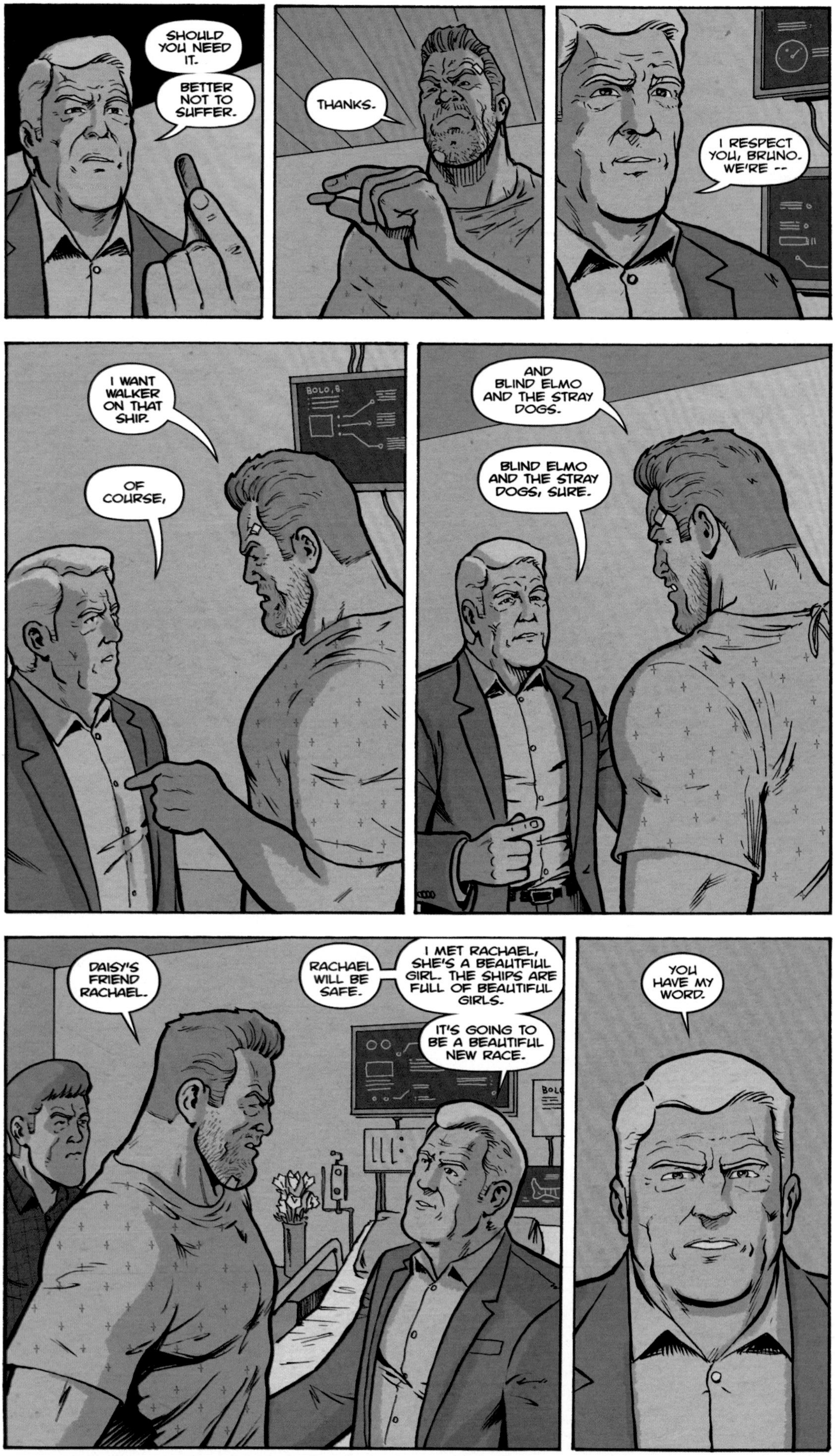
SHOULD YOU NEED IT.
BETTER NOT TO SUFFER.
THANKS.
I RESPECT YOU, BRUNO. WE'RE --
I WANT WALKER ON THAT SHIP.
OF COURSE,
AND BLIND ELMO AND THE STRAY DOGS.
BLIND ELMO AND THE STRAY DOGS, SURE.
DAISY'S FRIEND RACHAEL.
RACHAEL WILL BE SAFE.
I MET RACHAEL, SHE'S A BEAUTIFUL GIRL. THE SHIPS ARE FULL OF BEAUTIFUL GIRLS.
IT'S GOING TO BE A BEAUTIFUL NEW RACE.
YOU HAVE MY WORD.

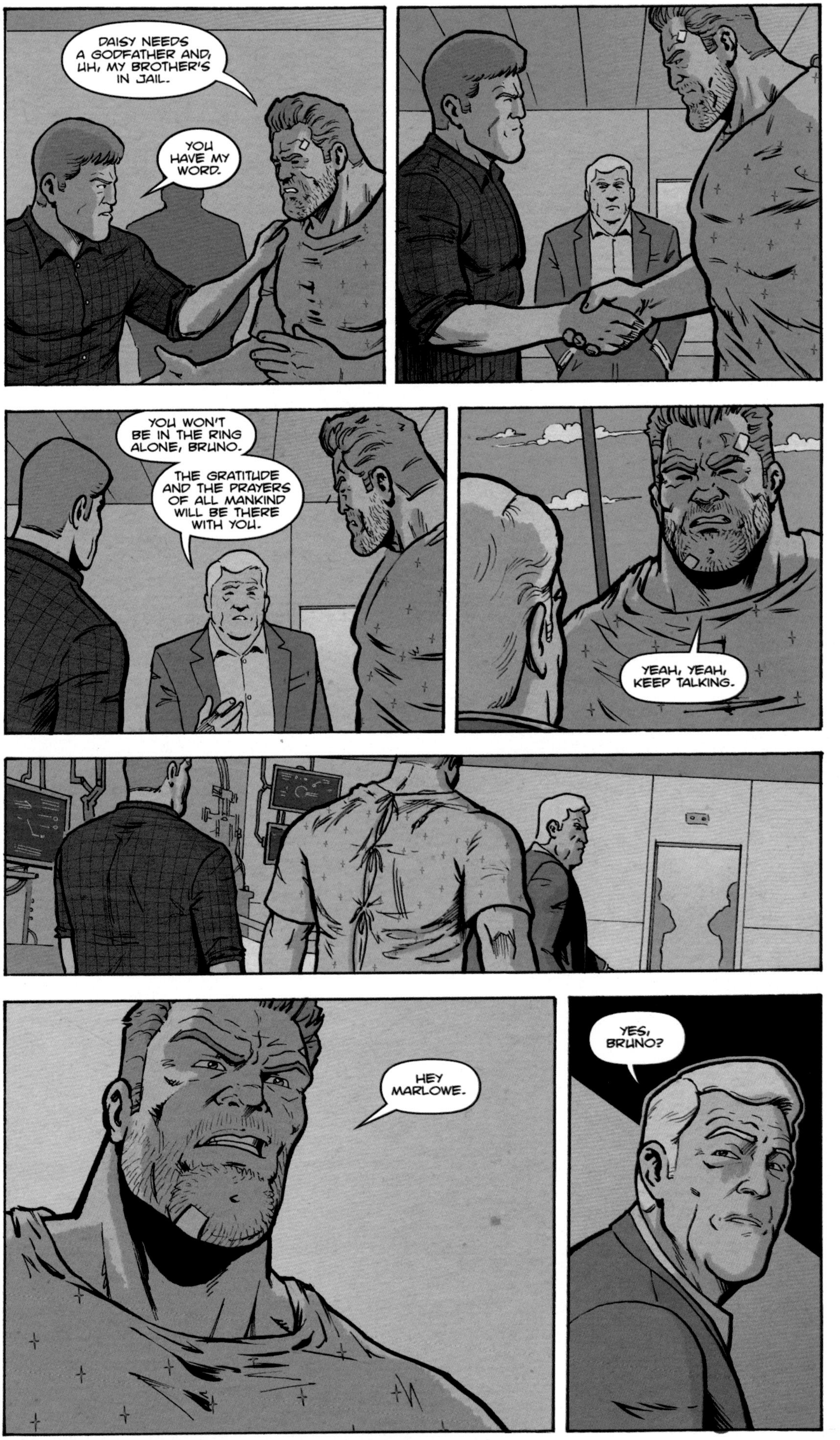
DAISY NEEDS A GODFATHER AND, UH, MY BROTHER'S IN JAIL.
YOU HAVE MY WORD.
YOU WON'T BE IN THE RING ALONE, BRUNO.
THE GRATITUDE AND THE PRAYERS OF ALL MANKIND WILL BE THERE WITH YOU.
YEAH, YEAH, KEEP TALKING.
HEY MARLOWE.
YES, BRUNO?

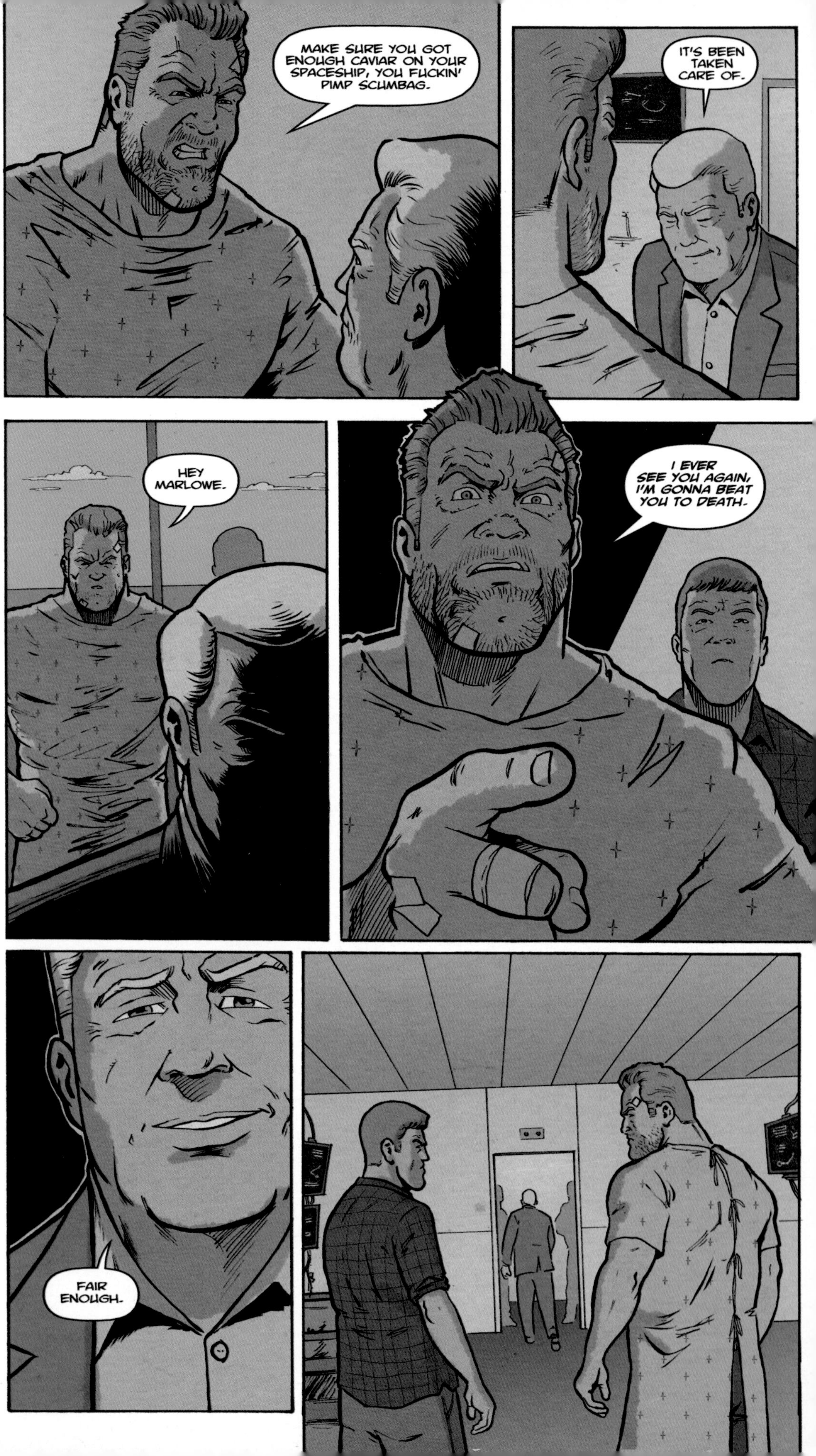
MAKE SURE YOU GOT ENOUGH CAVIAR ON YOUR SPACESHIP, YOU FUCKIN' PIMP SCUMBAG.
IT'S BEEN TAKEN CARE OF.
HEY MARLOWE.
I EVER SEE YOU AGAIN, I'M GONNA BEAT YOU TO DEATH.
FAIR ENOUGH.

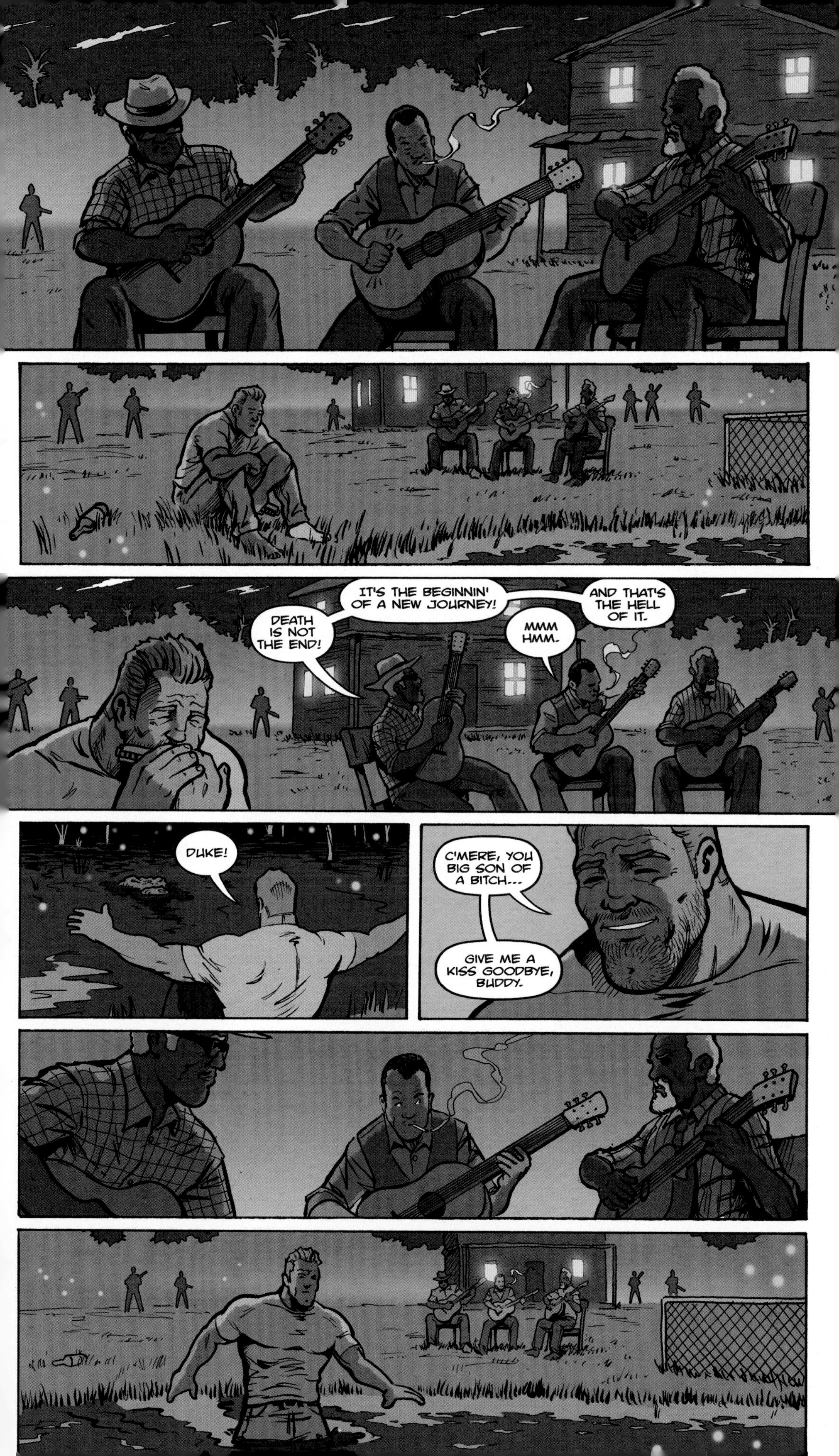
DEATH IS NOT THE END!
IT'S THE BEGINNIN' OF A NEW JOURNEY!
MMM HMM.
AND THAT'S THE HELL OF IT.
DUKE!
C'MERE, YOU BIG SON OF A BITCH...
GIVE ME A KISS GOODBYE, BUDDY.

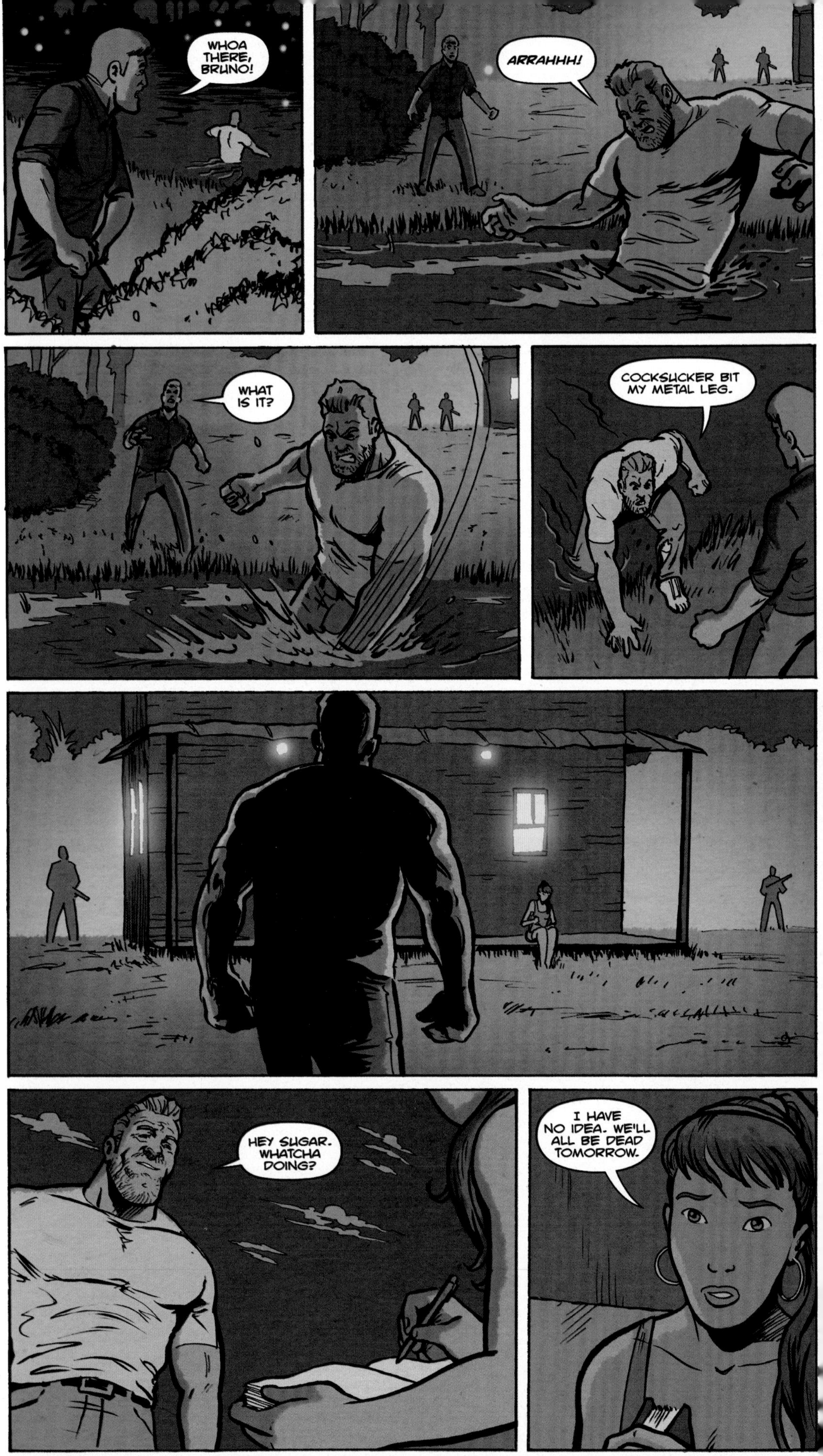
WHOA THERE, BRUNO!
ARRAHHH!
WHAT IS IT?
COCKSUCKER BIT MY METAL LEG.
HEY SUGAR. WHATCHA DOING?
I HAVE NO IDEA. WE'LL ALL BE DEAD TOMORROW.

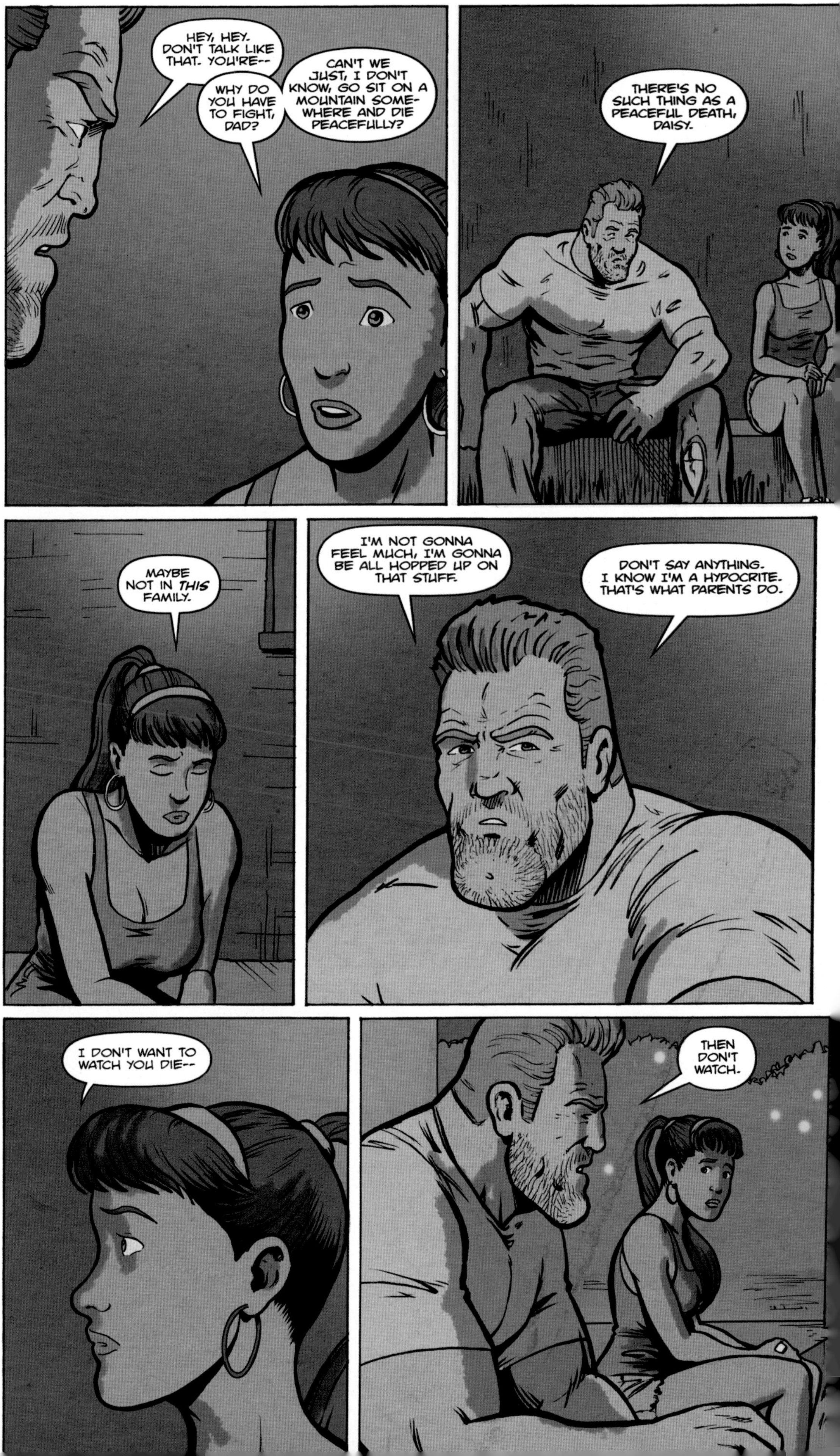
HEY, HEY. DON'T TALK LIKE THAT. YOU'RE--
WHY DO YOU HAVE TO FIGHT, DAD?
CAN'T WE JUST, I DON'T KNOW, GO SIT ON A MOUNTAIN SOMEWHERE AND DIE PEACEFULLY?
THERE'S NO SUCH THING AS A PEACEFUL DEATH, DAISY.
MAYBE NOT IN *THIS* FAMILY.
I'M NOT GONNA FEEL MUCH, I'M GONNA BE ALL HOPPED UP ON THAT STUFF.
DON'T SAY ANYTHING. I KNOW I'M A HYPOCRITE. THAT'S WHAT PARENTS DO.
I DON'T WANT TO WATCH YOU DIE--
THEN DON'T WATCH.

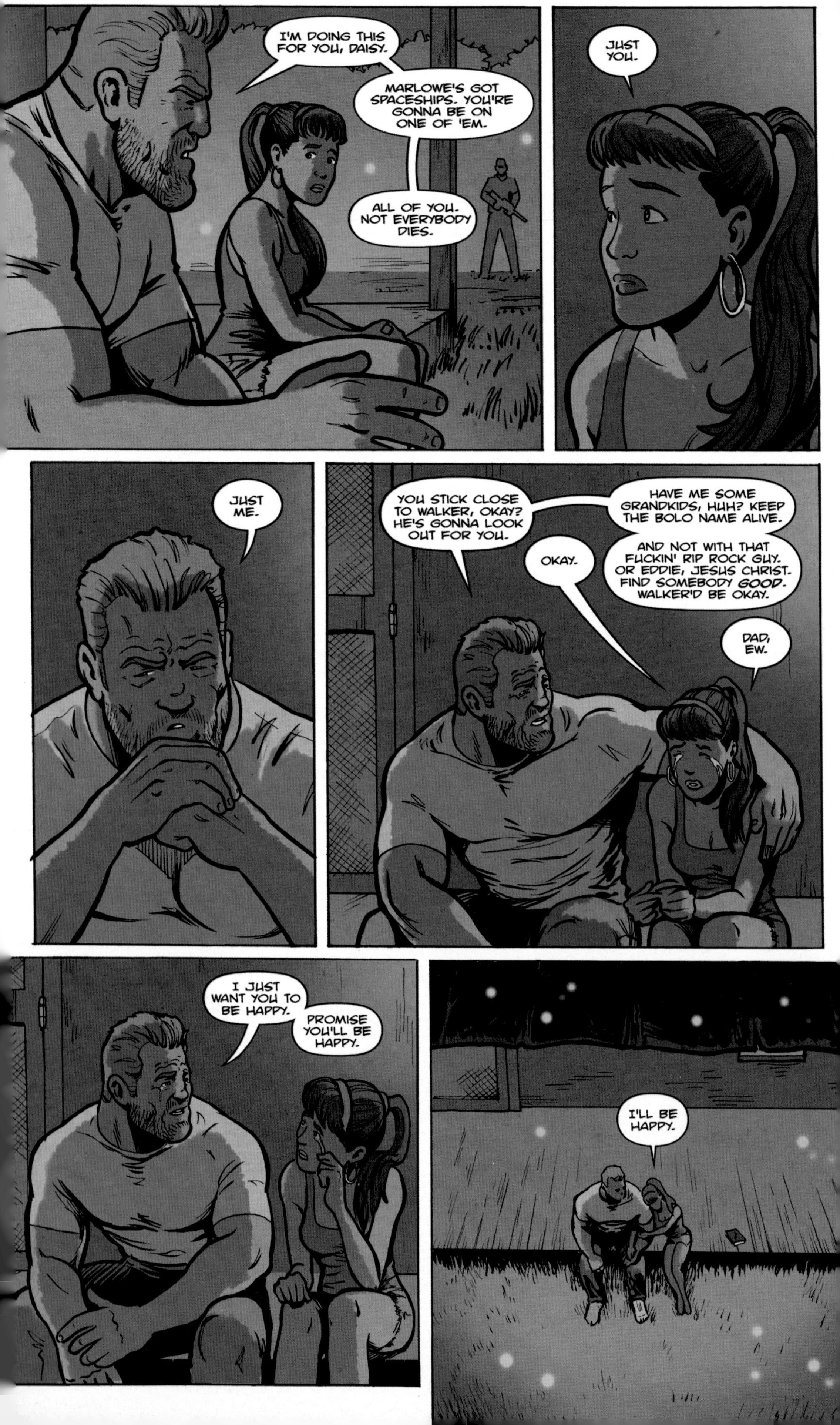
I'M DOING THIS FOR YOU, DAISY.
MARLOWE'S GOT SPACESHIPS. YOU'RE GONNA BE ON ONE OF 'EM.
ALL OF YOU. NOT EVERYBODY DIES.
JUST YOU.
JUST ME.
YOU STICK CLOSE TO WALKER, OKAY? HE'S GONNA LOOK OUT FOR YOU.
OKAY.
HAVE ME SOME GRANDKIDS, HUH? KEEP THE BOLO NAME ALIVE.
AND NOT WITH THAT FUCKIN' RIP ROCK GUY. OR EDDIE, JESUS CHRIST. FIND SOMEBODY GOOD. WALKER'D BE OKAY.
DAD, EW.
I JUST WANT YOU TO BE HAPPY.
PROMISE YOU'LL BE HAPPY.
I'LL BE HAPPY.

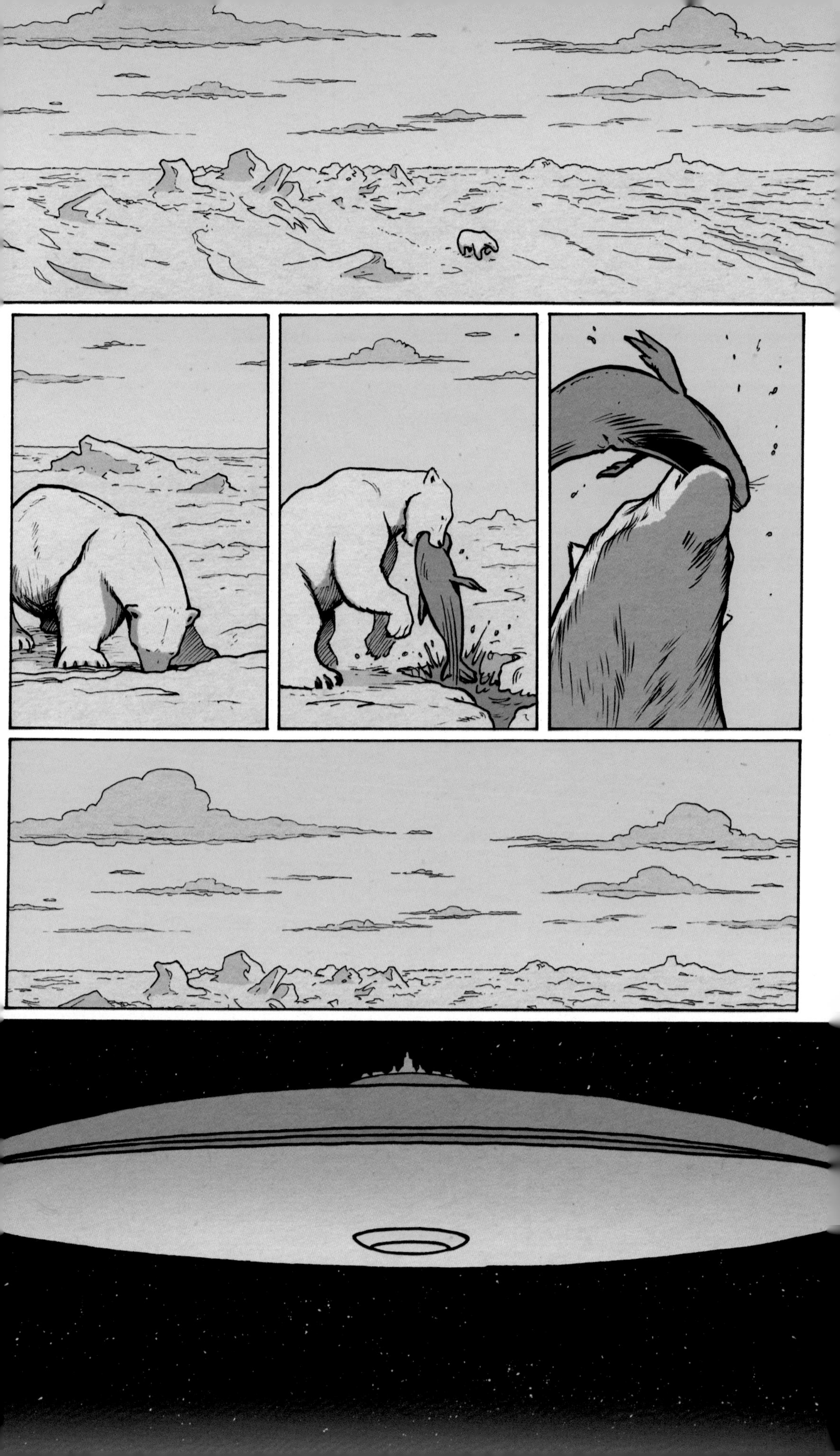

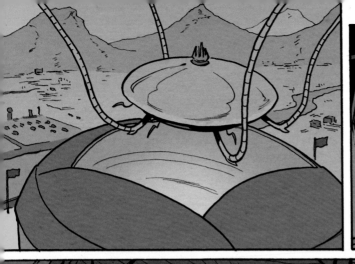

BRAAAAH! WRAAAAH!

BRAAAAH! WRAAAAH!

BRAAAAH! WRAAAAH!

I LOVE YOU, DAD.

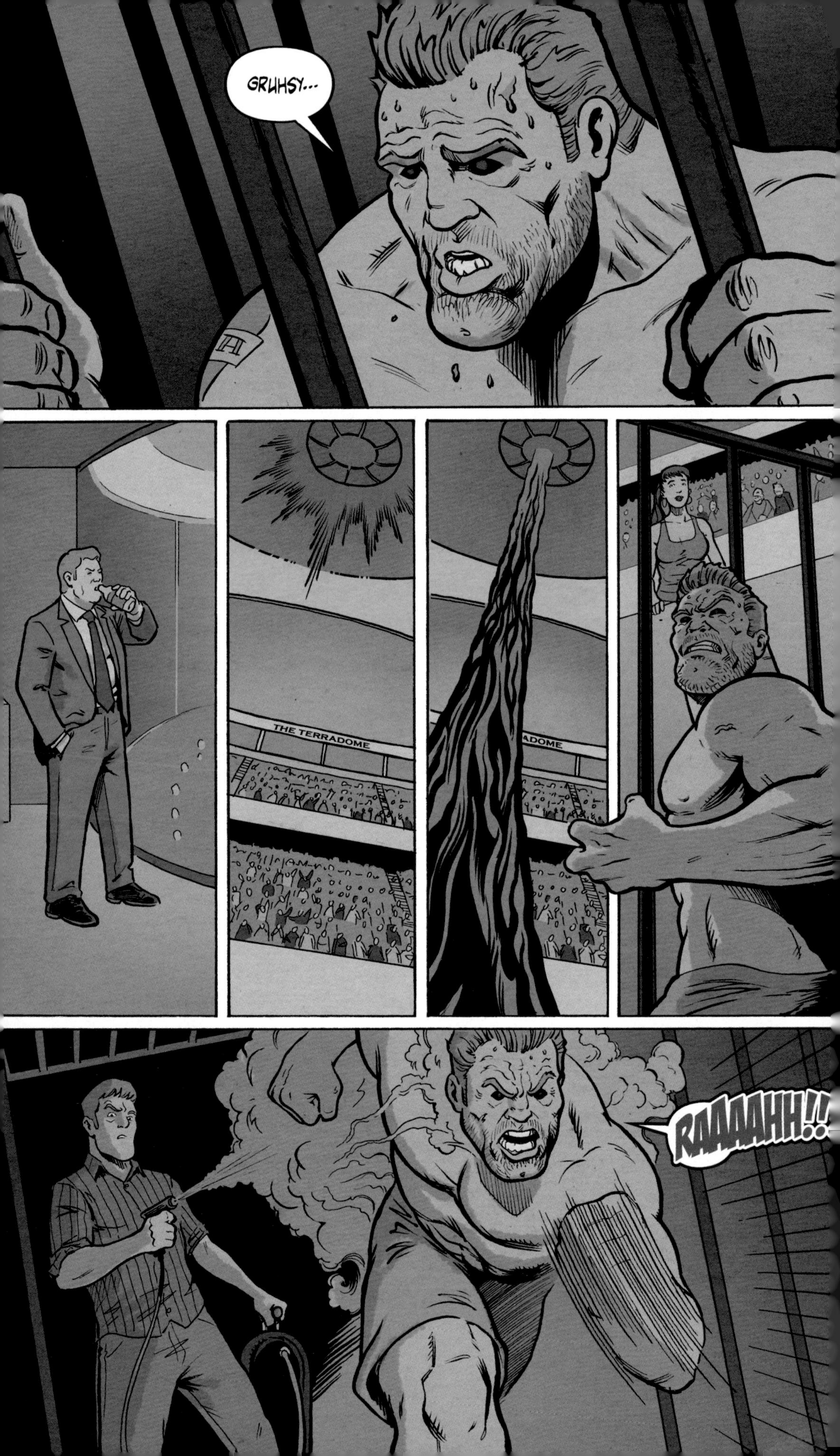
GRUHSY...
THE TERRADOME
RAAAAHH!!

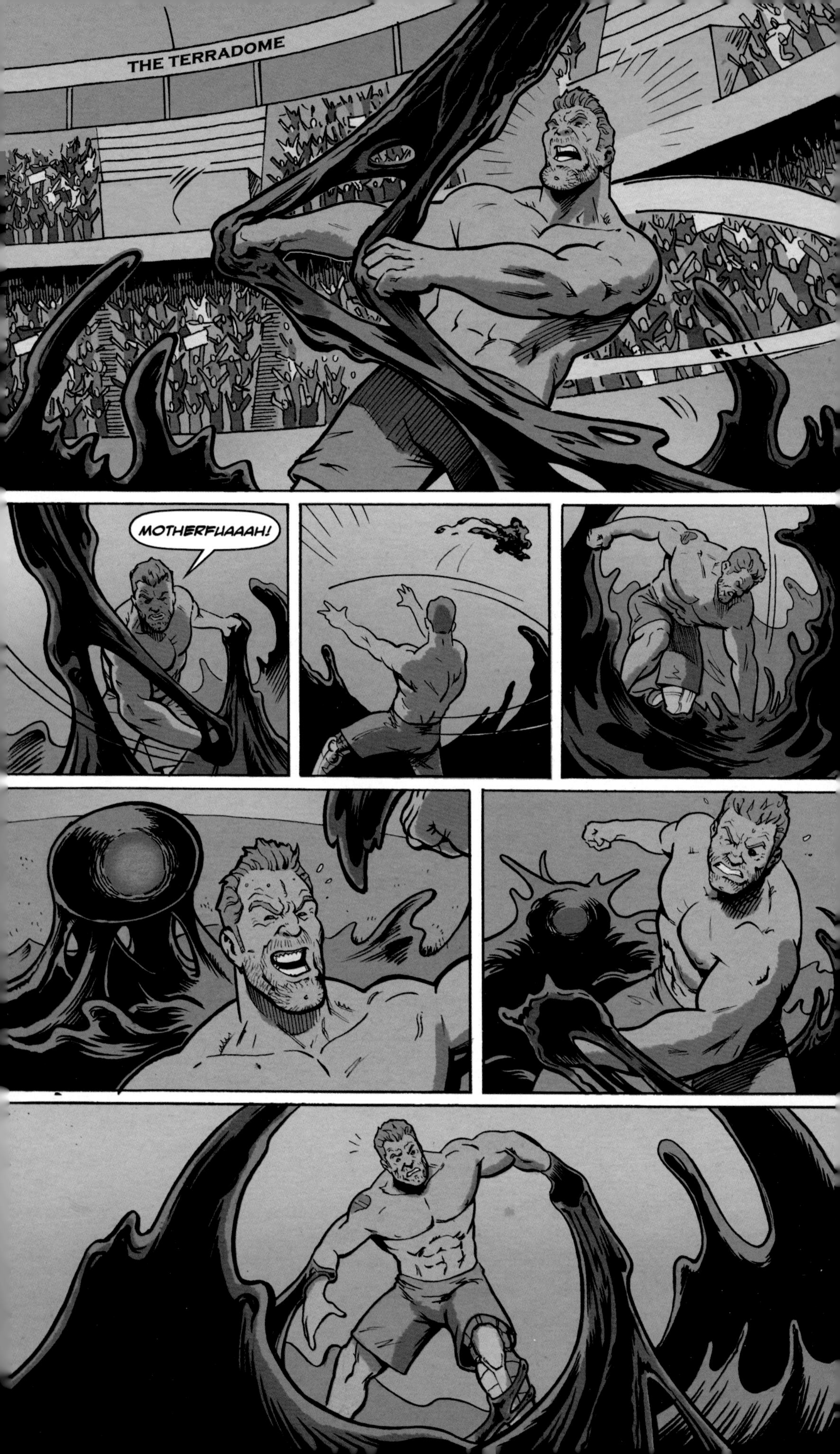
THE TERRADOME
MOTHERFUAAAH!

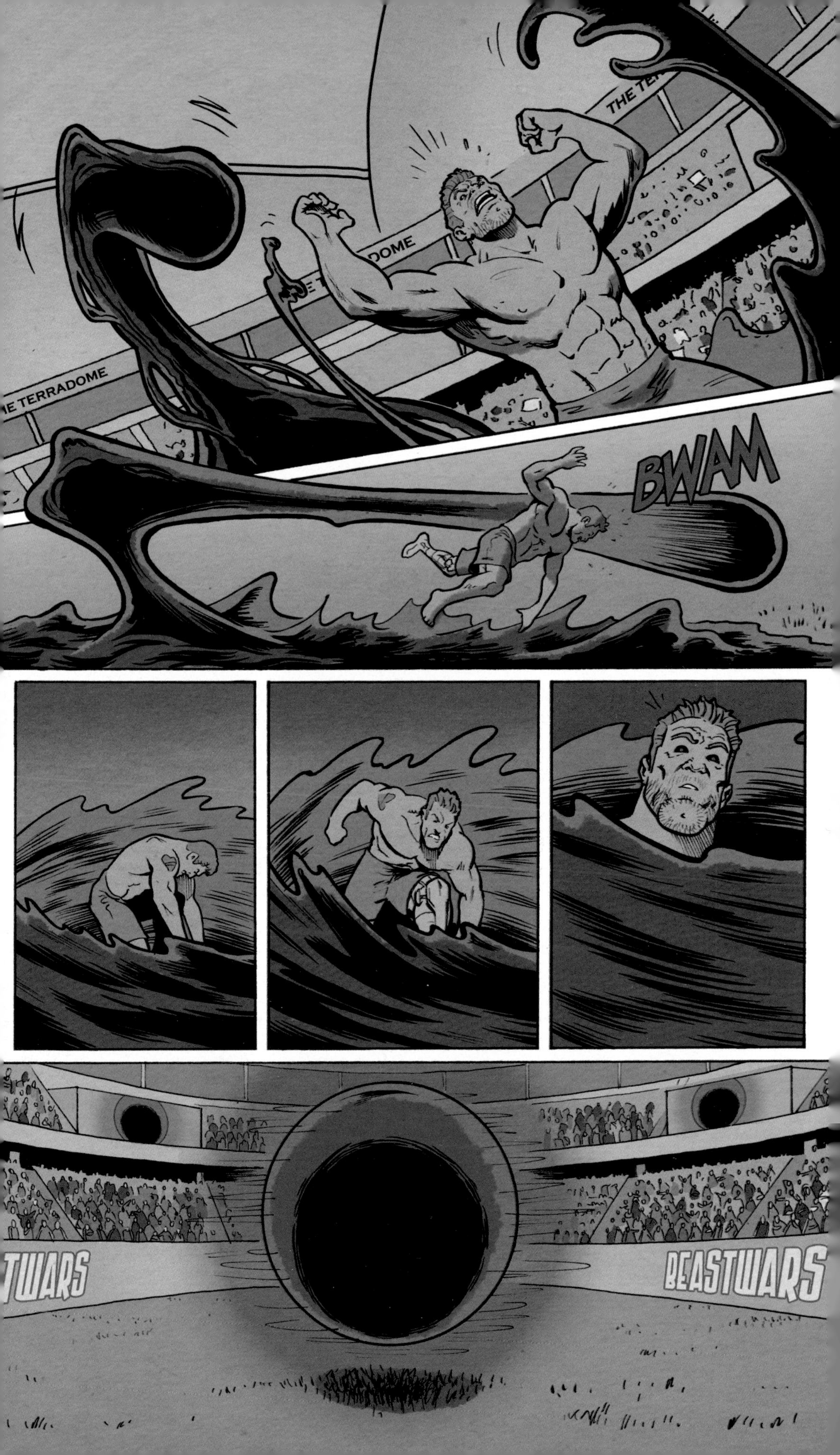
BWAM
BEASTWARS

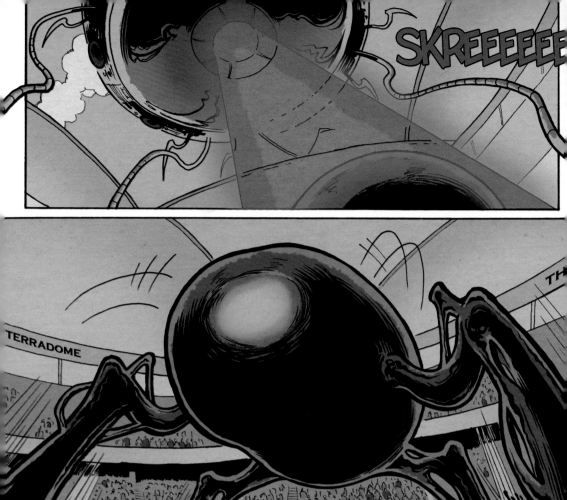

SKREEEEE

TERRADOME

THOOOOOM

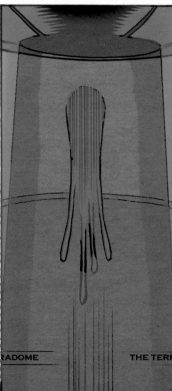

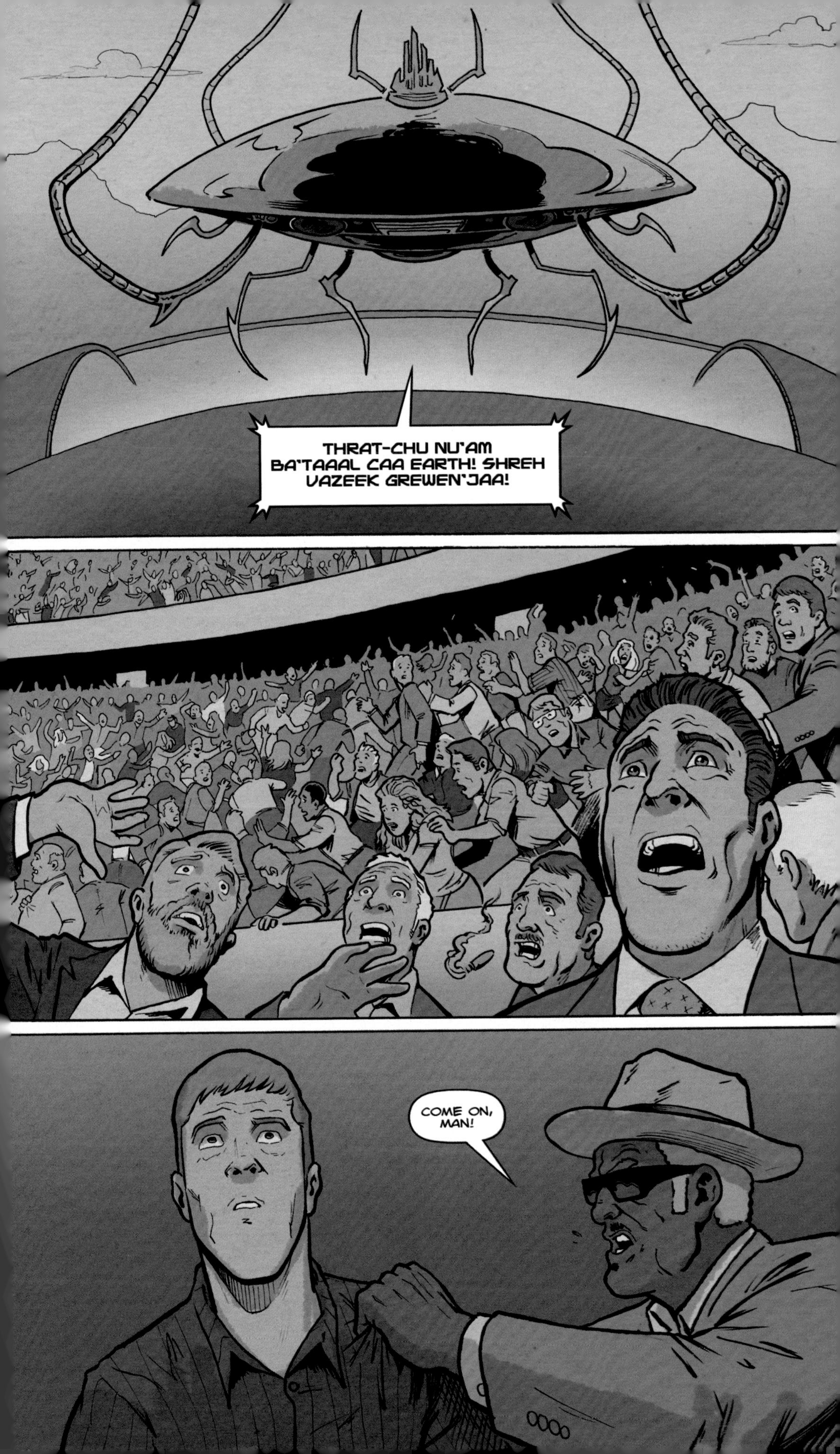
THRAT-CHU NU'AM BA'TAAAL CAA EARTH! SHREH VAZEEK GREWEN'JAA!
COME ON, MAN!

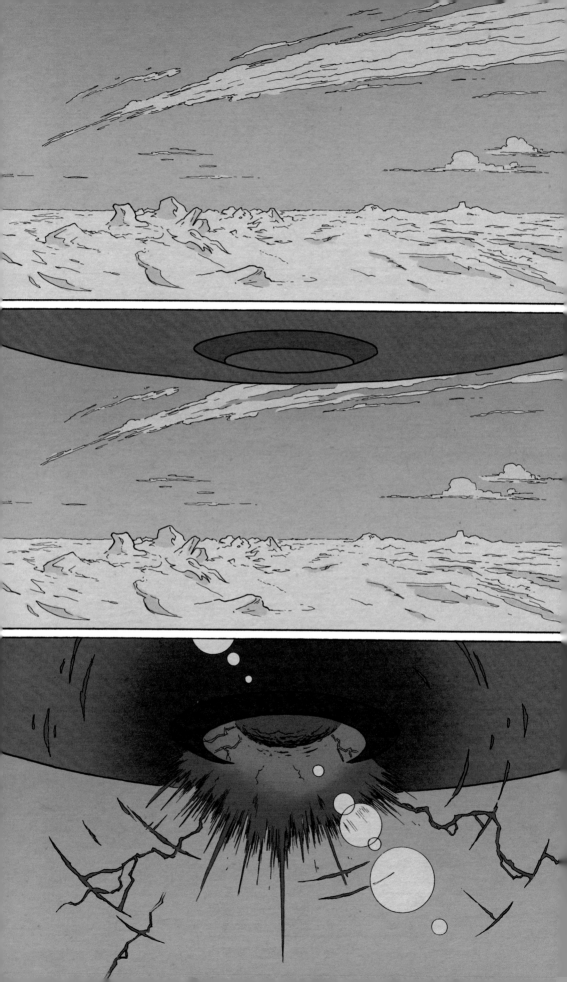

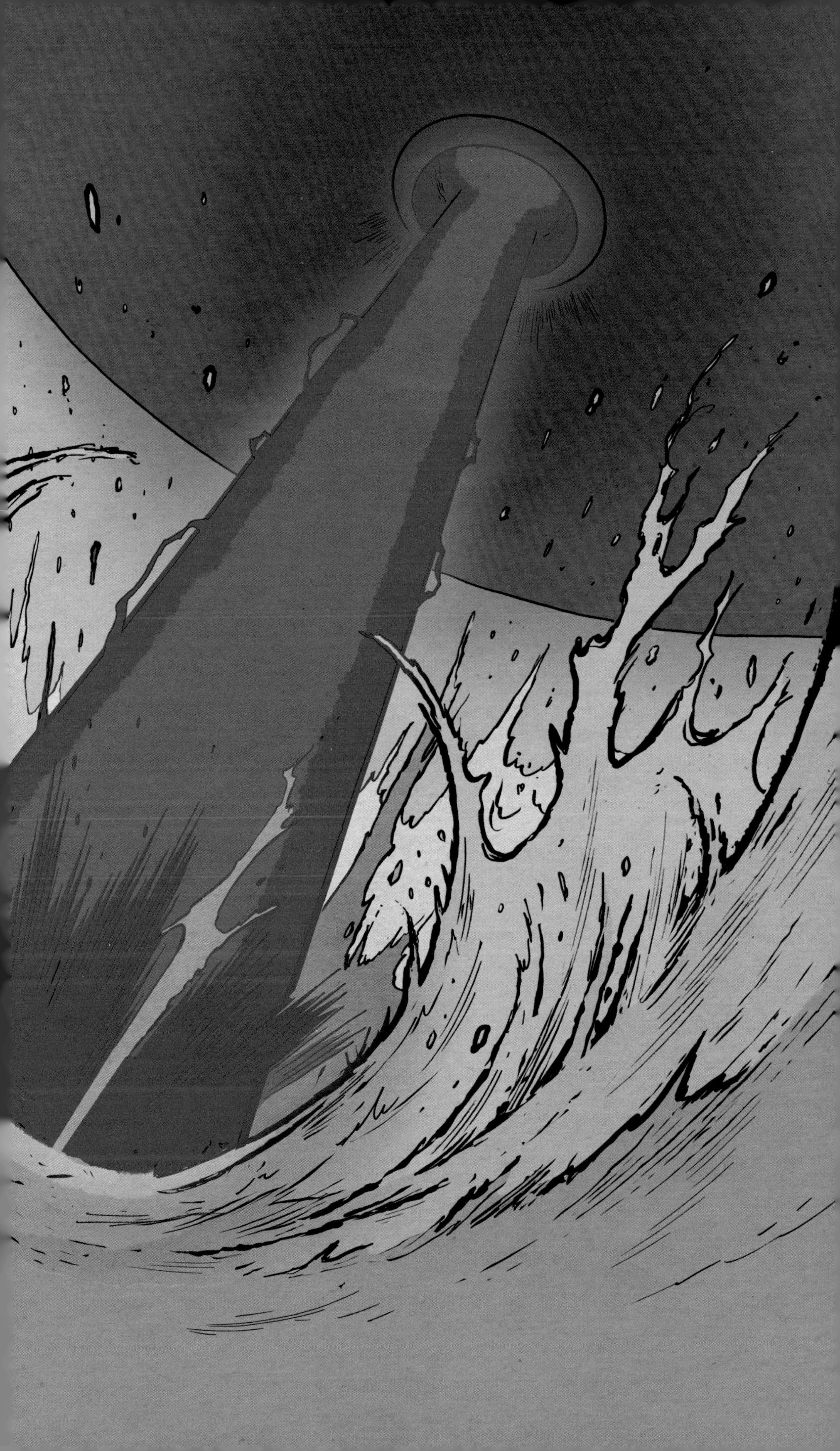

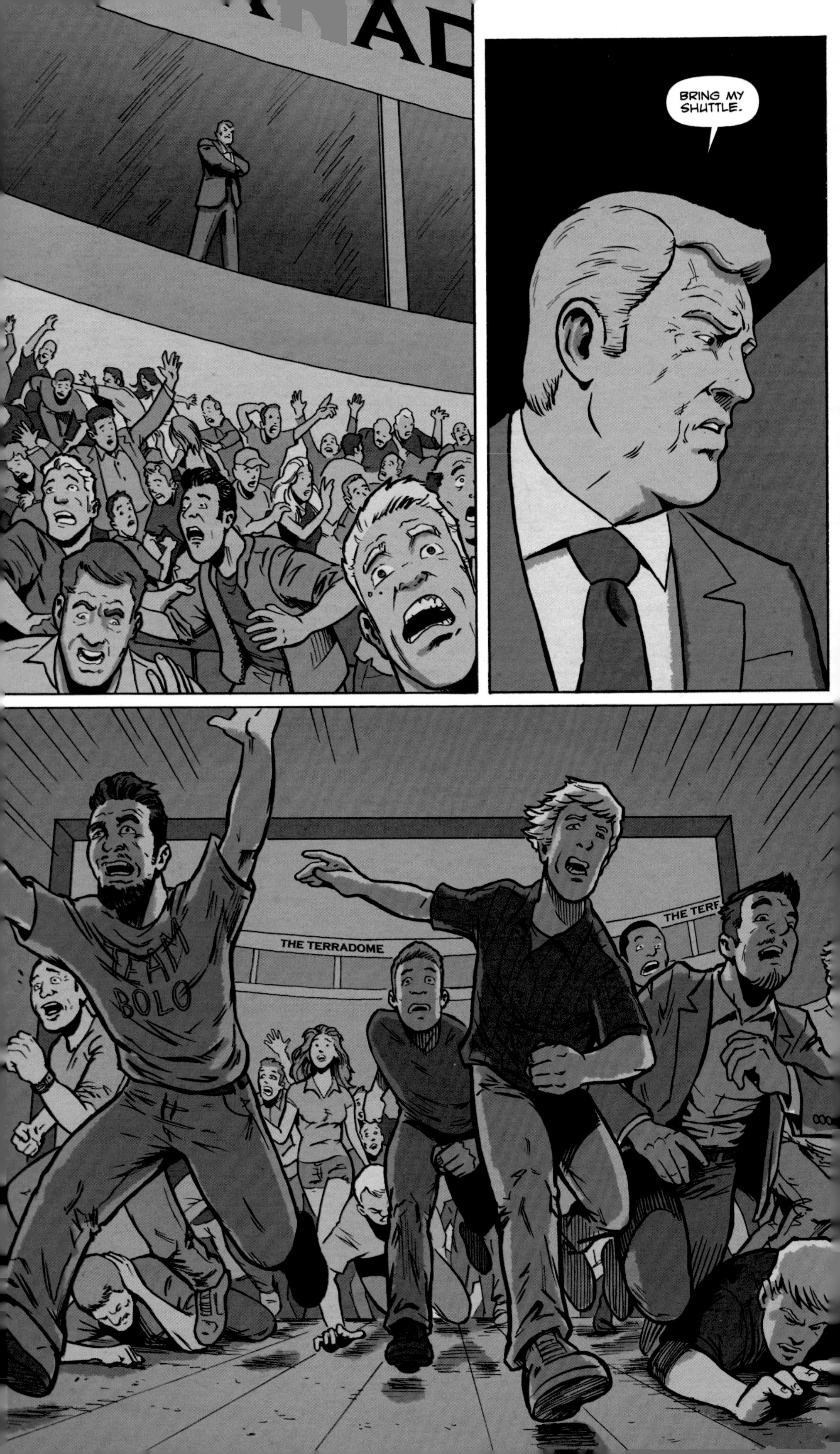
BRING MY SHUTTLE.
THE TERRADOME
TEAM BOLO

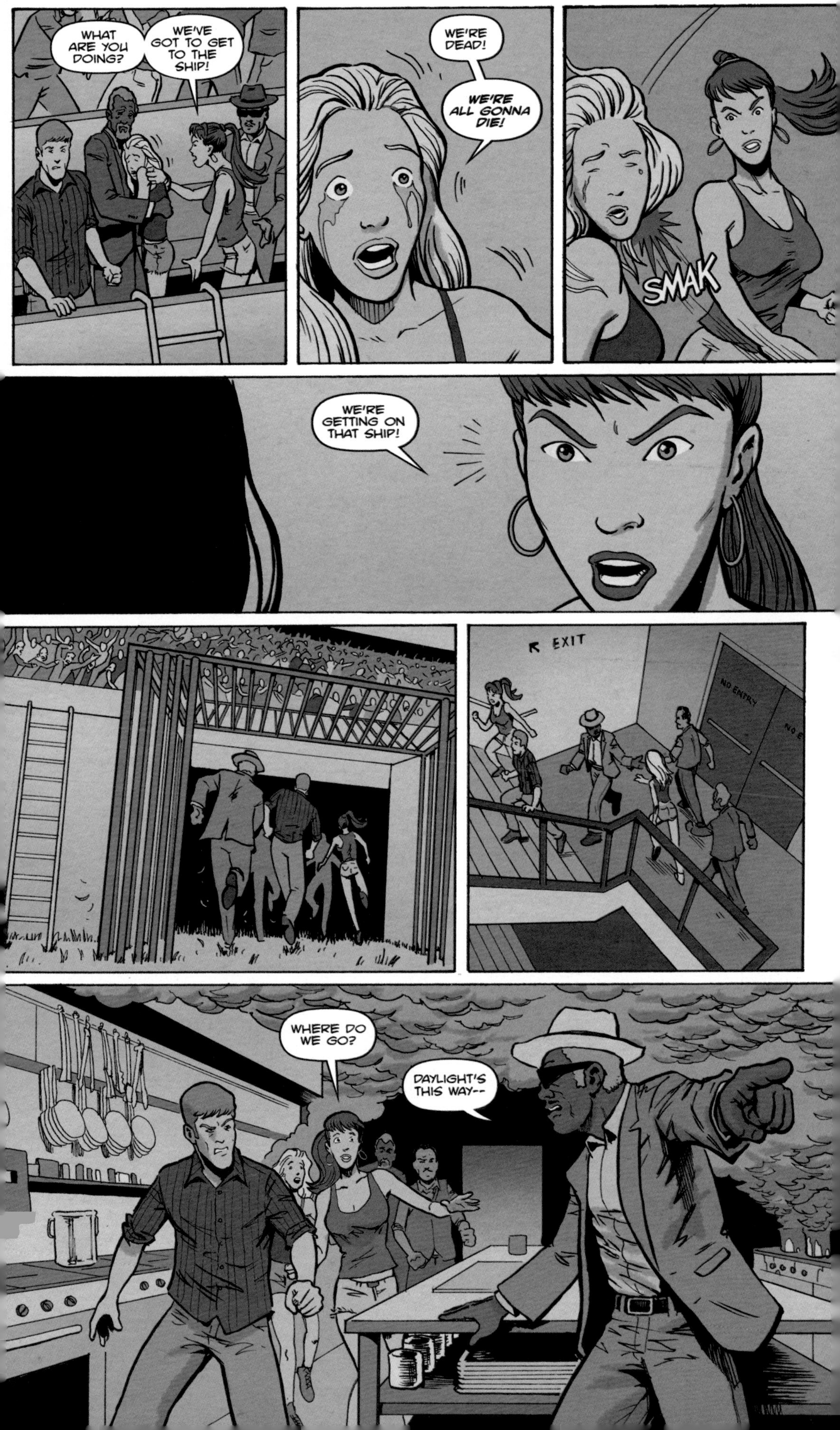
WHAT ARE YOU DOING?
WE'VE GOT TO GET TO THE SHIP!
WE'RE DEAD!
WE'RE ALL GONNA DIE!
SMAK
WE'RE GETTING ON THAT SHIP!
EXIT
NO ENTRY
WHERE DO WE GO?
DAYLIGHT'S THIS WAY--

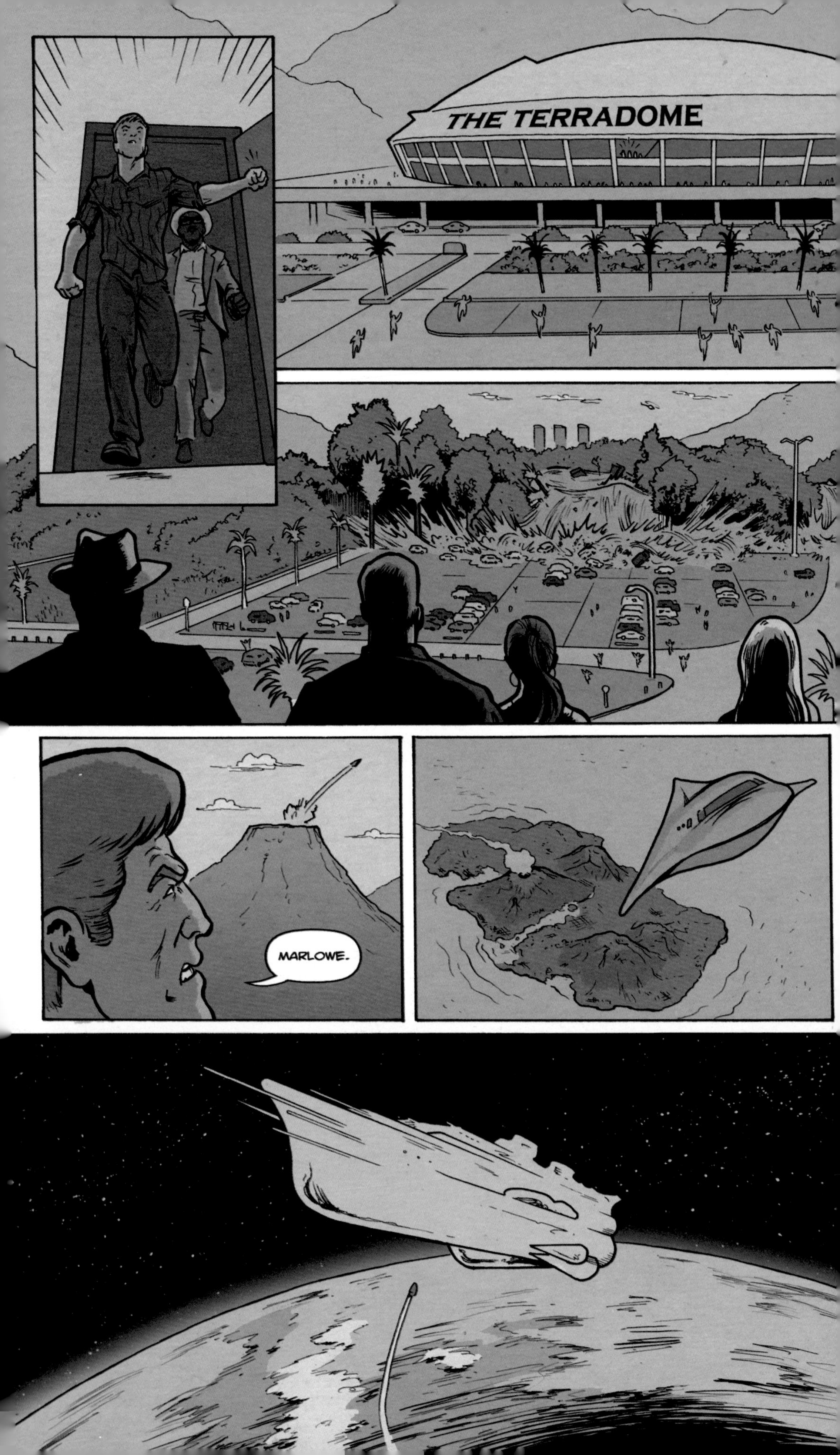
THE TERRADOME
MARLOWE.

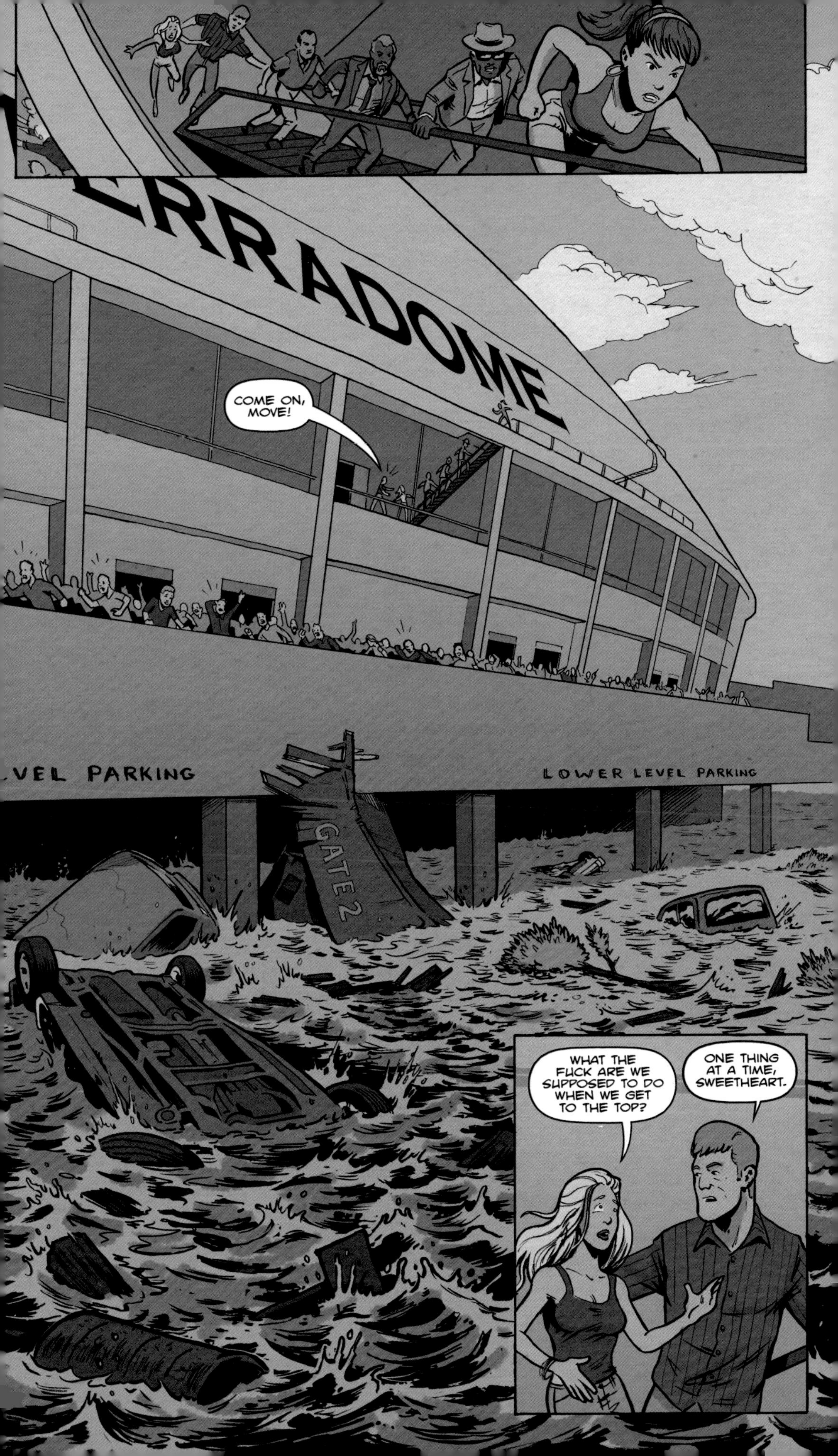
ERRADOME
COME ON, MOVE!
VEL PARKING
LOWER LEVEL PARKING
GATE 2
WHAT THE FUCK ARE WE SUPPOSED TO DO WHEN WE GET TO THE TOP?
ONE THING AT A TIME, SWEETHEART.

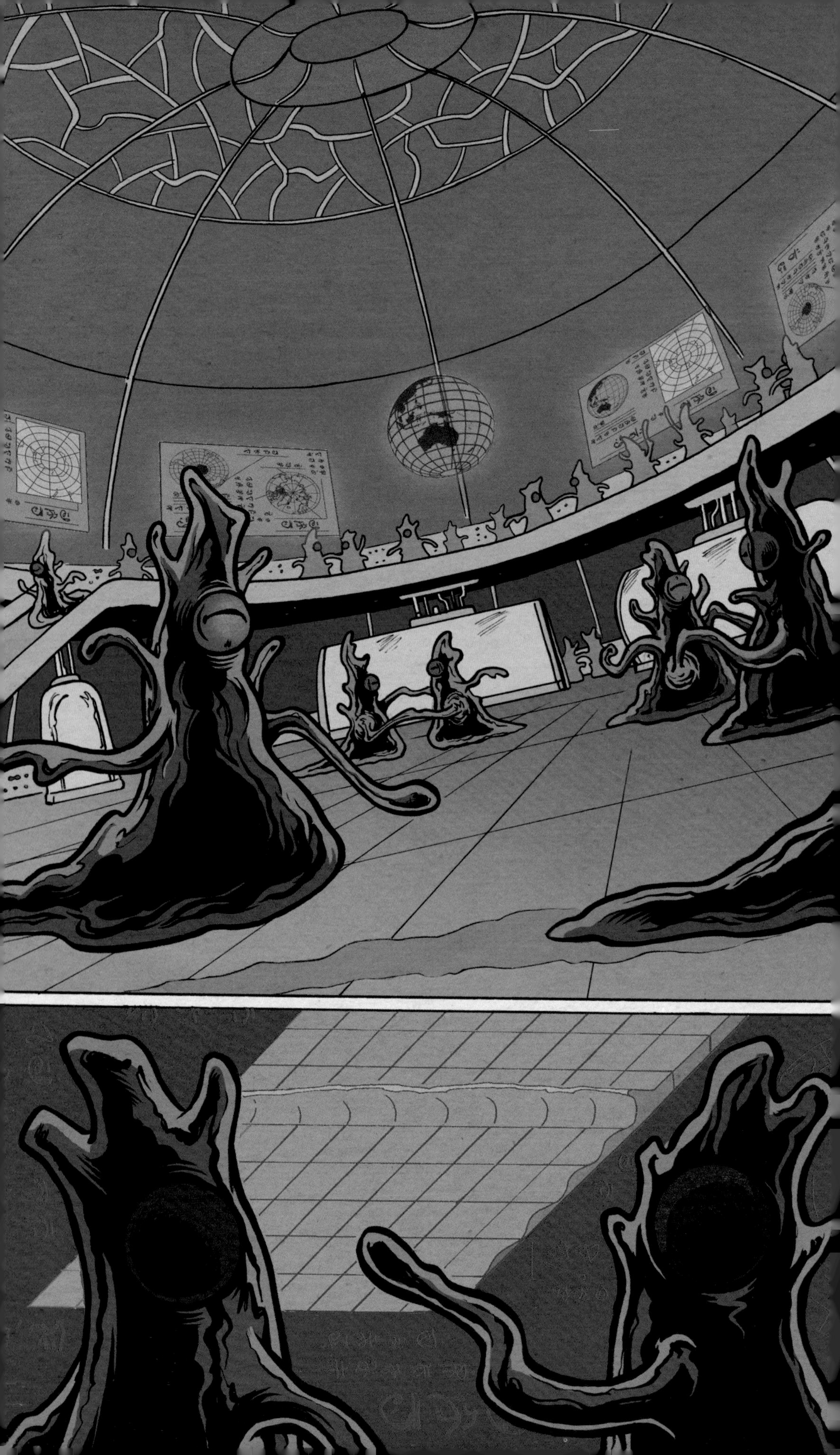

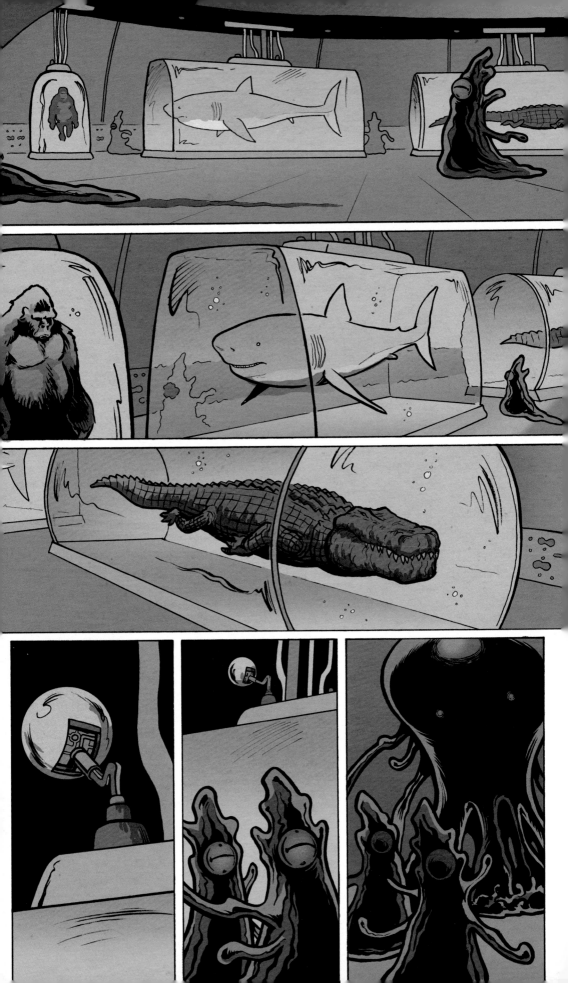

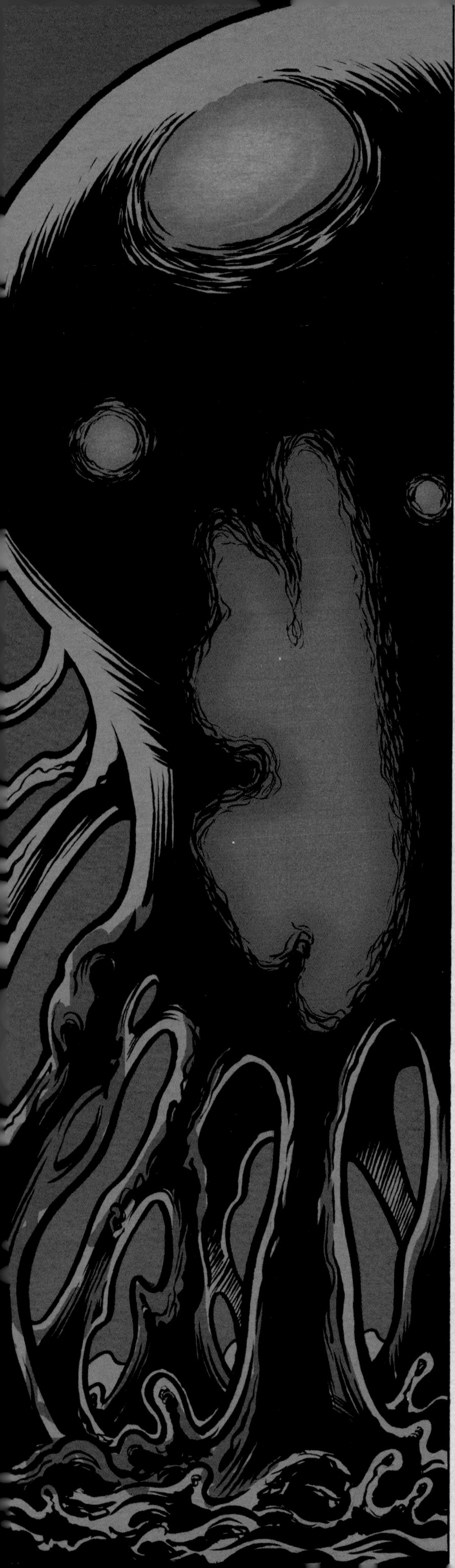
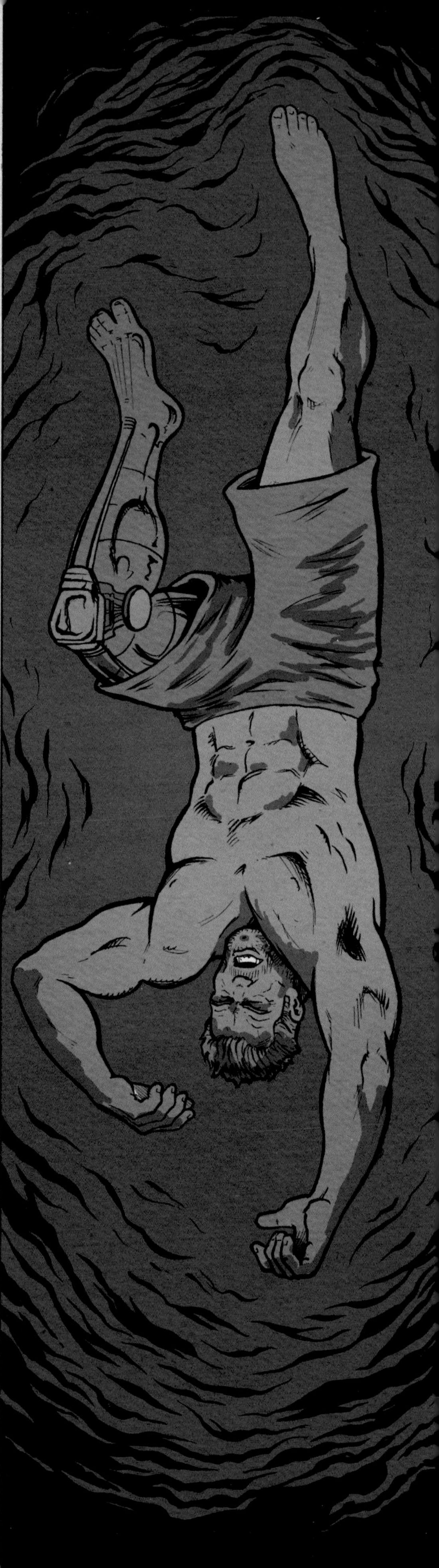

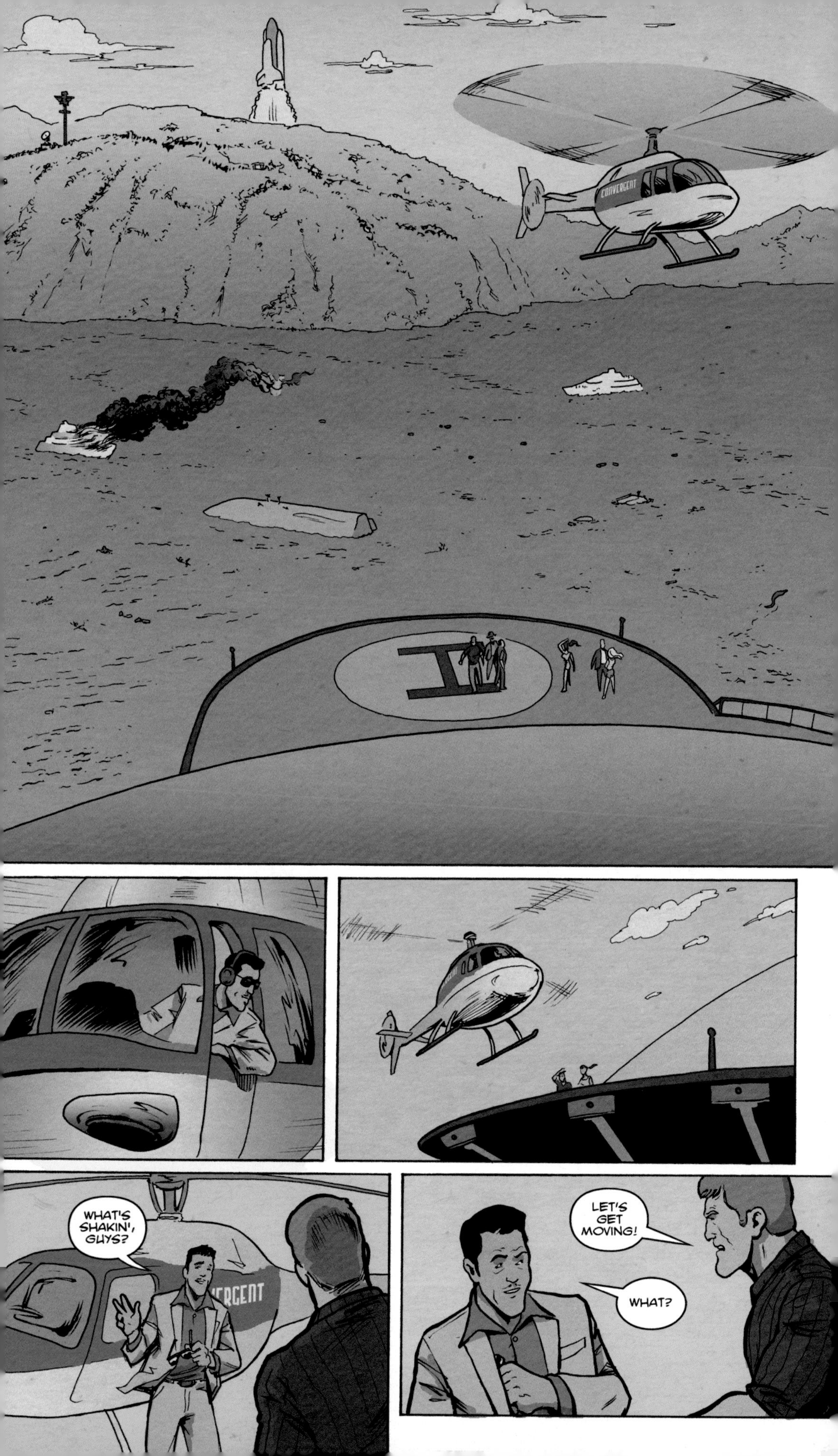
CONVERGENT
WHAT'S SHAKIN', GUYS?
LET'S GET MOVING!
WHAT?

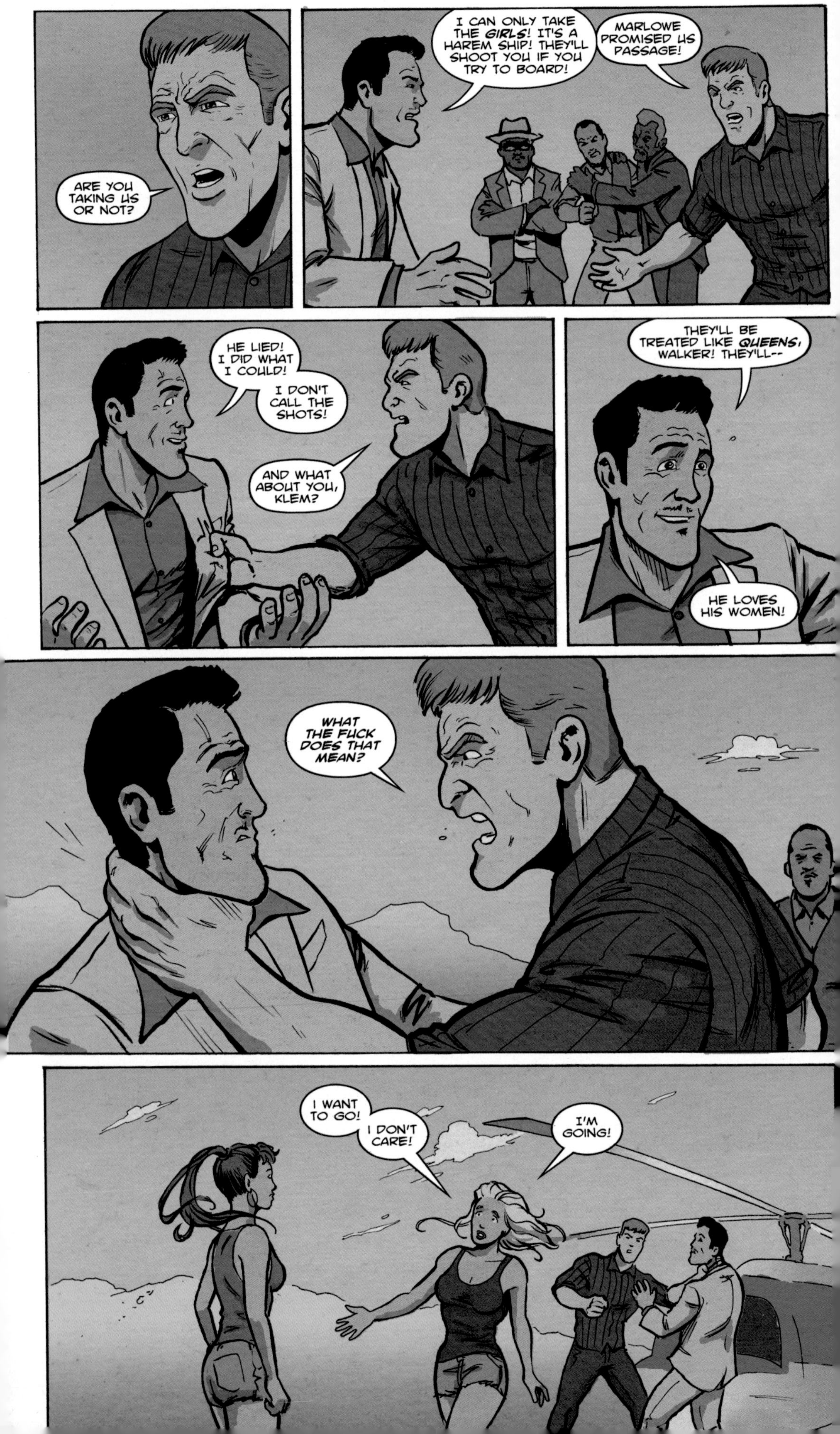

ARE YOU TAKING US OR NOT?
I CAN ONLY TAKE THE GIRLS! IT'S A HAREM SHIP! THEY'LL SHOOT YOU IF YOU TRY TO BOARD!
MARLOWE PROMISED US PASSAGE!
HE LIED! I DID WHAT I COULD!
I DON'T CALL THE SHOTS!
AND WHAT ABOUT YOU, KLEM?
THEY'LL BE TREATED LIKE QUEENS, WALKER! THEY'LL--
HE LOVES HIS WOMEN!
WHAT THE FUCK DOES THAT MEAN?
I WANT TO GO!
I DON'T CARE!
I'M GOING!

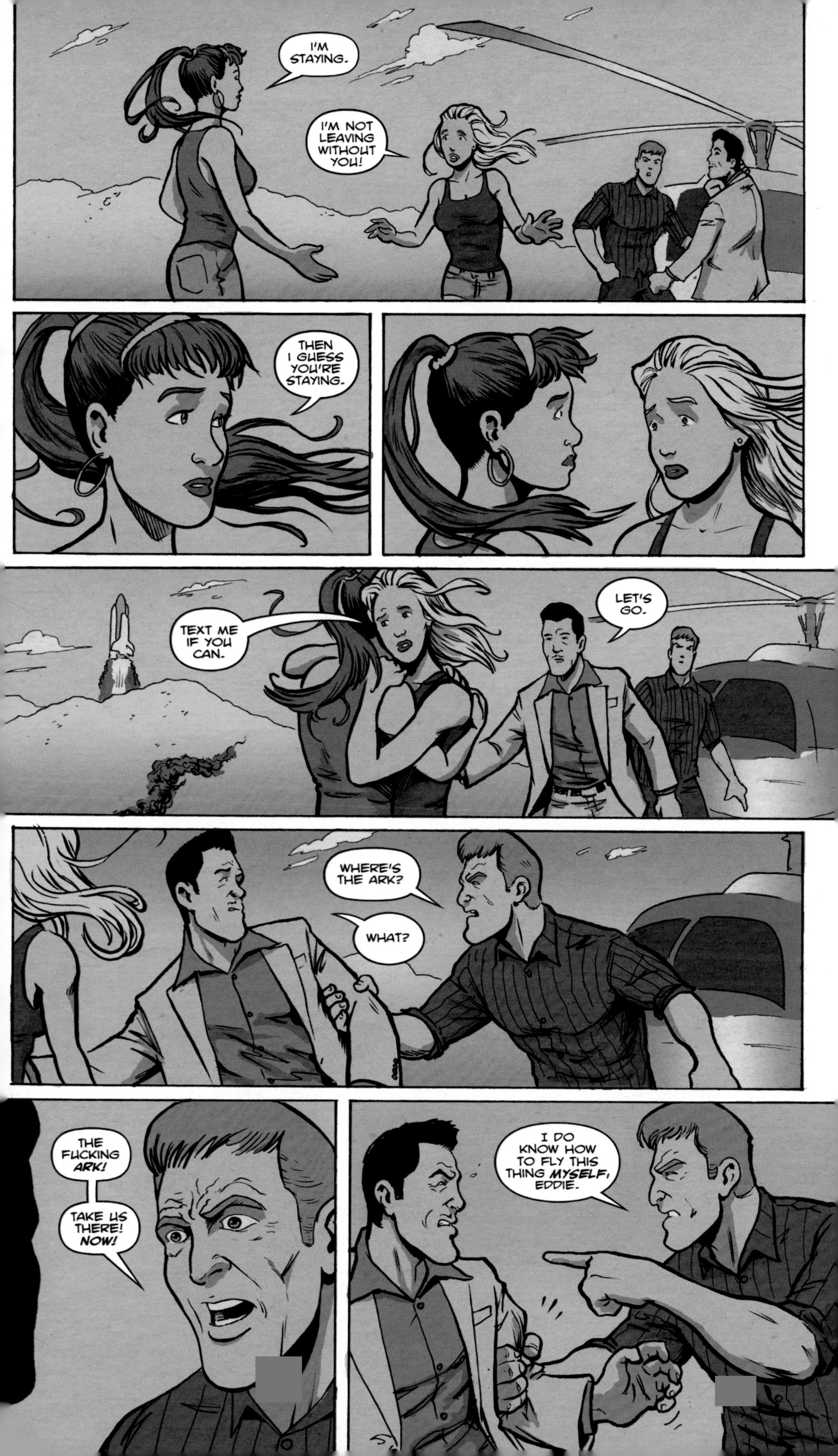

I'M STAYING.
I'M NOT LEAVING WITHOUT YOU!
THEN I GUESS YOU'RE STAYING.
TEXT ME IF YOU CAN.
LET'S GO.
WHERE'S THE ARK?
WHAT?
THE FUCKING *ARK!*
TAKE US THERE! *NOW!*
I DO KNOW HOW TO FLY THIS THING *MYSELF,* EDDIE.

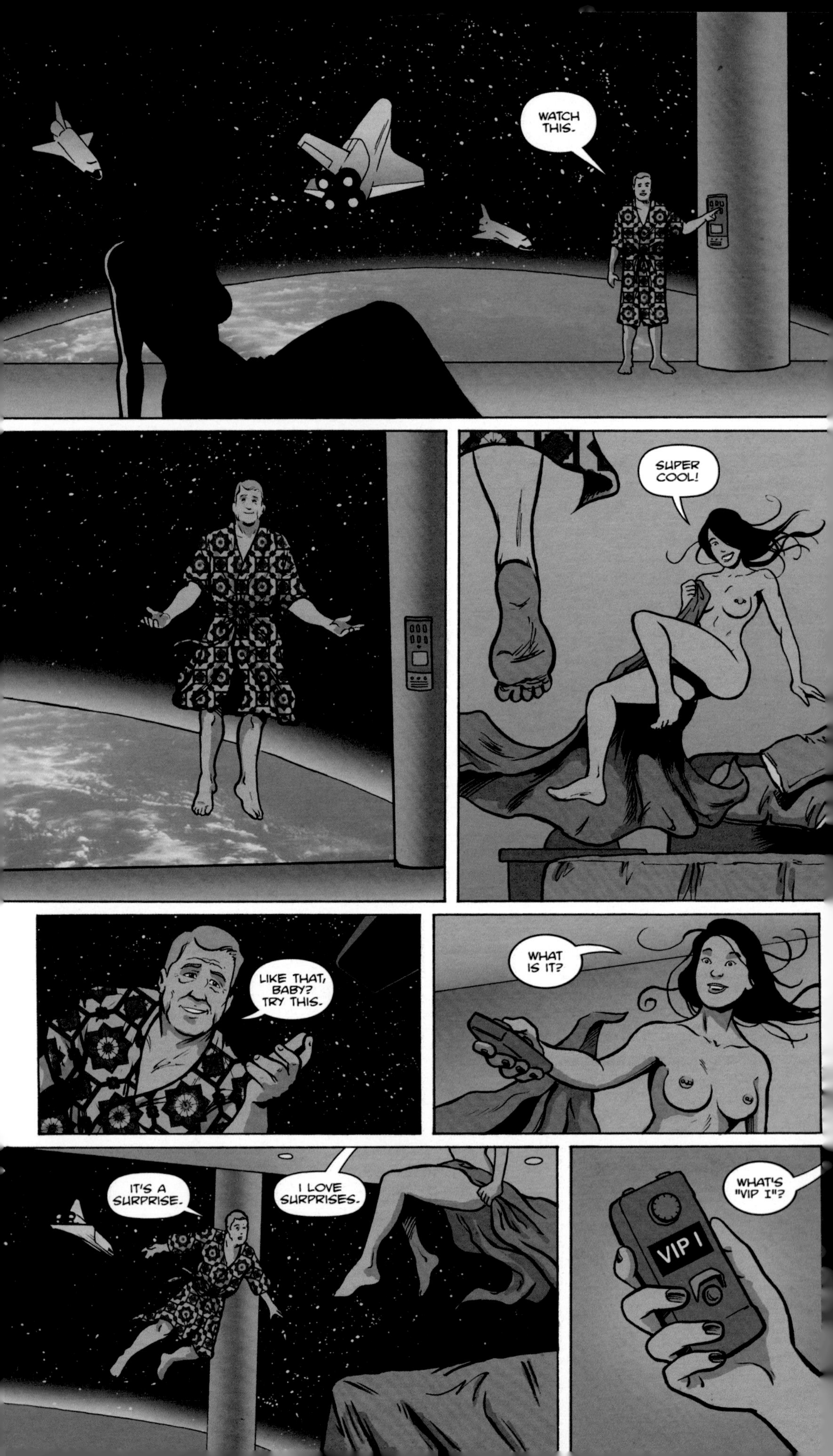
WATCH THIS.
SUPER COOL!
LIKE THAT, BABY? TRY THIS.
WHAT IS IT?
IT'S A SURPRISE.
I LOVE SURPRISES.
VIP I
WHAT'S "VIP I"?

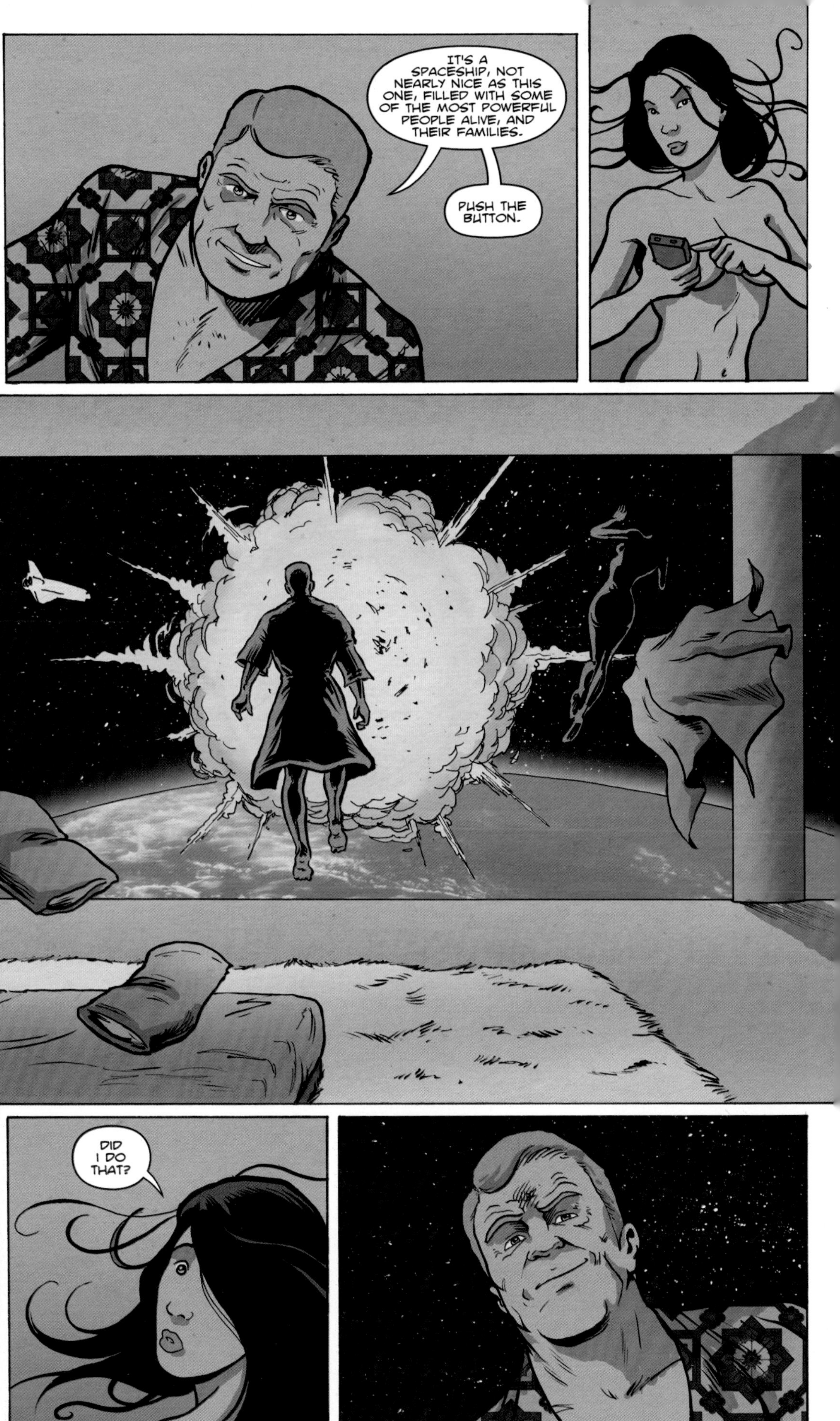
IT'S A SPACESHIP, NOT NEARLY NICE AS THIS ONE, FILLED WITH SOME OF THE MOST POWERFUL PEOPLE ALIVE, AND THEIR FAMILIES.
PUSH THE BUTTON.
DID I DO THAT?

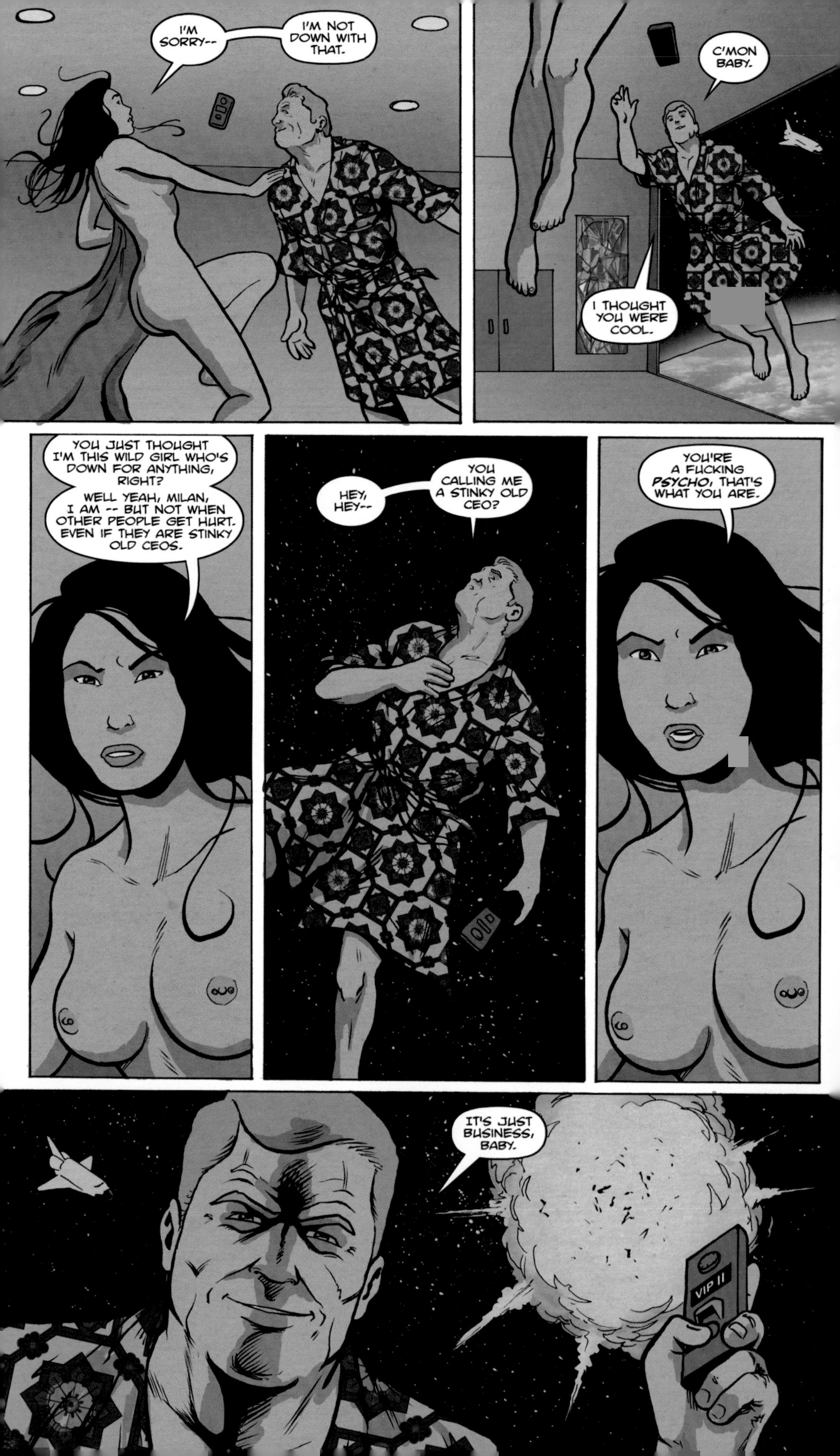
I'M SORRY--
I'M NOT DOWN WITH THAT.
C'MON BABY.
I THOUGHT YOU WERE COOL.
YOU JUST THOUGHT I'M THIS WILD GIRL WHO'S DOWN FOR ANYTHING, RIGHT?
WELL YEAH, MILAN, I AM -- BUT NOT WHEN OTHER PEOPLE GET HURT. EVEN IF THEY ARE STINKY OLD CEOS.
HEY, HEY--
YOU CALLING ME A STINKY OLD CEO?
YOU'RE A FUCKING *PSYCHO*, THAT'S WHAT YOU ARE.
IT'S JUST BUSINESS, BABY.
VIP II

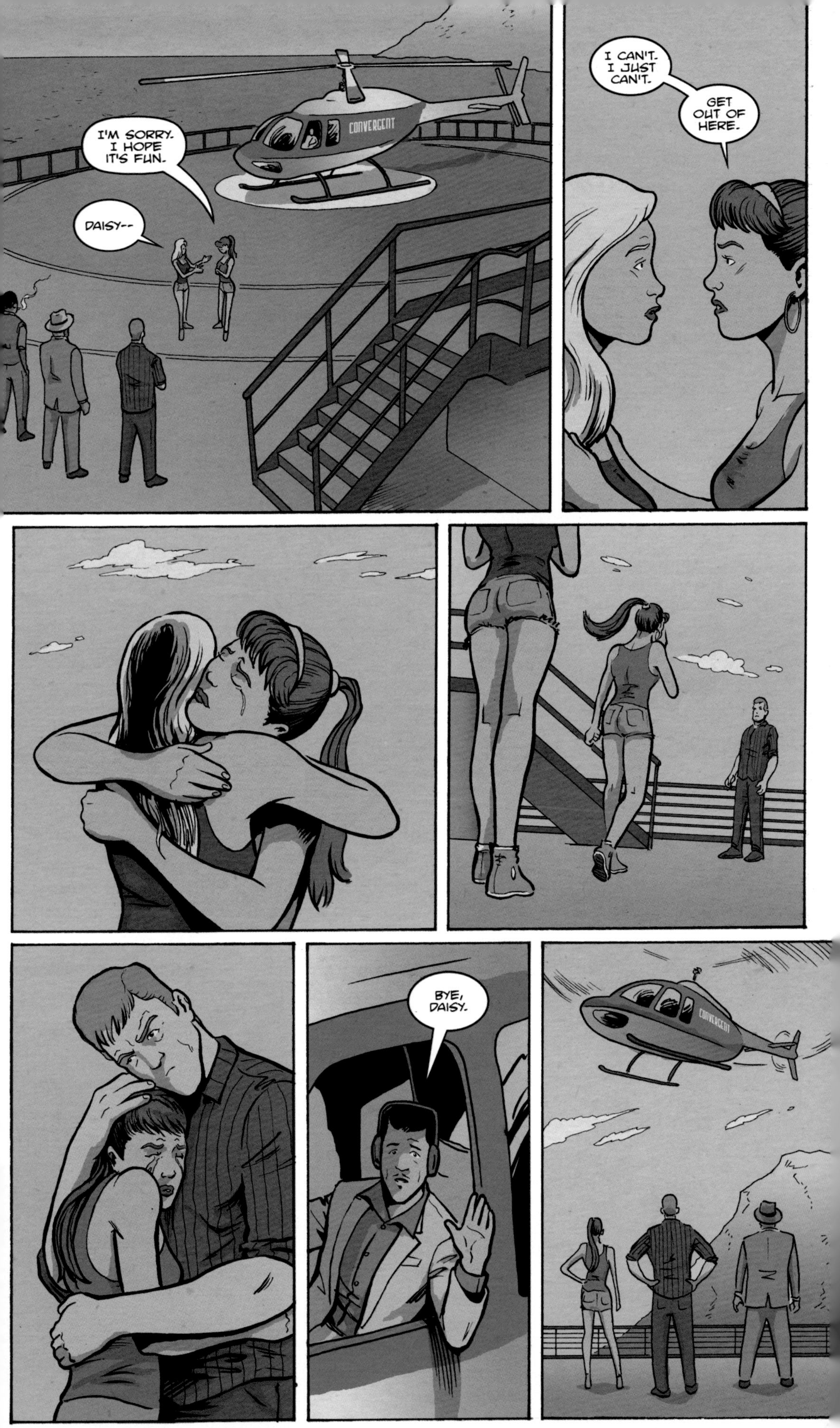
I'M SORRY. I HOPE IT'S FUN.
DAISY--
I CAN'T. I JUST CAN'T.
GET OUT OF HERE.
BYE, DAISY.
CONVERGENT

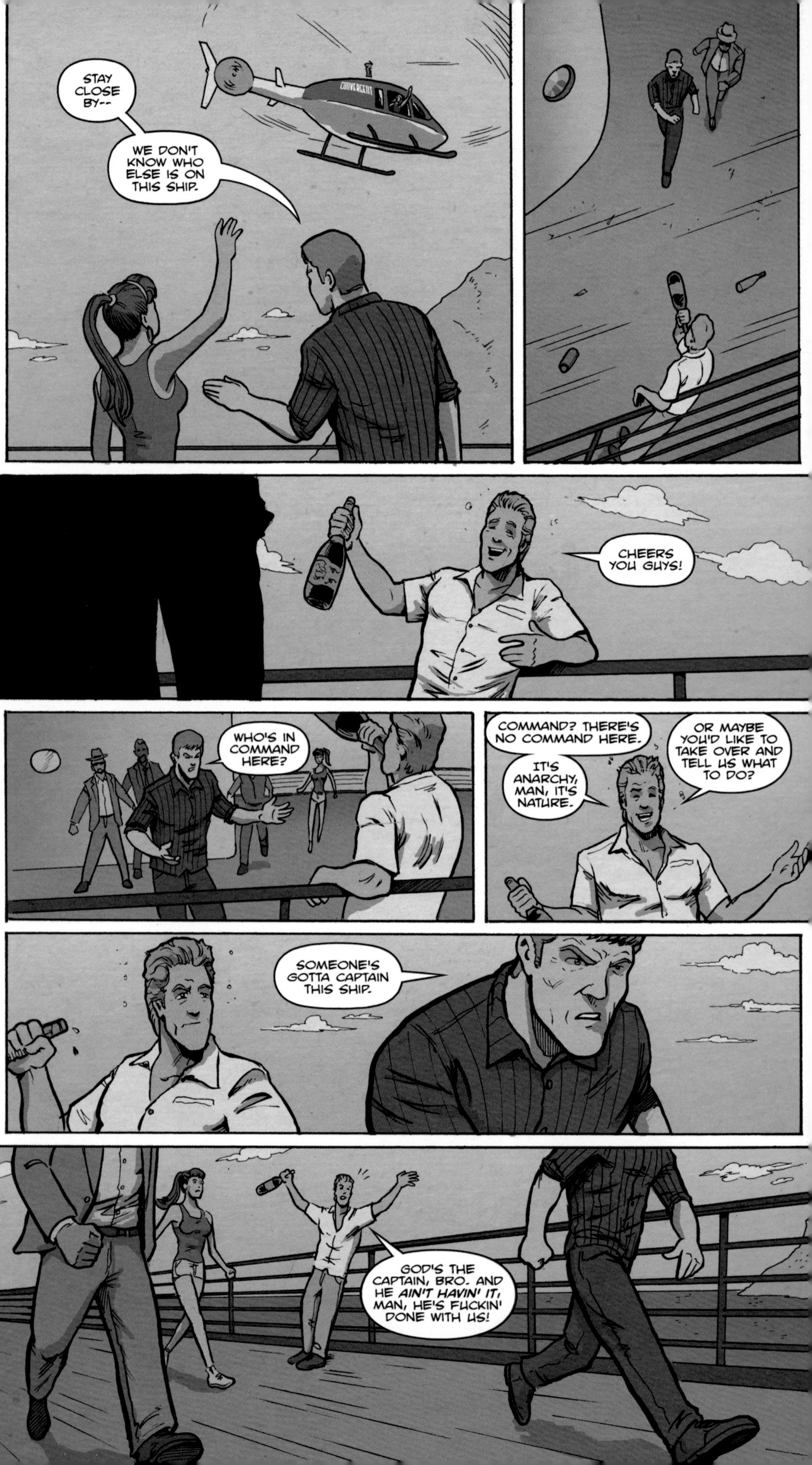
STAY CLOSE BY--
WE DON'T KNOW WHO ELSE IS ON THIS SHIP.
CHEERS YOU GUYS!
WHO'S IN COMMAND HERE?
COMMAND? THERE'S NO COMMAND HERE.
IT'S ANARCHY, MAN, IT'S NATURE.
OR MAYBE YOU'D LIKE TO TAKE OVER AND TELL US WHAT TO DO?
SOMEONE'S GOTTA CAPTAIN THIS SHIP.
GOD'S THE CAPTAIN, BRO. AND HE *AIN'T HAVIN' IT,* MAN, HE'S FUCKIN' DONE WITH US!

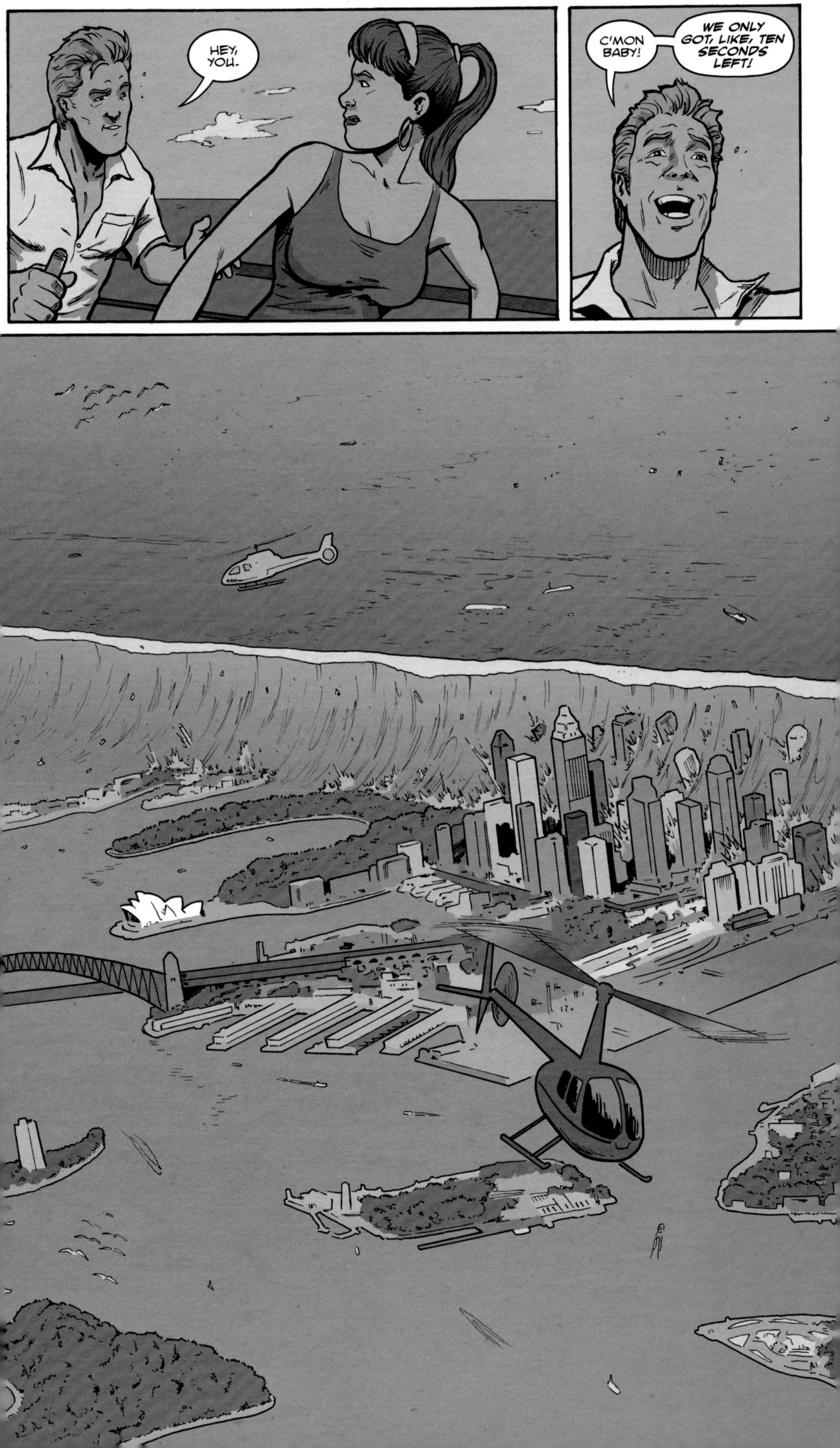
HEY, YOU.
C'MON BABY!
WE ONLY GOT, LIKE, TEN SECONDS LEFT!

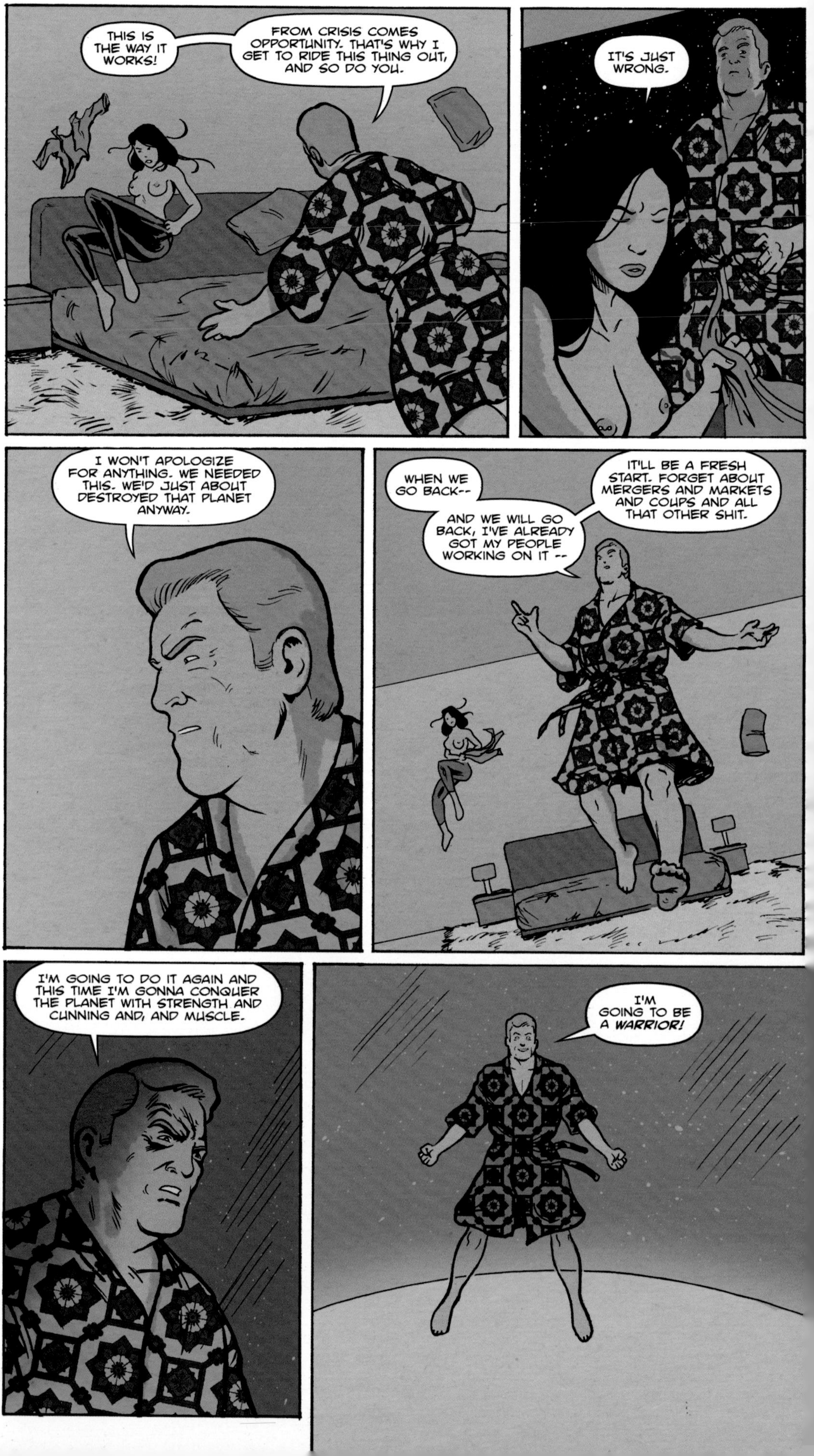
THIS IS THE WAY IT WORKS!
FROM CRISIS COMES OPPORTUNITY. THAT'S WHY I GET TO RIDE THIS THING OUT, AND SO DO YOU.
IT'S JUST WRONG.
I WON'T APOLOGIZE FOR ANYTHING. WE NEEDED THIS. WE'D JUST ABOUT DESTROYED THAT PLANET ANYWAY.
WHEN WE GO BACK--
AND WE WILL GO BACK, I'VE ALREADY GOT MY PEOPLE WORKING ON IT --
IT'LL BE A FRESH START. FORGET ABOUT MERGERS AND MARKETS AND COUPS AND ALL THAT OTHER SHIT.
I'M GOING TO DO IT AGAIN AND THIS TIME I'M GONNA CONQUER THE PLANET WITH STRENGTH AND CUNNING AND, AND MUSCLE.
I'M GOING TO BE A WARRIOR!

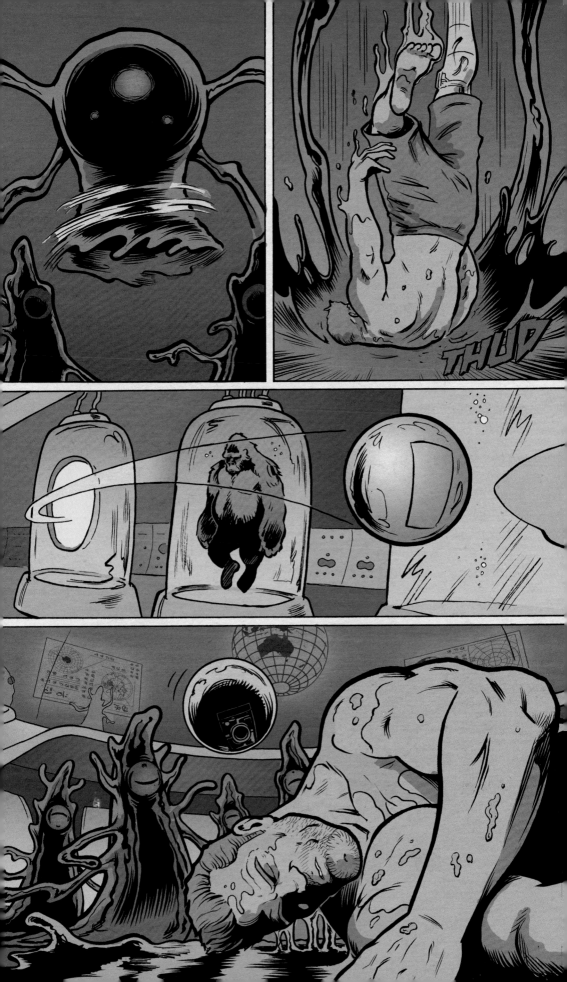

THUD

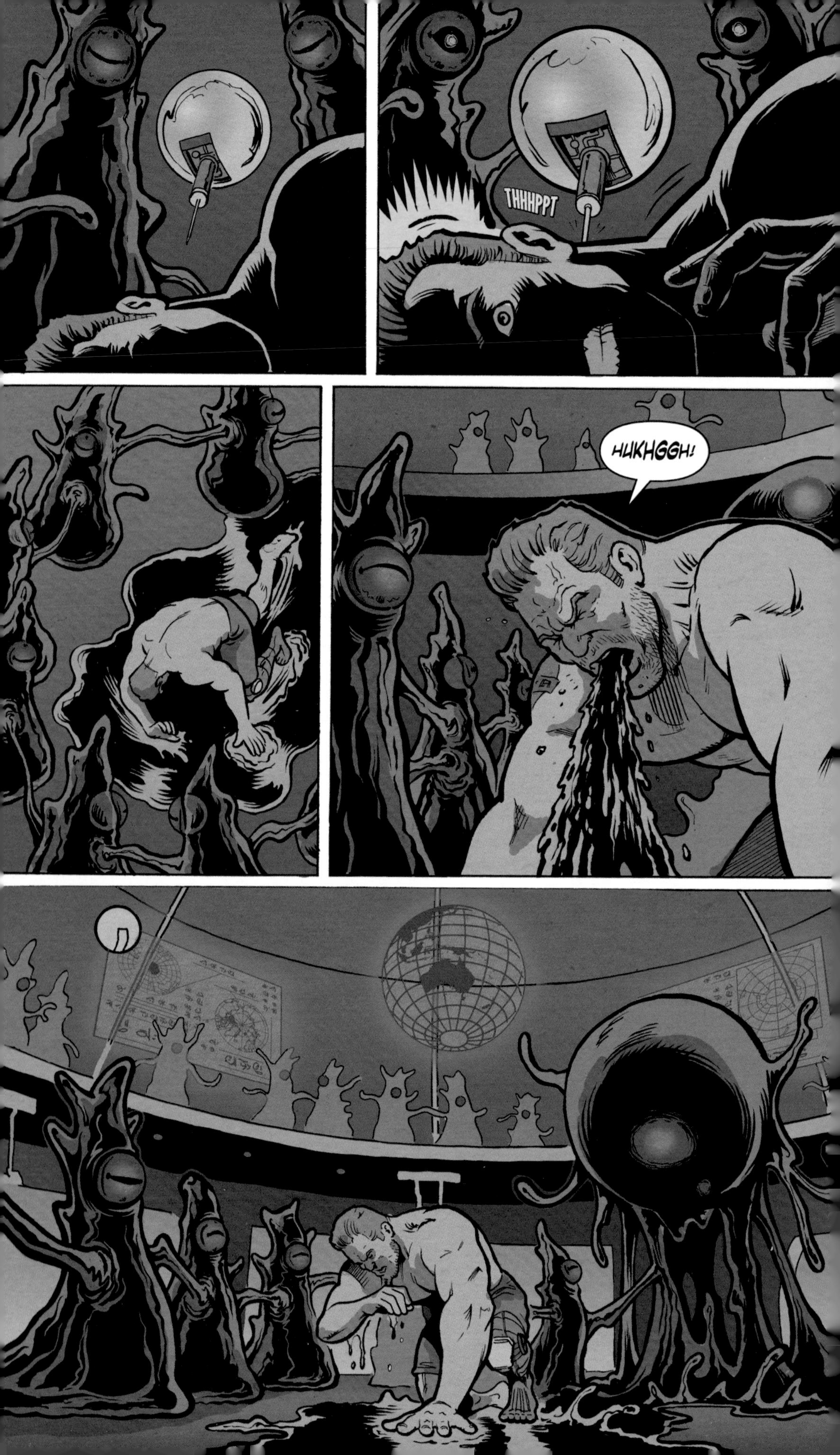
THHHPPT
HUKHGGH!

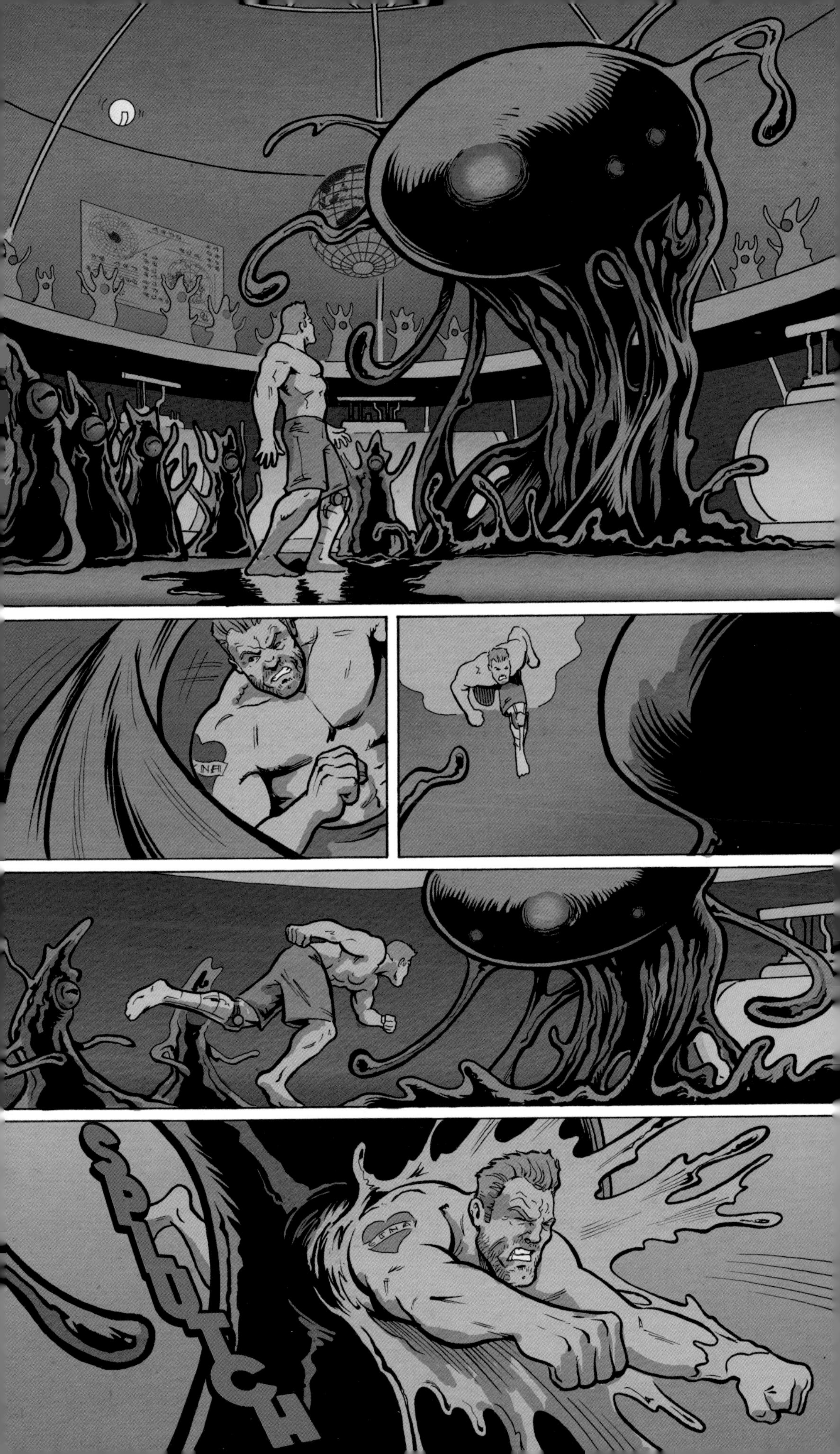
SPLUTCH

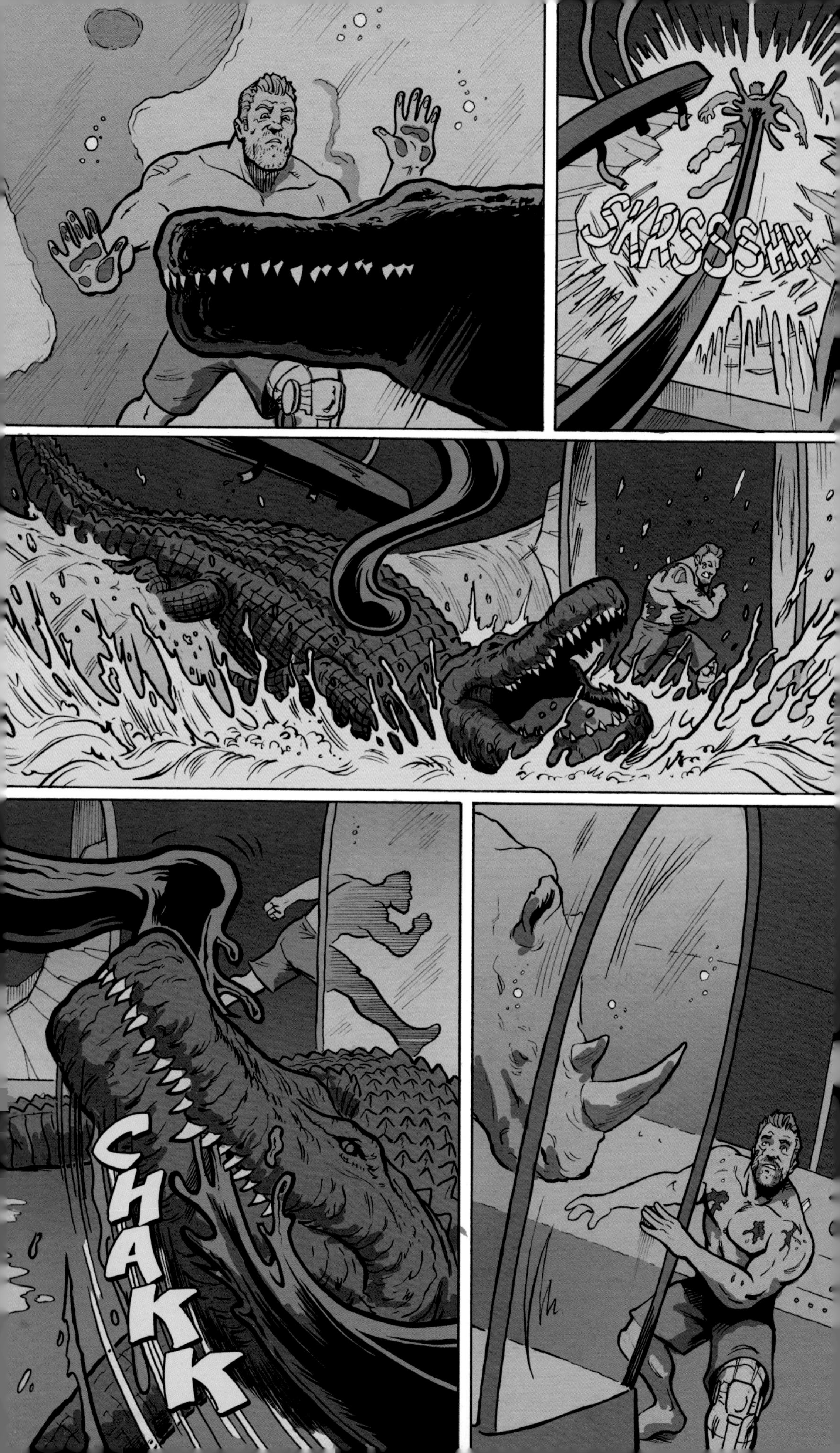
SKRSSSHH
CHAKK

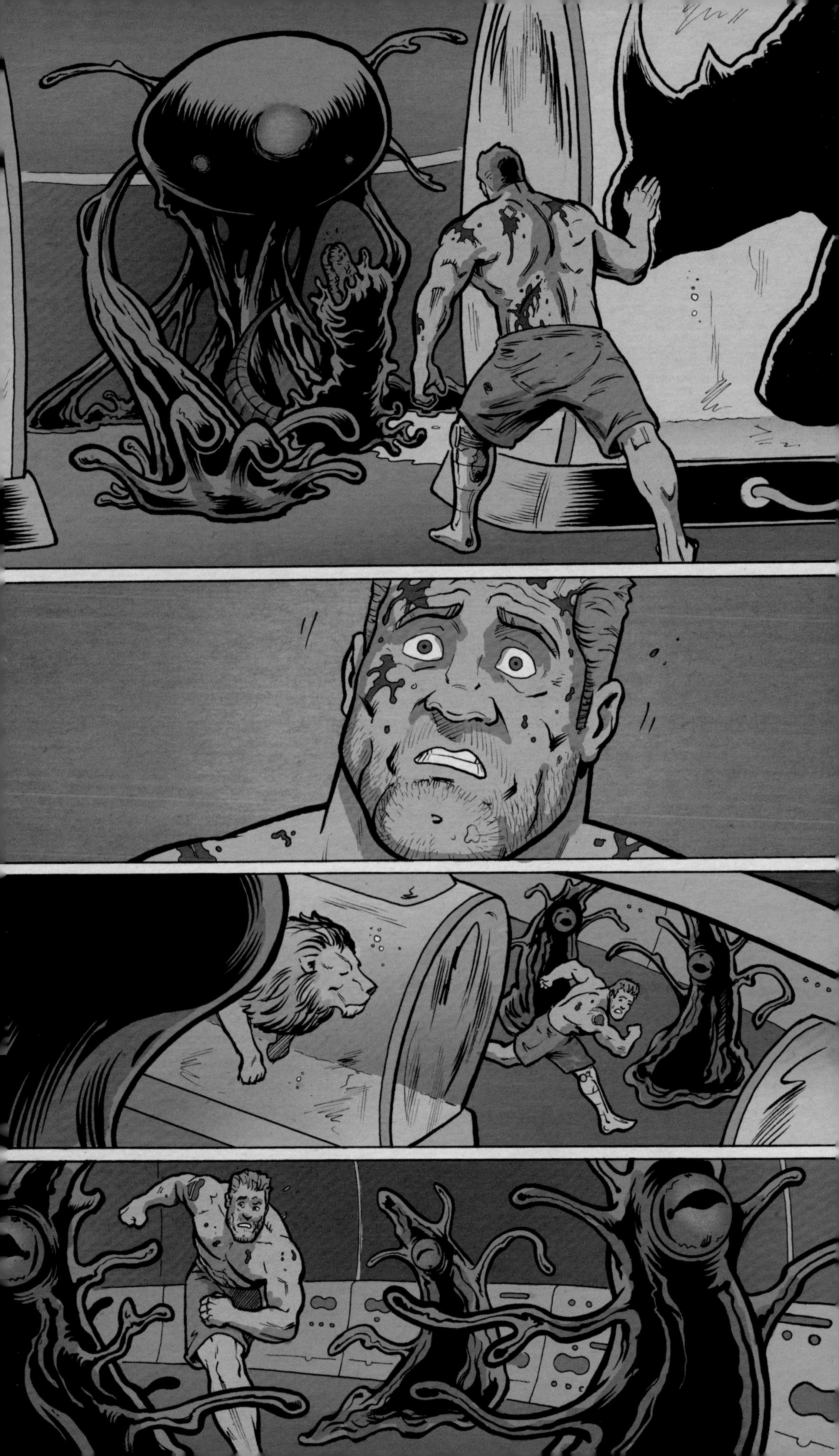

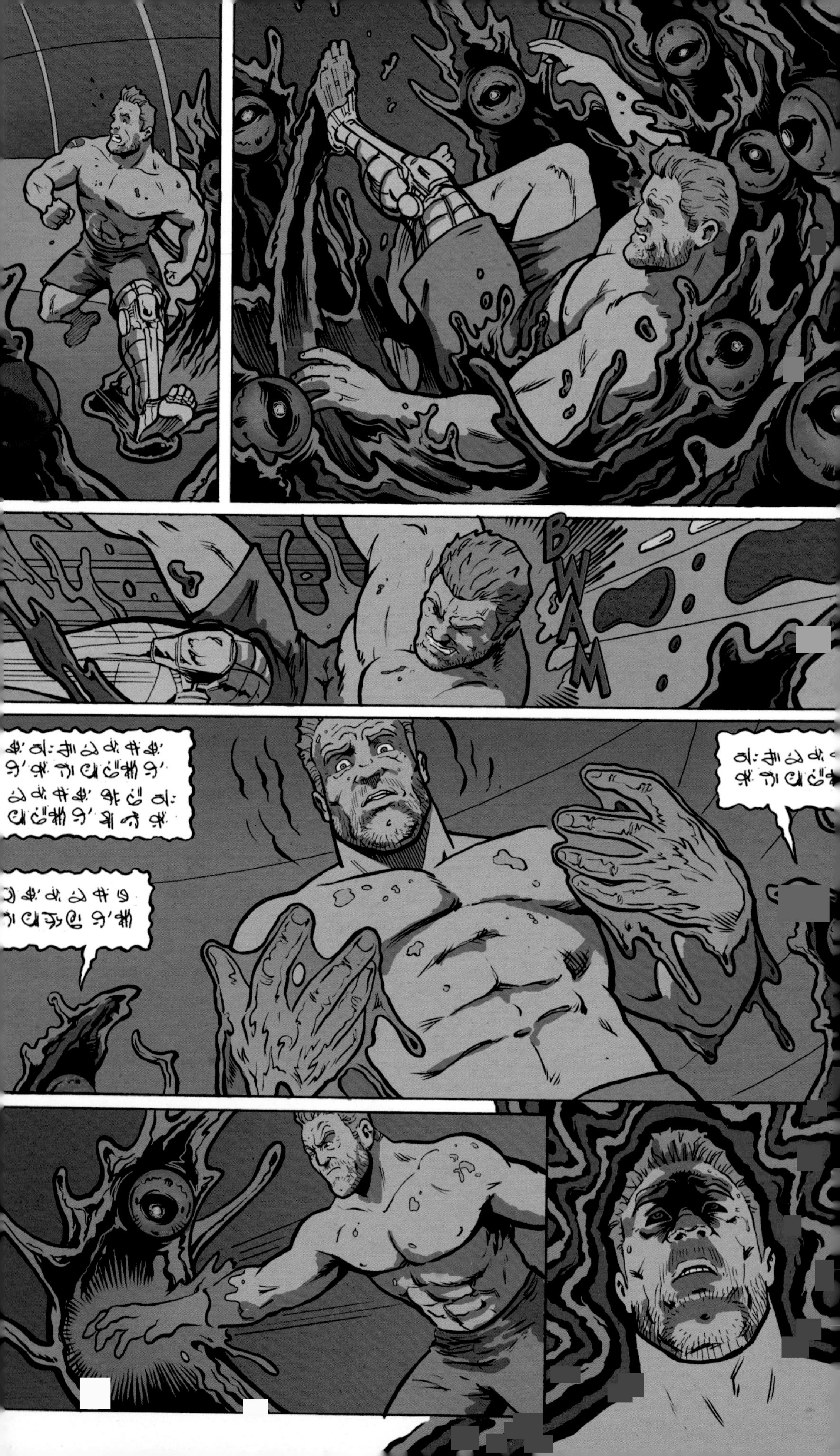
BWAM

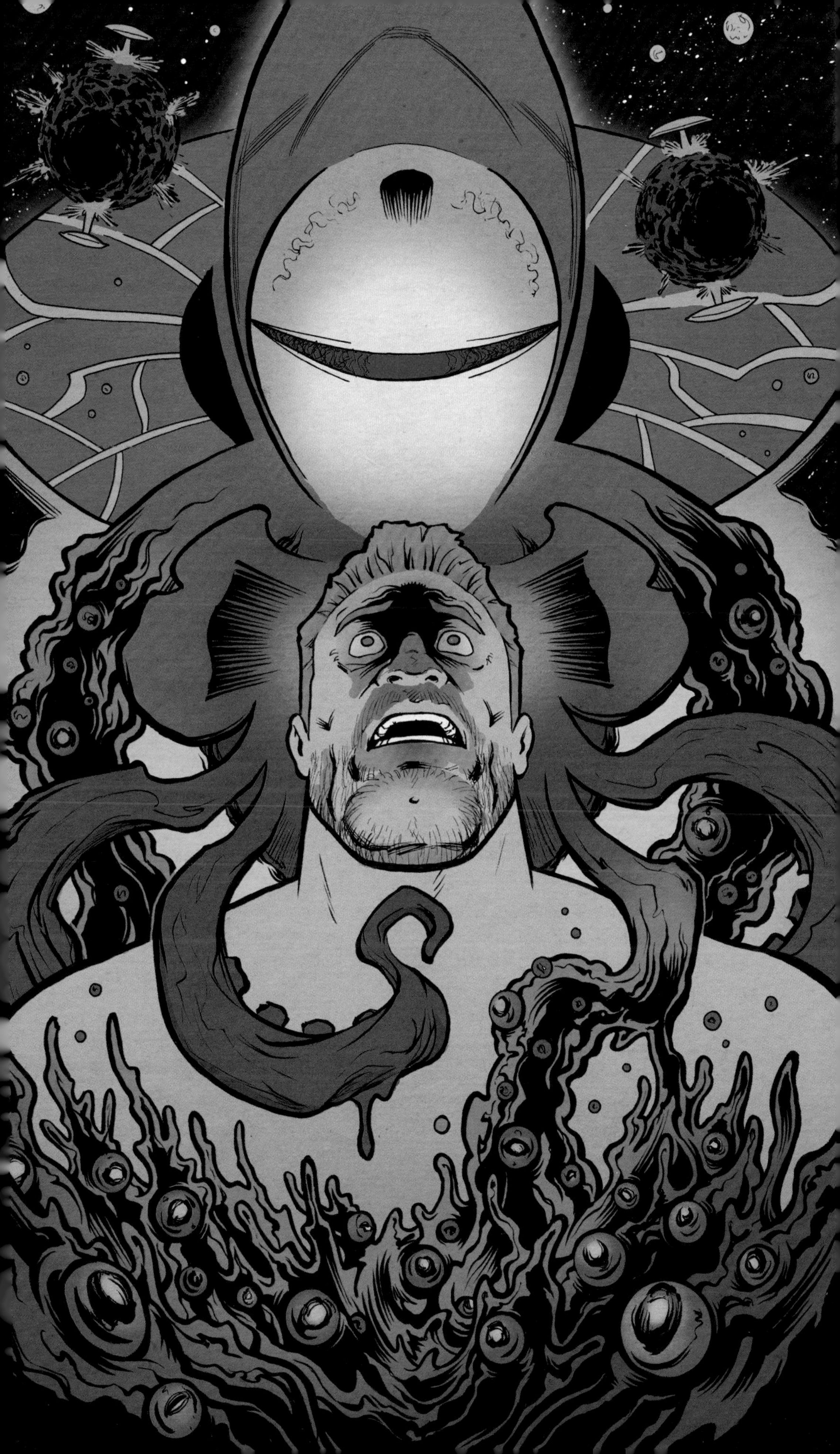

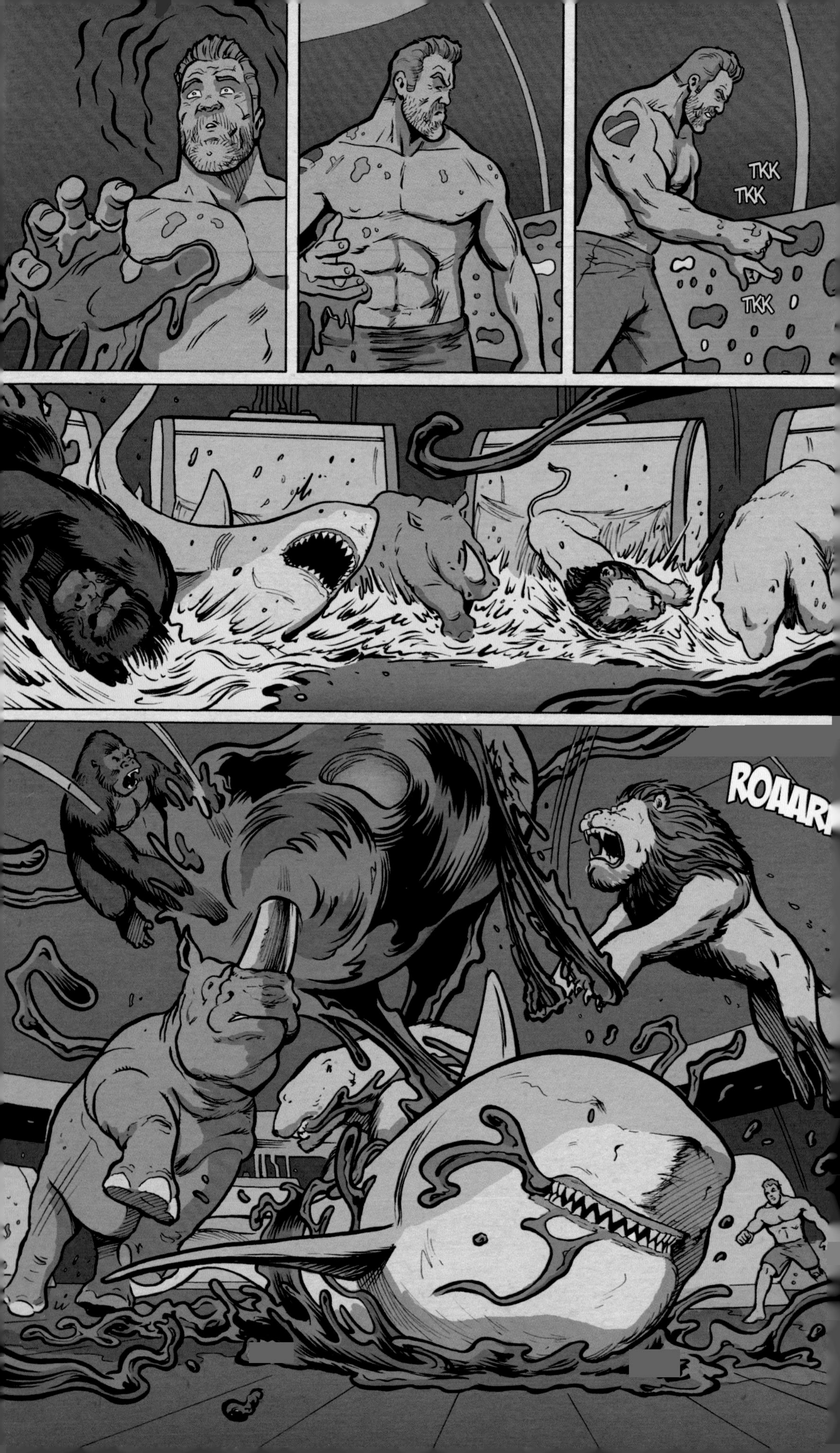
TKK
TKK
TKK
ROAAR

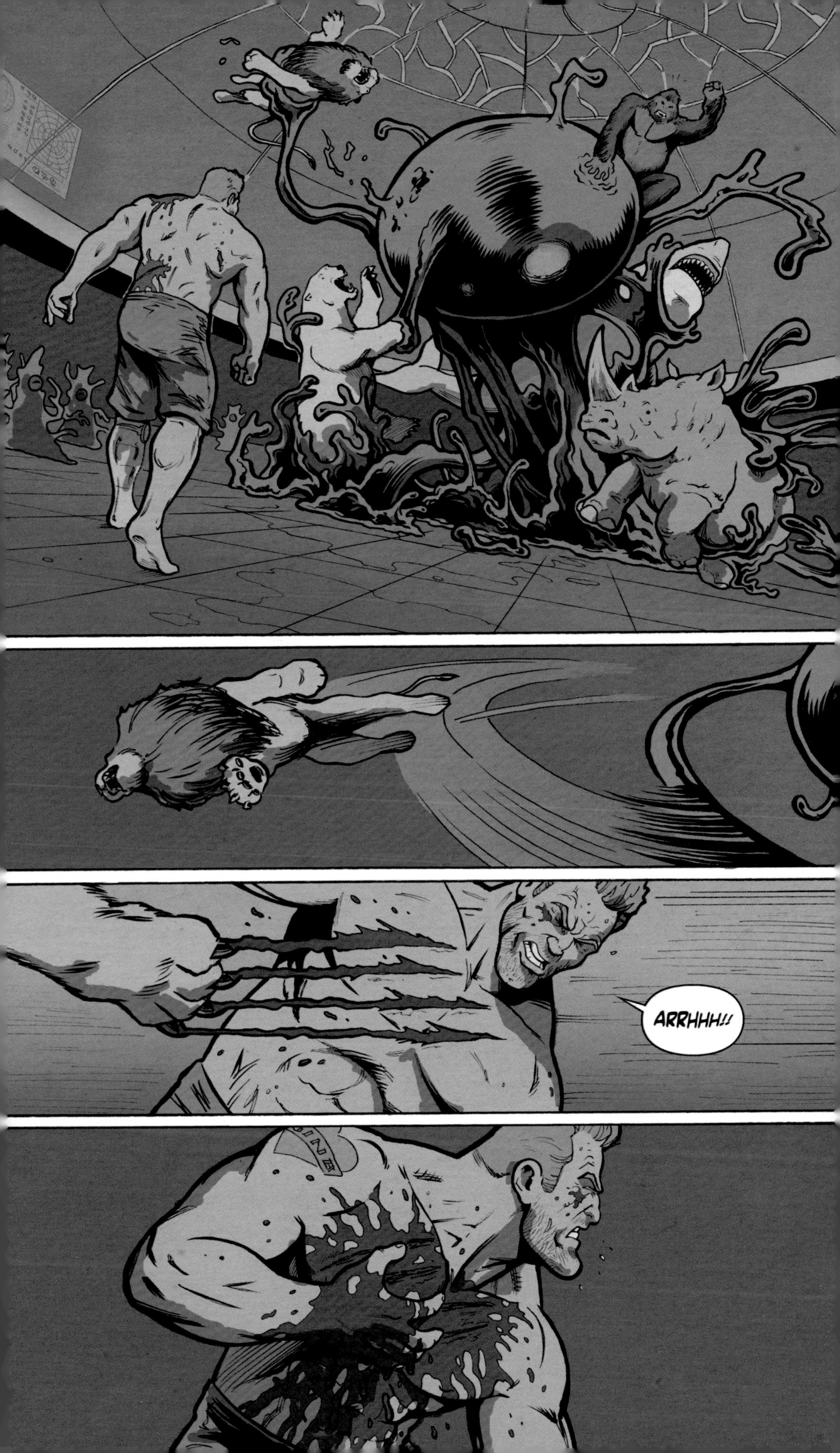
ARRHHH!!

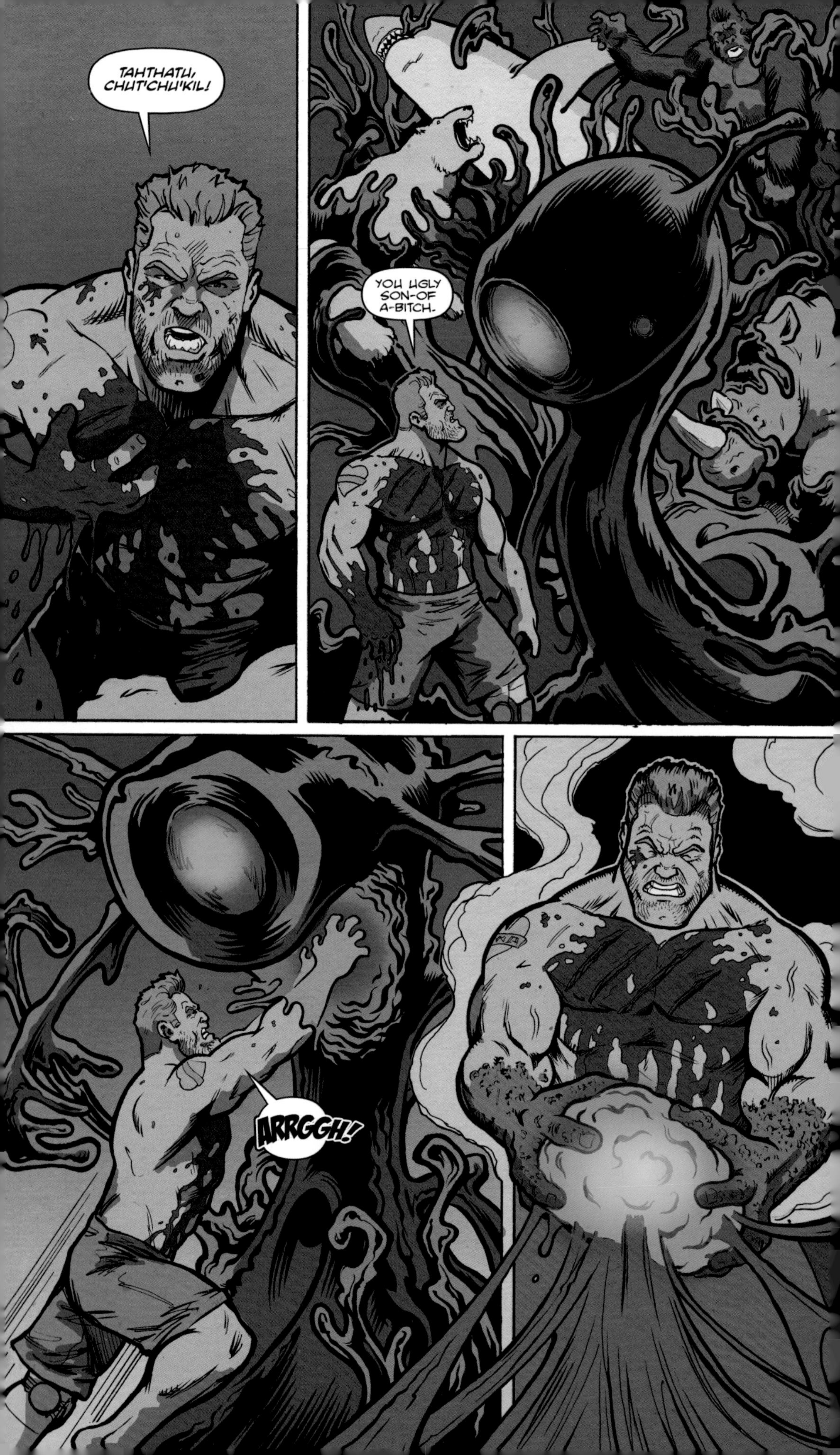
TAHTHATU, CHUT'CHU'KIL!
YOU UGLY SON-OF A-BITCH.
ARRGGH!

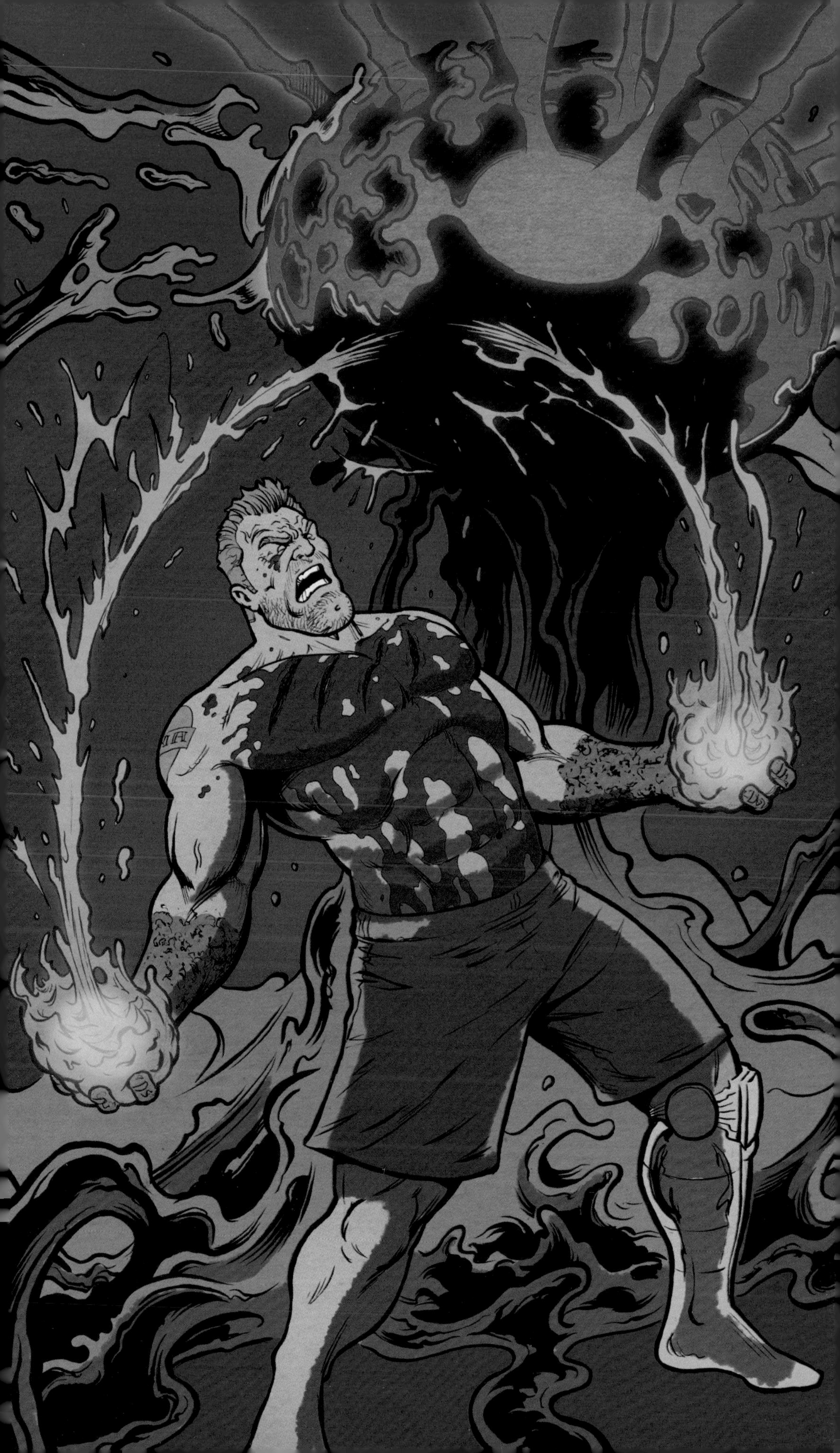

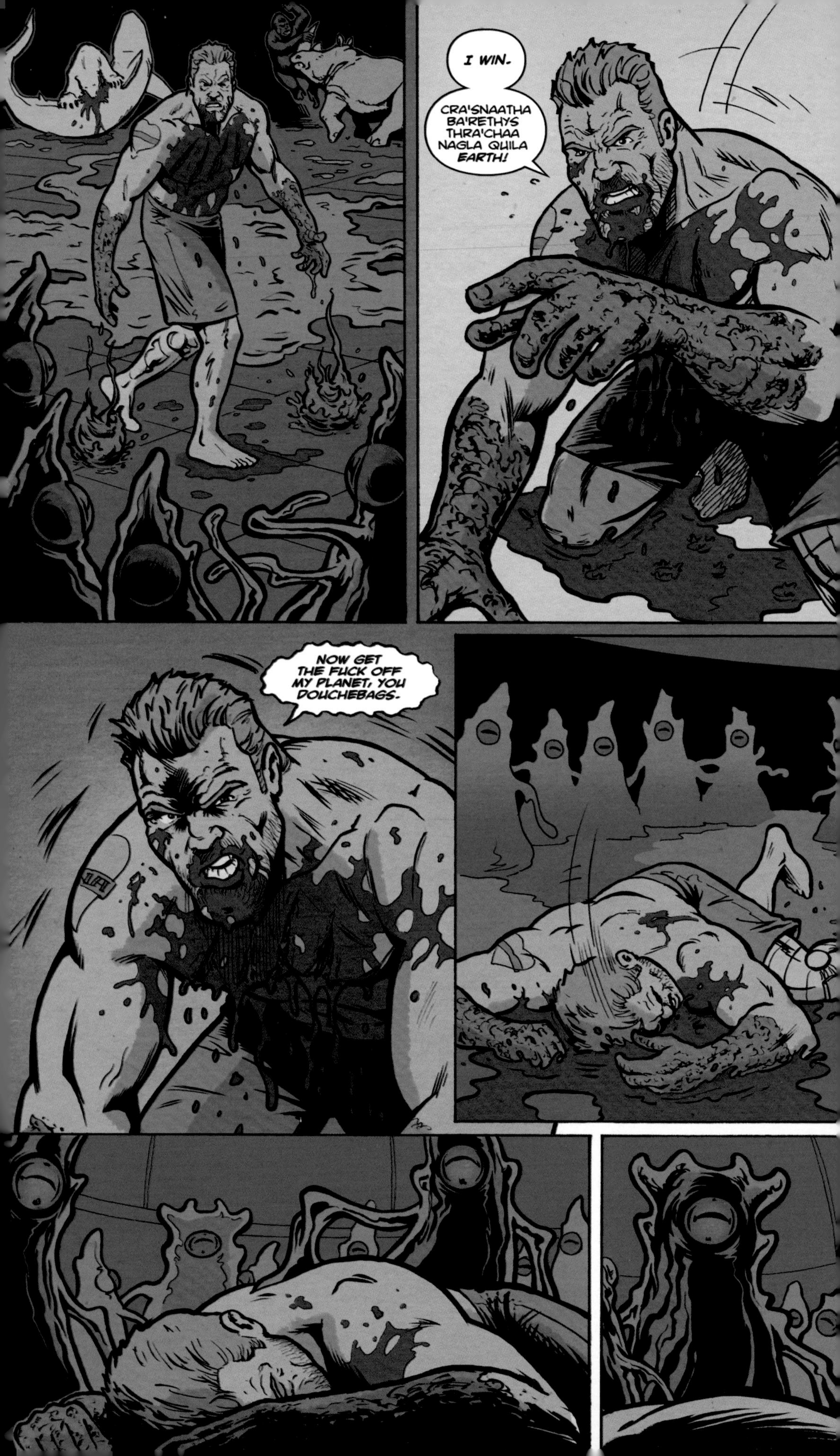
I WIN.
CRA'SNAATHA BA'RETHYS THRA'CHAA NAGLA QUILA EARTH!
NOW GET THE FUCK OFF MY PLANET, YOU DOUCHEBAGS.

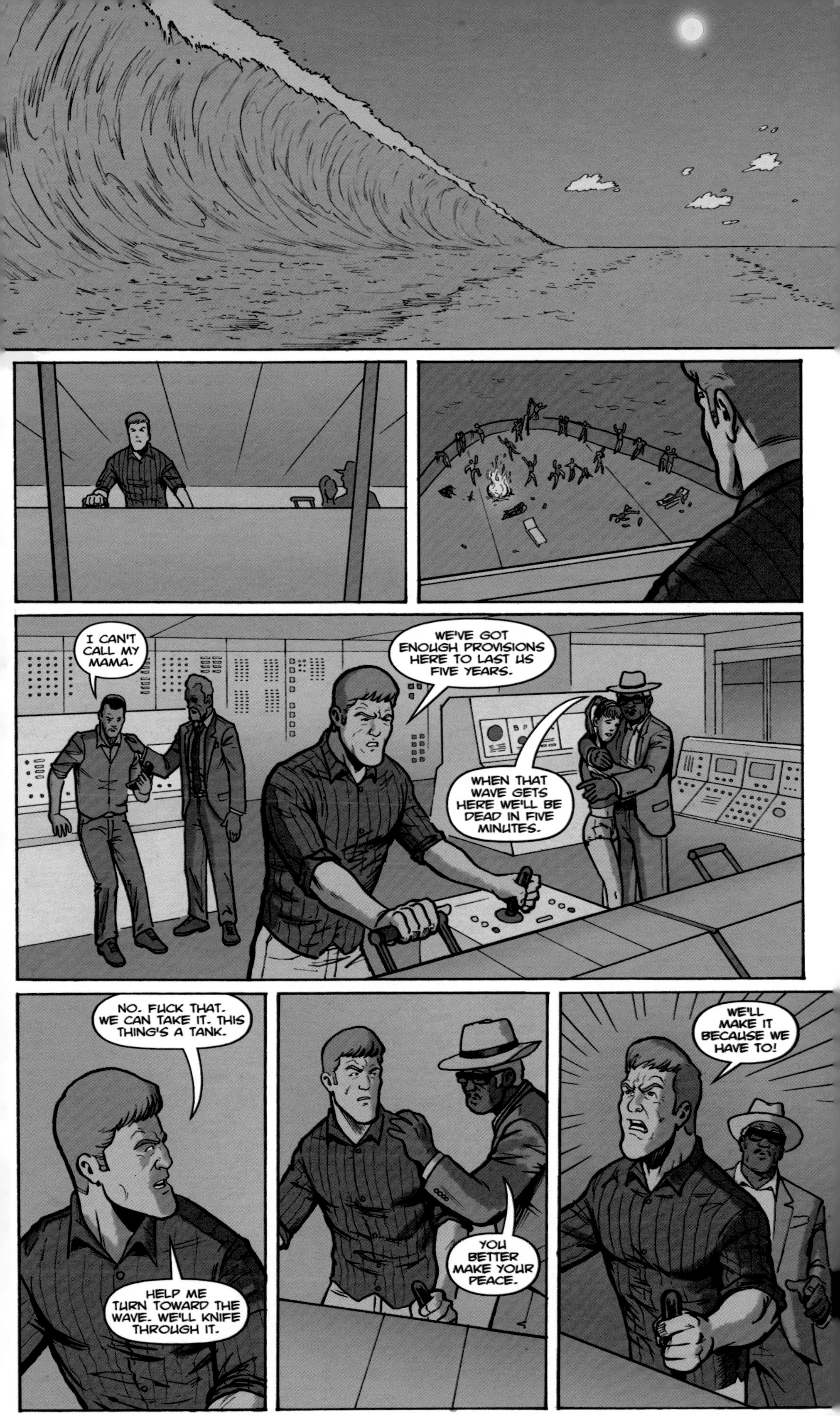
I CAN'T CALL MY MAMA.
WE'VE GOT ENOUGH PROVISIONS HERE TO LAST US FIVE YEARS.
WHEN THAT WAVE GETS HERE WE'LL BE DEAD IN FIVE MINUTES.
NO. FUCK THAT. WE CAN TAKE IT. THIS THING'S A TANK.
HELP ME TURN TOWARD THE WAVE. WE'LL KNIFE THROUGH IT.
YOU BETTER MAKE YOUR PEACE.
WE'LL MAKE IT BECAUSE WE HAVE TO!

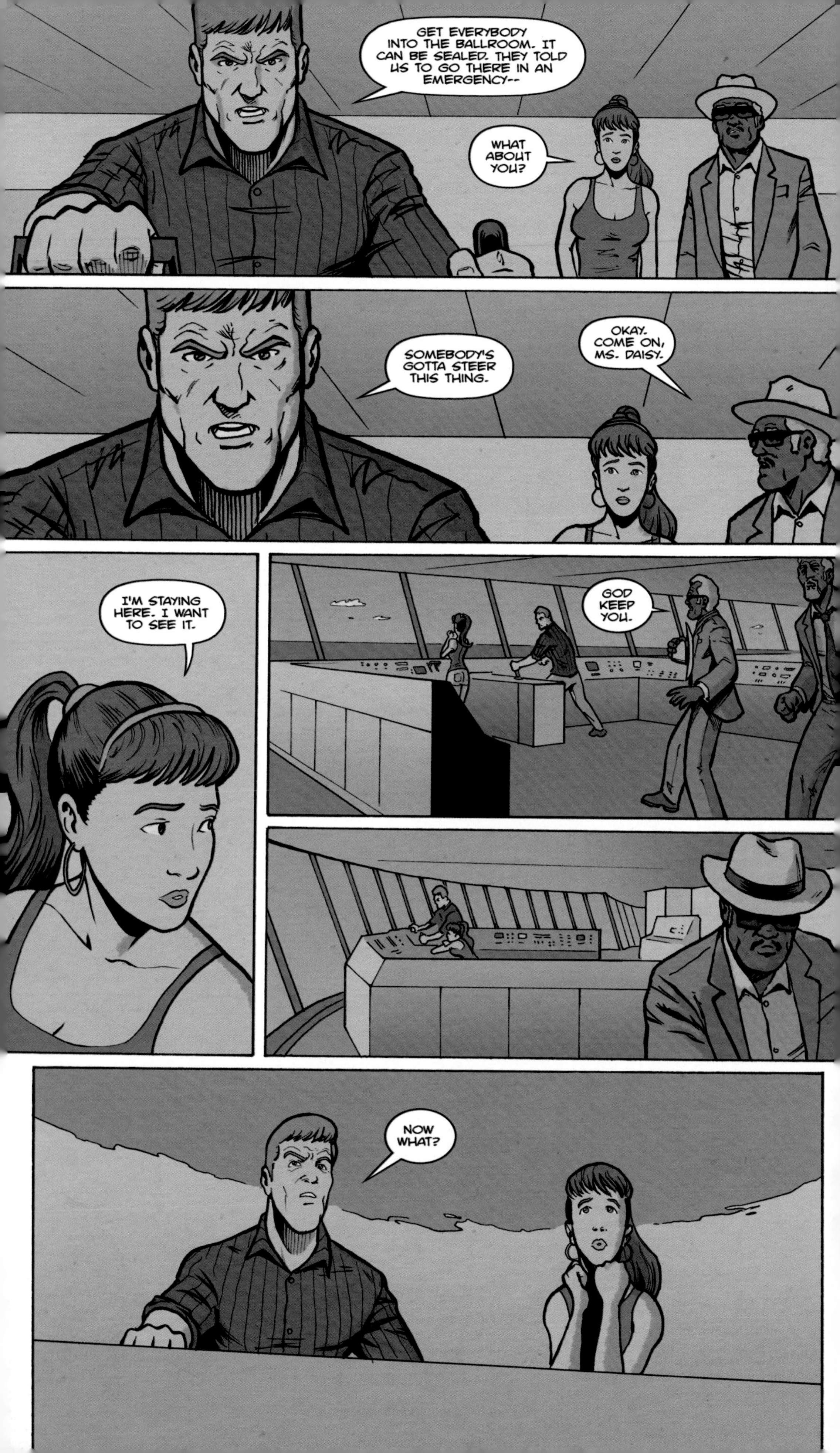
GET EVERYBODY INTO THE BALLROOM. IT CAN BE SEALED. THEY TOLD US TO GO THERE IN AN EMERGENCY--
WHAT ABOUT YOU?
SOMEBODY'S GOTTA STEER THIS THING.
OKAY. COME ON, MS. DAISY.
I'M STAYING HERE. I WANT TO SEE IT.
GOD KEEP YOU.
NOW WHAT?

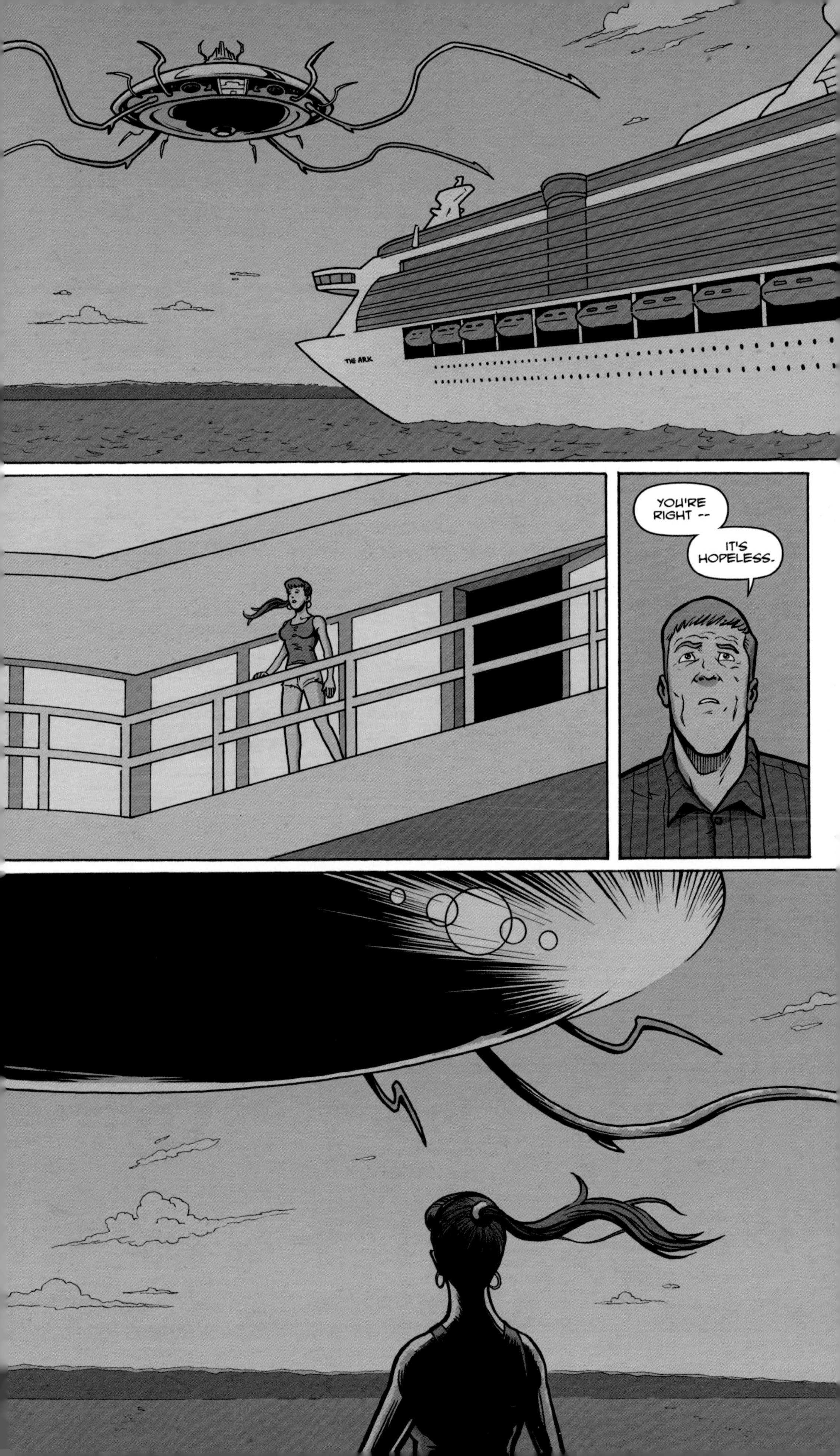
THE ARK
YOU'RE RIGHT --
IT'S HOPELESS.

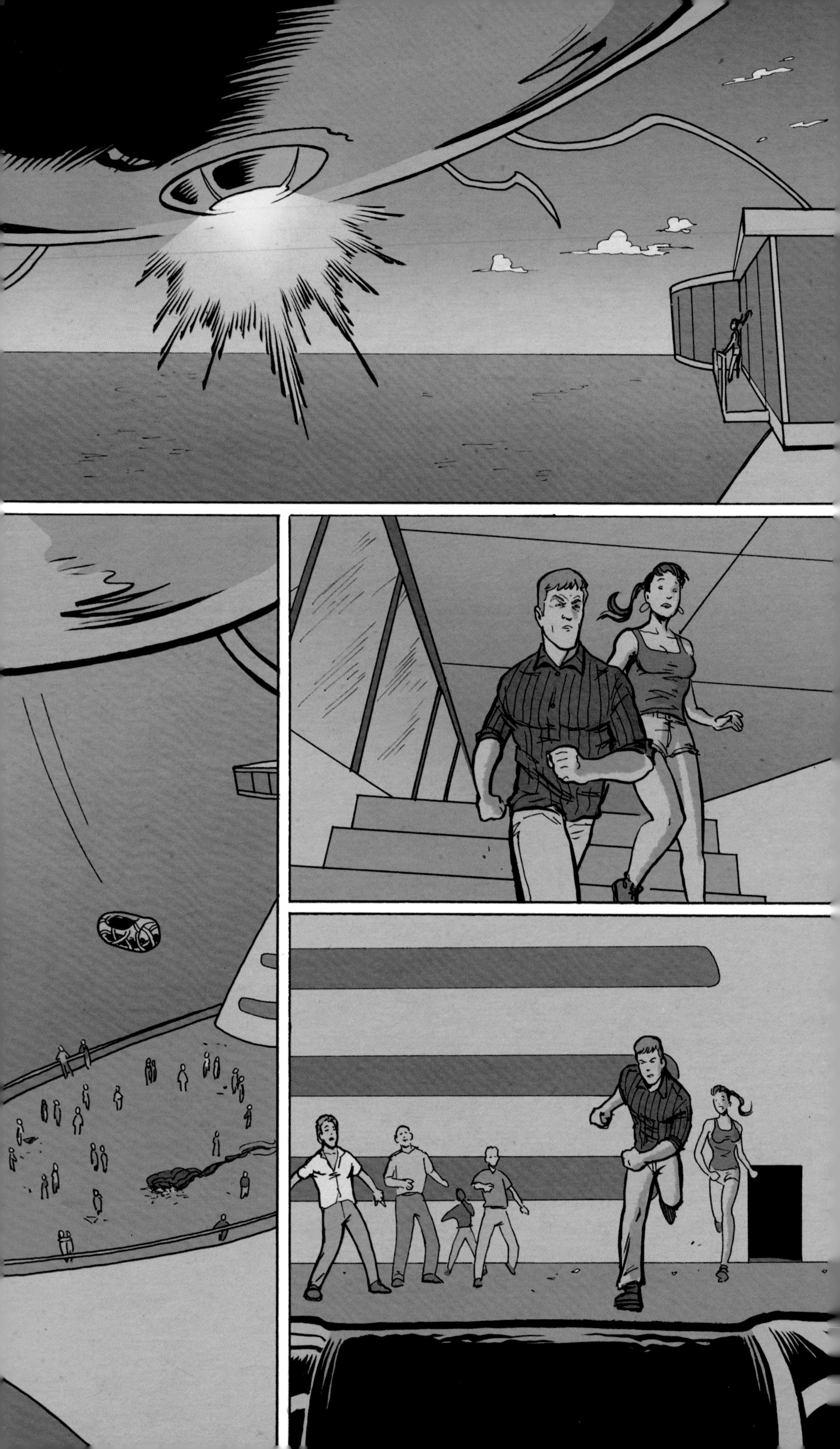

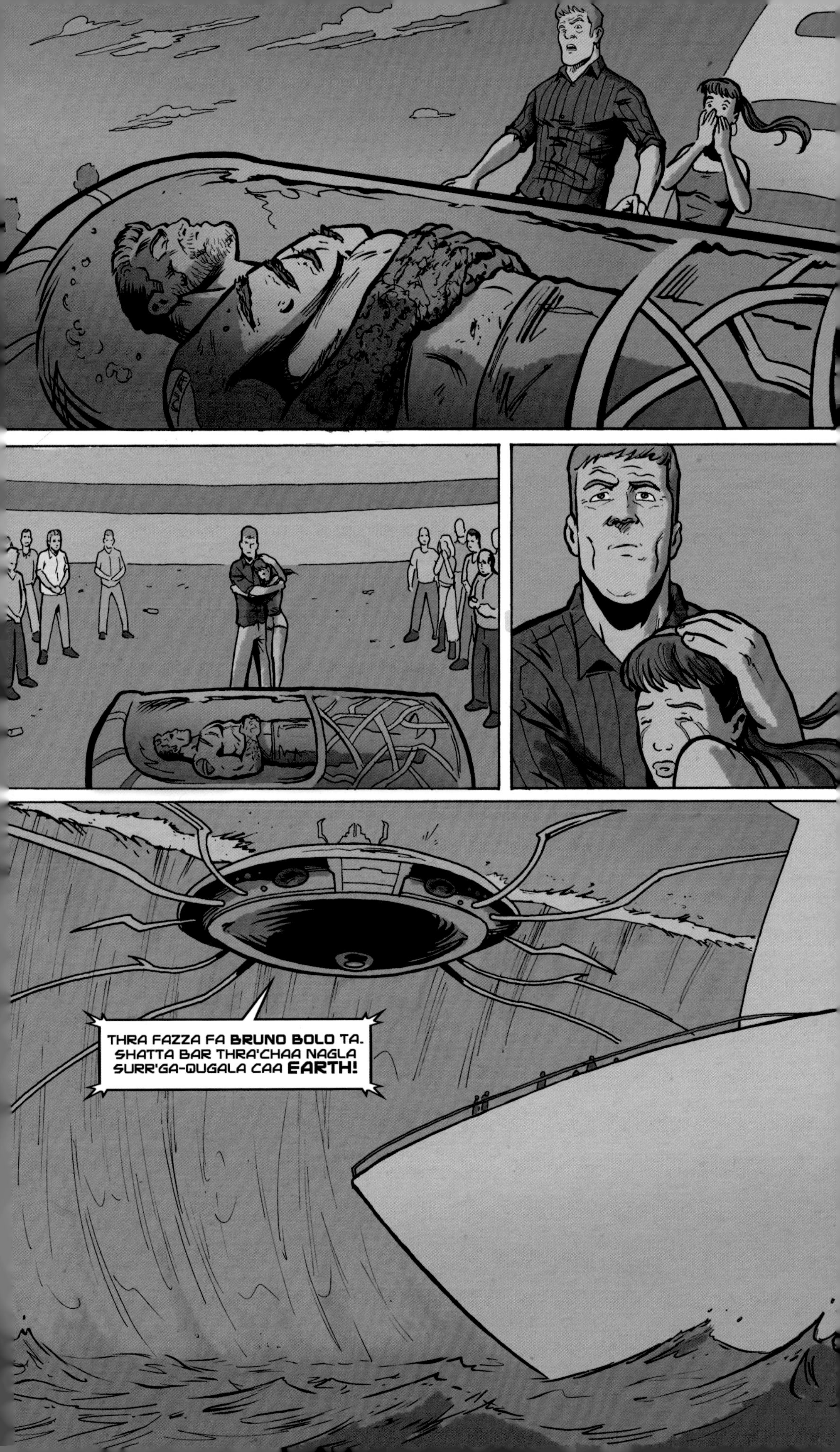
THRA FAZZA FA BRUNO BOLO TA. SHATTA BAR THRA'CHAA NAGLA SURR'GA-QUGALA CAA EARTH!

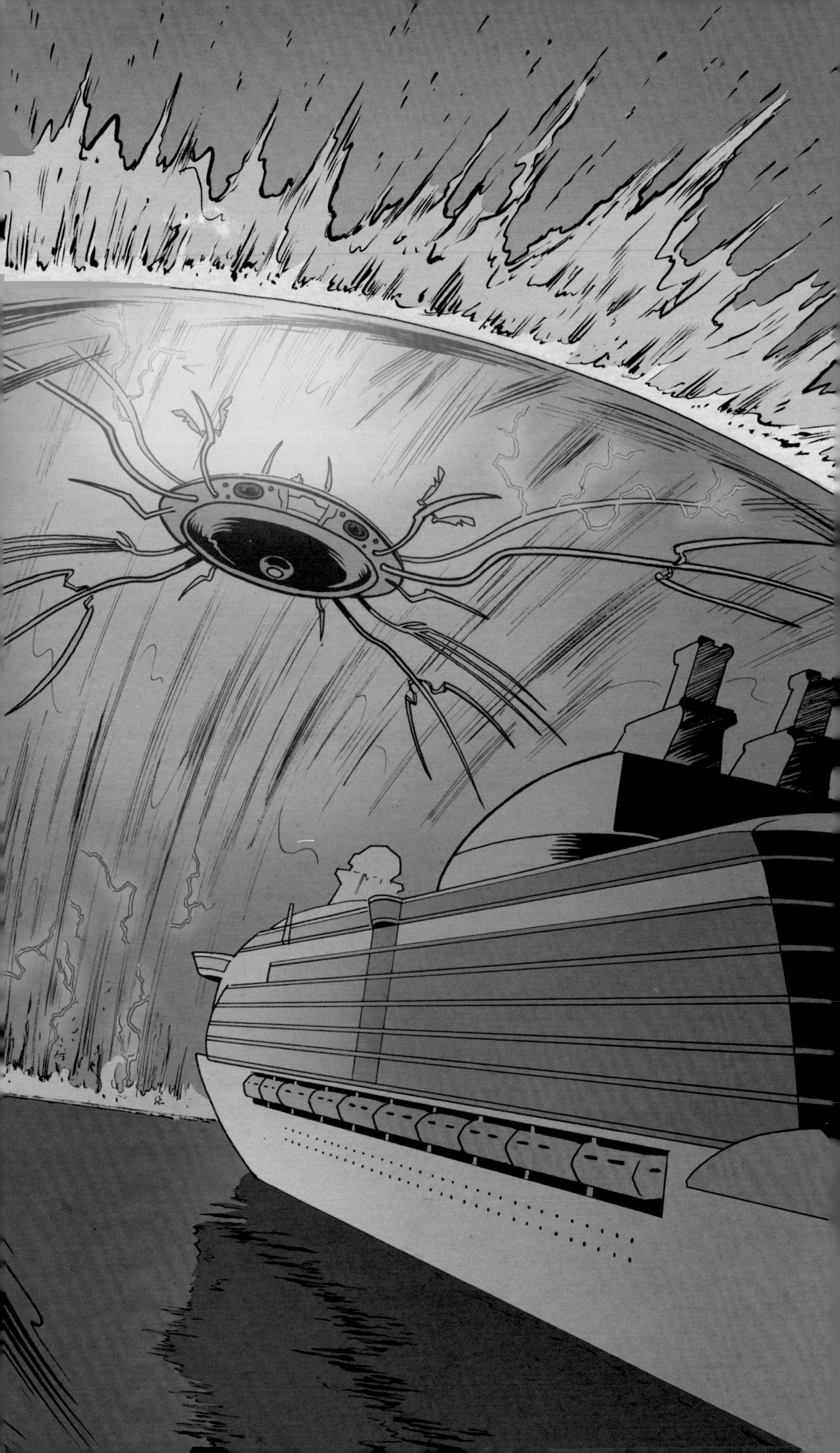

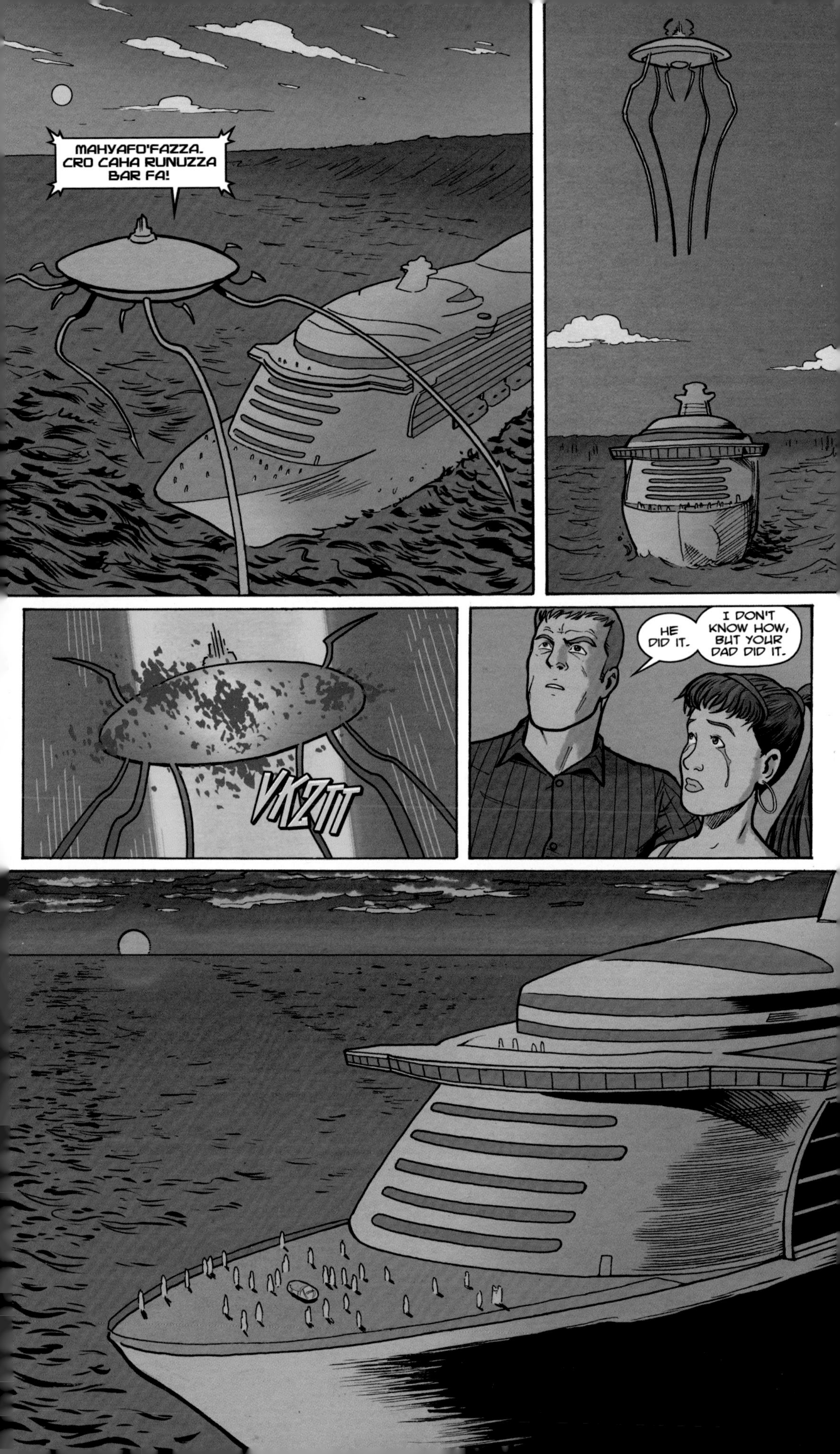
MAHYAFO'FAZZA. CRO CAHA RUNUZZA BAR FA!
VKZTT
HE DID IT.
I DON'T KNOW HOW, BUT YOUR DAD DID IT.

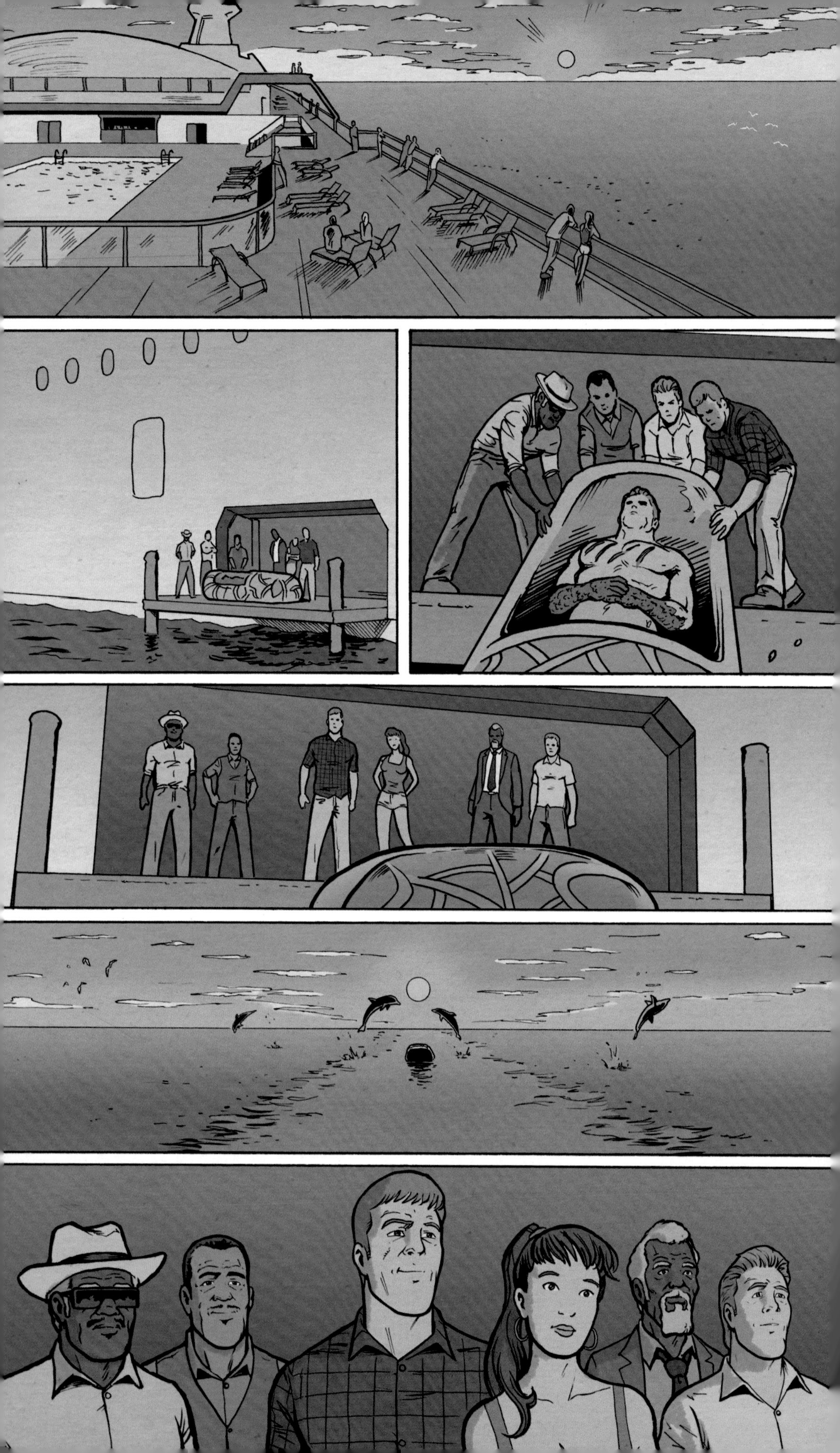

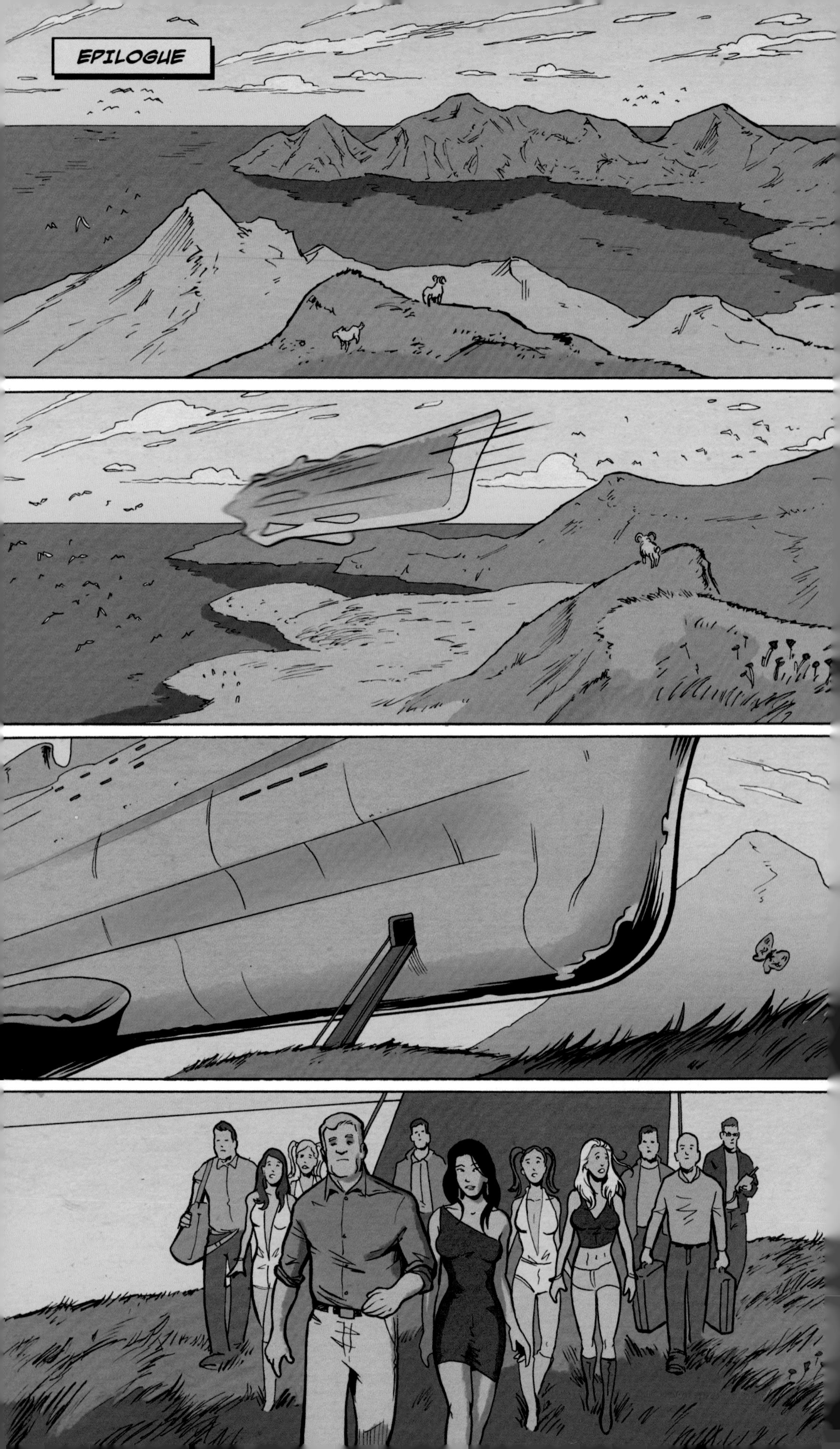
EPILOGUE

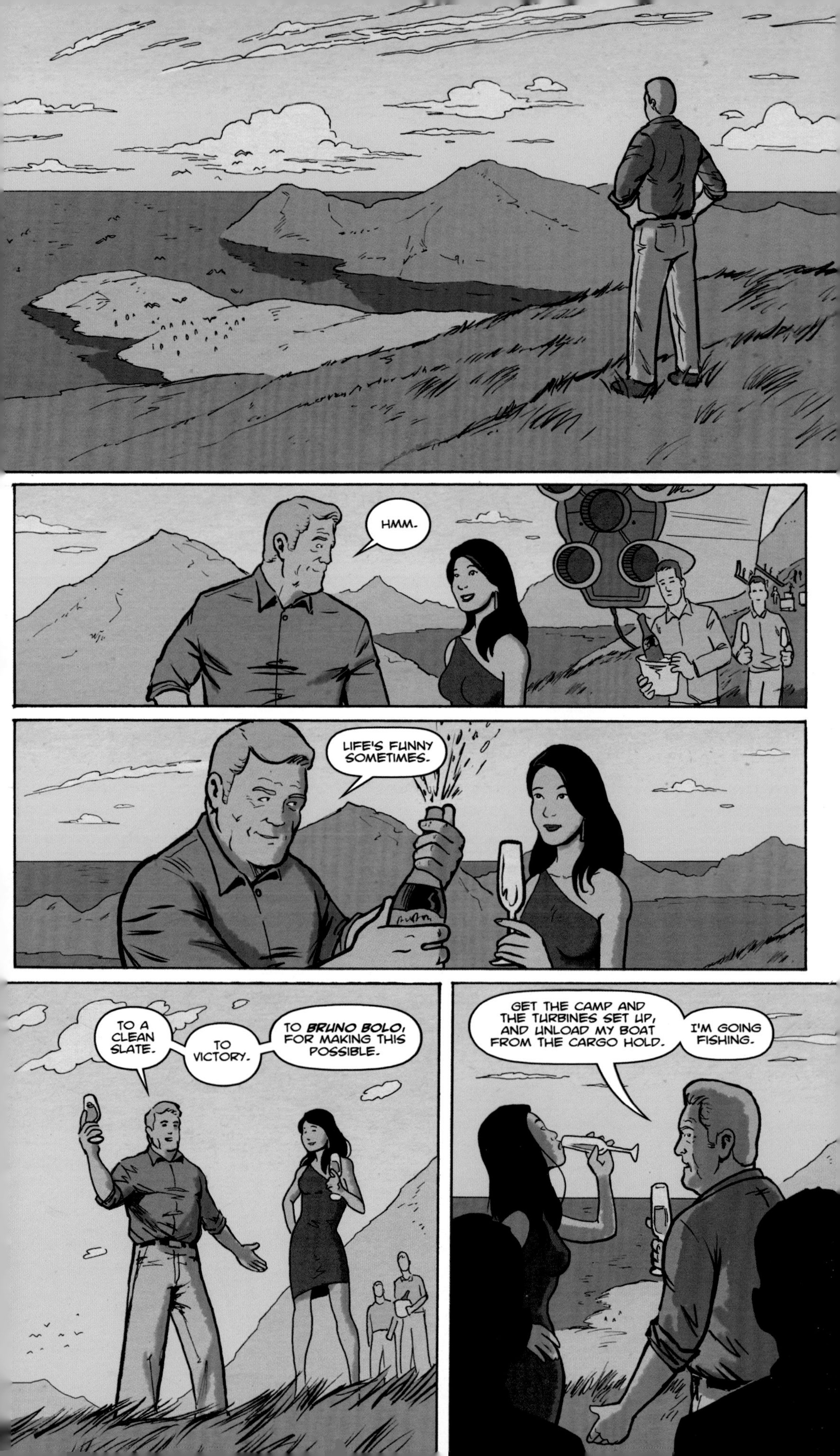
HMM.
LIFE'S FUNNY SOMETIMES.
TO A CLEAN SLATE.
TO VICTORY.
TO *BRUNO BOLO*, FOR MAKING THIS POSSIBLE.
GET THE CAMP AND THE TURBINES SET UP, AND UNLOAD MY BOAT FROM THE CARGO HOLD.
I'M GOING FISHING.

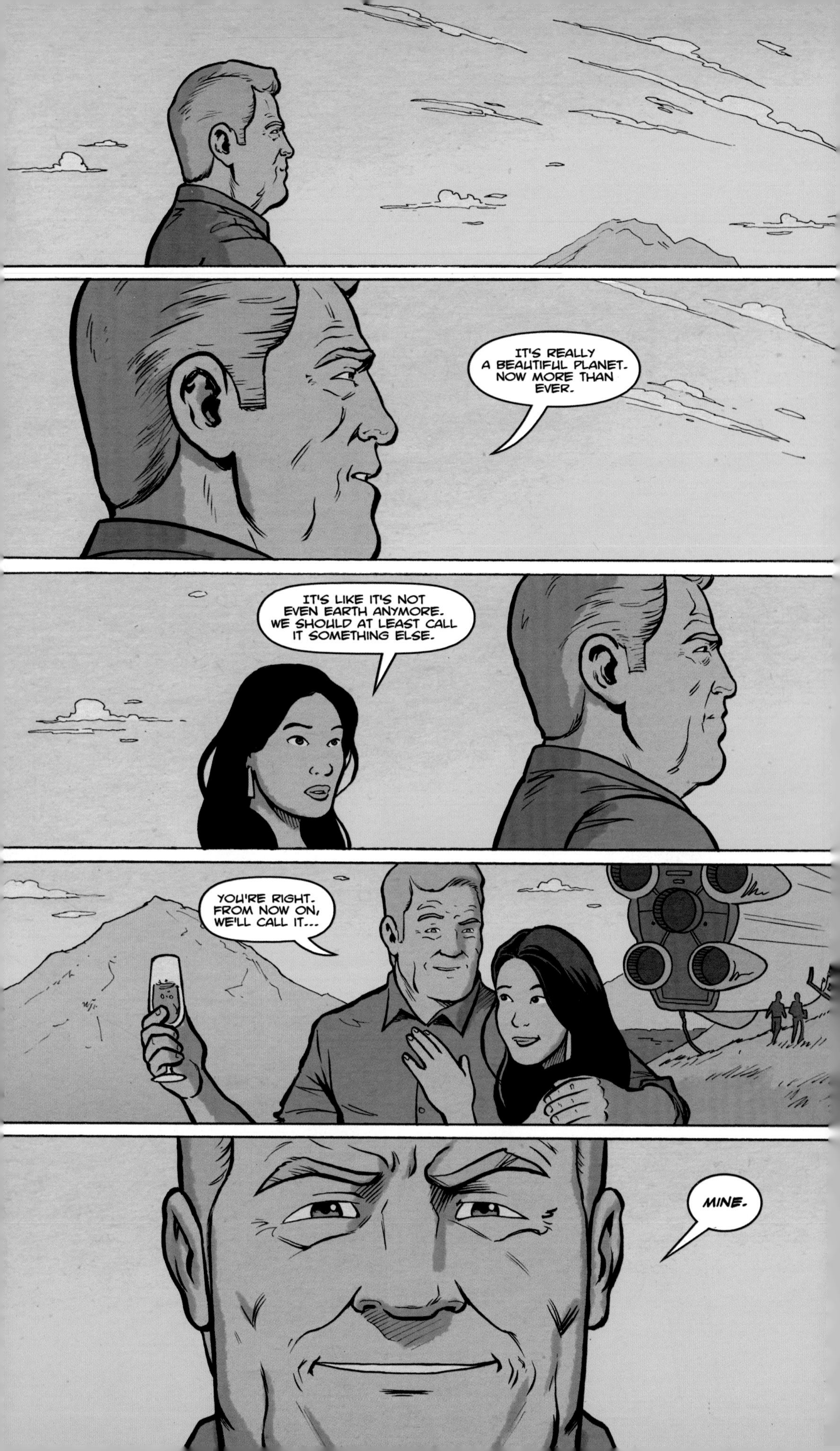
IT'S REALLY A BEAUTIFUL PLANET. NOW MORE THAN EVER.
IT'S LIKE IT'S NOT EVEN EARTH ANYMORE. WE SHOULD AT LEAST CALL IT SOMETHING ELSE.
YOU'RE RIGHT. FROM NOW ON, WE'LL CALL IT...
MINE.

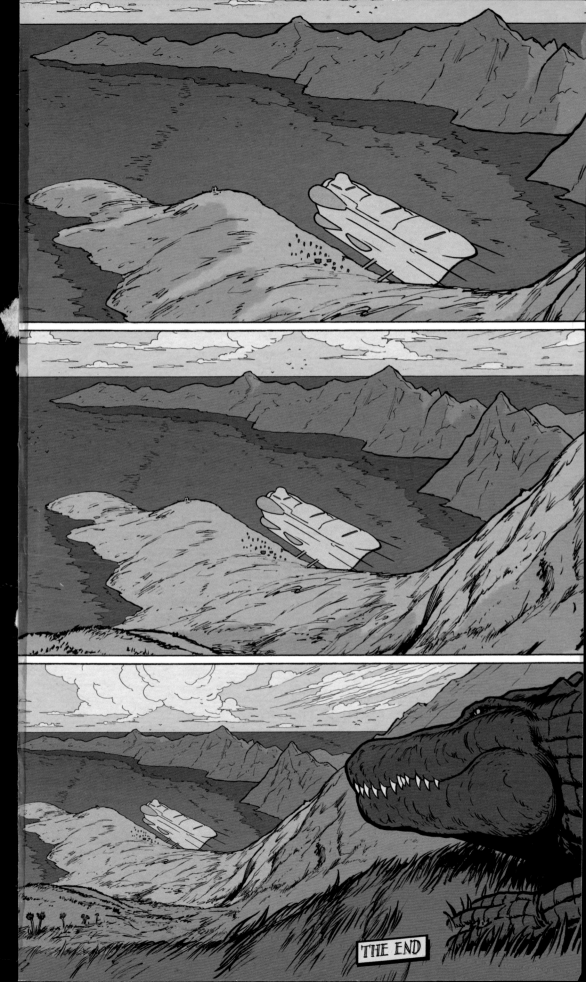

THE END

ABOUT THE CREATORS

Adam Mansbach's most recent book, Go the Fuck to Sleep, was a #1 New York Times bestseller. Published in thirty-six languages, it is forthcoming as a feature film from Fox 2000. His novels include The End of the Jews, winner of the California Book Award, and the cult classic Angry Black White Boy, which is taught at more than a hundred universities. His work has appeared in The New York Times Book Review, GQ, Esquire, The Believer, and on National Public Radio's All Things Considered.

Douglas Mcgowan is a filmmaker, record producer, and lifelong comic book fan.

Owen Brozman lives in Brooklyn with his wife. This is his first graphic novel. You can see more of his work at owenbrozman.com.